GOSPEL STUDIES SERIES

Your Study of

Isaiah

Made Easier

In the Bible and Book of Mormon

SECOND EDITION

GOSPEL STUDIES SERIES

Your Study of

Isaiah

Made Easier

In the Bible and Book of Mormon

SECOND EDITION

David J. Ridges

Springville, Utah

ISBN 13: 978-1-59955-388-7

Published by CFI, an imprint of Cedar Fort, Inc.
2373 W. 700 S., Springville, UT, 84663
Distributed by Cedar Fort, Inc., www.cedarfort.com

Cover design by Jen Boss
Cover design © 2009 by Lyle Mortimer

Printed in the United States of America

10 9 8 7 6 5 4 3 2

Printed on acid-free paper

Books
by David J. Ridges

The Gospel Studies Series:

- *Isaiah Made Easier, Second Edition*
- *The New Testament Made Easier, Part 1 (Second Edition)*
- *The New Testament Made Easier, Part 2 (Second Edition)*
- *Your Study of The Book of Mormon Made Easier, Part 1*
- *Your Study of The Book of Mormon Made Easier, Part 2*
- *Your Study of The Book of Mormon Made Easier, Part 3*
- *Your Study of The Doctrine and Covenants Made Easier, Part 1*
- *Your Study of The Doctrine and Covenants Made Easier, Part 2*
- *Your Study of The Doctrine and Covenants Made Easier, Part 3*
- *The Old Testament Made Easier, Part 1*
- *The Old Testament Made Easier—Selections from the Old Testament, Part 2*
- *The Old Testament Made Easier—Selections from the Old Testament, Part 3*
- *Your Study of the Pearl of Great Price Made Easier*
- *Your Study of Jeremiah Made Easier*
- *Your Study of The Book of Revelation Made Easier, Second Edition*

Additional titles by David J. Ridges:

- *Our Savior, Jesus Christ: His Life and Mission to Cleanse and Heal*
- *Mormon Beliefs and Doctrines Made Easier*
- *The Proclamation on the Family: The Word of the Lord on More Than 30 Current Issues*
- *65 Signs of the Times and the Second Coming*
- *Doctrinal Details of the Plan of Salvation: From Premortality to Exaltation*

These titles will soon be available through
Cedar Fort as e-books and on CD.

THE GOSPEL STUDIES SERIES

Welcome to this volume of the Gospel Studies Series, which will take you through Isaiah and the Isaiah chapters of the Book of Mormon with brief notes and commentary designed to keep you in the scripture while providing instruction and help along the way.

As with other study guides in the Gospel Studies Series, this work is intended to be a user-friendly, introductory study of Isaiah, as well as a refresher course for more advanced students of the scriptures. It is also designed and formatted to be a quick-reference resource that will enable readers to easily look up a particular verse or set of verses and gain additional understanding regarding them. It is hoped by the author that readers will write in the margins of their own scriptures some of the notes given in this study guide in order to assist them as they read and study Isaiah in the future.

—David J. Ridges

THE JST REFERENCES IN
STUDY GUIDES BY DAVID J. RIDGES

Note that some of the JST (The Joseph Smith Translation of the Bible) references I use in my study guides are not found in our LDS Bible in the footnotes or in the Joseph Smith Translation section in the reference section in the back. The reason for this, as explained to me while writing curriculum materials for the Church, is simply that there is not enough room to include all of the JST additions and changes to the King James Version of the Bible (the one we use in the English speaking part of the Church). As you can imagine, as was likewise explained to me, there were difficult decisions that had to be made by the Scriptures Committee of the Church as to which JST contributions were included and which were not.

The Joseph Smith Translation of the Bible in its entirety can generally be found in or ordered through LDS bookstores. It was originally published under the auspices of the Reorganized Church of Jesus Christ of Latter Day Saints in Independence, Missouri. The version of the JST I prefer to use is a parallel column version, *Joseph Smith's "New Translation" of the Bible*, published by Herald Publishing House, Independence, Missouri, in 1970. This parallel column version compares the King James Bible with the JST side by side and includes only the verses that have changes, additions, or deletions made by the Prophet Joseph Smith.

By the way, some members of the Church have wondered whether or not we can trust the JST since it was published by a breakaway faction from our Church. They worry that some changes from Joseph Smith's original manuscript might have been made to support doctrinal differences between us and the RLDS Church. This is not the case. Many years ago, Robert J. Matthews of the Brigham Young University Religion Department was given permission by leaders of the RLDS Church to come to their Independence, Missouri, headquarters and personally compare the original JST document word for word with their publication of the JST. Brother Matthews was thus able to verify that they had been meticulously true to the Prophet's original work.

CONTENTS

FOREWORD

Many people find the writings of Isaiah somewhat difficult or even impossible to understand. This presents a dilemma for them as they faithfully strive to read and study the scriptures, which include the words of Isaiah in both the Bible and the Book of Mormon. For example, when they come to the Isaiah chapters in First and Second Nephi, especially in Second Nephi where there are several such chapters, they find themselves wondering if it will count as having read the entire Book of Mormon if they just glance through the chapters of Isaiah and then carefully read the rest of the book.

In Third Nephi, chapter 22, the Savior quoted an entire chapter from the writings of the prophet Isaiah. He immediately followed that by giving a commandment regarding studying Isaiah's words. He said, "And now, behold, I say unto you, that ye ought to search these things. Yea, a commandment I give unto you that ye search these things diligently; for great are the words of Isaiah." With this commandment from the Savior in mind, people often struggle to find ways to better understand Isaiah.

This study guide is designed to bring you quickly and pleasantly to a basic understanding of Isaiah's words. Rather than giving hints and suggestions coupled with examples as to how one might better come to understand Isaiah's writings, this study guide will take you directly into Isaiah, chapter by chapter and verse by verse, as found in the Bible and in the Book of Mormon. Thus, you are actually reading the full text of Isaiah, with helpful hints and explanations right in the verse or between the verses and **bold** lettering to emphasis important scriptural messages. It provides an immediate, threshold-level understanding. With this basic understanding in place, the faithful member of the Church can study other guides and scholarly works on Isaiah to increase understanding.

The format used in this book is intentionally simple. As mentioned above, there are brief notes of explanation in brackets right in the verses. Short notes between verses are also provided. They are often somewhat conversational, designed to help you feel that you are having a chat with me as a teacher in a class on Isaiah. Thus, as you read the actual text of Isaiah, as found in the Bible and Book of Mormon, you get instant help in understanding. Please note that the title of this study guide reads Isaiah made "easier," not "easy." As with most worthwhile endeavors, it still requires some thought and work on your part.

Sources for the explanatory notes in brackets and between the verses are the footnotes in the LDS edition of the Bible; the JST (Joseph Smith Translation of the Bible); Book of Mormon; Doctrine and Covenants; *Teachings of the Prophet Joseph Smith,* compiled by Joseph Fielding Smith (Deseret Book, 1977); *Isaiah: Prophet, Seer and Poet,* by Victor L. Ludlow (Deseret Book, 1982); *Great are the Words of Isaiah,* by Monte S. Nyman (Bookcraft, 1980); various dictionaries; the Religion 302 *Old Testament Student Manual, 1 Kings—Malachi* for institute of religion students, published by the Church Educational System; and the Martin Luther edition of the German Bible.

This second edition of *Isaiah Made Easier in the Bible and Book of Mormon* contains hundreds of additional notes, clarifications, and explanations beyond those given in the first edition, including notes between the verses that were not provided there. Many of the readers of the first edition have written a number of the brief notes into their own scriptures for future reference in their ongoing scripture study.

—David J. Ridges

THE BOOK OF THE PROPHET
ISAIAH

General Background

Isaiah began his ministry about 740 B.C. (see chronology chart in the Bible Dictionary in the back of your LDS Bible). He continued until about 701 B.C. He is one of the greatest prophets who ever lived. You can read a summary about him in the Bible Dictionary under "Isaiah." We will quote one portion of that summary here:

Isaiah

"The Lord is salvation. Son of Amoz, a prophet in Jerusalem during 40 years, 740–701 B.C. He had great religious and political influence during the reign of Hezekiah, whose chief advisor he was. Tradition states that he was "sawn asunder" during the reign of Manasseh; for that reason he is often represented in art holding a saw."

The Savior quoted Isaiah more often than He quoted any other prophet in the Old Testament. This fact alone testifies of the importance of the writings and teachings of Isaiah. During the Savior's ministry to the Nephites on the American continent, He quoted Isaiah (in 3 Nephi 22) and then said (**bold** added for emphasis):

3 Nephi 23:1

1 AND now, behold, I say unto you, that **ye ought to search these things. Yea, a commandment I give unto you that ye search these things diligently; for great are the words of Isaiah**.

There are obviously many reasons that the teachings of Isaiah are vital to us. We will quote again from the Book of Mormon to see two major reasons to study Isaiah, according to Nephi. We will use **bold** to point out Nephi's reasons for quoting Isaiah to his people, including his wayward brothers Laman and Lemuel.

1 Nephi 19:23–24

23 And I did read many things unto them which were written in the books of Moses; but that I might **more fully persuade them to believe in the**

Lord their Redeemer I did read unto them that which was written by the prophet Isaiah; for I did liken all scriptures unto us, that it might be for our profit and learning.

24 Wherefore I spake unto them, saying: Hear ye the words of the prophet, ye who are a remnant of the house of Israel, a branch who have been broken off; hear ye the words of the prophet, which were written unto all the house of Israel, and liken them unto yourselves, **that ye may have hope** as well as your brethren from whom ye have been broken off; for after this manner has the prophet written.

Thus we are taught that Isaiah's teachings can greatly strengthen our testimonies of Jesus Christ, our Redeemer, and provide wonderful hope and assurance in our hearts that we can be found among those who are saved.

Knowing what Isaiah can do for us is one thing, but for many members of the Church, understanding the writings of Isaiah is quite another thing. Many years ago when I first remember reading 3 Nephi 23:1 (quoted above) I thought to myself, "If the Savior says that the words of Isaiah are great, then there must be something wrong with me because I don't understand most of them. Perhaps I am not spiritual enough, or the Holy Ghost can't work with me, or whatever." At any rate, it was a concern to me that I found Isaiah so difficult to understand.

Several years later, I attended a summer class for seminary and institute of religion teachers that was being taught by Brother Ellis Rasmussen of the BYU religion department. With Brother Rasmussen's first words, Isaiah came alive for me. As I recall, he quoted the first line of Isaiah 53:1 where Isaiah says, "Who hath believed our report?" And then he explained that it is just another way of saying, "Who believes us prophets anyway?"

Just like that, the key for understanding Isaiah was turned for me. It was possible to understand it! I listened with rapt attention and made many tiny, short notes in my scriptures during Brother Rasmussen's classes.

My intent is to make Isaiah "easier," not necessarily "easy," for students of the scriptures. The notes provided are intentionally brief, for two main reasons. One: They allow you to read the actual Bible text, with minimal interruption, and get a quick threshold understanding of Isaiah's teachings. Two: You may wish to write some of these brief notes in your own scriptures.

In order to keep the notes brief and somewhat conversational, considerable license has been taken with respect to capitalization and punctuation. The explanations and interpretations provided are not intended to be the final word on Isaiah. I am hopeful that readers will begin to see many other possibilities for interpretation and application of this great prophet's words, for the symbolism and messages of Isaiah do indeed lend themselves to multiple interpretations in various settings.

By the way, the references for the notes in brackets that say "German" are a reference to the translation found in the Martin Luther edition of the German Bible.

We will now proceed with our study of Isaiah.

ISAIAH 1

Background

Chapter 1 is a preface to the whole book of Isaiah, much like Doctrine and Covenants, section one, is to the whole Doctrine and Covenants, or like the superscription at the beginning of First Nephi is, which says "An account of Lehi . . ."

1 **The vision of Isaiah** the son of Amoz, which he saw **concerning Judah and Jerusalem** in the days of Uzziah, Jotham, Ahaz, and Hezekiah, kings of Judah [*The kings mentioned above reigned from about 740 B.C. to 701 B.C.*].

Isaiah states the main problem, in verses 2–4, next.

2 Hear, O heavens, and give ear, O earth: for the Lord hath spoken, **I have nourished and brought up children, and they have rebelled against me.**

3 The ox knoweth his owner, and the ass his master's crib [*manger*]: but **Israel doth not know** [*know God*], my people doth not consider [*think seriously, Israel—animals are wiser than you are!*].

4 Ah **sinful nation**, a **people laden with iniquity** [*loaded down with wickedness*], a seed of evildoers, children that are **corrupters**: they **have forsaken the Lord**, they have provoked the Holy One of Israel unto anger, they **are gone away**

backward [*retrogressing; they are "in the world" and "of the world"*].

5 ¶ **Why should ye be stricken any more** [*why do you keep asking for more punishment*]? ye will revolt more and more: **the whole head** [*leadership*] **is sick**, and the whole heart [*the people*] faint [*is diseased; in other words, the whole nation is spiritually sick*].

Isaiah continues the theme that the whole nation is riddled with wickedness and is thus spiritually sick. He uses repetition to drive home the point.

6 **From the sole of the foot even unto the head there is no soundness in it** [*you are completely sick*]; but **wounds, and bruises, and putrifying** [*filled with pus*] **sores** [*symbolically saying that the people are spiritually beaten and infected with sin*]: **they have not been closed, neither bound up, neither mollified with ointment** [*you are sick and you don't even care; you won't try the simplest first aid (the Atonement of Christ)*].

Old Testament prophets often spoke prophetically of the future as if it had already taken place. Isaiah uses this technique next, as he prophesies of the impending captivity of these wicked people.

7 **Your country is desolate**, your

cities are **burned** with fire: your land, strangers [*foreigners*] devour it in your presence, and it is desolate as overthrown by strangers [*foreigners, specifically the Assyrians*].

8 And **the daughter of Zion** [*Israel*] **is left as a cottage** [*temporary shade structure built of straw and leaves*] in a vineyard, as a lodge [*same as cottage*] in a garden of cucumbers, as a besieged city [*you are about as secure as a flimsy shade shack in a garden*].

9 **Except the Lord of hosts had left unto us a very small remnant** [*if God hadn't intervened and saved a few of Israel*], **we should have been as Sodom**, and we should have been like unto Gomorrah [*completely destroyed*].

10 ¶ **Hear the word of the Lord, ye rulers of Sodom** [*"Listen up, you wicked leaders!"*]; **give ear unto the law of our God, ye people of Gomorrah** [*Sodom and Gomorrah symbolize total wickedness*].

11 **To what purpose is the multitude of your sacrifices unto me** [*what good are your insincere, empty rituals*]? saith the Lord: I am full [*"I've had it to here!"*] of the burnt offerings of rams, and the fat of fed beasts; and I delight not in the blood of bullocks, or of lambs, or of he goats.

12 When ye come to appear before me, who **hath required this at your hand, to tread my courts** [*who authorized you hypocrites to act religious and pretend to worship Me*]?

13 **Bring no more vain** [*useless*] **oblations** [*offerings*]; incense is an abomination unto me; the new moons [*special Sabbath ritual at beginning of month—see Bible Dictionary, page 738 under "New Moon"*] and sabbaths, the calling of assemblies, I cannot [*"I can't stand it!"*] away with; it is iniquity, even the solemn meeting [*solemn assembly*].

14 **Your new moons and your appointed feasts** [*your hypocritical worship*] **my soul hateth**: they are a trouble unto me; I am weary to bear them.

15 And **when ye spread forth your hands** [*when you pray*], **I will hide mine eyes from you**: yea, when ye make many prayers, **I will not hear**: your hands are full of blood [*bloodshed; murder—see verse 21*].

Next, in spite of the gross wickedness of these people, as described by Isaiah, they are invited by a merciful Savior to repent and return to Him.

Major Message

If you want to repent but you think your sins have put you

beyond the reach of the Savior's Atonement, think again.

16 ¶ **Wash you** [*be baptized*], make you clean; put away the evil of your doings from before mine eyes [*repent*]; cease to do evil;

17 **Learn to do well** [*don't just cease to do evil but replace evil with good in your lives*]; seek judgment [*be fair in your dealings with others*], relieve the oppressed, judge the fatherless [*be kind and fair to them*], plead for [*stand up for, defend*] the widow.

Verse 18, next, is among the most well-known of all quotes from Isaiah. With verses 1–15 as a backdrop, this verse wonderfully and clearly teaches the power of the Atonement of Jesus Christ to cleanse and heal completely.

18 Come now, and let us reason together, saith the Lord: **though your sins be as scarlet** [*cloth dyed with scarlet, a colorfast dye*], **they shall be as white as snow** [*even though you think your sins are "colorfast," the Atonement can cleanse you*]; **though they be red like crimson, they shall be as wool** [*a long process is required to get wool white, but it can be done*].

19 **If ye be willing** [*agency, choice*] **and obedient**, ye shall eat the good of the land [*you will prosper*]:

20 **But if ye refuse and rebel**, ye shall be devoured with the sword: for the mouth of the Lord hath spoken it.

The word "harlot" (or prostitute), in verse 21, next, is a play on the imagery of a husband whose wife commits adultery against him. In the symbolism of the Bible, the husband represents Christ, and the wife represents Israel. They are bound together by covenant, but Israel cheats on her husband by being loyal to false gods, including wickedness and self-indulgence.

21 ¶ **How is** [*did*] **the faithful city** [*Jerusalem*] **become an harlot** [*unfaithful to the Lord; a willful sinner*]! it was full of judgment [*justice*]; righteousness lodged in it; but now murderers.

22 Thy silver is become dross [*surface scum on molten metal*] thy wine mixed with water [*you are polluted!*]:

23 **Thy princes** [*leaders, rulers*] **are rebellious**, and companions of thieves: **every one loveth gifts** [*bribes*], and followeth after rewards: they judge not [*do not do justice to*] the fatherless, neither doth the cause of the widow come unto them [*never penetrates their hearts*].

24 **Therefore saith the Lord**, the Lord of hosts, the mighty One of Israel, Ah, **I will ease me of** [*be rid of*] **mine adversaries**, and

avenge me of mine enemies [*in other words, the Lord will turn the wicked people of Israel over to the law of justice, since they have chosen to become His enemies*]:

25 ¶ And **I will turn my hand upon thee** [*repeatedly chastise you*], and purely purge away thy dross, and take away all thy tin [*slag; I will refine thee; in other words, put you through the refiner's fire to burn your impurities and sins out of you*]:

26 And **I will restore thy judges as at the first** [*among other things, a reference to the future when the gospel is restored by Joseph Smith*], and thy counsellors as at the beginning: **afterward thou shalt be called, The city of righteousness, the faithful city** [*the future gathering of Israel*].

27 **Zion shall be redeemed** [*a prophetic fact*] with judgment, and her converts with righteousness [*message of hope*].

28 **And the destruction of the transgressors and of the sinners shall be together** [*at the same time*], and they that forsake the Lord shall be consumed [*at the Second Coming*].

29 For **they shall be ashamed of** [*put to shame because of*] **the oaks** [*trees and gardens used in their idol worship*] which ye have desired, and **ye shall be confounded for the** [*because of the*] **gardens** [*used in idol worship*] that ye have chosen.

30 For **ye shall be as an oak whose leaf fadeth, and as a garden that hath no water** [*drought; destruction will come upon you because of your wickedness*].

31 And **the strong** [*the mighty wicked among you*] **shall be as tow** [*as a tuft of inflammable fibers*], and the maker of it as a spark, and **they shall both burn together, and none shall quench them** [*destruction of the wicked is sure to happen*].

ISAIAH 2

Background

Chapters 2, 3, and 4 go together. Chapter 2 is a multi-faceted prophecy of the latter-day gathering to the tops of the Rocky Mountains (Salt Lake City), the building of latter-day temples, the Millennium, and the destruction of the wicked at the Second Coming. Isaiah saw these things in vision (as stated in verse 1).

1 **The word that Isaiah the son of Amoz saw** concerning Judah and Jerusalem.

2 And it shall come to pass **in the last days**, that **the mountain** of the Lord's house shall be established in the top of the mountains [*"high*

place"—temples will be established; also, the Church will be established in the tops of the mountains in the last days], and shall be exalted above the hills [symbolism: you can get higher, closer to God in the temples than on the highest mountains]; and **all nations shall flow unto it** [the gathering of Israel in the last days, coming to the true gospel, with headquarters in the "top of the mountains"].

3 And **many people shall go and say, Come ye, and let us go up to the mountain of the Lord,** to the house [temples] of the God of Jacob; and **he will teach us of his ways, and we will walk in his paths**: for out of Zion shall go forth the law, and the word of the Lord from Jerusalem ["law" and "word" are synonyms; this seems to be a reference to the Millennium, when there will be two headquarters of Christ's kingdom, Zion (the New Jerusalem), built in Independence, Missouri, and Old Jerusalem; the Lord's word will go out from both cities].

Verse 4, next, is a direct reference to the Millennium.

4 **And he** [Christ] **shall judge** [rule] **among the nations**, and shall rebuke many people: and **they shall beat their swords into plowshares, and their spears into pruninghooks** [there will be peace]: **nation shall not lift up sword against nation, neither shall they learn war any more** [Millennium].

Isaiah now switches from the future back to his own time and people. It is a common practice (and somewhat confusing to us) for Isaiah to switch from the future to the past, or the present, and then back and forth, with no notice. It is part of "the manner of prophesying among the Jews" (2 Nephi 25:1).

Having told the people what will happen to their descendants in the far-distant future, and given them a glimpse of the beautiful peace and joy of living with the Savior during the Millennium, he now invites them to repent and prepare themselves to be worthy of living with Him forever.

5 **O house of Jacob** [another name for Israel], **come ye, and let us walk in the light of the Lord.**

Next, Isaiah reminds these wicked people why they are not currently enjoying the blessings of the Lord.

6 Therefore [this is why] thou [the Lord] hast forsaken thy people the house of Jacob [the Israelites], **because they be replenished from the east** [they are adopting false eastern religions], **and are soothsayers** [are into witchcraft, sorcery, and so forth] like the Philistines, and **they please themselves in the**

children of strangers [*are mixing with and marrying foreigners, people not of covenant Israel*].

7 Their land also is full of silver and gold, neither is there any end of their treasures [*they have become materialistic*]; their land is also full of horses, neither is there any end of their chariots [*horses and chariots represent armaments of war*]:

8 Their land also is full of idols; they worship the work of their own hands, that which their own fingers have made [*Isaiah is pointing out how absurd worshiping idols is*]:

The Book of Mormon adds a very important word in two places in verse 9, next. The Book of Mormon passages of Isaiah came from the Brass Plates and were thus of much earlier date and accuracy than the manuscripts from which our Old Testament is taken.

9 And the mean man [*poor, low in social status*] boweth [*not, see 2 Nephi 12:9*] down, and the great [*high in social status and influence*] man humbleth himself [*not*]: therefore forgive them not [*no one is humble*].

The main message in verse 10, next, is that it is impossible to hide from God.

10 Enter into the rock [*go ahead and try to find a place to hide from the Lord in the rocks, you*] wicked people], and hide thee in the dust, for fear of the Lord and for [*2 Nephi 12:10 does not have "for"*] the glory of his majesty [*2 Nephi 12:10 adds "shall smite thee"*].

One other thing we learn from verse 10, above, with the Book of Mormon additions, is that the wicked will be destroyed by the glory of the coming Savior, at the time of the Second Coming (compare with D&C 5:19).

11 The lofty looks of man [*pride*] shall be humbled, and the haughtiness of men shall be bowed down, and the Lord alone shall be exalted in that day [*the Lord will demonstrate power over all things at the Second Coming*].

Verse 12, next, is yet another reminder to you that Isaiah uses repetition to emphasize a point he wishes to make.

12 For the day of the Lord of hosts [*Second Coming*] shall be upon [*against*] every one that is proud and lofty, and upon [*against*] every one that is lifted up [*full of pride*]; and he shall be brought low [*humbled*]:

Trees are often used by Isaiah and other Old Testament prophets to represent people. We see this technique in verse 13, next.

13 And upon all the cedars [*people*] of Lebanon, that are high

and lifted up, and upon all the oaks [*people*] of Bashan,

14 And upon all the high mountains, and upon all the hills that are lifted up,

15 And upon every high tower, and upon every fenced wall [*man-made defenses*],

16 And **upon all the ships of Tarshish** [*symbolic of materialism and earthly power; noted for ability to travel long distances and carry large cargoes, and for their strength as warships*], **and upon all pleasant pictures** [*pleasure craft upon which the wealthy traveled*].

17 And **the loftiness** [*pride*] **of man shall be bowed down**, and the haughtiness of men shall be made low: and **the Lord alone shall be exalted in that day** [*at the time of the Second Coming*].

18 And **the idols he shall utterly abolish**.

The terror in the hearts of the wicked at the time of the Second Coming is depicted in verses 19 and 21, next.

19 And **they** [*the wicked*] **shall go into the holes of the rocks** [*caves*], and into the caves of the earth, **for fear of the Lord, and for the glory of his majesty**, when he ariseth to shake terribly the earth [*at the time*

of the Second Coming].

20 **In that day** [*Second Coming*] **a man shall cast his idols** of silver, and his idols of gold, which they made each one for himself to worship [*a reminder that idol worship is completely absurd*], **to the moles and to the bats** [*a play on words, pointing out that wicked people live in "darkness" also*];

21 **To go into the clefts of the rocks, and into the tops of the ragged rocks, for fear of the Lord**, and for the glory of his majesty, when he ariseth to shake terribly the earth [*at the time of the Second Coming*].

22 **Cease ye from man** [*stop trusting in man*], **whose breath is in his nostrils** [*who is mortal*]: **for wherein is he to be accounted of** [*in other words, why trust in man rather than God*]?

ISAIAH 3

Background

In this chapter Isaiah describes the downfall of Jerusalem because of wickedness. In a significant way, it is a pattern that applies to any nation or society in which personal sin and wickedness become a way of life for the majority of citizens.

Beginning with verse 16 and continuing to the end of the chapter, Isaiah points out, in effect, that women are generally the last stronghold against the downfall of a nation, and that when they also turn to pride and personal wickedness as a lifestyle, the nation is doomed.

We will be introduced to an ancient writing technique in this chapter called "chiasmus." It is a writing form in which the author says certain things and then intentionally repeats them in reverse order for emphasis.

Chiasmus was not discovered by scholars until after the time the Book of Mormon was published. This is significant because the Book of Mormon has several passages in which chiasmus is used (for example, 2 Nephi 29:13, Mosiah 3:18–19, and Alma 36). Such use of chiasmus as a writing style in the Book of Mormon is strong evidence that it is of ancient origin, which of course it is. We will include one example from the Book of Mormon. You will in fact see two short chiastic structures within this one verse. In this case, the structure consists of **A B C C' B' A,'** and it is repeated twice.

2 Nephi 29:13

13 And it shall come to pass that the **Jews** **[A]** shall have the **words** **[B]** of the **Nephites** **[C]**, and the **Nephites** **[C']** shall have the **words** **[B']** of the **Jews** **[A]**; and the **Nephites and the Jews** **[A]** shall have the **words** **[B]** of the **lost tribes of Israel** **[C]**; and the **lost tribes of Israel** **[C]** shall have the **words** **[B']** of the **Nephites and the Jews** **[A']**.

Often, but not necessarily always, the pivot point or midpoint of the chiasmus is the main message. For example, in the chiasmus used by Isaiah here in the first eight verses, the main message is found in verse 5, where he emphasizes that when a society collapses because of wickedness, everyone is persecuted and oppressed by everyone else.

We will now proceed with this chapter. The chiastic structure begins in verse 1 and ends at the beginning of verse 8. You may wish to read only the words of the chiasmus (in **underlined bold**), and then come back and read the complete verses. It will help you get the feel of a chiasmus.

1 For, behold, the Lord, the Lord of hosts, doth **take away from Jerusalem** **[A]** and from Judah the stay [*supply*] and the staff [*support*], the whole stay of **bread** **[B]**, and the whole stay of water [*the Lord is going to pull the props out and the whole thing will collapse*],

2 The **mighty man** [*the powerful leader*] **[C]**, and the man of war [*your military power will crumble*],

the judge, and the prophet, and the prudent, and the ancient,

3 The captain of fifty, and **the honourable man, and the counsellor [D]** [*no competent leaders*], and the cunning artificer [*skilled craftsman*], and the eloquent orator [*all the stable, dependable people who are the mainstays of a stable society will be gone*].

4 And I will give **children to be their princes [E]** [*leaders*], and babes [*immature people*] shall rule over them [*immature, irresponsible leaders will take over*].

5 And **the people shall be oppressed, every one by another [F]**, [*this is the pivot point of this chiasmus*] and every one by his neighbour [*anarchy*]: the **child shall behave himself proudly against the ancient [E']**, and the base [*crude and rude*] against the honourable [*no respect for authority; public acceptance of coarseness, crudeness, rudeness*].

Economic conditions will become so bad that people will be asked to serve as leaders if they happen to have a decent set of clothes.

6 When a man shall take hold of his brother of the house of his father, saying, **Thou hast clothing, be thou our ruler [D']**, and let [*let not; see 2 Nephi 13:6*] this ruin be under thy hand [*be our leader, don't let this happen to us*]:

7 In that day shall he [*the man asked to be the leader in verse 6, above*] swear [*protest*], saying, **I will not be an healer [C']** [*I can't lead you and fix your problems!*]; for in my house is neither **bread [B']** nor clothing: make me not a ruler of the people [*I can't solve your problems. I've got my own problems*].

8 For **Jerusalem is ruined [A']**, and Judah is fallen: because their tongue and their doings are against the Lord, to provoke the eyes of his glory [*in word and actions, the people are completely against the Lord*].

Next, Isaiah tells us that the faces of the truly wicked and evil "radiate" their wickedness to all.

9 ¶ **The shew of their countenance doth witness against them**; and **they declare their sin as Sodom, they hide it not** [*blatant sin; they show no embarrassment nor shame for what they are doing*]. **Woe unto their soul!** for they have rewarded evil unto themselves [*they are sinning against themselves, preparing an evil harvest for themselves*].

Next, the Lord assures the righteous among the wicked that they will reap the sweet harvest of their goodness.

The **bolded** text in verses 10 and 11, next, summarizes a major message found throughout

Isaiah's teachings.

10 **Say ye to the righteous, that it shall be well with him**; for they shall eat the fruit of their doings [*righteousness will pay off*].

11 **Woe unto the wicked! it shall be ill with him**: for the reward of his hands shall be given him. [*"As ye sow, so shall ye reap."*]

12 ¶ As for my people, **children are their oppressors, and women rule over them** [*breakdown of traditional family; men are weak leaders, women have to fill in; can also reflect the deep bitterness and powerful influence of many women when they turn wicked*]. O my people, **they which lead thee cause thee to err**, and destroy the way of thy paths [*leadership without basic gospel values can be devastating*].

13 **The Lord standeth up to plead** [*to try your case as in a court of law; implying that the evidence is against you*], and standeth to judge the people.

14 **The Lord will enter into judgment** [*in effect, you will stand before the Lord to answer for your behaviors*] with the ancients of his people, and the princes [*leaders*] thereof: for **ye have eaten up the vineyard; the spoil of** [*things you have taken from*] **the poor is in your houses** [*you were supposed to protect them but instead you preyed on them*].

15 **What mean ye** [*what have you got to say for yourselves*] that **ye beat my people to pieces, and grind the faces of the poor**? saith the Lord God of hosts.

Isaiah now says that society is lost when women also turn to evil. From this we can better understand the devil's strategy in our day as he works to convince women to join in the evils of men and pull away from home and family.

16 ¶ Moreover the Lord saith, **Because the daughters of Zion** [*women of the Church particularly, and women in general*] **are haughty** [*full of pride*], and **walk with stretched forth necks** [*prideful*] and **wanton eyes** [*lustful*], walking and **mincing as they go** [*walking in such a way as to attract men's lustful thoughts*], and **making a tinkling with their feet** [*a reference to wearing expensive, high-fashion shoes (in Isaiah's day) with little bells on them to attract attention to their wealthy status*]:

17 **Therefore** [*for these reasons*] **the Lord will smite** with a scab the crown of the head [*will take away their beauty*] of **the daughters of Zion**, and the Lord will discover [*uncover*] their secret parts [*expose their evil deeds*].

Scholars do not always agree

on the nature of the female ornaments mentioned in verses 18–23, next. We will supply definitions from a variety of sources, realizing that many of them are simply best guesses.

18 **In that day** [*when destruction comes*] **the Lord will take away** the bravery [*beauty*] of their tinkling **ornaments** about their feet, and their **cauls**, and their **round tires like the moon** [*possibly crescent-shaped necklaces*],

19 The **chains**, and the **bracelets**, and the **mufflers** [veils],

20 The **bonnets**, and the **ornaments** of the legs, and the *headbands*, and the **tablets** [*perfume boxes*], and the **earrings**,

21 The **rings**, and **nose jewels**,

22 The **changeable suits of apparel** [*beautiful clothing*], and the *mantles*, and the **wimples** [*shawls*], and the crisping pins [*money purses*],

23 The **glasses** [*see-through clothing; see Isaiah 3:23, footnote a in your Bible*], and the **fine linen**, and the **hoods** [*turbans*], and the **vails**. [*Isaiah has described female high-society fashions, accompanied by arrogance and materialism, in terms of such things in his day.*]

24 **And it shall come to pass, that instead** [*in place of*] **of sweet smell there shall be stink** [*from corpses of people killed by invading armies*]; and instead of a girdle [*high-fashion clothing*] a **rent** [*torn clothing, rags*], and instead of well set hair **baldness** [*invading armies customarily shaved the heads of captives whom they enslaved for the purposes of humiliation, identification, and sanitation*]; and instead of a **stomacher** [*nice robe*] a girding of sackcloth [*coarse clothing worn by slaves and the poor class*]; and burning [*branding; conquerors often branded their slaves*] instead of [*in the place of*] beauty.

25 **Thy men shall fall by the sword**, and thy mighty in the war [*invasion*].

The above-mentioned slaughter of men will set the stage for the plural marriage mentioned in Isaiah 4:1. With so few men left, the widows and other women in Jerusalem will plead with men to marry several wives, so that they can have a proper place in society. They will offer to pay their own way so they will not become a financial burden on their husbands. Remember that plural marriage was common in that culture at the time.

26 **And her** [*Jerusalem's*] **gates shall lament and mourn**; and **she** being desolate [*empty, defeated*] **shall sit upon the ground** [*a sign of defeat and humility*].

ISAIAH 4

Background

Both the Joseph Smith Translation and the Hebrew Bible put verse one of chapter 4 at the end of chapter 3, which puts it in the context of Jerusalem's destruction and the scarcity of men resulting from the war prophesied in Isaiah 3:25–26. Footnote 4:1a in your Bible, says "because of scarcity of men due to wars. See 3:25." Footnote b likewise refers the reader to chapter 3.

Verses 2–6 deal with the Millennium.

1 **And in that day** [*the time of the destruction of Jerusalem spoken of in Isaiah 3:25–26*] **seven women shall take hold of one man, saying,** We will eat our own bread, and wear our own apparel [*we will pay our own way*]: only let us be called by thy name [*please marry us*], to take away our reproach [*the stigma in that society of being unmarried and childless*].

Verse 2, next, starts a new topic, namely, conditions during the Millennium.

2 **In that day** [*Millennium*] **shall the branch of the Lord** [*Christ—see Jeremiah 23:5*] **be beautiful and glorious**, and the fruit of the earth shall be excellent and comely [*pleasant to look at*] for them that are escaped of Israel [*for those*

who have escaped wickedness—the righteous remnant of Israel*].

3 And it shall come to pass, that **he that is left in Zion, and he that remaineth in Jerusalem, shall be called holy**, even every one that is written among the living [*those saved by approval of the Messiah*] in Jerusalem:

4 **When the Lord shall have washed away the filth of the daughters of Zion** [*after the Lord has cleansed the earth of the wicked at the Second Coming*], and shall have purged the blood of Jerusalem from the midst thereof by the spirit of judgment, and by the spirit of burning [*earth will be cleansed by fire*].

The Angel Moroni quoted verses 5 and 6 to Joseph Smith in reference to the last days. (See *Messenger and Advocate*, April 1835, page 110.) The imagery in verse five symbolizes the presence of the Lord on earth during the Millennium.

5 And **the Lord will create upon every dwelling place of mount Zion, and upon her assemblies, a cloud and smoke by day** [*represents the presence of the Lord as in Exodus 19:16–18*], and the shining of a **flaming fire by night**: for upon all [*everyone*] the glory shall be a defence.

6 And **there shall be a tabernacle**

[*shelter*] **for a shadow** [*shade*] in the daytime from the heat, and for a place of refuge, and **for a covert** [*protection*] from storm and from rain [*Millennial peace and protection*].

ISAIAH 5

Background
In this chapter we will see Isaiah's marvelous intellect and poetic talent at work as he composes a song or poetic parable of a vineyard, symbolizing God's mercy and Israel's unresponsiveness to Him.

1 **Now will I sing** [*compose a song or poetic parable*] to my well-beloved **a song of my beloved** [*Christ*] touching **his vineyard** [*Israel—see verse 7*]. My wellbeloved hath a vineyard in a fruitful hill [*in a place where they have great potential to grow and produce the desired fruit*]:

2 And **he fenced it, and gathered out the stones thereof** [*took away the stumbling blocks and obstacles to progression*], **and planted it with the choicest vine** [*the men of Judah—see verse 7; symbolic of His covenant people*], and **built a tower** [*set prophets*] in the midst of it, and also **made a winepress therein** [*planning for a good harvest*]: and **he looked that it should bring forth grapes** [*the desired product, faithful people*], **and it brought forth wild grapes** [*apostasy*].

3 And now, O inhabitants of Jerusalem, and men of Judah, **judge, I pray you, betwixt me and my vineyard** [*I'll give you the facts; you be the judge*].

4 **What could have been done more** to my vineyard, **that I have not done** in it [*the main question—compare with Jacob 5:47 and 49*]? **wherefore** [*why*], when I looked [*planned*] that it should bring forth grapes [*the desired result, faithful people*], **brought it forth wild grapes** [*wicked people; apostasy*]?

5 And now go to; **I will tell you what I will do to my vineyard** [*Israel*]: **I will take away the hedge** [*divine protection*] thereof, **and it shall be eaten up** [*destroyed*]; and **break down the wall** [*protection*] thereof, **and it shall be trodden down** [*by enemies*]:

6 And **I will lay it waste: it shall not be pruned** [*will not have sins, false doctrines, and so forth pruned out of the lives of its people by living prophets*], **nor digged** [*nourished; the Spirit withdraws, no prophets*]; **but there shall come up briers and thorns** [*apostate doctrines and behaviors*]: I will also command the clouds that they rain **no rain** upon it [*famine*].

Next, in verse 7, Isaiah defines some of the symbolism in this parable.

7 For **the vineyard** of the Lord of

hosts **is the house of Israel**, and the **men of Judah his pleasant plant**: and **he looked for judgment** [*fairness, honesty, and so forth*], **but behold oppression; for righteousness, but behold a cry** [*found riotous living instead*].

Verse 8, next, has actually been misinterpreted on occasions to mean that building row houses and condominiums is sinful. Of course, such is not the meaning but it is interesting how far astray things can go.

8 ¶ **Woe unto them** [*the powerful, wealthy*] that join house to house [*cheat the poor and unfortunate out of their homes and take them from them*], **that lay field to field, till there be no place, that they** [*the poor*] may be placed alone in the midst of the earth [*those in power push the poor farmers off their land by unscrupulous means*].

9 In mine ears said the Lord of hosts, Of a truth **many houses shall be desolate**, even great and fair [*the homes and palaces of the great and powerful wicked*], without inhabitant [*troubles are coming because of your wickedness*].

Next, Isaiah uses stark imagery to prophesy that a famine is coming.

10 Yea, **ten acres of vineyard shall yield one bath** [*about 8¼ U.S. gallons*], and **the seed of an homer**

[*6½ bushel of seed*] **shall yield an ephah** [*½ bushel of harvest; in other words, famine is coming*].

Next, we see a warning against riotous living, which generally accompanies sin and wickedness in society.

11 ¶ **Woe unto them that rise up early in the morning, that they may follow strong drink; that continue until night**, till wine inflame them!

Next, in verse 12, Isaiah points out that these people "go to church" and go through all the motions of the true religion (law of Moses, for them), but they are hypocrites and do not live the gospel in their daily lives.

12 And **the harp**, and the **viol** [*lyre*], the **tabret** [*drums*], and **pipe** [*instruments associated with worship of the Lord in Bible times*], and **wine**, are in their feasts: **but they regard not the work of the Lord** [*their worship is empty, hypocritical*], neither consider the operation of his hands [*they do not actually acknowledge God*].

Next, Isaiah speaks prophetically of the future as if it has already happened. This way of speaking is quite common in Old Testament prophecies.

13 ¶ **Therefore** [*that is why*] **my people are gone into captivity, because they have no knowledge**

[*Amos 8:11–12 famine of hearing words of the Lord*]: and **their honourable men are famished, and their multitude dried up** with thirst [*the prophesied destructions and famine have taken their toll*].

14 **Therefore** [*that is why*] **hell hath enlarged herself** [*they've had to add on to hell to make room for you*], and opened her mouth without measure [*more than anyone thought possible*]: **and their glory, and their multitude, and their pomp, and he that rejoiceth** [*in wickedness and riotous living*], **shall descend into it.**

15 And **the mean** [*poor*] **man shall be brought down** [*humbled*], and **the mighty man shall be humbled**, and the eyes of the lofty shall be humbled [*everyone needs humbling*]:

16 **But the Lord of hosts shall be exalted in judgment** [*you will see that the Lord is correct*], and God that is holy shall be sanctified in righteousness [*the Lord will triumph*].

17 **Then** [*after the destruction that is coming to Israel*] **shall the lambs feed** [*graze where the Lord's vineyard once stood—destruction is complete*] after their manner, **and the waste places** [*ruins*] **of the fat ones** [*the former prosperous inhabitants*] shall strangers [*foreigners*] eat [*in other words,*

foreign enemies will take over your land].

Next, in verse 18, Isaiah uses yet another image to describe the bondage of sin among the covenant people of Israel.

18 **Woe unto them that draw iniquity with cords of vanity, and sin as it were with a cart rope** [*you are tethered to your sins; they follow you like a cart follows the animal pulling it*]:

19 **That say, Let him** [*the Lord*] make speed, and **hasten his work, that we may see it** [*it is up to God to prove to us that He exists*]: and **let the counsel** [*plans*] **of the Holy One of Israel** [*the Lord*] draw nigh and come [*come to pass*], that we may know it [*if He wants us to know Him, He will have to be more obvious about His existence*]!

Verse 20, next, is well-known and often used in our lessons and sermons. We see much of this switching of things around in the world today.

20 ¶ **Woe unto them that call evil good, and good evil**; that **put darkness for light, and light for darkness**; that put bitter for sweet, and sweet for bitter!

21 **Woe unto them that are wise in their own eyes** [*full of evil pride*], and prudent in their own sight!

22 **Woe unto them that are mighty**

to drink wine, and men of strength to mingle strong drink:

23 **Which justify the wicked for reward** [*bribes, corrupt judicial system*], **and take away the righteousness of the righteous from him** [*ruin the good reputations of righteous people*]!

Next, in verse 24, Isaiah describes serious ultimate consequences of rebellion and sin.

24 Therefore as the fire devoureth the stubble, and the flame consumeth the chaff, so **their root shall be as rottenness, and their blossom shall go up as dust** [*shall not bear fruit, shall have no posterity in the next life and destruction of many in this life*]: **because they have cast away the law of the Lord** of hosts, and despised the word of the Holy One of Israel.

The unfathomable depth of the love and mercy that the Savior has for us is brought out at the end of verse 25, next. In this we see the power of the Atonement of Jesus Christ to cleanse and heal. You may wish to reread Isaiah 1:18 as you read this verse.

25 **Therefore** [*for these reasons*] **is the anger of the Lord kindled against his people** [*covenant Israel*], and **he hath stretched forth his hand against them**, and hath smitten them: and the hills did tremble, and their carcases were torn in the midst of the streets [*great destruction is coming*]. For all this [*because of all this wickedness*] his anger is not turned away, **but his hand is stretched out still** [*you can still repent—compare with Jacob 6:4*].

In verses 26–30, next, we see a prophecy of the gathering of Israel in the last days. We see modern transportation bringing members and new converts great distances to gather together as Saints. Isaiah's imagery shows us that none will stop the work of the Lord and the gathering of Israel in these marvelous times. Surely, we are witnessing this in our day.

26 ¶ And **he will lift up an ensign** [*flag, rallying point; the true gospel*] **to the nations from far**, and will hiss [*whistle; a signal to gather*] unto them from the end of the earth: and, behold, **they shall come with speed swiftly** [*modern transportation*]:

27 **None shall be weary nor stumble** among them; **none shall slumber nor sleep**; neither shall the girdle of their loins be loosed [*change clothes*], nor the latchet of their shoes be broken [*they will travel so fast that they won't need to change clothes or even take their shoes off*]:

28 **Whose arrows are sharp, and all their bows bent** [*perhaps

describing the body of a sleek airliner, like an arrow, and the swept back wings like a bow], **their horses' hoofs shall be counted like flint** [*making sparks like the wheels on a train?*], and their wheels like a whirlwind [*airplanes, trains?*]:

29 **Their roaring shall be like a lion** [*the noise of airplanes, trains, and so on?*], they shall roar like young lions: yea, they shall roar, and **lay hold of the prey** [*take in their passengers?*], **and shall carry it away safe, and none shall deliver it** [*the converts—none will stop the gathering of Israel in the last days*].

30 **And in that day** [*the last days*] they shall roar against them like the roaring of the sea: and **if one look unto the land, light is darkened in the heavens thereof** [*conditions in the last days: war, smoke, pollution, spiritual darkness?*].

ISAIAH 6

Background

Chapter 6 contains rich Atonement symbolism, especially verses 6 and 7. Without an understanding of symbolism, these two verses seem strange and mysterious. With it, they show the wonderful power of the Atonement of Christ to cleanse and heal, and to enable us to accept difficult callings with assurance and faith.

Most scholars agree that this chapter is an account of Isaiah's call to serve as a prophet of the Lord. Some feel that it is a later calling to a major assignment. Either way, Isaiah feels completely inadequate and overwhelmed (verse 5).

Verse 1 identifies the date of this revelation to Isaiah.

1 **In the year that king Uzziah died** [*about 740 B.C.*] **I** [*Isaiah*] **saw** also **the Lord** [*Jesus—see footnote 6c in your Bible*] **sitting upon a throne, high and lifted up** [*exalted*], and **his train** [*skirts of his robe; authority; power. Hebrew: wake, light*] **filled the temple** [*symbolic of heaven—see Revelation 21:22, where the celestial kingdom does not need a temple but, in effect, is a temple itself*].

2 **Above it** [*the throne*] **stood the seraphims** [*angelic beings*]: **each one had six wings** [*wings are symbolic of power to move, act, and so forth, in God's work—see D&C 77:4*]; **with twain** [*two*] **he covered his face** [*symbolic of a veil, which shows reverence and respect toward God in biblical culture*], and **with twain he covered his feet**, and **with twain he did fly**.

3 And **one cried unto another, and said, Holy, holy, holy, is the Lord of hosts** [*a word repeated three times forms the superlative in*

Hebrew, meaning the very best]: **the whole earth is full of his glory.**

4 **And the posts of the door moved** [*shook*] **at** the voice of him that cried, **and the house was filled with smoke** [*shaking and smoke are symbolic of God's presence in biblical culture, as at Sinai, Exodus 19:18*].

Next, Isaiah tells us that he was completely overwhelmed by the experience of seeing the Savior.

5 ¶ **Then said I, Woe is me! for I am undone** [*completely overwhelmed*]; because **I am a man of unclean lips** [*I am so imperfect*], and I dwell in the midst of a people of unclean lips: **for mine eyes have seen the King, the Lord of hosts.**

6 **Then flew one of the seraphims unto me, having a live coal** [*symbolic of the Atonement; also symbolic of the Holy Ghost who guides us to the Atonement; we often say that the Holy Ghost "cleanses by fire"*] **in his hand,** which he had taken with the tongs **from** off **the altar** [*the "altar cross," representing the Savior's sacrifice for our sins*]:

7 **And he laid it** [*the Atonement*] **upon my mouth** [*inadequacies, sins, imperfections*], **and said, Lo, this** [*the Atonement*] **hath touched thy lips** [*Isaiah's sins and imperfections—see verse 5, above*]; and **thine iniquity is taken away, and thy sin purged** [*the results of the Atonement*].

Watch now as the blessings of the Atonement give Isaiah confidence to accept his mission from the Lord. It can do the same for us in our callings.

8 Also [*then*] **I heard the voice of the Lord, saying, Whom shall I send, and who will go for us? Then said I** [*Isaiah*], **Here am I; send me** [*the cleansing power of the Atonement and help of the Spirit gave Isaiah the needed confidence to accept the call*].

Next, in verses 9–12, the Savior gives Isaiah an idea of the kinds of people he will be working with as a prophet. It will be a tough assignment. We will use a quote from Isaiah in the Book of Mormon to help with verse 9.

9 ¶ **And he** [*the Lord*] **said, Go** [*this is the official call*], **and tell this people, Hear** ye indeed, but understand not; **and see** ye indeed, but perceive not.

The Book of Mormon makes significant changes to the above verse of Isaiah.

2 Nephi 16:9
9 And he said: Go and tell this people—Hear ye indeed, **but they understood not**; and see ye indeed, **but they perceived not** [*Isaiah's task will not be easy with that kind of people*].

In verse 10, next, (*which contains a chiasmus—see notes in chapter 3 of this study guide*) the Lord gives Isaiah some additional insights as to the type of people he will be preaching to. In effect, the Savior appears to be telling him to imagine this type of people in his mind's eye.

10 [*In your imagination*] Make the **heart** [A] of this people fat [*unfeeling, insulated from truth*], and make their **ears** [B] heavy [*deaf to spiritual matters*], and shut their **eyes** [C] [*spiritually blind*]; lest they see with their **eyes** [C'], and hear with their **ears** [B'], and understand with their **heart** [A'], and convert, and be healed.

There is a quote in Matthew in which the Savior basically quoted the above verse of Isaiah. Note that Matthew records that the people have refused to hear the gospel message.

Matthew 13:15

15 For this people's heart is waxed gross, and *their* ears are dull of hearing, and their eyes **they have closed**; lest at any time they should see with *their* eyes, and hear with *their* ears, and should understand with *their* heart, and should be converted, and I should heal them.

The Lord's description of the people with whom Isaiah would be working appears to have startled and concerned him somewhat, causing him to ask the following question:

11 **Then said I, Lord, how long** [*will people be like this*]? **And he answered,** Until the cities be wasted without inhabitant, and the houses without man, and the land be utterly desolate [*in other words, as long as people are around*],

12 **And the Lord have removed men far away** [*people are gone*], and there be a great forsaking [*many deserted cities*] in the midst of the land.

In verse 13, next, Isaiah is assured that the time will never come when there are no more people, as mentioned in the scenario given in verses 11–12, above. Instead, a remnant of Israel will survive and will be pruned by the Lord and gathered.

13 ¶ **But yet in it** [*the land*] **shall be a tenth** [*a remnant*], **and it** [*Israel*] **shall return** [*includes the concept of repenting*], **and shall be eaten** [*in other words, pruned—as by animals eating the limbs, leaves, and branches; in other words, the Lord "prunes" his vineyard or cuts out old apostates, false doctrines, and so forth; He destroys old unrighteous generations so new may have a chance to grow*]: **as a teil** [*lime?*] **tree, and as an oak, whose substance** [*sap*] **is in them,**

when they cast their leaves [*trees that shed the old, non-functioning leaves and look dead in winter but are still alive*]: **so the holy seed shall be the substance thereof** [*Israel may look dead, but there is still life in it*].

ISAIAH 7

Background
In this chapter, we see a plot by Israel (the northern ten tribes who became the "lost ten tribes," also known as "Ephraim" at this time in history) and Syria to attack Judah (Jerusalem and the surrounding area). Their plan is to conquer Judah and place a puppet king on the throne in Jerusalem who will be loyal to them.

You will see different names used to refer to Syria, the northern kingdom (Israel) and the southern kingdom (Judah), and this can be confusing. We will list some of these plus the names of kings, to help you keep things straight:

Syria
- Damascus (the capital city of Syria)
- Rezin (the king)

Israel (the ten tribes)
- Ephraim
- Samaria (the capitol city of Israel)
- Pekah (the king)

Judah (the tribes of Judah and Benjamin)
- House of David
- Jerusalem
- Ahaz (the king)

In verse 1, next, we are told that this plot took place about 734 B.C., which is about twelve years before the Assyrians conquered Israel and carried them away captive (thus they became the lost ten tribes).

1 And **it came to pass in the days of Ahaz** [*about 734 B.C.*] the son of Jotham, the son of Uzziah, **king of Judah**, that Rezin **the king of Syria, and** Pekah **the** son of Remaliah, **king of Israel** [*the ten tribes in northern Israel*], **went up toward Jerusalem to war against it**, but could not prevail against it [*didn't win, but they did kill 120,000 men of Judah and take 200,000 captives in one day; see 2 Chronicles 28:6–15*].

Next, in verse 2, we learn that the inhabitants of Judah found out about the plot against them.

2 And **it was told the house of David** [*Judah, Jerusalem*], saying, **Syria is confederate** [*joining forces*] **with Ephraim** [*Israel, the northern ten tribes*]. **And his** [*King Ahaz's*] **heart was moved** [*shaken*], **and the heart of his people, as the trees of the wood are moved with the wind** [*they were "shaking in their boots"; scared*].

Next, the Lord sends Isaiah to wicked King Ahaz to tell him not to worry about the plot, because it will not amount to anything.

3 **Then said the Lord unto Isaiah, Go forth now to meet Ahaz** [*king in Jerusalem*]**,** thou, and Shear-jashub [*Hebrew: "the remnant shall return"*] thy son, at the end of the conduit of the upper pool **in the highway of the fuller's field** [*where the women wash clothes— Ahaz is hiding among the women*];

4 **And say unto him,** Take heed, and **be quiet** [*settle down*]**; fear not,** neither be fainthearted [*don't worry about continued threats from Syria and Israel*] **for** [*because of*] **the two tails of these smoking firebrands** [*these two kings who think they are really something but are nothing but smoldering stubs of firewood*], for [*because of*] the fierce anger of Rezin with Syria, and of the son of Remaliah [*referring to Pekah, king of Israel*].

5 **Because Syria, Ephraim** [*the ten tribes*], and the son of Remaliah [*the ten tribes' king*], **have taken evil counsel** [*have evil plans*] **against thee, saying,**

6 **Let us go up against Judah,** and vex [*cause trouble for*] it, **and let us** make a breach therein for us, and **set a king in the midst of it** [*set up our own king in Jerusalem*], even the son of Tabeal [*the name of the fellow they had in mind to install as a puppet king*]:

7 **Thus saith the Lord God, It shall not stand, neither shall it come to pass** [*the plot will fail, so don't worry about it*].

8 For **the head** [*capital city*] **of Syria is Damascus, and the head** [*leader*] **of Damascus is Rezin**; and **within threescore and five years** [*sixty-five years*] **shall Ephraim** [*the ten tribes*] be **broken,** that it be not a people [*in sixty-five years, the ten tribes will be lost; apparently it took several years after Assyria captured the ten tribes (about 722 B.C.) until they were lost to the knowledge of other people*].

9 And **the head** [*capital city*] **of Ephraim is Samaria,** and **the head** [*leader*] **of Samaria is Remaliah's son** [*Pekah; apparently Isaiah had such disdain for Pekah that he refused to use his name, preferring instead to call him "Remaliah's boy"*]. **If ye** [*Ahaz and his people, the tribe of Judah*] **will not believe** [*in the Lord*], surely **ye shall not be established** [*not be saved by the Lord's power*].

Next, the Lord has Isaiah invite King Ahaz to ask for a sign to prove that what Isaiah has told him about the plot is true. Watch how this weak king reacts to this rare invitation from the Lord.

10 ¶ **Moreover** the Lord spake

again unto Ahaz, saying,

11 **Ask thee a sign** [*to strengthen your faith*] **of the Lord** thy God; ask it either in the depth, or in the height above [*ask anything you want*].

12 **But Ahaz said, I will not ask, neither will I tempt** [*test*] **the Lord** [*refuses to follow prophet's counsel; he is deliberately evasive, and is already secretly depending on Assyria for help*].

13 **And he** [*Isaiah*] **said, Hear ye now, O house of David** [*Ahaz and his people, Judah*]; Is it a small thing for you to weary men, but **will ye weary my God also** [*try the patience of God*]?

Next, Isaiah prophesies of the coming of Jesus Christ in the meridian of time—see heading to chapter 7 in your Bible. Verse 14 emphasizes that because of their wickedness, these people desperately need the Savior.

14 **Therefore** [*because of your disobedience*] the Lord himself shall give you a sign; Behold, **a virgin shall conceive, and bear a son, and shall call his name Immanuel** [*the day will come when the Savior will be born*].

15 **Butter and honey** [*curd and honey, the only foods available to the poor at times*] **shall he eat, that he may know to refuse the**

evil, and choose the good.

Next, in verse 16, Isaiah explains that in the same number of years it will take the future Savior to grow from an infant to the point of being able to choose between right and wrong, the kings of Syria and Israel will fall from power.

16 For **before the child shall know to refuse the evil, and choose the good** [*before he is old enough to choose right from wrong—in just a few years*], **the land** [*both Israel and Syria*] **that thou abhorrest** [*that causes you fear*] **shall be forsaken of both her kings**.

17 **The Lord shall bring upon thee** [*Ahaz*]**, and upon thy people, and upon thy father's house** [*the royal family*], days that have not come [*trouble like never before*], from the day that Ephraim departed from Judah [*when the ten tribes comprising Israel split into the northern kingdom under Jeroboam I, and the tribes of Judah and Benjamin under Rehoboam, about 975 B.C.*]; even **the king of Assyria** [*the king of Assyria and his armies will come upon you*].

18 And it shall come to pass **in that day, that the Lord shall hiss** [*signal, call for*] **for the fly** [*associated with plagues, troubles and so forth*] **that is in the uttermost part of the rivers of Egypt, and for the bee that is in the land of Assyria.**

19 And **they shall come, and shall rest** all of them **in the desolate valleys, and in the holes of the rocks, and upon all thorns, and upon all bushes** [*you will have enemies in your land like flies; they will overrun the land*].

Verse 20, next, says, in effect, that the people of Judah will become slaves.

20 **In the same day shall the Lord shave with a razor** [*fate of captives, slaves—who are shaved for humiliation, sanitation, identification*] **that is hired** [*Assyria will be "hired" to do this to Judah*], **namely**, by them beyond the river, by **the king of Assyria**, the head, and the hair of the feet: and it shall also consume the beard [*they will shave you clean—conquer you; beards were a sign of dignity in ancient Israel*].

The imagery used by Isaiah in verses 21–25, next, shows us that, after the conquering enemy armies have done their work, the land will be relatively empty of inhabitants.

21 And **it shall come to pass in that day** [*after much devastation in Judah*], **that a man shall nourish a young cow, and two sheep;**

22 And it shall come to pass, **for the abundance of milk that they** [*the domestic animals*] **shall give he shall eat butter**: for butter and honey shall every one eat that is left in the land [*not many people left, so a few animals can supply them well*].

23 And it shall come to pass in that day, that every place shall be, **where there were a thousand vines at a thousand silverlings** [*worth a thousand pieces of silver*], **it shall even be for briers and thorns** [*uncultivated land where it used to be cultivated and productive; symbolic of apostasy*].

24 **With arrows and bows shall men come thither**; because all the land shall become briers and thorns [*previously cultivated land will become wild and overgrown so hunters will hunt wild beasts there*].

25 **And on all hills that shall be digged** [*that were once cultivated*] with the mattock [*hoe*] there [*you*] shall not come thither [*because of*] the fear of briers and thorns: but **it shall be for the sending forth** [*pasturing*] **of oxen, and for the treading of lesser cattle** [*sheep or goats*].

ISAIAH 8

Background

We mentioned in Isaiah 7:12 that King Ahaz was secretly planning on alliances and treaties for protection, rather than repenting and turning to the Lord for help. In this chapter, we will see the Lord warn Judah against such alliances.

Isaiah will have the uncomfortable and very unpopular role of telling the people that such treaties will do no good, and that they should repent instead and thus qualify for the help of the Lord.

Isaiah will also prophesy of the coming destruction of Syria and Israel (verse 4).

As the chapter begins, we see Isaiah's use of imagery and symbolism to carry his message. In verse 1, he is told that he and Sister Isaiah will have a son. They are to give him a name (verse 3) that means that enemy armies will carry swift destruction upon the cities of Judah (except Jerusalem).

1 Moreover **the Lord said unto me, Take thee a great** [*large*] **roll** [*scroll*]**, and write in it** with a man's pen **concerning Maher-shalal-hash-baz** [*"to speed to the spoil, he hasteneth the prey"—see footnote 1d in your Bible*].

Isaiah invites two men to witness this prophecy, as it is written upon the scroll.

2 And I [*Isaiah*] took unto me faithful **witnesses** to record, **Uriah** the priest, and **Zechariah** the son of Jeberechiah.

3 And I went unto the prophetess [*Isaiah's wife*]; and she conceived, and bare a son. **Then said the Lord to me, Call his name Maher-shalal-hash-baz**.

4 For **before the child shall have knowledge to cry, My father, and my mother** [*before their son is old enough to talk*]**, the riches of Damascus** [*Syria*] **and the spoil** [*wealth*] **of Samaria** [*northern Israel; the ten tribes*] **shall be taken away before the king of Assyria** [*before Isaiah's son is old enough to say "Daddy," "Mommy," Assyria will attack and ravage northern Israel and Syria*].

Now the topic turns to the people of Judah, with Jerusalem as their capital city.

5 The Lord spake also unto me again, saying,

6 **Forasmuch as** [*since*] **this people** [*Judah, Jerusalem*] **refuseth the waters of Shiloah** [*the gentle help of Christ, John 4:14*] that go softly, **and rejoice in Rezin** [*heed Syria instead of the Lord*] **and Remaliah's son** [*northern Israel's king*];

7 Now **therefore**, behold, **the Lord bringeth up upon them the waters of the river, strong** [*terrifying*] **and many** [*armies and so forth*], even the king of Assyria, and all his glory [*pomp fanfare and ceremony of coming enemy armies*]: and **he shall come up over all his channels, and go over all his banks** [*you'll be*

"flooded" with Assyrians]:

8 And **he** [*Assyria*] **shall pass through Judah**; he shall overflow and go over, he shall reach even to the neck [*to Jerusalem*]; and the stretching out of his wings shall fill the breadth of thy land, O Imman-uel [*or, the land of the future birth of Christ*].

9 ¶ **Associate yourselves** [*if you form political alliances for protection rather than turning to God*], **O ye people, and ye shall be broken in pieces**; and **give ear, all ye of far countries** [*listen up, foreign nations who might rise against Judah*]: **gird yourselves** [*prepare for war against Judah*], **and ye shall be broken in pieces;** gird yourselves, and ye shall be broken in pieces [*note that "broken in pieces" is repeated three times for emphasis; repeating something three times indicates the Hebrew superlative*].

Perhaps you have noticed that Isaiah makes considerable use of repetition as a means of empha-sizing his messages. This is a common part of the "manner of prophesying among the Jews" (2 Nephi 25:1). We see an example of this type of repetition in verse 10, next.

10 **Take counsel together, and it shall come to nought** [*your plans to destroy Judah will not succeed ultimately*]; **speak the word** [*make*

decrees], **and it shall not stand**: for God is with us [*Judah won't be destroyed completely*].

Next, beginning with verse 11, Isaiah is given the difficult task of taking a stand opposite to that which was popular among the people. It was politically popular among the people at this time to advocate making alliances for safety with other nations, espe-cially Assyria. Isaiah tells them this is a mistake.

11 ¶ For **the Lord spake thus to me** [*Isaiah*] **with a strong hand** [*firmly*], **and instructed me that I should not walk in the way of this people** [*that I should not go along with popular opinion among the people of Judah*], **saying,**

12 **Say ye not, A confederacy** [*be allies with Assyria*], **to all them** to whom this people shall say, A confederacy; **neither fear ye their fear, nor be afraid.** [*"Isaiah, don't endorse Judah's plan for confed-eracy with Assyria. Don't tell them what they want to hear."*]

13 **Sanctify the Lord of hosts himself; and let him be your fear, and let him be your dread.** [*"Isaiah, you rely on the Lord, not public approval."*]

14 **And he** [*the Lord*] **shall be for a sanctuary** [*for you, Isaiah*]; **but for a stone of stumbling and for a rock of offence to** [*the Lord*

will stand in the way of] **both the houses of Israel** [*Israel (the northern ten tribes) and Judah*], for a gin [*a trap*] and for **a snare to the inhabitants of Jerusalem.**

Note Isaiah's great skill with words as he describes the downfall of Judah with hammer-like driving force, next, in verse 15.

15 And many among them [*Judah*] shall **stumble**, and **fall**, and be **broken**, and be **snared**, and be **taken**.

16 **Bind up the testimony** [*record your testimony against these wicked people, Isaiah*], seal the law among my disciples [*followers*].

Next, in verses 17–18, Isaiah pledges his loyalty to the Lord, in the face of much public opposition.

17 **And I** [*Isaiah*] **will wait upon the Lord** [*I will trust the Lord*], **that hideth his face from the house of Jacob** [*who has had to withdraw His blessings from the house of Israel*], and I will look for him [*will watch for His blessings and guidance in my life*].

18 **Behold, I and the children whom the Lord hath given me are for signs and for wonders in Israel from the Lord of hosts,** which dwelleth in mount Zion [*in other words, Isaiah and his family serve as a witness of the Lord among these Israelites*].

Many people turn to the occult for messages from beyond the veil. It seems to be easier to do this than to repent and gain revelation from the Lord. Isaiah speaks of this turning to the dark side in verse 19, next.

19 ¶ And **when they** [*the wicked*] **shall say unto you, Seek unto them** [*spiritualists, mediums, and so forth*] **that have familiar spirits, and unto wizards that peep** [*into their crystal balls and so forth*], **and that mutter: should not a people seek unto their God?** for the living to the dead [*why consult the dead on behalf of the living*]?

20 **To the law and to the testimony** [*the scriptures*]: **if they** [*sorcerers, wizards, mediums, and so forth*] **speak not according to this word** [*the scriptures*], it is because there *is no light in them.*

Next, Isaiah foretells what will happen to these people if they continue in the direction they are heading.

21 **And they** [*Israel, who will be taken into captivity*] **shall pass through it** [*the land*], **hardly bestead** [*severely distressed*] **and hungry**: and it shall come to pass, that when they shall be hungry, **they shall fret themselves** [*become enraged*], **and curse their king and their God, and look upward** [*be cocky, defiant; not humbled by their troubles*].

22 **And they shall look unto the earth** [*will look around them*]; **and behold** [*see only*] **trouble and darkness, dimness of anguish** [*gloom*]; **and they shall be driven to darkness** [*thrust into utter despair; spiritual darkness as the result of wickedness*].

ISAIAH 9

Background

This is a continuation of the topic in chapter 8. King Ahaz of Judah ignored the Lord's counsel and made an alliance with Assyria anyway. Symbolism here can include that Assyria would represent the devil and his evil, prideful ways. King Ahaz could symbolize foolish and wicked people who make alliances with the devil or his evil ways and naively think that they are thus protected from destruction spiritually and often physically.

In this chapter, Isaiah gives one of the most famous and beautiful of all his messianic prophecies. He prophesies that Christ will come. Handel's "Messiah" puts some of this chapter to magnificent music. You will likely recognize verse 6.

Verse 1 is positioned as the last verse of chapter 8 in the Hebrew Bible. It serves as a transition from the end of chapter 8 to the topic of the Savior's mortal mission, in chapter 9.

Verse 1 is somewhat complex and basically prophesies that the Savior will come to earth and prepare a way for people to escape from spiritual darkness and despair. It helps to know that two of the twelve tribes of Israel, the tribes of Zebulun and Naphtali, were located in what became known as Galilee in the Savior's day. Thus, verse 1 says that the humbling of haughty Israel, which took place when the Assyrians swept down upon them, will someday be softened when the Savior walks and teaches there during His mortal mission.

1 **Nevertheless the dimness** [*the despair and spiritual darkness referred to in 8:22*] **shall not be such as was in her vexation** [*distress*], **when at the first** [*Assyrian attacks in Isaiah's day*] **he lightly afflicted** [*NIV: "humbled"*] **the land of Zebulun** [*in northern Israel*] and the land of Naphtali [*in northern Israel*], **and afterward did more grievously afflict** [*Hebrew: gloriously bless; German: bring honor to*] **her** [*NIV: Galilee*] by the way of the sea, beyond Jordan, **in Galilee** of the nations [*blessed her via Jesus walking and teaching in Galilee*].

Next, Isaiah speaks prophetically of the future as if it has already happened. As we mentioned before, this was a common form of prophesying among the Jews.

2 **The people that walked in darkness** [*apostasy and captivity*] **have seen a great light** [*the Savior and His teachings*]: they that dwell in the land of the shadow of death, **upon them hath the light shined.**

3 **Thou hast multiplied the nation, and** not [*"not" is a mistake in translation and doesn't belong here; see 2 Nephi 19:3 where it is rendered correctly in this chapter of Isaiah as found in the Book of Mormon*] **increased the joy**: they joy before thee according to the joy in harvest, and as men rejoice when they divide the spoil [*Christ and His faithful followers will ultimately triumph*].

4 **For thou hast broken the yoke of his burden** [*Thou hast set them free*], and the staff of his shoulder, the rod [*symbolic of power*] of his oppressor, as in the day of Midian [*just like with Gideon and his three hundred; Judges 7:22*].

Next, Isaiah looks ahead to the destruction of the wicked at the time of the Second Coming and points out that their destruction will be different than that found in a normal battle.

5 For **every battle of the warrior** [*of man against man*] **is with confused noise, and garments rolled in blood** [*normal battles involve much noise and bloodshed*]; **but this** [*the final freedom from the wicked*] **shall be with burning**

and fuel of fire [*the burning at the Second Coming*].

6 **For unto us a child** [*Christ*] **is born, unto us a son is given: and the government shall be upon his shoulder: and his name shall be called Wonderful, Counsellor, The mighty God, The everlasting Father, The Prince of Peace.**

7 **Of the increase of his government and peace there shall be no end, upon the throne of David** [*during the Millennium, Christ will rule on earth*], **and upon his** kingdom, to order it, and to establish it with judgment [*fairness*] and with justice from henceforth even for ever. The zeal [*energy, power*] of the Lord of hosts will perform this.

The topic now switches back to Isaiah's day as he prophesies of the pride and wickedness that will continue to plague the northern ten tribes, often referred to at this point in history as "Israel" or "northern Israel." You will see that Isaiah uses several different ways of referring to the ten tribes.

8 **The Lord sent a word into Jacob** [*Israel*], and it hath lighted upon Israel.

9 And **all the people shall know,** even Ephraim [*northern Israel*] and the inhabitant of Samaria [*northern Israel*], **that say in the**

pride and stoutness of heart,

Next, in verse 10, Isaiah points out how full of pride rebellious Israel is. In effect, they boast that God's punishments won't humble them. They don't need God and they are not afraid of Him. They are basically saying to the Lord, "Go ahead and tear down our cities. We will simply rebuild them and with better materials than ever!"

10 **The bricks are fallen down, but we will build with hewn stones** [*boastful northern Israel claims they can't be destroyed but would simply rebuild with better materials than before*]: **the sycomores are cut down, but we will change them into cedars** [*we will rebuild with better wood than before*].

11 **Therefore the Lord shall set** up the adversaries of Rezin [*Syria*] **against him** [*Israel*], and join his enemies together [*the enemies of Syria will also come against Israel*];

One of the most important and consistent messages of Isaiah is that the wicked can still repent. We see this sweet message at the end of verse 12, next.

Major Message

The wicked can still repent. It is not too late for these wicked Israelites.

12 **The Syrians before** [*on the*

east], and **the Philistines behind** [*on the west*]; **and they shall devour Israel with open mouth.** For all this his anger is not turned away, **but his hand is stretched out still** [*the Lord will still let you repent if you will turn to Him. Compare with Jacob 6:4–5*].

Sadly, as Isaiah prophesies next, these people refuse the offer to repent.

13 ¶ For **the people turneth not unto him** [*the Lord*] that smiteth them [*who is punishing them*], **neither do they seek the Lord of hosts.**

14 **Therefore the Lord will cut off from Israel head** [*leaders*] and **tail** [false prophets], **branch** [*palm branch, meaning triumph and victory in Hebrew culture*] and **rush** [*reed, meaning people low in social status in the Hebrew culture*], in one day [*it will happen fast*].

Next, Isaiah defines some of the terms he used in verse 14, above, which were familiar to people in his day but not to us.

15 **The ancient and honourable, he is the head**; and **the** [*false*] **prophet that teacheth lies, he is the tail.**

16 For **the leaders of this people cause them to err; and they that are led of them are destroyed.**

Verse 17, next, shows us that the entire society was corrupt through and through.

17 Therefore the Lord shall have no joy [*pleasure, satisfaction*] in their young men, neither shall have mercy on their fatherless and widows [*all levels of society have gone bad*]: for every one is an hypocrite and an evildoer, and every mouth speaketh folly [*evil, corruption*]. For all this his anger is not turned away, but his hand is stretched out still [*please repent!*].

18 For wickedness burneth as the fire [*wickedness destroys like wildfire*]: it shall devour the briers and thorns [*the people of apostate Israel*], and shall kindle in the thickets of the forest [*destroy the people*], and they shall mount up like the lifting up of smoke.

19 Through the wrath of the Lord of hosts is the land darkened [*awful conditions*], and the people shall be as the fuel of the fire: no man shall spare his brother.

Wickedness inevitably destroys a society and nation. Verse 20, next, describes the desperate conditions that eventually overtake a wicked people.

20 And he [*the wicked*] shall snatch on the right hand, and be hungry; and he shall eat on the left hand, and they shall not be satisfied: they shall eat every man the flesh of his own arm [*the wicked will turn on each other*]:

Verse 21, next, speaks of the civil wars between the northern ten tribes and the people of Judah, which Isaiah has been discussing.

21 Manasseh, Ephraim [*Israel, the ten tribes*]; and Ephraim, Manasseh: and they together shall be against Judah. For all this his anger is not turned away, but his hand is stretched out still [*you can still repent; please do!*]

ISAIAH 10

Background

In the heading to chapter 10 in your Bible, you find the phrase, *"Destruction of Assyria is a type of destruction of the wicked at the Second Coming."* The word "type" means something that is symbolic of something else. For example, both Joseph who was sold into Egypt and Isaac were "types" of Christ; in other words, many things that happened to them were symbolic of the Savior. The following charts show some of the ways in which these great prophets were "types" of Christ:

Joseph in Egypt	Christ
Was sold for the price of a common slave	Was sold for the price of a common slave
Was thirty years old when he began his mission as prime minister to save his people	Was thirty years old when He began His formal mission to save His people
Gathered food for seven years to save his people	Used seven "days" to create the earth in which to offer salvation to us
Forgave his persecutors	Forgave His persecutors

Isaac	Christ
Was the only begotten of Abraham and Sarah	Is the Only Begotten of the Father
Was to be sacrificed by his father	Was allowed to be sacrificed by His Father
Carried the wood for his sacrifice	Carried the cross for His sacrifice
Volunteered to give his life (Abraham was too old to restrain him.)	Gave His life voluntarily

Another example of a "type" of Christ is found in Leviticus 14 where the priest is a "type" of Christ as he presents the privilege of being cleansed to the leper (who is a "type" of all sinners—that is to say, the leper can be symbolic of the need we all have to be cleansed from sin). We will include Leviticus 14:1–9 here as a brief lesson on the power of understanding the use of "types" in the scriptures.

Leviticus 14:1–9

1 And the LORD spake unto Moses, saying,

2 This shall be **the law of the leper** [*the rules for being made clean; symbolic of serious sin and great need for help and cleansing*] **in the day of his cleansing** [*symbolic of the desire to be made spiritually clean and pure*]: **He shall be brought unto the priest** [*authorized servant of God; bishop, stake president, who holds the keys of authority to act for God*]:

3 And **the priest shall go forth out of the camp** [*the person with leprosy did not have fellowship with the Lord's people and was required to live outside the main camp of the children of Israel; the bishop symbolically goes out of the way to help sinners who want to repent*]; and **the priest shall look, and, behold,** *if* **the plague of leprosy be healed in the leper** [*the bishop serves as a judge to see if the repentant sinner is ready to return to full membership privileges*];

4 Then shall the priest command to take for him that is to be cleansed [*the person who has repented*] **two birds** [*one represents the Savior during His mortal mission, the other represents the person who has repented*] alive *and* clean, and **cedar wood** [*symbolic of the cross*], and **scarlet** [*associated with mocking Christ before his crucifixion, Mark 15:17*], and **hyssop** [*associated with Christ on the cross, John 19:29*]:

5 And the priest shall command that **one of the birds** [*symbolic of the Savior*] be **killed in an earthen vessel** [*Christ was sent to earth to die for us*] **over running water** [*Christ offers "living water," the gospel of Jesus Christ—John 7:37–38—which cleanses us when we come unto Him*]:

6 **As for the living bird** [*representing the person who has repented*],

he [*the priest; symbolic of the bishop, stake president, one who holds the keys of judging*] **shall take it** [*the living bird*], **and the cedar wood,** and the **scarlet,** and the **hyssop** [*all associated with the Atonement*], **and shall dip them and the living bird in the blood of the bird** *that was* **killed over the running water** [*representing the cleansing power of the Savior's blood, which was shed for us*]:

7 And he shall **sprinkle upon him that is to be cleansed from the leprosy** [*symbolically, being cleansed from sin*] **seven times** [*seven is the number that, in biblical numeric symbolism, represents completeness, perfection*], **and shall pronounce him clean** [*he has been forgiven*], **and shall let the living bird** [*the person who has repented*] **loose into the open field** [*representing the wide open opportunities again available in the kingdom of God for the person who truly repents*].

8 And **he that is to be cleansed shall wash his clothes** [*symbolic of cleaning up your life from sinful ways and pursuits—compare with Isaiah 1:16*], and **shave off all his hair** [*symbolic of becoming like a newborn baby; "born again;" fresh start*], and **wash himself in water** [*symbolic of baptism*], **that he may be clean** [*cleansed from sin*]: and **after that he shall come into the camp** [*rejoin the Lord's*

covenant people], and shall tarry abroad out of his tent seven days.

9 But it shall be on the seventh day, that he shall shave all his hair off his head and his beard and his eyebrows, even all his hair he shall shave off [symbolic of being "born again"]: and he shall wash his clothes [clean up his life], also he shall wash his flesh in water [symbolic of baptism], and he shall be clean [a simple fact, namely that we can truly be cleansed and healed by the Savior's Atonement].

Having considered the use of "types" (sometimes called "types and shadows") in the scriptures, we will now proceed with chapter 10 and watch as Assyria is used as a "type" of the destruction of the wicked at the Second Coming.

1 **Woe unto them that decree unrighteous decrees** [unrighteous laws], **and that write grievousness** [oppression] **which they have pre-scribed;**

2 **To turn aside the needy from judgment** [fair treatment], **and to take away the right from the poor of my people, that widows may be their prey** [victims], **and that they may rob the fatherless!**

3 And **what will ye do in the day of visitation** [punishment], and in the desolation which shall come from far [from Assyria]? to whom

will ye flee for help? and where will ye leave your glory [wealth and so forth]?

4 **Without me** [the Lord] **they shall bow down under the prisoners** [huddle among the prisoners], **and they shall fall under the slain.** For all this his anger is not turned away, but **his hand is stretched out still** [you can still repent].

Have you noticed how often, in Isaiah's writings, the Lord says that "His hand is stretched out still"? It means that they can still repent. This is one of the major themes in the Lord's teachings through His prophet, Isaiah. We will quote from the Book of Mormon to verify that this is the meaning of that phrase:

<u>Jacob 6:4–5</u>
4 And how merciful is our God unto us, for he remembereth the house of Israel, both roots and branches; and **he stretches forth his hands unto them all the day long**; and they are a stiffnecked and a gainsaying people [always opposing God]; but as many as will not harden their hearts shall be saved in the kingdom of God.

5 Wherefore, my beloved brethren, I beseech of you in words of soberness that ye would **repent**, and come with full purpose of heart, and cleave unto God as he cleaveth unto you. And **while**

his arm of mercy is extended towards you in the light of the day, harden not your hearts.

5 ¶ **O Assyrian, the rod of mine anger** [*the tool of destruction used by the Lord to "hammer" Israel*], and the staff in their hand is mine indignation.

6 **I will send him** [*Assyria*] **against an hypocritical nation** [*Israel*], and against the people of my wrath will I give him a charge, to take the spoil, and **to take the prey, and to tread them** [*Israel*] **down** like the mire of the streets.

7 **Howbeit** [*however*] **he meaneth not so**, neither doth his heart think so [*king of Assyria doesn't realize he is a tool in God's hand, thinks he's very important on his own*]; but it is in his heart to destroy and cut off nations not a few.

Isaiah depicts the boasting and bragging of the prideful king of Assyria, in verse 8, next.

8 For **he** [*Assyrian king*] **saith** [*brags*], Are not my princes [*commanders*] altogether kings [*just like kings in other countries*]?

Next, Isaiah depicts the king boasting about cities his armies have already conquered.

9 Is not **Calno** as **Carchemish**? is not **Hamath** as **Arpad**? is not **Samaria** as **Damascus?** [*Assyria*

has already taken these cities.]

Next, the king boastfully declares that the gods of the above cities were powerless to save them, and they were more powerful than the God of Judah and Israel.

10 As my hand hath found the kingdoms of **the idols, and** whose **graven images did excel** [*were more powerful than*] **them of Jerusalem and of Samaria**;

11 **Shall I not, as I have done unto Samaria and her idols, so do to Jerusalem and her idols** [*a boast; I'll do the same to Jerusalem*]?

In verse 12, next, Isaiah explains what the Lord will do to the king of Assyria and his armies, when He is through using him to punish His rebellious covenant people.

12 Wherefore it shall come to pass, that **when the Lord hath performed his whole work upon mount Zion and on Jerusalem, I will punish** the fruit of the stout heart of **the king of Assyria**, and the glory of his high looks [*when I'm through using Assyria against Israel, then Assyria will get its just punishments*].

13 **For he** [*Assyrian king*] **saith, By the strength of my hand I have done it**, and by my wisdom; for I am prudent: and I have removed

the bounds of the people, and have robbed their treasures, and I have put down the inhabitants like a valiant man [*bragging*]:

14 **And my hand hath found as a nest the riches of the people**: and as one gathereth eggs that are left, have I gathered all the earth; and **there was none that moved the wing, or opened the mouth, or peeped** [*everybody is afraid of me!*].

15 **Shall the axe** [*Assyria*] **boast itself against him** [*the Lord*] **that heweth therewith** [*is it reasonable for the ax to claim that it swings itself*]? or shall the saw magnify itself against him that shaketh it [*uses it*]? as if the rod should shake itself against them that lift it up, or as if the staff should lift up itself, as if it were no wood [*how foolish for people to say they don't need the Lord*].

16 **Therefore shall the Lord, the Lord of hosts, send among his fat ones** [*Assyria's powerful armies*] **leanness** [*trouble is coming*]; and under his [*Assyria's*] glory **he** [*Christ*] **shall kindle a burning like the burning of a fire** [*the fate of Assyria*].

17 And **the light of Israel** [*Christ*] **shall be for a fire**, and his Holy One [*Christ*] for a flame: and **it shall burn and devour his** [*Assyria's*] **thorns and his briers** [*armies*]

in one day [*Example: 185,000 Assyrians died of devastating sickness in one night as they prepared to attack Jerusalem; see 2 Kings 19:35–37*];

18 **And shall consume the glory of his forest** [*symbolic of his armies, people*], and of his fruitful field, both soul and body: and they shall be **as when a standardbearer fainteth** [*as when the last flag-carrying soldier falls and the flag with him, the Assyrians will waste away, be destroyed*].

Next, Isaiah uses an interesting image to foretell that the Assyrians will be reduced to few people, so few that a small child who is just learning how to count and write numbers could count them and write the number down.

19 **And the rest of the trees** [*people*] **of his forest shall be few, that a child may write them.**

Attention now turns to the remnant of Israel remaining after the Assyrians are through with them. It is a prophecy of the gathering of Israel in the last days.

20 ¶ And it shall come to pass **in that day** [*the last days*], that **the remnant of Israel**, and such as are escaped of the house of Jacob [*Israel*], **shall no more again stay** [*depend*] **upon him** [*Assyria; symbolic of Satan and*

his evil front organizations] that smote them; **but shall stay upon the Lord, the Holy One of Israel, in truth**.

21 **The remnant shall return**, even the remnant of Jacob, **unto the mighty God** [*1. A remnant remains in the land after Assyrian destruction. 2. A future righteous remnant*].

22 For though thy people Israel be as the sand of the sea, yet **a remnant of them shall return**: the consumption decreed [*at end of the world*] shall overflow with righteousness [*Christ; the glory of the Savior will consume the wicked at the Second Coming; see D&C 5:19, 2 Nephi 12:10*].

23 **For the Lord God of hosts** [*Jehovah, Jesus Christ*] **shall make a consumption**, even determined, in the midst of all the land.

The topic now turns again to the fate of the Assyrians.

24 ¶ Therefore thus saith the Lord God of hosts, O my people that dwellest in Zion, **be not afraid of the Assyrian: he shall smite thee with a rod, and shall lift up his staff against thee**, after the manner of Egypt [*like Egypt did in earlier times*].

25 **For yet a very little while**, and the indignation shall cease, and mine anger in their destruction

[*then the Assyrian kingdom will fall via the anger of the Lord*].

26 And **the Lord of hosts shall stir up a scourge for him** according to the slaughter of Midian at the rock of Oreb: and as his rod was upon the sea [*the parting of the Red Sea*], so shall he lift it up after the manner of Egypt [*God will stop Assyria like he stopped the Egyptians*].

27 And it shall come to pass **in that day**, that **his burden** [*Assyria's rule; Satan's oppression*] **shall be taken away from off thy shoulder**, and his yoke from off thy neck, and **the yoke shall be destroyed because of the anointing** [*the Savior*].

Beginning with verse 28, next, Isaiah foretells how the Assyrian armies will gobble up city after city, and will come right up to the gates of Jerusalem, and then will be stopped in their tracks by the Lord. What remains of their army will then go home.

Isaiah speaks of the future as if it has already happened. He is a master at building dramatic tension.

28 He [*Assyria*] **is come to Aiath**, he is passed **to Migron**: at **Michmash** he hath laid up his carriages [*horses and chariots are symbolic of military might in biblical symbolism*].

29 They are gone over the passage: they have taken up their lodging at **Geba**; **Ramah** is afraid; **Gibeah** of Saul is fled.

30 Lift up thy voice, O daughter of **Gallim**: cause it to be heard unto **Laish**, O poor **Anathoth** [*Jeremiah's hometown; see Jeremiah 1:1*].

31 **Madmenah** is removed; the inhabitants of **Gebim** gather themselves to flee.

32 As **yet shall he** [*Assyria*] **remain at Nob** that day [*Assyria will take city after city, getting closer and closer to Jerusalem until they come to Nob, just outside Jerusalem*]: **he shall shake his hand** [*threaten*] **against** the mount of the daughter of Zion [*Jerusalem*], the hill of **Jerusalem**.

33 **Behold, the Lord, the Lord of hosts, shall lop** [*cut off*] **the bough with terror** [*when the Assyrian armies get right to Jerusalem, the Lord will "trim them down to size," "clip their wings," and stop them in their tracks*]: **and the high ones of stature** [*leaders of Assyrian armies*] **shall be hewn down, and the haughty shall be humbled**.

34 **And he shall cut down the thickets of the forest** [*the Assyrians*] **with iron** [*an axe*], and Lebanon shall fall by a mighty one [*see 2 Kings 19:32*].

ISAIAH 11

Background

Joseph Smith recorded that Moroni quoted this chapter, saying that it was about to be fulfilled. We find this statement in the Pearl of Great Price, Joseph Smith—History, as follows:

Joseph Smith–History 1:40

40 In addition to these, **he quoted the eleventh chapter of Isaiah, saying that it was about to be fulfilled**. He quoted also the third chapter of Acts, twenty-second and twenty-third verses, precisely as they stand in our New Testament. He said that that prophet was Christ; but the day had not yet come when "they who would not hear his voice should be cut off from among the people," but soon would come.

In Isaiah, chapter 11, we are taught that powerful leaders will come forth in the last days to lead the gathering of Israel. We are instructed in Christlike qualities of leadership. We will be shown the peace that will abound during the Millennium and Isaiah will also teach about the gathering of Israel in the last days.

1 And **there shall come forth a rod** [*Hebrew: twig or branch; D&C 113:3–4 defines this "rod" as "a servant in the hands of Christ"*]

out of the stem [*root*] of Jesse [*Christ—see heading to this chapter in your Bible*], and a Branch shall grow out of his roots:

Perhaps, the imagery here in verse one grows out of the last two verses of chapter 10, where the wicked leaders end up, in effect, as "stumps" and have been destroyed. In the last days, new, righteous, powerful leaders will be brought forth to replace the "stumps" of the past and will have their origins in the "roots" of Christ. Roots can symbolically represent being solid and firmly rooted in God.

Next, we see a description of Christlike qualities of leadership.

2 And the spirit of the Lord shall rest upon him, the **spirit of wisdom** and **understanding**, the spirit of **counsel** and **might**, the spirit of **knowledge** and of the **fear of** [*respect, honoring of*] **the Lord**;

3 And shall make him of **quick understanding in the fear of the Lord**: and **he shall not judge after the sight of his eyes, neither reprove after the hearing of his ears**:

Verse 4, next, makes a transition into describing powers held exclusively by the Savior.

4 But **with righteousness shall he judge the poor**, and **reprove with equity** for the meek of the earth:

and he shall **smite the earth** with the rod of his mouth, and with the breath of his lips shall he **slay the wicked**.

5 And **righteousness shall be the girdle of his loins** [*He will be clothed in righteousness*], and faithfulness the girdle of his reins [*desires, thoughts*].

Next, we are taken into the Millennium, where we are shown conditions of peace.

6 **The wolf also shall dwell with the lamb,** and **the leopard shall lie down with the kid** [*young goat*]; and **the calf and the young lion** and the fatling together; **and a little child shall lead** [*herd*] **them** [*Millennial conditions*].

7 And **the cow and the bear shall feed** [*graze*]; their young ones shall lie down together: and **the lion shall eat straw like the ox.**

8 And **the sucking** [*nursing*] **child shall play on the hole of the asp** [*viper*], and the weaned child shall put his hand on the cockatrice' [*venomous serpent's*] den.

9 **They shall not hurt nor destroy in all my holy mountain** [*throughout the earth*]: for **the earth shall be full of the knowledge of** [*Hebrew: "devotion to"*] **the Lord**, as the waters cover the sea.

10 **And in that day there shall be a root of Jesse** [*probably Joseph*

Smith—see Doctrine and Covenants Student Manual for Institutes of Religion of the Church, page 284], **which shall stand for an ensign** [*a rallying point for gathering*] of the people; **to it shall the Gentiles seek**: and his rest shall be glorious.

11 And it shall come to pass in that day, that **the Lord shall set his hand again the second time** [*dual meaning: after Babylonian captivity; also last days*] **to recover** [*gather*] **the remnant of his people**, which shall be left, from Assyria, and from Egypt, and from Pathros, and from Cush, and from Elam, and from Shinar, and from Hamath, and from the islands of the sea [*in other words, Israel will be gathered throughout the earth*].

12 And **he shall set up an ensign** [*the Church in the last days*] for the nations, **and shall assemble the outcasts of Israel, and gather together the dispersed of Judah** from the four corners of the earth.

13 The envy also of Ephraim shall depart, and the adversaries of Judah shall be cut off: **Ephraim shall not envy Judah, and Judah shall not vex Ephraim** [*U.S.A. and others will work with the Jews*].

14 **But they** [*the Jews with Ephraim's help*] **shall fly upon the shoulders of the Philistines toward the west** [*will attack the western slopes that were Philistine*

territory]; **they shall spoil them of the east** together: they shall lay their hand upon Edom and Moab; and the children of Ammon shall obey them [*the Jews will be powerful in the last days rather than easy prey for their enemies*].

15 **And the Lord shall utterly destroy the tongue of the Egyptian sea** [*perhaps meaning that the productivity of the Nile River will be ruined; see Isaiah 19:5–10*]; **and with his mighty wind shall he shake his hand over the river** [*perhaps the river referred to in Revelation 16:12; symbolically, the Euphrates, representing preparation for the Battle of Armageddon*], and shall smite it in the seven streams, and make men go over dryshod.

16 And **there shall be an highway** [*God will prepare a way for them to return; gathering*] **for the remnant of his people**, which shall be left, from Assyria; like as it was to Israel in the day that he came up out of the land of Egypt.

ISAIAH 12

Background

This short but beautiful chapter refers to the Millennium. It describes the faithful who survive the destruction at the Second Coming of Christ as praising the Lord and rejoicing at the salvation that has come to them.

1 And **in that day** [*during the Millennial reign of the Savior*] **thou** [*Israel*] **shalt say**, O Lord, I will praise thee: though thou wast angry with me [*in times past, because of my rebellions*], thine anger is turned away, and thou comfortedst me.

2 Behold, God is my salvation; I will trust, and not be afraid: for **the Lord JEHOVAH** [*Jesus Christ*] **is my strength and my song**: he also is become my salvation.

3 **Therefore** [*because Christ is your King during the Millennium*] **with joy shall ye draw water** [*"living water"; see John 4:10, 7:38–39*] **out of the wells of salvation**.

4 And **in that day shall ye say, Praise the Lord**, call upon his name, declare his doings among the people, make mention that his name is exalted.

5 **Sing unto the Lord; for he hath done excellent things**: this is known in all the earth [*knowledge of the gospel will permeate the whole earth during the Millennium*].

6 **Cry out** [*sing it out with great joy*] **and shout**, thou inhabitant of Zion [*the people who dwell on earth during the Millennium*]: **for great is the Holy One of Israel** [*Christ*] **in the midst of thee** [*the Savior will be on earth among the people during the Millennium*].

ISAIAH 13

Background

In chapter 10, the destruction of Assyria was described as a "type" of (meaning "symbolic of") the destruction of the wicked at the Second Coming of Christ. We discussed the definition of "type" in the notes at the beginning of that chapter. In this chapter, the destruction of Babylon is likewise a "type" of the destruction of Satan's kingdom at the time of the Second Coming.

It will be helpful for you to understand that the ancient city of Babylon was a huge city full of wickedness and evil. Over time, Babylon has come to symbolize the wickedness of the world. A brief description of Babylon is given in your Bible Dictionary under "Babylon" as follows (**bold** added for emphasis):

Bible Dictionary, Babylon

The capital of Babylonia. According to Gen. 10:8–10 it was founded by Nimrod, and was one of the oldest cities of the land of Shinar; in 11:1–9 we have the record of the Tower of Babel and the "Confusion of Tongues." (See Ether 1:3–5, 34–35.) During the Assyrian supremacy (see *Assyria*) it became part of that empire, and was destroyed by Sennacherib. After the downfall of Assyria, Babylon became

Nebuchadnezzar's capital. He built an enormous city, of which the ruins still remain. The city was square, and the Euphrates ran through the middle of it. According to Herodotus **the walls were 56 miles in circumference, 335 feet high, and 85 feet wide**. A large part of the city consisted of beautiful parks and gardens. The chief building was the famous temple of Bel. Inscriptions that have been recently deciphered show that the Babylonians had accounts of the Creation and the Deluge in many ways similar to those given in the book of Genesis. Other inscriptions contain accounts of events referred to in the Bible histories of the kingdoms of Israel and Judaea, and also give valuable information as to the chronology of these periods.

You can find a brief sketch of the history of the Babylonian empire in the Bible Dictionary, under "Assyria."

In verse 1, Isaiah tells us that this prophecy is essentially a message of doom to Babylon, which he saw in vision. It applies to ancient Babylon, as a nation, and to the "Babylon" of evil in the last days before the Second Coming.

1 **The burden of Babylon** [*message of doom to Babylon*], which Isaiah the son of Amoz did see.

In verses 2–5, next, Isaiah explains that The Lord will gather his righteous forces (as stated in verse 4) in the last days to do battle with the forces of evil (Babylon).

2 **Lift ye up a banner upon the high mountain** [*raise up an ensign to the righteous*], **exalt** [*raise*] **the voice unto them** [*the righteous*], **shake the hand** [*wave to them; signal to them*], **that they may go into the gates of the nobles** [*gather with the righteous*].

Next, Isaiah speaks of the future as if it had already happened. The Book of Mormon makes a significant change to verse 3, next.

3 **I have commanded my sanctified ones** [*the righteous who are worthy to be in the presence of the Lord*], **I have also called my mighty ones for mine anger** [*2 Nephi 23:3 adds "is not upon them"*], **even them that rejoice in my highness** [*exalted and glorious status*].

4 **The noise of a multitude in the mountains** [*gathering*], like as of **a great people**; a tumultuous noise of the **kingdoms** of **nations gathered together: the Lord of hosts mustereth the host of the battle** [*the Lord rallies the righteous together to do battle with evil*].

5 **They come from a far country, from the end of heaven, even the Lord, and the weapons of his indignation**, to destroy the whole land [*the wicked*].

Next, in effect, Isaiah suggests that the wicked in the last days would do well to begin practicing their howling and screaming in preparation for the Second Coming.

6 ¶ **Howl ye** [*the wicked*]; **for the day of the Lord** [*the Second Coming*] **is at hand** [*is getting close*]; it shall come as a destruction from the Almighty.

7 **Therefore shall all hands be faint** [*hang limp*], **and every man's heart shall melt** [*wicked men's courage will falter*]:

8 And **they shall be afraid**: pangs and sorrows shall take hold of them; they shall be in pain as a woman that travaileth [*like a woman in labor, they can't get out of it now*]: **they shall be amazed** [*will look in fear*] one at another; **their faces shall be as flames** [*burn with shame at the thought of facing the Lord*].

9 **Behold, the day of the Lord** [*Second Coming*] **cometh, cruel** [*as viewed by the wicked*] both with wrath and fierce anger, to lay the land desolate: **and he shall destroy the sinners thereof out of it** [*a purpose of the Second Coming*].

Next, Isaiah mentions a few signs of the times, which will precede the Second Coming.

10 For **the stars of heaven** and the constellations thereof **shall not give their light: the sun shall be darkened** in his going forth, and **the moon shall not** cause her light to **shine**.

11 And **I will punish the world for their evil**, and the wicked for their iniquity; and **I will cause the arrogancy of the proud to cease**, and will lay low the haughtiness of the terrible [*will humble the tyrants; typical Isaiah repetition to drive home a point*].

12 **I will make a man** [*survivor of the burning at the Second Coming*] **more precious** [*scarce*] **than fine gold**; even a man than the golden wedge of Ophir [*a land rich in gold, possibly in southern Arabia; in other words, there will be relatively few survivors of the Second Coming because of widespread wickedness at the time*].

13 **Therefore** [*because of gross wickedness on earth*] **I will shake the heavens, and the earth shall remove out of her place**, in the wrath of the Lord of hosts, and in the day of his fierce anger.

In verse 14, next, Isaiah turns his attention back to the nation of Babylon in ancient times. But the prophecy can also refer to the wicked in general. Huge numbers of the wicked, including foreigners, had gravitated to Babylon because of the opportunity for wickedness there.

14 **And it** [*dual meaning: Baby-lon; also the wicked in general*] **shall be as the chased roe** [*hunted deer*], **and as a sheep that no man taketh up** [*no shepherd,* no one defending them]: **they shall every man turn to his own people, and flee every one into his own land** [*foreigners who have had safety in Babylon because of Babylon's great power will return back to their homelands because Babylon is no longer powerful and safe*].

15 **Every one that is found** [*"every-one that is proud," 2 Nephi 23:15*] **shall be thrust through** [*with the sword*]; and **every one that is joined unto them** [*who has gath-ered with the wicked in Babylon*] **shall fall by the sword.**

16 **Their children also shall be dashed to pieces before their eyes** [*refers only to conditions in Babylon and among the wicked before the Second Coming, not at the Second Coming; young children will not be harmed by the Second Coming of the Savior*]; **their houses shall be spoiled, and their wives ravished** [*the fate of Babylon; conditions among the wicked in the last days*].

Next, Isaiah prophesies that the Medes will be the army that conquers the ancient city of Babylon.

17 Behold, **I will stir up the Medes against them** [*a specific*

prophecy; Medes from Persia con-quered Babylon easily in 538 B.C.*], **which shall not regard silver; and as for gold, they shall not delight in it** [*you Babylonians will not be able to bribe the Medes not to destroy you*].

18 **Their bows also shall dash the young men to pieces; and they shall have no pity on the fruit of the womb** [*babies*]; **their eye shall** not spare children.

19 **And Babylon** [*a huge city with 335-foot high walls; see Bible Dic-tionary, under "Babylon"*], the glory of kingdoms, the beauty of the Chaldees' excellency [*Babylonian's pride*], **shall be as** when God over-threw **Sodom and Gomorrah** [*Bab-ylon will be completely destroyed and never inhabited again*].

20 **It shall never be inhabited,** neither shall it be dwelt in from generation to generation: neither shall the Arabian pitch tent there; neither shall the shepherds make their fold there.

21 **But wild beasts of the desert shall lie there**; and their houses [*the ruins of ancient Babylon*] shall be full of doleful creatures [*lonely, solitary creatures*]; and **owls shall dwell there**, and satyrs [*male goats; can also mean demons—see footnote 21b in your Bible*] shall dance [*leap about*] there.

Have you noticed that whenever

Isaiah desires to communicate the complete destruction of a city, people, or nation, he describes the ruins that are left as places where owls live? Owls tend to prefer to live in lonely places, away from human habitation.

22 And **the wild beasts of the islands** [*NIV: "hyenas"*] **shall cry** [*howl*] **in their desolate houses** [*the ruins*], and dragons [*hyenas, wild dogs, jackals*] in their pleasant [*in their once-pleasant*] palaces: and **her time is near to come, and her days shall not be prolonged** [*Babylon's time is nearly up, her days are almost over*].

The rest of verse 22, above, was apparently left out of the Bible. We will turn to the Book of Mormon for it.

2 Nephi 23:22
22 And the wild beasts of the islands shall cry in their desolate houses, and dragons in their pleasant palaces; and her time is near to come, and her day shall not be prolonged. **For I will destroy her speedily; yea, for I will be merciful unto my people, but the wicked shall perish.**

ISAIAH 14

Background
In this chapter, Isaiah uses colorful style and imagery as he prophesies concerning the future downfall of the King of Babylon and, symbolically, the downfall of Satan's kingdom. Verse 12 is a particularly well-known verse.

There are several possible fulfillments of verse 1, next.

1 **For the Lord will have mercy on Jacob** [*Israel*], and will yet choose Israel [*bless Israel; another definition of "choose" is to "elect for eternal happiness"; see 1828 Noah Webster Dictionary, under "choose"*], **and set them in their own land** [*One historical fulfillment was when Cyrus the Great of Persia allowed captives in Babylon to return in 538 B.C.; another group returned in 520 B.C. This is also being fulfilled in our day.*]: **and the strangers shall be joined with them** [*foreigners will live with them*], and they shall cleave to the house of Jacob [*possibly meaning that Gentiles will join with Israel in the last days*].

2 **And the people** [*many nations who will help Israel return*] **shall take them** [*Israel*], **and bring them to their place:** and **the house of Israel shall possess them** [*nations who used to dominate Israel*] in the land of the Lord for servants and handmaids: **and they** [*Israel*] **shall take them** [*nations who used to dominate Israel*] **cap-tives**, whose captives they [*Israel*] were; **and they shall rule over**

their oppressors [*the tables will be turned in the last days*].

In verse 3, next, we are taught that righteous Israel will finally have peace during the Millennium.

3 And **it shall come to pass in the day** [*"in that day," 2 Nephi 24:3*] **that the Lord shall give thee rest from thy sorrow, and from thy fear, and from the hard bondage** wherein thou wast made to serve [*Israel will finally be free from subjection by foreigners and enemies during the Millennium*],

Several of the verses that follow now can be considered as dual in meaning. Many of them can refer to the king of Babylon. And they can also refer to Satan, as his kingdom comes to an end for a thousand years at the time of the Second Coming.

Verse 4 is a continuation of verse 3, with Isaiah holding forth the thought to Israel, in order to make a point, that when they are set free by the fall of Babylon, and ultimately by the fall of Satan and his kingdom, they will be in a position to taunt their former adversaries. The message is that ultimately, the righteous will triumph over all their enemies, because they have sided with the Lord.

4 That **thou shalt take up this proverb** [*a taunting*] against the king of Babylon [*dual: literally King of Babylon. Refers to Satan also, plus any wicked leader*], **and say, How hath the oppressor ceased** [*what happened to you!*]! the golden city ceased [*your unconquerable city, kingdom, is gone!*]!

The answer to the question in verse 4, above, is found in verse 5, next. One of the important doctrines in the answer is that God has power over Satan and any members of his evil kingdom.

5 **The Lord hath broken the staff of the wicked**, and the sceptre [*power*] of the rulers.

6 *He* [*Babylon; Satan*] **who smote the people in wrath with a continual stroke** [*constantly*], **he that ruled the nations in anger, is persecuted** [*punished*], **and none hindereth** [*nobody can stop it*].

7 **The whole earth is at rest, and is quiet: they break forth into singing** [*during the Millennium*].

8 Yea, **the fir trees** [*cyprus trees; symbolic of people*] **rejoice** at thee, and the cedars [*people*] of Lebanon, saying, **Since thou art laid down** [*since you got chopped down; compare with 10:33–34*], **no feller** [*tree cutter; destruction*] **is come up against us.**

9 **Hell** [*spirit prison*] **from beneath is moved for thee** [*is getting ready

to receive you] to meet thee at thy coming: it stirreth up the dead for thee, even all the chief ones of the earth [*wicked leaders*]; it hath raised up from their thrones all the kings of the nations.

In verses 9 and 10, Isaiah creates a scene in our minds wherein all the wicked leaders of the earth (who by the time this vision is foretelling are in spirit prison) are taunting the devil and the king of Babylon at the time they arrive in hell.

10 **All they shall speak and say unto thee, Art thou also become weak as we** [*What happened to your power, Satan; king of Babylon*]? **art thou become like unto us** [*how is it that you are no better off than we are*]?

11 **Thy pomp is brought down to the grave** [*was destroyed with you*], and the noise of thy viols [*royal harp music*]: **the worm is spread under thee, and the worms cover thee** [*your dead body is covered with maggots just like ours were; you're no better off here in hell than we are, so ha, ha, ha! (refers to the king of Babylon, since Satan has no physical body)*].

12 **How art thou fallen from heaven, O Lucifer** [*what happened to you; how were you dethroned*], son of the morning [*one who was high in authority—compare with D&C 76:25–26*]! **how art thou cut down to the ground, which didst weaken the nations** [*how did you get cut down to this; you used to destroy nations, now your power is destroyed*]!

Next, in verses 13–14, Isaiah explains to us Lucifer's motives that led to his rebellion.

13 For **thou hast said in thine heart** [*these were your motives*], I will ascend into heaven, **I will exalt my throne above the stars of God** [*I will be the highest*]: I will sit also upon the mount of the congregation, in the sides of the north [*mythical mountain in the north where gods assemble*]:

14 I will ascend above the heights of the clouds; **I will be like the most High** [*as described in Moses 4:1–3*].

We will quote from the scene given in Moses, in the Pearl of Great Price, in which Lucifer rebelled, and will add **bold** to point things out:

<u>Moses 4:1–3</u>
1 And I, the Lord God, spake unto Moses, saying: That **Satan**, whom thou hast commanded in the name of mine Only Begotten, is the same which was from the beginning, and he **came before me, saying**—Behold, here am I, **send me, I will be thy son** [*the Redeemer*], and I will redeem all mankind, that one soul shall

not be lost, and surely I will do it; **wherefore give me thine honor**.

2 But, behold, my Beloved Son, which was my Beloved and Chosen from the beginning, said unto me—Father, thy will be done, and the glory be thine forever.

3 Wherefore, because that **Satan** rebelled against me, and **sought** to destroy the agency of man, which I, the Lord God, had given him, and also, **that I should give unto him mine own power**; by the power of mine Only Begotten, I caused that he should be cast down;

We will now continue with Isaiah's teaching as to what will become of Satan when his kingdom (referred to as "the kingdom of the devil" in 1 Nephi 22:22) is brought down by the power of God.

15 **Yet thou** [*Lucifer*] **shalt be brought down to hell, to the sides of the pit** [*to the lowest part of the world of the dead, outer darkness*].

16 **They** [*the residents of hell*] **that see thee** [*Lucifer; King of Babylon*] **shall narrowly look upon thee** [*look at you with contorted faces and sneers*], and consider thee, **saying** [*with sarcasm*]**, Is this the man that made the earth to tremble,** that did shake kingdoms;

17 **That made the world as a wilderness, and destroyed the cities thereof;** that opened not the house of his prisoners [*who never freed his prisoners*]?

18 **All the kings of the nations,** even all of them, **lie in glory, every one in his own house** [*all other kings have magnificent tombs*].

19 **But thou** [*dual meaning: King of Babylon literally; Satan figuratively because he doesn't even have a physical body*] **art cast out of thy grave like an abominable branch** [*cut off and walked upon*], and as the raiment of those that are slain, thrust through with a sword [*ruined and discarded*], that go down to the stones of the pit [*the very bottom*]; as a carcase trodden under feet.

20 **Thou** [*King of Babylon/Satan*] **shalt not be joined with them in burial** [*you will not have a magnificent tomb like they do. Satan will not get a tomb because he does not have a physical body*], because thou hast destroyed thy land, and slain thy people: the seed of evildoers shall never be renowned [*none of your (king of Babylon) evil family will survive*].

21 **Prepare slaughter for his** [*king of Babylon's*] **children for** [*because of*] **the iniquity of their fathers** [*parents and ancestors*]; that they

do not rise, nor possess the land, nor fill the face of the world with cities [*none of your children will rule the earth like you have*].

22 **For I will rise up against them**, saith the Lord of hosts, **and cut off from Babylon the name, and remnant, and son, and nephew** [*I will destroy Babylon completely; Satan's kingdom on earth completely*], saith the Lord.

23 **I will also make it** [*Babylon*] **a possession for the bittern** [*owls*], and pools of water: and I will sweep it with the besom [*broom*] of destruction [*a "clean sweep"*], saith the Lord of hosts.

Next, beginning with verse 24, Isaiah begins a new topic. It is a prophecy concerning the fate of Assyria. Remember that Isaiah served as a prophet from about 740 B.C. to 701 B.C., which means that he was still alive when the Assyrians attacked and conquered the northern ten tribes (known as Israel during this period of history) in about 722 B.C. The Assyrian army will suffer a major defeat in Judah about 701 B.C.

His prophecy about the downfall of Babylon (the first part of this chapter) was for future fulfillment (about 538 B.C.).

24 **The Lord of hosts hath sworn** [*covenanted, promised*], **saying**,

Surely as I have thought [*planned*], so shall it come to pass [*here is something else I will do*]; and as I have purposed, so shall it stand [*it will happen*]:

25 That **I will break the Assyrian** [*the Assyrian army*] **in my land** [*Judah*], **and upon my mountains** [*the mountains of Judah*] **tread him** [*the Assyrians*] **under foot**: then shall his yoke [*bondage*] **depart from off them** [*my people*], and his burden depart from off their shoulders [*dual meaning: the Assyrian downfall in Judah in 701 B.C.; the forces of the wicked will be destroyed at the Second Coming and again, after the final battle at the end of the Millennium, when Satan and his followers will be cast out permanently; see D&C 88:111–15*].

26 **This is the purpose** [*the plan*] **that is purposed upon the whole earth: and this is the hand** [*the hand of the Lord*] **that is stretched out upon all the nations** [*the eventual fate of all wicked nations*].

27 **For the Lord of hosts hath purposed, and who shall disannul it** [*prevent it*]? **and his hand is stretched out, and who shall turn it back?**

Beginning with verse 28, next, the topic again changes, this time to the fate of the Philistines, who have also been enemies to the Lord's people.

28 In the year that king Ahaz died [*about 720 B.C.*] **was this burden** [*prophetic message of doom to the Philistines*].

29 Rejoice not [*don't start celebrating*], **whole Palestina** [*Philistia*], **because the rod** [*power*] **of him** [*Shalmaneser, King of Assyria from 727–722 B.C.*] **that smote thee is broken: for out of the serpent's root** [*"snakes lay eggs"—from the same source, Assyria*] **shall come forth a cockatrice** [*one "snake" is dead (Shalmaneser) and a worse one will yet come (Sennacherib), King of Assyria, 705–687 B.C. The Philistines rejoiced when Sargon, King of Assyria from 722–705 B.C. took over at Shalmaneser's death. Sargon was not as hard on them as his predecessor was.*], **and his** [*Sennacherib's*] **fruit shall be a fiery flying serpent.**

Next, in verse 30, the Lord describes the two options that are before the Philistines at this point.

30 And the firstborn of the poor shall feed, and the needy shall lie down in safety [*if you Philistines will repent and join with the Lord, you too can enjoy peace and safety, otherwise . . .*]: **and I will kill thy** [*Philistines'*] **root with famine, and he shall slay**

thy **remnant** [*you will be utterly destroyed, if you don't repent*].

Next, Isaiah speaks prophetically of the future, as if it had already happened.

31 Howl, O gate; cry, O city; thou whole Palestina [*Philistia*], **art dissolved** [*reduced to nothing*]: **for there shall come from the north a smoke** [*cloud of dust made by an enemy army*], **and none shall be alone in his appointed times** [*the enemy army will have no cowards in it*].

32 What shall one then answer the messengers of the nation [*Philistia—what will one say when people ask, "What happened to the Philistines"?*] [*Answer:*] **That the Lord hath founded Zion, and the poor of his people shall trust in it** [*the Lord is the one who caused the destruction of the wicked and established Zion*].

ISAIAH 15

Background

Next, we see a message of doom to the country of Moab, located east of the Dead Sea and named after the son of Lot's oldest daughter. There was constant warfare between the Moabites and the Israelites.

One of the major messages of these chapters of "doom" for the enemies of Israel is that all enemies of the Lord and His covenant people will ultimately fall. In other words, all members of Satan's kingdom, whose ultimate goal it is to destroy righteousness and the agency of others, will be overcome by the power of the Lord.

1 **The burden** [*message of doom*] **of Moab** [*descendants of Lot and his eldest daughter; see Genesis 19:37*]. Because in the night [*suddenly? unexpectedly?*] Ar of Moab [*a city in Moab*] is laid waste, and brought to silence; because in the night, Kir [*another city*] of Moab is laid waste, and brought to silence;

2 He [*Moab, the country east of the Dead Sea*] is gone up to Bajith [*a city*], and to Dibon, [*a city*], the high places [*pagan places of worship*], to weep: **Moab shall howl** over Nebo [*Mt. Nebo, north of Moab*], and over Medeba [*a city*]: **on all their heads shall be baldness** [*symbolic of slavery, captivity, and mourning*], **and every beard cut off** [disgrace, *slavery, captivity ,and mourning*].

3 **In their streets they shall gird** [*dress*] **themselves with sackcloth** [*symbolic of deep tragedy and mourning*]: **on** the tops of their houses [*flat-roofed buildings used like we use decks*, etc.], and **in their streets, every one shall howl, weeping abundantly**.

4 And Heshbon [*a city in Moab*] shall cry, and Elealeh [*a city*]: their voice shall be heard even unto Jahaz [*a city*]: therefore [*for this reason*] **the armed soldiers of Moab shall cry out**; his life shall be grievous [*miserable*] unto him.

5 **My heart shall cry out for Moab**; his fugitives shall flee unto Zoar [*a border city just south of the Dead Sea*], an heifer [*young cow*] of three years old [*Moab, including Zoar, is being destroyed in its prime*]: for by the mounting up of Luhith [*where you start climbing up to get to Luhith*] **with weeping shall they go** it up; for in the way of Horonaim they shall raise up a cry of destruction.

6 For **the waters of Nimrim shall be desolate** [*dried up*]: for **the hay is withered away, the grass faileth, there is no green thing** [*there will be a drought and resulting famine*].

7 Therefore the abundance they have gotten, and that which they have laid up, shall they carry away to the brook of the willows [*probably the border between Moab and Edom—land directly south of Moab*].

Again, as previously mentioned several times in this study guide, Isaiah is speaking of the future as if it had already happened. This is part of "the manner of prophesying among the Jews" mentioned by Nephi in 2 Nephi 25:1.

8 For **the cry is gone round about the borders of Moab** [*they are completely surrounded*]; the howling thereof unto Eglaim, and the howling thereof unto Beer-elim.

9 For the waters of Dimon shall be full of blood: for **I will bring more upon Dimon, lions upon him that escapeth of Moab**, and upon the remnant of the land [*those who manage to escape the enemy armies will be destroyed by other means, including lions.*]

ISAIAH 16

Background

A mood change now occurs. Isaiah indicates the time will come when Moab will come under the protection of Judah. This occurs under righteous King David. This is a great prophecy in light of the fact that in Isaiah's day, Judah and Moab were long-standing enemies.

1 **Send ye the lamb** [*send an appeal for help*] to the ruler of the land from Sela [*about sixty miles south of the Dead Sea*] to the wilderness, unto the mount of the daughter of Zion [*Jerusalem*].

2 For it shall be, that, **as a wandering bird cast out of the nest,** so the daughters of Moab shall be at the fords of Arnon [*a river on the northern border of Moab. Moab will have gone through some rough times.*]

Isaiah now prophesies that Moab will appeal to Judah for help. Their plea to Judah for help is given in verse 3, next.

3 Take counsel, execute judgment [*kindness and fairness*]; make thy shadow [*symbolic of protection and help*] as the night in the midst of the noonday; **hide the outcasts** [*protect the inhabitants of Moab*]; bewray [*betray*] not him that wandereth.

4 **Let mine outcasts dwell with thee, Moab** [*should say "Judah"; NIV "Let the Moabite fugitives stay with you"*]; **be thou a covert** [*protection*] **to them** [*Moab's inhabitants*] from the face of the spoiler [*German: destroyer*]; **for the extortioner** [*persecutor*] **is at an end, the spoiler ceaseth, the oppressors are consumed out of the land** [*thanks to help from Judah. Could also refer to destruction of wicked at Second Coming.*].

5 And **in mercy shall the throne be established: and he** [*Christ— see heading to this chapter in your Bible*] **shall sit upon it in truth in the tabernacle of David, judging, and seeking judgment, and hasting righteousness.** [*Conditions during the Millennium. Could also*

refer to Judah in the last days.]

Isaiah now returns to troubles to come upon Moab back then.

6 **We have heard of the pride of Moab; he is very proud**; even of his **haughtiness**, and his **pride**, and his **wrath**: but his **lies** shall not be so. [*Moab's unfounded boasts of strength and well-being will not work out in fact.*]

In the background notes accompanying Isaiah chapter 3 in this study guide, we introduced a writing technique called "chiasmus." You may wish to go back and reread those notes, because Isaiah uses chiastic structure again here, in verses 7 through 11. In this case, he lists several cities in order and then lists them in reverse order (the basic structure of a chiasmus). The last two cities of the chiasmus are out of order, but it still works.

7 Therefore [*because of these sins listed in verse 6*] shall Moab howl for **Moab** (A), every one shall howl: for the foundations of **Kir-hareseth** (B) shall ye mourn; surely they are stricken.

8 For the fields of **Heshbon** (C) languish, and the vine of **Sibmah** (D): the lords of the heathen [*enemy nations—Assyrians*] have broken down the principal plants thereof [*the Assyrians ruined terraced*

vineyards when they attacked Moab], they are come even unto **Jazer** (E), they wandered through the wilderness: her branches are stretched out, they are gone over the sea.

9 ¶ Therefore [*this is why*] I will bewail with the weeping of **Jazer** (E') the **vine** of **Sibmah** (D'): I will water thee with my tears, O **Heshbon** (C'), and Elealeh: for the shouting for thy summer fruits and for thy harvest is fallen.

10 And gladness is taken away, and joy out of the plentiful field; and in the vineyards there shall be no singing, neither shall there be shouting [*in other words, there will be great sadness*]: the treaders shall tread out no wine in their presses [*because the grapes and vines have been destroyed by the enemy soldiers*]; I have made their vintage shouting to cease.

11 Wherefore my bowels [*symbolic in Hebrew of the center of feeling and emotion*] shall sound like an harp for **Moab** (A'), and mine inward parts for **Kir-haresh** (B').

12 ¶ **And it shall come to pass, when it is seen that Moab is weary on the high place** [*places of worshipping idols and false gods*], that **he shall come to his**

sanctuary to pray; but he shall not prevail [*won't get the help he needs from his false gods*].

13 **This is the word that the Lord hath spoken concerning Moab since that time** [*the Lord has warned Moab through past prophets too*].

14 But now the Lord hath spoken, saying, **Within three years**, as the years of an hireling, and **the glory of Moab shall be contemned** [*scorned*], with all that great multitude; **and the remnant shall be very small and feeble** [*in three years, there won't be much left of Moab*].

ISAIAH 17

Background
Isaiah now tells what will happen to Syria and says a few more things about Israel.

1 **The burden** [*message of doom*] **of Damascus** [*a major city in Syria*]. Behold, **Damascus is taken away from being a city, and it shall be a ruinous heap** [*worthless pile of rubble*].

Isaiah is speaking prophetically of the future as if it had already taken place.

2 **The cities of Aroer** [*area near Damascus*] **are forsaken**: they shall be for flocks, which shall lie down, and none shall make them afraid [*animals will graze where cities now stand*].

3 **The fortress** [*fortified city*] **also shall cease from Ephraim** [*northern Israel, the northern ten tribes*], and the kingdom from Damascus, and the remnant of Syria: **they shall be as the glory of the children of Israel** [*will be cut down like Israel will be*], saith the Lord of hosts.

The topic now turns to Israel's coming troubles.

4 And in that day it shall come to pass, that **the glory of Jacob** [*Israel*] **shall be made thin**, and the fatness of his flesh [*his prosperity*] shall wax lean [*bad times are coming*].

5 And **it shall be as when the harvestman gathereth the corn** [*grain*], and reapeth the ears with his arm; and it shall be as he that gathereth ears in the valley of Rephaim [*a fertile valley northwest of Jerusalem well-known for good harvests—Israel will be "harvested," plucked up*].

6 ¶ **Yet gleaning grapes shall be left in it** [*a small remnant will be left after Assyria's attack on Israel*], as the shaking of an olive tree, two or three berries [*olives*] in the top of the uppermost bough, four or five in the outmost fruitful branches thereof, saith the Lord God of Israel [*remnants scattered here and there*].

7 **At that day shall a man look to his Maker** [*people will repent*], **and his eyes shall have respect to the Holy One of Israel** [*Jesus*].

8 **And he shall not look to the altars** [*of false gods*], **the work of his hands** [*idols he has made*], neither shall respect [*worship*] that which his fingers have made, either the groves [*locations used for idol worship*], or the images [*idols*]. [*This probably refers also to the last days and into the Millennium.*]

9 ¶ **In that day shall his** [*Syria's*] **strong cities be as a forsaken bough** [*limb*], and an uppermost branch, which they left because of the children of Israel: and there shall be desolation [*in Syria*].

10 **Because** [*this is why you have these problems*] **thou hast forgotten the God of thy salvation,** and hast not been mindful of the rock of thy strength [*the Lord*], therefore shalt thou plant pleasant plants [*continue idol worship*], and shalt set it with strange slips [*cuttings for grafting, symbolic of imported gods or idols*]:

11 **In the day** [*while things are going well*] **shalt thou make thy plant to grow** [*continue worshiping idols*], and in the morning shalt thou make thy seed to flourish: **but the harvest** [*results of idol worship*] **shall be a heap** [*worthless*] in the day of grief and of desperate sorrow [*your false gods will not help you*].

12 **Woe to the multitude of many people** [*nations, including Assyria, who attack the Lord's people*], which make a noise like the noise of the seas [*powerful*]; and to **the rushing of nations**, that make a rushing like the rushing of mighty waters!

13 **The nations shall rush like the rushing of many waters: but God shall rebuke them** [*will stop them*], and they shall flee far off, and shall be chased as the chaff of the mountains before the wind, and like a rolling thing [*tumbleweeds, etc.*] before the whirlwind [*wicked enemy nations are nothing compared to God's power; when the time is right, the Lord will stop them*].

14 And behold **at eveningtide trouble; and before the morning** [*unexpected, sudden disaster*] **he is not** [*the wicked are gone, destroyed; can refer to the destruction at the time of the Second Coming also*]. **This is the portion** [*the lot; in other words, they will get what is coming to them*] **of them that spoil us** [*the Lord's people*], and the lot of them that rob us.

ISAIAH 18

Background

This chapter uses symbolism to depict the gathering of Israel in the last days. You will see the missionaries (verse 2) going forth throughout the world, inviting all people to gather into the gospel fold. This is, in effect, the final pruning (verse 4) before the Second Coming.

As we begin with verse 1, we see a mistranslation with the first word.

1 **Woe** [*this is a mistranslation in the King James Version. The Hebrew word means "hark" or "greetings" and has no negative connotation—see footnote 1a in your Bible*] **to the land** [*most likely America*] **shadowing** [*overshadowed with God's protecting Spirit*] **with wings** [*wings often represent shelter or protection, as in the hen gathering her chicks under her wings in Matthew 23:37, and so forth. Wings also represent power in D&C 77:4; Also, North and South America look somewhat like wings*], **which is beyond the rivers of Ethiopia** [*America is beyond the "rivers" or oceans beyond Africa*].

2 **That sendeth ambassadors** [*missionaries*] by the sea, even in vessels of bulrushes upon the waters, **saying, Go, ye swift** [*modern transportation?*] **messengers, to a nation scattered** [*scattered Israel*] **and peeled,** to a people terrible from their beginning hitherto [*German: once powerful, perhaps meaning once righteous*]; **a nation meted out and trodden down** [*scattered Israel*], whose land the

rivers [*symbolic of enemy nations in Isaiah 8:7, 17:12*] have spoiled!

3 **All ye inhabitants of the world, and dwellers on the earth, see ye** [*pay attention*], **when he** [*the Lord*] **lifteth up an ensign** [*a signal to gather; the restored gospel*] **on the mountains** [*can symbolize Church headquarters; see Isaiah 2:2; also can symbolize temples*]; and when he bloweth a trumpet [*a clear, unmistakable sound, easy to distinguish from other sounds—the gospel message*], **hear ye.**

4 **For so the Lord said unto me** [*Isaiah*], I will take my rest, and I will consider in my dwelling place like a clear heat [*nourishing rays of light and truth*] upon herbs, and like a cloud of dew [*nourishing water*] in the heat of harvest [*right when it is needed*].

5 **For afore** [*before*] **the harvest** [*at the time of the Second Coming*], when the bud is perfect, and the sour grape [*immature grape*] is ripening in the flower, **he** [*the Lord*] **shall both cut off the sprigs with pruning hooks, and take away and cut down the branches** [*just before the millennial harvest, a final "pruning" will take place— the wicked will be destroyed, pruned away so the righteous can develop to their full potential*].

6 **They** [*the wicked*] **shall be left together** [*completely*] **unto the**

fowls of the mountains [*birds of prey*], and to the beasts of the earth: and the fowls shall summer upon them, and all the beasts of the earth shall winter upon them.

Isaiah now prophesies that the remnant, scattered Israel, will be gathered and brought back to the Lord, a righteous nation.

7 ¶ **In that time** [*probably the last days*] **shall the present** [*gift, gathered Israel*] **be brought unto the Lord** of hosts of a people scattered and peeled, and from a people terrible from their beginning hitherto; a nation meted out and trodden under foot, whose land the rivers have spoiled [*see verse 2*], to the place of the name of the Lord of hosts, the mount Zion [*the remnant, scattered Israel, will be gathered and brought back to the Lord a righteous nation; see verse 1*].

ISAIAH 19

Background

This chapter contains a rather detailed prophecy about Egypt, including civil war (verse 2). Of particular interest to us in modern times is the prophecy of the destruction that will occur against the productivity of the Nile River in the last days (verses 5–10). The building of the Aswan Dam, beginning in 1960, may be a substantial contributor to the fulfilling of this prophecy, because of the severe problems it caused downstream.

A beautiful prophecy, beginning with verse 18, informs us that the day will come when our Egyptian brothers and sisters will have the gospel of Jesus Christ, and that Egypt and Assyria will join together with Israel as covenant people of the Lord.

1 **The burden** [*message of doom*] **of Egypt.** Behold, the Lord rideth upon a swift cloud [*trouble coming quickly*], and shall come into Egypt: and the idols [*false religions*] of Egypt shall be moved at his presence, and the heart [*courage*] of Egypt shall melt in the midst of it [*they will be terrified*].

2 And **I will set the Egyptians against the Egyptians** [*civil war*]: and they shall fight every one against his brother, and every one against his neighbor; city against city, and kingdom against kingdom.

3 And **the spirit of Egypt shall fail** [*great despair*] in the midst thereof; and I will destroy the counsel [*plans*] thereof: and **they shall seek to the idols** [*they will seek help from their false gods*], and to the charmers, **and to them that have familiar spirits** [*spiritualists who claim to contact the dead*], and to the wizards [*the occult*].

4 **And the Egyptians will I give over into the hand of a cruel lord**

[*hard masters*]; and **a fierce king shall rule over them** [*we don't know who this is or was*], saith the Lord, the Lord of hosts.

5 And the waters shall fail from the sea, and **the river shall be wasted** and dried up [*the Nile River will be ruined*].

6 And **they** [*the Egyptians*] **shall turn the rivers far away** [*will ruin their own rivers*]; and the brooks of defence shall be emptied and dried up: the reeds and flags shall wither.

7 **The paper reeds** [*papyrus*] by the brooks, by the mouth of the brooks, **and every thing sown** [*planted*] **by the brooks, shall wither**, be driven away, and be no more [*the papyrus industry, crops, and so forth will be devastated*].

8 **The fishers also shall mourn**, and all they that cast angle [*fishhooks*] into the brooks shall lament, **and they that spread nets upon the waters shall languish** [*fishing industry will be ruined*].

9 **Moreover** [*in addition*] **they that work in fine flax** [*linen fabric is made from flax plant fibers*], **and they that weave networks** [*fine linen*], **shall be confounded** [*stopped; in other words, the textile industry will be ruined*].

10 **And they shall be broken** in the purposes [*will have no success*]

thereof, all **that make sluices** [*dams*] **and ponds for fish.**

11 **Surely the princes** [*nobles; leaders*] of Zoan [*Tanis, ancient capital of the Nile Delta*] **are fools**, the **counsel** of the wise counsellors of Pharaoh **is become brutish** [*absurd*] [*Pharaoh has received bad counsel from those who are supposed to be wise*]: **how say ye unto Pharaoh, I am the son of the wise, the son of ancient kings** [*how do you counselors to Pharaoh dare to claim to be wise*]?

12 Where are they? **where are thy wise men** [*to whom you have turned instead of the Lord*]? and **let them tell thee now**, and let them know what the Lord of hosts hath purposed upon [*against*] Egypt.

13 **The princes** [*leaders*] **of Zoan are become fools**, the princes of Noph [*Memphis, capital of northern Egypt*] are deceived; **they have also seduced Egypt** [*led her astray*], even they that are the stay [*support*] of the tribes thereof.

14 The Lord hath mingled [*has allowed, because of agency*] a perverse spirit in the midst thereof: and **they have caused Egypt to err in every work thereof**, as a drunken man staggereth in his vomit.

15 **Neither shall there be any work for Egypt**, which the head [*leaders, high society*] or tail [*poor, low society*], branch [*palm branch,*]

high society] or rush [*papyrus reed, low society, poor*], may do.

16 **In that day** [*the last days*] **shall Egypt be like unto women** [*the worst insult in Egyptian culture of that day*]: **and** it [*Egypt*] **shall be afraid and fear because of the shaking of the hand of the Lord** of hosts, which he shaketh over it.

Next, in verse 17, Isaiah tells us that, in the last days, the Jews will become a terror to Egypt. This is the exact opposite of what the situation has been throughout history, where the Egyptians were a terrifying power in the eyes of the Jews.

17 And **the land of Judah shall be a terror unto Egypt** [*a complete turnabout; tremendous prophecy!*], every one that maketh mention thereof shall be afraid in himself, because of the counsel [*plan*] of the Lord of hosts, which he hath determined against it [*Egypt*].

Next, Isaiah prophesies that the day will come when relations will improve between Egypt and Israel. He also foretells the day in which the Egyptians will have the true gospel and will make covenants with the Lord.

18 **In that day** [*last days*] **shall five** [*several*] **cities in the land of Egypt speak the language of Canaan** [*Israel; a prophecy of greatly improved relationship*

between Egypt and Judah in the last days], **and swear** [*make covenants*] **to the Lord of Hosts** [*make covenants with Jesus Christ*]; one shall be called, The city of destruction [*not a good translation; could be "city of the sun"*].

Verse 19, next, tends to make us think that there will someday be a temple to the Lord built in Egypt.

19 **In that day** [*last days*] **shall there be an altar** [*a temple?*] **to the Lord in the midst of the land of Egypt**, and a pillar [*symbolic of a temple*] at the border thereof to the Lord.

20 **And it** [*the altar and the pillar*] **shall be for a sign and for a witness** [*reminder*] **unto** [*of*] **the Lord of hosts in the land of Egypt**: for they [*Egyptians*] shall cry [*pray*] unto the Lord because of the oppressors, and **he shall send them a saviour**, and a great one, **and he shall deliver them** [*the Egyptians will hear and live the gospel*].

21 **And the Lord shall be known to Egypt, and the Egyptians shall know the Lord in that day** [*the last days*], and shall do sacrifice [*3 Nephi 9:20; broken heart and contrite spirit*] and oblation [*D&C 59:12*]; yea, **they shall vow a vow** [*make covenants*] **unto the Lord, and perform it** [*and will be faithful to them*].

Often, the Lord has to first humble people and then heal them. Otherwise they won't listen to Him. We see this in verse 22, next.

22 And **the Lord shall smite Egypt**: he shall smite **and heal it** [*first humble it, then heal it*]: **and they shall return even to the Lord**, and he shall be intreated [*prayed to*] of [*by*] them, and shall heal them [*wonderful blessings are in store for Egypt*].

23 ¶ **In that day shall there be a highway out of Egypt to Assyria** [*Iraq?*], and the Assyrian shall come into Egypt, and the Egyptian into Assyria, and **the Egyptians shall serve** [*the Lord; see verse 25*] **with the Assyrians.**

24 **In that day** [*the last days*] **shall Israel be the third with Egypt and with Assyria** [*all three will be allied, with Israel as a blessing in the midst of them*], even a blessing in the midst of the land:

25 Whom the Lord of hosts shall bless, saying, **Blessed be Egypt my people, and Assyria the work of my hands, and Israel mine inheritance** [*all three nations will worship the true God and be part of the Lord's people*].

ISAIAH 20

Background
Isaiah 20 seems to have no particular references to the future. It

deals with ancient Egypt and is a prophecy that Assyria will overrun Egypt.

1 **In the year** [*about 711 B.C.*] **that Tartan** [*an Assyrian general*] **came unto Ashdod** [*when Sargon the king of Assyria sent him, Ashdod was a coastal city about forty miles west of Jerusalem*] **and fought against Ashdod** [*the center of a revolt against Assyria*], **and took it;**

In verse 2, next, Isaiah uses a rather dramatic method of communicating what is in store for Egypt, when the Assyrians attack them.

2 At the same time [*about 711 B.C.—see verse 1*] **spake the Lord by Isaiah** the son of Amoz, **saying, Go and loose the sackcloth** [*symbolic of mourning already*] **from off thy loins, and put off thy shoe from thy foot.** And he did so, walking naked [*without an upper garment; symbolic of slavery and exile; see verse 4*] and barefoot [*like a slave*].

3 **And the Lord said, Like as my servant Isaiah hath walked naked** [*stripped to the waist*] **and barefoot three years** [*we don't know whether this means constantly during the three years, or occasionally during the three years to remind the people of the message*] **for a sign and wonder upon Egypt and upon Ethiopia**

[symbolic of what will happen to Egypt and Ethiopia];

4 So shall the king of Assyria lead away the Egyptians prisoners, and the Ethiopians captives, young and old, naked and barefoot, even with their buttocks *[upper thighs]* uncovered, to the shame of Egypt.

The Jews at this time had been depending on Egypt and Ethiopia for protection from Assyria, rather than repenting and turning to the Lord for help, as counseled by their prophets. In verse 5, next, the Lord tells them that their hopes are in vain.

5 And they *[Judah]* **shall be afraid and ashamed of** *[disappointed by]* **Ethiopia their expectation** *[hope]*, **and of Egypt their glory** *[as mentioned above, Judah was hoping for protection from Egypt and Ethiopia, rather than repenting and turning to God]*.

6 And the inhabitant of this isle *[nation; in other words, Jerusalem, Judah]* **shall say in that day, Behold, such is our expectation** *[our hope is destroyed!]*, **whither we flee for help to be delivered from the king of Assyria**: and how shall we escape *[if that can happen to Ethiopia and Egypt, our "protection" from Assyria, what do we do now]*?

ISAIAH 21

Background

This chapter is another prophecy about the destruction of Babylon. As mentioned in verses 2–4, this was a particularly difficult vision for Isaiah to watch.

1 The burden *[message of doom]* **of the desert of the sea** *[Babylon]*. As whirlwinds *[which are devastating in the desert]* in the south pass through; so it cometh from the desert, from a terrible land.

2 A grievous vision is declared unto me *[Isaiah; this was extra hard for Isaiah to watch]*; the treacherous dealer dealeth treacherously, and the spoiler spoileth. Go up, O Elam *[a country east of Babylon]*: **besiege** *[attack]*, **O Media** *[a country northeast of Babylon; the Medes conquered Babylon in about 538 B.C.]*; **all the sighing thereof** *[groaning Babylon has caused]* **have I** *[the Lord]* **made to cease.**

3 Therefore are my *[Isaiah's]* **loins** *[whole being]* **filled with pain**: pangs have taken hold upon me, as the pangs of a woman that travaileth *[is in labor]*: **I was bowed down at the hearing of it** *[the vision]*; **I was dismayed at the seeing of it** *[this vision of the destruction of Babylon overwhelmed Isaiah]*.

4 **My heart panted** [*faltered*], fearfulness affrighted me [*made me tremble*]: **the night of my pleasure hath he turned into fear unto me** [*I can't get to sleep at night*].

5 Prepare the table, watch in the watchtower, eat, drink: arise, ye princes, and anoint the shield [*oil your shields, get ready for action*].

6 For thus hath the Lord said unto me [*Isaiah*], **Go, set a watchman, let him declare what he seeth.**

7 **And he saw** a chariot with a couple of horsemen, a chariot of asses, and a chariot of camels; **and he hearkened diligently with much heed** [*paid close attention to what he saw*]:

8 And he cried, A lion: My lord, I stand continually [*day after day*] upon the watchtower in the daytime, and I am set in my ward whole nights [*I am keeping watch constantly like you told me to*]:

9 And, behold, here cometh a chariot of men, with a couple of horsemen [*messengers*]. **And he answered and said, Babylon is fallen, is fallen** [*dual meaning: Babylon has fallen; Satan's kingdom will likewise eventually fall*]; and all the graven images of her gods he hath broken unto the ground [*the Medes joined the Persians and Elamites and conquered Babylon, about 538 B.C.*].

10 **O my threshing** [*O my crushed one*], and the corn [*grain*] of my floor [*the son of my threshing floor, that is, the Israelites who will survive Babylon's downfall*]: **that which I have heard of the Lord of hosts, the God of Israel, have I declared unto you.**

It seems that no wicked nation is escaping Isaiah's prophecies of destruction. Next, we see the message of doom to the Edomites in Dumah.

11 **The burden of Dumah** [*message of doom to the Edomites who live in Dumah, a desert oasis about 250 miles southeast of the Dead Sea*]. **He calleth to me out of Seir** [*mountain range southeast of the Dead Sea*], **Watchman, what of the night** [*how long until daylight? In other words, how long will this oppression last*]? Watchman, what of the night?

12 The watchman said, **The morning cometh, and also the night** [*the end of Babylonian captivity will come but another oppressor will follow*]: if ye will enquire, enquire ye [*ask for more information later*]: return, come.

13 **The burden upon Arabia** [*difficulties caused Arabia by the Babylonian conquests*]. In the forest [*oasis*] in Arabia shall ye lodge, O ye travelling companies of Dedanim [*an area about 150 miles*

east of the Sea of Galilee].

14 **The inhabitants of the land of Tema** [*about 250 miles south of Jerusalem, in the Arabian Desert*] **brought water to him** [*Kedar, that is, refugees from Kedar*] **that was thirsty, they prevented** [*met; "prevent" is used seventeen times in King James Version, always in the obsolete sense of "go before," "meet," "precede," and so forth. See Psalm 119:147, where "prevented" means "got up before dawn." See also Matthew 17:25, where Jesus spoke first, before Peter spoke*] **with their bread him that fled** [*refugees from Kedar fleeing the Babylonians, Dedan and Tema need to prepare to take care of later refugees from Kedar*].

15 **For they** [*refugees from Kedar*] **fled from the swords**, from the drawn sword, and from the bent bow, and from the grievousness of war.

16 For thus hath the Lord said unto me [*Isaiah*], **Within a year**, according to the years of an hireling [*a wage earner, who can be fired for poor performance just as Kedar, in one year, will be "fired" for poor performance with respect to God*], and **all the glory of Kedar shall fail.**

17 And **the residue of the number of archers, the mighty men** of

the children of Kedar, **shall be diminished** [*Kedar will be devastated and have few warriors left*]: **for the Lord God of Israel hath spoken it.**

ISAIAH 22

Background
This prophecy deals with the wicked inhabitants of Jerusalem. If you read the heading to this chapter in your Bible, you see that it prophesies of the coming captivity of the Jews. It also deals with the power of Christ to free captives from sin.

1 **The burden of the valley of vision** [*message of doom to Jerusalem*]. **What aileth thee now, that thou art wholly gone up to the housetops** [*"What's wrong with you! Can't you see what's coming? How can you be so insensitive, always partying when your future is so bleak!"*]?

2 **Thou that art full of stirs** [*noise*], **a tumultuous city, a joyous city** [*always partying; false sense of security*]: **thy slain men are not slain with the sword**, nor dead in battle [*are easily captured and killed*].

Remember, as in many cases previously pointed out in this study guide, Isaiah is speaking prophetically of the future as if it has already taken place. We see that the partying and lack of vigilance on the part of the Jewish soldiers has made it easy for the enemy to capture them.

3 **All thy rulers are fled together, they are bound by the archers** [*captured easily; tied up by the archers, who don't normally do the actual hand-to-hand combat and capturing*]: all that are found in thee are bound together, which have fled from far.

4 **Therefore said I** [*this is the reason Isaiah said*], **Look away from me** [*don't try to get me to party with you*]; **I will weep bitterly, labour not to comfort me** [*don't try to comfort me because I see what's coming*], **because of the spoiling of the daughter of my people** [*Jerusalem*].

5 For **it is a day of trouble**, and of treading down, and of perplexity by the Lord God of hosts in the valley of vision [*Jerusalem*], breaking down the walls, and of crying to the mountains.

6 And **Elam bare the quiver with chariots** [*symbolic of war*] **of men and horsemen** [*horse is symbolic of conquering, victory*], **and Kir uncovered the shield** [*Jerusalemites hope the soldiers of Elam and Kir—on the main road between Elam and Babylon—will defeat the Assyrians before they reach Jerusalem*].

Isaiah is pointing out the futility of the efforts of the Jews to defend themselves against these enemies. They have been weakened by wickedness and riotous living. Their only effective defense is to repent and turn to the Lord (verse 11).

7 ¶ And it shall come to pass, that **thy choicest valleys shall be full of chariots**, and the horsemen shall set themselves in array at the gate [*enemy soldiers will be everywhere in your land*].

8 And **he discovered** [*stripped off*] **the covering** [*defense*] **of Judah**, and thou didst look in that day to the armour of the house of the forest [*Jerusalem's defense is inadequate*].

9 **Ye have seen also the breaches** [*cracks, breaks in the wall*] **of the city of David** [*Jerusalem*], **that they are many** [*Isaiah points out weaknesses in Jerusalem's defenses*]: and ye gathered together the waters of the lower pool [*Hezekiah's tunnel; you dug a tunnel to bring water into the city during siege*].

10 **And ye have numbered** [*taken stock of things*] **the houses of Jerusalem, and the houses have ye broken down to fortify the wall** [*dismantled houses for stone to fortify city walls and so forth*].

11 Ye made also a ditch between the two walls for the water of the old pool: but **ye have not looked**

unto the maker thereof [*the Lord*], neither had respect unto him that fashioned it long ago [*you have not turned to the Lord and repented, wherein your only reliable protection lies*].

Verse 12 again reminds them that humility and repentance are the only way out of the coming destruction.

12 **And in that day did the Lord God of hosts call to weeping,** and to **mourning**, and to **baldness**, and to **girding with sackcloth** [*God said, "Repent, humble yourselves!"*]:

13 **And behold** [*instead of repenting and humbly turning to the Lord for protection, the people continued in*] **joy and gladness** [*partying*], **slaying oxen, and killing sheep, eating flesh, and drinking wine**: let us **eat and drink; for to morrow we shall die** [*people ignore God, don't repent, continue riotous living*].

14 And it was revealed in mine ears by the Lord of hosts, **Surely this iniquity shall not be purged from you till ye die**, saith the Lord God of hosts [*the way you're heading, you will die in your sins*].

Next, Isaiah illustrates the negative influence that foreign lifestyles, philosophies and religions, and so forth, are having upon the Lord's people at this time.

15 **Thus saith the Lord God of hosts, Go, get thee unto** [*go see*] **this treasurer, even unto Shebna** [*leader of the king's court, probably a foreigner; perhaps symbolic of foreign religions, lifestyles, and so forth, taking hold of Jews but eventually driven out by the Messiah; see verses 19–20*], **which is over the house, and say,**

16 **What hast thou here? and whom hast thou here, that thou hast hewed thee out a sepulchre here** [*foreign influences attempting to become permanent; Shebna is a vain man carving out a great monument to himself*], as he that heweth him out a sepulchre on high, and that graveth an habitation for himself in a rock?

17 Behold, the Lord will carry thee away with a mighty captivity, and will surely cover thee [*you won't be famous*].

18 **He will surely violently turn and toss thee like a ball into a large country: there shalt thou die** [*you will die in a foreign land (likely Assyria—see footnote 18a in your Bible), symbolic of the fate of Jerusalem's inhabitants as they are carried away into a foreign land*], and there the chariots of thy glory shall be the shame of thy lord's house.

19 And **I will drive thee from thy station**, and from thy state shall he pull thee down.

20 And it shall come to pass **in that day**, that **I will call my servant Eliakim** [*a real person in Jerusalem, symbolic of the Messiah—see footnote 20a in your Bible*] the son of Hilkiah:

21 And **I will clothe him with thy robe, and strengthen him with thy girdle** [*he will take your place*], **and I will commit thy government into his hand**: and he [*Messiah*] shall be a father to the inhabitants of Jerusalem, and to the house of Judah.

22 And **the key of the house of David will I lay upon his shoulder; so he shall open, and none shall shut; and he shall shut, and none shall open** [*symbolic of Christ's power*].

23 And **I will fasten him as a nail in a sure place** [*the Messiah is absolutely reliable*]; and he shall be for a glorious throne to his father's house [*dual meaning: Eliakim's family depends on him for their temporal salvation; we depend on Christ for our spiritual salvation*].

24 **And they shall hang upon him all the glory of his father's house, the offspring and the issue**, all vessels of small quantity, from the vessels of cups, even to all the vessels of flagons [*dual meaning: Eliakim's relatives, small and great, depend on him; Christ carries all mankind, small and great,*

upon the cross; Atonement*].

The symbolism in verse 25, next, does not apply to the Savior, rather, only to Eliakim.

25 **In that day, saith the Lord of hosts, shall the nail that is fastened in the sure place be removed**, and be cut down, and fall; and the burden that was upon it shall be cut off: for the Lord hath spoken it [*Eliakim will eventually fall from office and his family with him*].

ISAIAH 23

Background

This is the last of the set of prophecies against foreign nations that began with chapter 13.

1 **The burden** [*prophecy of doom*] **of Tyre** [*located about 120 miles north of Jerusalem, on the coast of the Mediterranean Sea; a leading sea power of Isaiah's time*]. **Howl, ye ships of Tarshish** [*large ships of trade*]; **for it** [*Tyre*] **is laid waste**, so that there is no house, no entering [*harbor*] in: from the land of Chittim [*Cyprus*] it is revealed to them.

2 **Be still** [*stunned*], ye inhabitants of the isle [*seaport of Tyre or Cyprus?*]; thou whom the merchants of Zidon, that pass over the sea, have replenished [*made rich*].

3 And by great waters the seed [*grain from the Nile*] of Sihor [*city in Egypt*], the harvest of the river,

is her revenue; and she is a mart [*marketplace*] of nations.

4 **Be thou ashamed** [*German: terrified—Sidon's commerce will be interrupted via Tyre's downfall*], **O Zidon**: for the sea hath spoken, even the strength of the sea, saying, I travail not, nor bring forth children, neither do I nourish up young men, nor bring up virgins [*Tyre is not producing anymore*].

5 **As at the report concerning Egypt** [*as the report comes to Egypt*], **so shall they** [*the Egyptians*] **be sorely pained at the report of Tyre** [*Egypt will be in anguish upon hearing what has happened to Tyre*].

6 Pass ye over to Tarshish [*probably in Spain*]; howl, ye inhabitants of the isle.

7 **Is this your joyous** [*riotous*] **city**, whose antiquity is of ancient days? **her own feet shall carry her afar off to sojourn** [*she creates her own downfall like we do when we go against God*].

8 **Who hath taken this counsel** [*who is planning this*] **against Tyre**, the crowning city, whose merchants are princes [*mighty leaders*], whose traffickers [*traders*] are the honourable [*famous*] of the earth?

Verse 9, next, has the answer to the question posed by Isaiah, in verse 8, above.

9 **The Lord of hosts hath purposed** [*planned*] **it**, to stain the pride of all glory, and to bring into contempt [*to humble*] all the honourable [*unrighteous famous*] of the earth.

10 Pass through thy land as a river, O daughter of Tarshish : **there is no more strength** [*you are ruined*].

11 **He** [*the Lord*] **stretched out his hand over the sea, he shook the kingdoms: the Lord hath given a commandment against the merchant city** [*Tyre*], to destroy the strong holds thereof [*merchandising networks; Tyre is doomed*].

12 And he said, **Thou shalt no more rejoice**, O thou oppressed virgin [*unconquered until the fulfillment of this prophesy*], daughter of Zidon: arise, pass over to Chittim [*Cyprus*]; **there also shalt thou have no rest** [*Tyre's downfall ruins other economies too*].

13 **Behold** [*look at*] **the land of the Chaldeans** [*Babylon*]; **this people was not, till** [*was not ruined, until*] **the Assyrian founded it** [*set it up*] **for them** [*desert creatures*] **that dwell in the wilderness** [*the Assyrians destroyed Babylon to the point that it is now nothing more than a place for desert creatures to live*]: they set up the towers [*siege towers*] thereof, they raised [*razed; destroyed*] up the palaces thereof; and he [*Assyria*] brought it to ruin.

14 **Howl, ye ships of Tarshish: for your strength is laid waste** [*via Tyre's downfall*].

15 And it shall come to pass in that day, that **Tyre shall be forgotten seventy years,** according to the days of one king: **after the end of seventy years shall Tyre sing as an harlot** [*will "prostitute" the ways of God again*].

16 Take an harp, go about the city, thou harlot that hast been forgotten; make sweet melody, sing many songs, that thou mayest be remembered.

17 And it shall come to pass **after the end of seventy years,** that the Lord will visit **Tyre,** and she **shall turn** [*return*] **to her hire** [*wicked ways*], **and shall commit fornication** [*symbolic of intense and total disloyalty to God; see Bible Dictionary, under "Adultery"*] **with all the kingdoms of the world upon the face of the earth** [*Tyre will be an evil influence to many nations*].

18 **And her merchandise and her hire shall be holiness to the Lord** [*perhaps referring to the future when the wicked will be gone and the good things and wealth of the earth will be for the righteous and the building up of the kingdom of God*]: it shall not be treasured nor laid up; for her merchandise shall be for them that dwell before the Lord [*the righteous*], to eat sufficiently, and for durable clothing [*righteousness blesses people for eternity*].

ISAIAH 24

Background

In the first part of this chapter, Isaiah emphasizes the consequences of wickedness. The punishment for sin (if they don't repent) will eventually come upon all, regardless of social status (verse 3). Isaiah will again use chiasmus (see notes in the background for chapter 3 in this study guide) as a means of providing emphasis. It will be a simple chiasmus, consisting of **A, B, C, B,' A.'**

Other messages in this chapter also include the seriousness of breaking covenants (beginning with verse 5), and the burning of the wicked at the time of the Second Coming.

We will begin our study now by noting the chiasmus, which begins in verse 1.

1 Behold, **the Lord (A)** maketh the **earth empty (B)**, and maketh it waste, and turneth it upside down, and scattereth abroad the inhabitants thereof.

2 And it shall be, as with the **people (C)**, so with the priest; as with the servant, so with his master; as with

the maid, so with her mistress; as with the buyer, so with the seller; as with the lender, so with the borrower; as with the taker of usury [interest on loans], so with the giver of usury to him [*no one who is wicked will escape, regardless of social status*].

3 The <u>land shall be utterly emptied</u> (**B'**), and utterly spoiled: for **the Lord** (**A'**) hath spoken this word.

Verse 4, next, reminds us that pride is a devastating sin for individuals and nations.

4 The earth mourneth and fadeth away, **the world languisheth** [*wastes away*] and fadeth away, **the haughty** [*prideful*] **people of the earth do languish**.

The main problem that is causing the people of the world (verse 4) to waste away is described by Isaiah in verse 5.

5 **The earth** also **is defiled** under the inhabitants thereof; **because they have transgressed the laws, changed the ordinance, broken the everlasting covenant** [*they have gone into apostasy*].

In verse 6, next, Isaiah explains that apostasy with its accompanying personal and national wickedness will be the cause of the burning at the Second Coming.

6 **Therefore** [*this is why*] **hath the curse** [*the punishments of God*]

devoured the earth, and they that dwell therein are desolate: **therefore** [*this is why*] **the inhabitants of the earth are burned, and few men left** [*at the Second Coming*].

The glory of the Lord will be the source of the burning at the Second Coming, according to D&C 5:19 and 2 Nephi 12:10, 19, and 21.

In verses 7–12, next, Isaiah uses several different ways to say, in effect, that the party is over for the wicked.

7 **The new wine mourneth** [*fails, runs out*], the vine languisheth [*fails*], **all the merryhearted do sigh** [*"the party's over!"*].

8 **The mirth** [*merriment*] **of tabrets** [*drums; tambourines*] **ceaseth**, the noise of them that rejoice [*party, revel in riotous living*] endeth, the joy of the harp ceaseth.

9 **They shall not drink wine with a song** [*drunken singing*]; strong drink shall be bitter to them that drink it.

10 **The city of confusion is broken down** [*towns are broken down*]: every house is shut up, that no man may come in.

11 **There is a crying for wine in the streets** [*people still want their wicked lifestyle*]; all joy is darkened, the mirth of the land is gone.

12 **In the city is left desolation**, and the gate is smitten with destruction [*Isaiah has "painted" a verbal picture that the "party" is very over, in verses 7–12. This is an excellent example of his inspired brilliance and use of repetition in his prophesying*].

13 **When thus it shall be in the midst of the land among the people** [*nations*], **there shall be as the shaking of an olive tree, and as the gleaning grapes when the vintage is done** [*a few righteous will be separated, or gleaned from the wicked*].

14 **They** [*the relatively few righteous*] **shall lift up their voice, they shall sing** [*praises*] **for the majesty of the Lord**, they shall cry aloud from the sea.

15 **Wherefore glorify ye the Lord in the fires** [*probably should say "islands"—see footnote 15a in your Bible*], even the name of the Lord God of Israel in the isles of the sea [*nations of the earth; a few righteous, a remnant, are scattered throughout the earth*].

16 **From the uttermost part of the earth have we heard songs, even glory to the righteous**. But I [*Isaiah*] said, My leanness, my leanness [*my inability to change things!*], woe unto me! the treacherous dealers have dealt very treacherously; yea, the treacherous dealers have dealt treacherously

[*wickedness continues despite Isaiah's efforts to warn them and get them to change*].

17 **Fear** [*terror*], and **the pit** [*a trap*], and **the snare** [*a trap*], **are upon thee, O inhabitant** [*wicked people*] **of the earth**.

In verse 18, next, Isaiah teaches that, ultimately, there is no escape for the wicked.

18 And it shall come to pass, that **he who fleeth from the noise of the fear shall fall into the pit** [*as stated in verse 17, above*]; **and he that cometh up out** [*escapes*] **of the midst of the pit shall be taken in the snare** [*sometimes the wicked think that they have escaped the justice of God, but they haven't*]: **for the windows from on high are open** [*heaven is watching*], and the foundations of the earth do shake.

19 The earth is utterly broken down, the earth is clean dissolved, the earth is moved exceedingly [*will "reel to and fro"; see verse 20*].

20 **The earth shall reel to and fro like a drunkard**, and shall be removed like a cottage [*flimsy temporary shade structure built in a garden; see Isaiah 1:8*]; and the transgression thereof shall be heavy upon it; and it shall fall, and not rise again [*German: not remain standing*].

21 And it shall come to pass **in that day, that the Lord shall punish**

the host of the high ones [*wicked, proud*] that are on high, and the kings of the earth upon the earth [*the wicked will be punished*].

The doctrine of missionary work in the postmortal spirit world prison is clearly taught in verse 22, next.

22 And **they shall be gathered together, as prisoners are gathered in the pit** [*spirit prison—see footnotes 22a and 22b in your Bible*], and shall be shut up in the prison, **and after many days shall they be visited** [*by missionaries who come to the spirit prison; see D&C 138*].

Next, in verse 23, Isaiah explains to us that the glory of the Savior, as He comes to earth at the time of His Second Coming, will be beyond anything we have ever experienced.

23 **Then the moon shall be confounded, and the sun ashamed** [*moon and sun's majesty are nothing compared to radiant glory and majesty of Christ when He comes; see D&C 133:49*], **when the Lord of hosts shall reign in mount Zion, and in Jerusalem** [*during the Millennium*], and before his ancients gloriously.

ISAIAH 25

Background

One of the major messages in this chapter is that it is worth being righteous. Those who are worthy to be with the Savior will receive the very best of blessings and enjoy the results of their righteous efforts.

As we begin, we see the righteous praising God for the plan of salvation.

1 **O Lord, thou art my God**; I will exalt thee, **I will praise thy name**; for thou hast done wonderful things; **thy counsels of old** [*plans made in Council in Heaven*] are faithfulness and truth.

Next, the righteous praise and acknowledge the Lord for His power over the wicked. This is an important doctrine, since some people are of the opinion that the forces of evil, with Satan at the helm, have a chance to ultimately triumph over the Savior. They don't.

2 For **thou hast made of a** [*wicked*] **city an heap** [*pile of rubble*]; **of a defenced city a ruin: a palace of strangers** [*symbolic of kingdoms of the wicked*] **to be no city**; it shall never be built [*rebuilt; symbolic of the fall of Babylon, and the eventual fall of Satan's kingdom*].

3 **Therefore shall** [*this is why*] **the strong** [*powerful wicked*] **people glorify** [*acknowledge*] **thee**, the city of the terrible [*tyrant; German: powerful Gentile*] nations shall fear thee [*God has power over the wicked*].

4 **For thou hast been a strength to the poor, a strength to the needy in his distress, a refuge from the storm, a shadow** [*shade; protection*] **from the heat, when the blast of the terrible ones** [*the wicked*] **is as a storm against the wall** [*you have helped the righteous poor and needy*].

5 **Thou shalt bring down** [*humble*] **the noise** [*unrighteous revelry*] of strangers [*foreigners; people whose lifestyle is "foreign" to the gospel*], as the heat in a dry place [*strangers who have been fierce like the heat in the desert against the righteous*]; even the heat with the shadow [*shade*] of a cloud [*God subdues the wicked like He subdues desert heat with clouds*]: **the branch** [*German Bible: victory song of tyrants*] **of the terrible ones** [*tyrants*] **shall be brought low** [*humbled*].

6 ¶ **And in this mountain** [*mount Zion—see heading to this chapter in your Bible; probably a reference to the Millennium—see D&C 133:56*] **shall the Lord of hosts make unto all people** [*nations; the righteous*] **a feast of fat things** [*the best*], a feast of wines on the lees [*thickest, best part of the wine, in other words, the best blessings of the gospel are made available to the righteous*], of fat things full of marrow, of wines on the lees well refined.

7 And **he will destroy** in this mountain the face of the covering [*veil*] cast over all people, and **the vail that is spread over all nations** [*veil of spiritual darkness will be taken away*].

We see the blessed and happy state of the righteous, because of the resurrection and Atonement of Jesus Christ, highlighted in verse 8, next.

8 **He** [*Christ*] **will swallow up death in victory** [*the resurrection*]; **and the Lord God will wipe away tears from off all faces** [*through the Atonement come happiness and eternal life for the righteous; sharp contrast with the fate of wicked in verses 2, 10, 11, 12, and so forth*]; and the rebuke [*troubles, persecutions, problems*] of his people shall he take away from off all the earth: for **the Lord hath spoken it** [*it will happen!*].

9 **And it shall be said in that day** [*future*], **Lo, this is our God; we have waited for him, and he will save** [*has saved*] **us: this is the Lord; we have waited for him, we will be** [*are*] **glad** and rejoice in his salvation.

In verses 10–12, next, Isaiah yet again emphasizes the fact that the Lord will triumph over the wicked.

10 **For in this mountain shall the hand of the Lord rest, and Moab**

[*symbolic of the wicked*] **shall be trodden down under him**, even as straw is trodden down for the dunghill [*fate of the wicked*].

11 And **he shall spread forth his hands in the midst of them** [*the wicked*], as he that swimmeth spreadeth forth his hands to swim: and **he shall bring down their pride** together with the spoils of their hands [*He will humble the wicked and take away their ill-gotten gain*].

12 **And the fortress of the high fort** [*supposedly invincible domains of the wicked*] of thy walls **shall he** [*the Lord*] **bring down, lay low, and bring to the ground, even to the dust** [*kingdoms of the wicked destroyed completely!*].

ISAIAH 26

Background

This chapter consists of a message of encouragement to the righteous and a warning against wickedness. It depicts the righteous singing and praising Jehovah.

1 **In that day** [*last days*] **shall this song** [*of praise to the Lord*] **be sung in the land of Judah**; We have a strong city; **salvation will God appoint for walls and bulwarks** [*"salvation is all around us"*].

2 **Open ye the gates** [*several possible meanings: implies peaceful times when the city gates can be left open; can mean the gates of heaven; "gate" can also mean baptism*], **that the righteous nation** [*the righteous people*] **which keepeth the truth may enter in.**

3 **Thou wilt keep him** [*the righteous nation; individual*] **in perfect peace, whose mind is stayed** [*based, supported, supplied by*] **on thee**: because he trusteth in thee.

4 **Trust ye in the Lord for ever: for in the Lord JEHOVAH** [*the Savior*] **is everlasting strength**.

5 ¶ **For he** [*JEHOVAH in verse 4, above*] **bringeth down** [*humbles*] **them that dwell on high** [*the "high and mighty," that is, the proud wicked*]; the lofty city, he layeth it low; he layeth it low, even to the ground; he bringeth it even to the dust [*will completely destroy the wicked*].

6 **The foot shall tread it** [*the lofty city, that is, the wicked*] **down,** even the feet of the poor, and the steps of the needy [*the tables are turned; the oppressed now triumph and the wicked get their just dues*].

7 The way of the just [*righteous*] is uprightness: **thou, most upright** [*Christ*], **dost weigh the path of the just** [*make the path smooth, bless the righteous*].

8 Yea, **in the way of thy judgments, O Lord, have we waited for thee** [*we've been living righteously*];

the desire of our soul is to thy name [*our hearts are right; see D&C 64:22*], and to the remembrance of thee.

9 **With my soul have I desired thee in the night; yea, with my spirit within me will I seek thee early** [*I seek Thee day and night, in other words, always*]; **for when thy judgments** [*teachings and commandments*] **are in the earth, the inhabitants of the world will learn righteousness.**

Next, in verse 10, Isaiah points out to us that the problem with the wicked is that they do not want to do right.

10 **Let favour be shewed to the wicked, yet will he not** [*does not want to*] **learn righteousness:** in the land of uprightness [*among the righteous*] will he deal unjustly [*the wicked are always looking for ways to cheat the righteous*], and **will not** [*does not want to*] **behold the majesty of the Lord** [*even when the Lord shows kindness to the wicked, they don't repent because they don't desire righteousness; their hearts are not right*].

11 **Lord, when thy hand is lifted up** [*when Your power and existence are obvious*], **they** [*the wicked*] **will not see** [*don't want to see*]: **but they shall see** [*every knee shall bow and every tongue confess; see D&C 76:110*], **and be ashamed** [*put to shame*] for their envy at the people [*because of thy zeal for thy people*]; yea, **the fire of** [*reserved for*] **thine enemies shall devour them** [*the wicked; Second Coming*].

12 ¶ Lord, thou wilt ordain peace for us: for **thou also hast wrought all our works in us** [*all we have is from Thee; gratitude—compare with D&C 59:21*].

13 O Lord our God, **other lords** [*secular leaders, including wicked rulers*] beside thee **have had dominion over us: but by thee only will we make mention of thy name** [*Thou only do we honor and worship*].

Next, Isaiah speaks of the fact that the wicked will not be resurrected with the righteous. He speaks of the future as if it had already happened.

14 **They** [*the wicked rulers*] **are dead, they shall not live** [*until the resurrection of the wicked at the end of the Millennium—see D&C 88:101*]; **they are deceased, they shall not rise** [*their power is ended*]: **therefore** [*because of their wickedness*] **hast thou visited** [*punished*] **and destroyed them**, and made all their memory to perish.

15 **Thou hast increased the nation** [*the righteous—see verse 2*], O Lord, thou hast increased the

nation: **thou art glorified: thou hadst** [*hast*] **removed** [*spread*] **it far unto all the ends of the earth** [*there will be a tremendous increase in the number of righteous during the Millennium*].

16 **Lord, in trouble have they** [*the righteous*] **visited thee** [*come unto thee*], **they poured out a prayer when thy chastening was upon them** [*the righteous turn to God in times of trouble*].

17 **Like as a woman with child, that draweth near the time of her delivery, is in pain, and crieth out in her pangs: so have we been in thy sight, O Lord** [*when unavoidable trouble came, we turned to thee*].

Next, Israel, in effect, confesses that they have not always acted like the Lord's covenant people, which includes the responsibility of blessing others with the gospel and taking the gospel and the priesthood to all the world (see Abraham 2:9–11).

18 **We have been with child** [*we have had pain and suffering as part of our mortal probation*], **we have been in pain, we have as it were brought forth wind** [*nothing—sometimes we have turned from Thee, and pain and suffering have not produced desired results, fruits of righteousness in our lives*], **we have not wrought any deliverance in the earth** [*we have not*

brought salvation to people of the earth like we were called to do as Thy covenant people]; neither have the inhabitants of the world fallen [*been humbled*].

Next, in verse 19, the Savior teaches that the righteous, who have died before His resurrection, will be resurrected with Him (see also D&C 133:54–55).

19 **Thy dead men shall live** [*be resurrected*], **together with my** [*Christ's*] **dead body shall they arise** [*they will be resurrected with Christ*]. **Awake and sing, ye that dwell in dust** [*lie in graves*]: for thy dew is as the dew of herbs, and **the earth shall cast out the dead** [*resurrection*].

20 ¶ **Come, my people** [*the righteous, 19:25*], **enter thou into thy chambers, and shut thy doors about thee: hide thyself as it were for a little moment, until the indignation** [*cleansing of the earth*] **be overpast.** [*This verse is full of Passover symbolism. The Israelites closed their doors and put lamb's blood (symbolic of the Atonement) on doorposts, which provided them safety from the Lord's destruction among the Egyptians. Through righteous homes where the gospel is lived and the Atonement used, we can be spared God's punishments. God punishes only those who merit punishment.*]

21 For, behold, the Lord cometh out of his place [*heaven*] **to punish the inhabitants of the earth for their iniquity** [*the destruction of the wicked at the Second Coming as well as many destructions of the wicked previous to that time*]: **the earth also shall disclose her blood, and shall no more cover her slain** [*the bloodshed and crimes of the wicked will be exposed and punishment given out*].

ISAIAH 27

Background

This chapter is a prophecy of the gathering of Israel in the last days. The Church will flourish and spread throughout the earth (verse 6), as prophesied in Daniel 2:35, 44–45. The "kingdom of the devil" spoken of in 1 Nephi 22:22, will ultimately be destroyed by Christ.

1 **In that day** [*spoken of in chapter 26, above*] **the Lord with his sore** [*hard, fierce*] **and great and strong sword shall punish leviathan** [*Satan; can also include all forces of evil, all who serve Satan*] the piercing serpent, even leviathan **that crooked serpent** [*the devil— see Revelation 12:9*]; **and he shall slay the dragon** that is in the sea [*Leviathan was a legendary sea monster representing evil*].

2 **In that day sing ye unto her** [*Israel*], **A vineyard of red wine** [*symbolizing a productive people to the Lord*].

3 **I the Lord do keep it** [*my vineyard, Israel*]; **I will water it every moment: lest any hurt it, I will keep it night and day** [*so that it will do verse 6*].

4 Fury is not in me: **who would set the briers and thorns** [*the wicked*] **against me in battle** [*who dares to fight against the Lord*]? I would go through them, **I would burn them together** [*all of them*].

5 **Or let him** [*Israel*] **take hold of my strength** [*repent and come unto Me*], that he may make peace with me; and **he shall make peace with me** [*prophetic!*].

6 **He** [*God*] **shall cause them** [*Israel*] **that come of Jacob** [*the father of the twelve sons who became the twelve tribes of Israel*] **to take root** [*Israel will be restored*]: **Israel shall blossom and bud, and fill the face of the world with fruit** [*the blessings of righteousness and salvation*].

Without help, the pronouns in verse 7, next, can be quite confusing.

7 ¶ Hath **he** [*God*] smitten **him** [*Israel*], as **he** [*God*] smote **those** [*Israel's enemies*] that smote **him** [*Israel*]? or is **he** [*Israel*] slain according to [*like*] the slaughter of **them** [*Israel's enemies*] that are slain by **him** [*God*]? [*Has God*

been as hard on his people, Israel, as on her enemies? Answer: No!]

8 **In measure** [*moderation*], **when it** [*Israel*] **shooteth forth, thou wilt debate with it** [*prune it, discipline it*]: **he** [*God*] **stayeth his rough wind in the day of the east wind** [*God could destroy you with a really "rough" wind, but instead he sends the terrible east wind, a hot, dry wind off the Arabian Desert that devastates crops and helps humble you. In German, this says "You mete to them what is needed to set them straight so you can set them free." Jeremiah 30:11 in the King James Version says the same thing and is much clearer than the King James translation of verse 8, above.*]

We will include Jeremiah 30:11 here, so you can read it along with verse 8, above:

Jeremiah 30:11

11 **For I *am* with thee**, saith the LORD, to save thee: though I make a full end of all nations whither **I have scattered thee, yet will I not make a full end of thee** [*you will not be destroyed completely*]: but **I will correct** [*discipline*] **thee in measure**, and will not leave thee altogether unpunished.

9 **By this** [*the rough times, refiner's fire referred to in verse 8*] **therefore shall the iniquity** [*wickedness*] **of Jacob** [*Israel*] **be purged** [*rooted out*]; **and this is all the fruit** [*the product of Israel's wickedness—the consequences designed by God to purge wickedness out of them*] **to take away his** [*Israel's*] **sin;** when he [*God*] maketh all the stones of the altar [*used in idol worship*] *as* chalkstones that are beaten in sunder [*into pieces*], the groves [*used in idol worship*] and images [*used in idol worship*] shall not stand up [*your false religions, upon which you have relied, will crumble*].

10 **Yet** [*the time will come that*] **the defenced city** [*established wickedness*] **shall be desolate**, and the habitation forsaken [*abandoned*], and left like a wilderness: **there shall the calf feed** [*in effect, where you once lived will become a place for animals to live*], and there shall he [*the calf*] lie down, and consume the branches thereof [*nothing will be left of you and your wickedness*].

11 When the boughs thereof are withered, they shall be broken off: the women come, and set them on fire [*women will use what is left for cooking fires; symbolically, wickedness will be destroyed completely by fire*]: for **it is a people of no understanding** [*of the gospel, because they don't want it*]: **therefore** [*that is why*] **he that made them will not have mercy on them**, and he [*God*] that formed

them will shew them no favour.

Isaiah now switches topics somewhat, and prophesies of the latter-day gathering of Israel, "one by one."

12 ¶ And **it shall come to pass in that day** [*the last days*], that the Lord shall beat [*glean*] off from the channel of the river [*from Mesopotamia*] unto the stream of Egypt [*the Nile River; gather Israel out of the whole world*], and **ye shall be gathered one by one**, O ye children of Israel [*the righteous shall be gathered to Christ from the whole earth*].

13 And it shall come to pass **in that day**, that **the great trumpet shall be blown** [*to signal the gathering*], **and they shall come which were ready to perish in the land of Assyria** [*symbolic of the wicked world*], and the outcasts in the land of Egypt [*the righteous, who have been "outcasts" in the wicked world*], **and shall worship the Lord in the holy mount at Jerusalem** [*in the holy temples*].

ISAIAH 28

Background

Isaiah speaks to Israel (the northern ten tribes in his day, also referred to as "Ephraim") in verses 1–4. This message came probably somewhere around 724 B.C., before the ten tribes were taken captive by

the Assyrians in 722 B.C.

1 **Woe to the crown of pride** [*the haughty Ephraimites at Samaria, capital city of Israel, who have not yet come under Assyrian control and have boasted about their invincibility*], **to the drunkards of Ephraim** [*northern Israel is "drunk," out of control with wickedness*], **whose glorious beauty is a fading flower** [*on the way out*], which are on the head of the fat valleys [*rich, productive land area in Samaria*] of them that are overcome with wine [*you are out of control with wickedness*]!

2 **Behold, the Lord hath a mighty and strong one** [*Shalmaneser, the Assyrian king and his armies*], **which as a tempest of hail and a destroying storm, as a flood of mighty waters overflowing** [*compare with Isaiah 8:7*], **shall cast down** to the earth with the hand [*the Assyrians will flood your land and conquer you*].

3 **The crown of pride, the drunkards of Ephraim, shall be trodden under feet** [*Israel, the northern ten tribes, will be destroyed; this happens in 722 B.C. via Assyria*]:

We have mentioned several times that one of the techniques used by ancient prophets was repetition. We are seeing another example of that in the verses that follow.

4 **And the glorious beauty, which is on the head of the fat valley, shall be a fading flower**, and **as the hasty fruit** [*early fruit; the first ripe fruit on the tree*] **before the summer; which when he that looketh upon it seeth, while it is yet in his hand he eateth it up** [*it doesn't last long once someone has spotted it, in other words, you will be "gobbled up" quickly like the first ripe fruit of the season*].

5 **In that day** [*last days or Millennium*] **shall the Lord of hosts be for a crown of glory, and for a diadem** [*crown*] **of beauty, unto the residue** [*the righteous who are left*] **of his people** [*the Savior will lead you, as opposed to the proud, haughty drunkards referred to in verse 1*],

6 And for a spirit of judgment to him that sitteth in judgment, and **for strength to them that turn the battle to the gate** [*Christ will provide strength to overcome all enemies and "push them back to where they came from"*].

7 ¶ **But they** [*Israel's leaders*] **also have erred** through wine, and through strong drink are out of the way; the [*false*] **priest** and the [*false*] **prophet** have erred through strong drink, they are swallowed up of wine, they are out of the way through strong drink; **they err in vision**, they **stumble in judgment** [*apostasy; out of control literally and symbolically*].

8 For **all tables are full of vomit and filthiness, so that there is no place clean** [*apostasy has completely penetrated the nation*].

9 ¶ **Whom shall he** [*the Lord*] **teach knowledge** [*of the gospel*]? and **whom shall he make to understand doctrine?** [*answer:*] them that are weaned from the milk, and drawn from the breasts [*toddlers; in other words, start teaching them while very young*].

Verse 10, next, is a rather well-known quote from Isaiah.

10 For precept must be upon precept, **precept upon precept; line upon line, line upon line; here a little, and there a little** [*a lifelong process starting very young*]:

11 **For with stammering** [*not understandable*] **lips and another tongue** [*a tongue "foreign" to the wicked; in other words, through the Holy Ghost*] **will he speak to this people.**

12 **To whom he said**, This is the rest [*peace of God*] wherewith ye may cause the weary to rest; and **this is the refreshing** [*available from God through righteous living*]: **yet they** [*Israel*] **would not** [*didn't want to*] **hear** [*in verse 10, the Lord tells them how he would help them bit by bit, not overwhelm them, but they don't want to hear such stuff*].

Next, in verse 13, Isaiah repeats again that the stubborn people of the northern ten tribes (Israel) had plenty of opportunity to hear and understand the gospel. They were given the opportunity so that they would be accountable for the consequences when they rebelled. This is the law of justice in action.

Remember that at this point in history, the northern ten tribes are called "Israel," and the southern two tribes (Judah and Benjamin) are called "Judah."

13 But **the word of the Lord was unto them precept upon precept,** precept upon precept; **line upon line,** line upon line; here a little, and there a little; **that they might go, and fall backward** [*apostasy isn't just "falling"; it is retrogressing—falling backward*], and **be broken,** and **snared,** and **taken** [*by Satan; in other words, when ignored, the word of God condemns*].

Next, Isaiah turns his attention to the haughty people of Judah.

14 ¶ **Wherefore hear the word of the Lord, ye scornful men** [*scoffers*], **that rule this people** which is in Jerusalem [*Isaiah now speaks to the people in Jerusalem in his day*].

15 **Because ye have said** [*boasted*], **We have made a covenant with death, and with hell are we at agreement** [*we have an*

"*agreement*" *with death and hell*]; **when the overflowing scourge** [*that all the prophets keep saying will come*] **shall pass through, it shall not come unto us: for we have made lies our refuge** [*we have found that wickedness **does** pay!*], **and under falsehood have we hid ourselves** [*we will live wickedly and get away with it!*]:

16 ¶ **Therefore** [*because of your wickedness, boasting, and so forth*] **thus saith the Lord God, Behold, I lay in Zion for a foundation a stone** [*the Savior*], **a tried** [*proven reliable*] **stone, a precious corner stone** [*Ephesians 2:20*], **a sure foundation** [*the Lord is the only one with whom you can strike agreements and have guaranteed results*]: **he that believeth shall not make haste** [*will not flee; he that lives righteously will not have to flee before the face of the Lord*].

17 **Judgment also will I lay to the line** [*carpenter's line, used to build straight and true*], **and righteousness to the plummet** [*plumb bob (carpenter's tools used to build precisely); symbolic of the fact that all things about the Savior and His gospel are exact and true*]: **and the hail shall sweep away the refuge** of lies [*in other words, you won't get away with your boast in verse 15*], **and the waters** [*can refer to the Assyrians, see 8:7; could also refer to Christ as "living water,"*

as in John 4:10] shall overflow the hiding place [*of the wicked*].

18 ¶ And **your covenant with death** [*verse 15*] **shall be disannulled** [*canceled*], and **your agreement with hell shall not stand**; when the overflowing scourge [*referred to boastfully in verse 15*] shall pass through, then **ye shall be trodden down** by it [*the wicked will be destroyed*].

19 **From the time that it** [*the punishment of God*] **goeth forth it shall take you: for morning by morning shall it pass over, by day and by night** [*continuously*]: **and it shall be a vexation** [*pure terror*] **only to understand the report** [*God's judgments*].

Isaiah now refers to the proud boast in verse 15 that they could be comfortable and protected in sin. He uses the imagery of a bed that is too short for the person trying to sleep in it.

20 For **the bed is shorter than that a man can stretch himself on it** [*you can't ever get completely comfortable in the bed of sin you've made for yourselves to lie in*]: **and the covering** [*the blanket of lies you made for yourselves*] **narrower than that he can wrap himself in it** [*you can't get completely comfortable in your blanket of sin!*].

21 **For the Lord shall rise up as in mount Perazim** [*David attacked and smote the Philistines*

there, with the Lord's help], **he shall be wroth as in the valley of Gibeon** [*where the Lord killed Joshua's enemies, the Amorites, with huge hailstones*], that he may do his work, his strange work; and bring to pass his act, his strange [*unusual*] act.

Next, Isaiah issues a strong warning to these arrogant people.

22 **Now therefore be ye not mockers** [*don't scoff at God's word*], **lest your bands be made strong** [*lest you be totally enslaved by wickedness*]: **for I** [*Isaiah*] **have heard from the Lord God of hosts a consumption, even determined upon the whole earth** [*I've heard God will annihilate the wicked*].

23 ¶ **Give ye ear, and hear my voice; hearken, and hear my speech.**

24 **Doth the plowman** [*farmer; symbolic of God*] **plow all day to sow** [*getting ready to plant*]: **doth he open and break the clods of his ground** [*continuously*]? [*Does the Lord just keep plowing, preparing and preparing the ground forever, or does he go on to the next steps, planting, harvesting, and so forth? In other words, "Do you think Judgment Day will never come, that the Lord will never get around to harvest time?"*]

Isaiah answers his own question in verse 25, next.

25 **When he** [*the farmer*] **hath made plain the face thereof** [*has the ground plowed and leveled*], **doth he not cast abroad** [*plant, throw the seeds by hand*] the fitches [*dill seeds*], and scatter the cummin, and cast in the principal wheat [*the main crop*] and the appointed [*planned on*] barley and the rie in their place [*doesn't the farmer plan carefully and then work his plan*]?

26 For **his** [*the plowman's*] **God doth instruct him to discretion, and doth teach him.**

Next, Isaiah uses some different methods of harvesting used in his day to illustrate that the Lord carefully applies differing harvesting methods to harvest His people, depending on their personalities.

27 For **the fitches** [*a plant producing small seeds that were harvested and used like we use pepper*] **are not threshed with a threshing instrument, neither is a cart wheel** [*used in harvesting larger grain seeds such as wheat*] **turned about** [*around and around*] **upon the cummin** [*very small seeds*]; but the fitches are beaten out with a staff, and the cummin with a rod [*God will use appropriate methods to "harvest" all the righteous out from the wicked, according to their personalities, aptitudes, talents, and so forth*].

28 Bread corn [*cereal grain*] is bruised [*ground in a mill*]; because he will not ever [*forever*] be threshing it, nor break it with the wheel of his cart, nor bruise it with his horsemen. [*In the Martin Luther German Bible, this verse says basically that cereal grain is ground to make bread, not threshed to the point of destruction when it is threshed with wagon wheels and horses.*]

29 **This also cometh forth from the Lord of hosts** [*this is how the Lord goes about harvesting the righteous*], which is wonderful in counsel [*who is wonderful in how He plans His work; see 19:3, 25:1*], and excellent in working [*German: carries it out wonderfully*].

ISAIAH 29

Background
This chapter compares with 2 Nephi 27 in the Book of Mormon. The Book of Mormon rendition provides many changes for this chapter in the Bible. We will draw heavily from it as we proceed.

This prophecy was given by Isaiah about 700 B.C., near the end of his ministry. It deals with the last days, including the restoration of the gospel through the Prophet Joseph Smith, giving many specific details about the coming forth of the Book of Mormon. It is a chapter of scripture that bears extra strong witness of the truthfulness of prophecies given by the Lord through His chosen servants, such as Isaiah.

Isaiah begins by prophesying about the out-of-control wickedness that will prevail among all peoples upon the earth in the last days.

1 **Woe to Ariel** [*Jerusalem; Zion in 2 Nephi 27:3*], to Ariel, **the city where David dwelt!** add ye year to year; let them kill sacrifices [*keep right on going as you are with your wickedness and empty rituals; it will do you no good!*].

2 **Yet I will** [*I will continue to*] **distress Ariel**, and there shall be heaviness and sorrow: and **it shall be unto me as Ariel** [*it shall become a proper Zion*].

3 And **I will camp against thee** [*the Lord will humble his rebellious covenant people*] round about, and will lay siege against thee with a mount [*mound of dirt*], and I will raise forts against thee [*as is the case in a planned military action; in other words, you will be chastened until you repent*].

4 **And thou** [*Ariel*] **shalt be brought down** [*humbled*], and shalt speak out of the ground, and **thy speech shall be low out of the dust**, and **thy voice shall be, as of one** that hath a familiar spirit [*a dead relative speaking from the*

spirit world], **out of the ground**, and thy speech shall whisper out of the dust [*the Book of Mormon came "out of the ground" and in it, the Nephites, our dead Israelite "relatives" who came from Ariel; in other words, Jerusalem, speak to us as from the dust*].

5 Moreover **the multitude of thy strangers** [*the number of your enemies*] **shall be like small dust** [*countless*], and the multitude of the terrible ones [*tyrants*] shall be as chaff that passeth away [*that blows away in the wind, in other words, countless*]: yea, **it shall be at an instant suddenly** [*the things that humble you; see first part of verse 4; will catch you off guard so that you will hardly be able to believe they are happening so rapidly and nobody is stopping them*].

6 **Thou shalt be visited of** [*disciplined or punished by*] **the Lord** of hosts with thunder, and with earthquake, and great noise, with storm and tempest, and the flame of devouring fire.

In verses 7–8, next, Isaiah describes the ultimate failure and frustration of the wicked who fight against the work of the Lord.

7 ¶ And the multitude of **all the nations that fight against Ariel** [*the Lord's people; Zion, 2 Nephi 27:3*], even all that fight against

her and her munition, and that distress her, **shall be as a dream of a night vision.**

8 It [*their persecution of the Saints*] **shall even be** [*unto them, 2 Nephi 27:3 —enemy nations*] **as when an hungry man dreameth, and, behold, he eateth; but he awaketh, and his soul is empty** [*he is still hungry*]: **or as when a thirsty man dreameth, and, behold, he drinketh** [*in his dream*]; **but he awaketh, and, behold, he is faint, and his soul hath appetite: so shall the multitude of all the nations be, that fight against mount Zion** [*persecutors of the Saints never feel satisfied, are still "hungry and thirsty" for more, can't leave us alone*].

9 ¶ **Stay yourselves, and wonder** [*you wicked people, stop and think*]; **cry ye out,** and cry: **they** [*the wicked, 2 Nephi 27:4*] **are drunken** [*out of control*], **but not with wine;** they stagger [*stumble around*], but not with strong drink [*in other words, they are "drunk" with wickedness, out of control because they have no prophets to lead them, as mentioned in verse 10, next*].

The Book of Mormon makes an important doctrinal correction to the Bible, in verse 10, next. It is not the Lord who causes spiritual darkness to come upon people; rather, it is the people themselves who close their eyes

to truth and light and who are the cause of spiritual darkness.

10 **For the Lord hath poured out upon you the spirit of deep sleep** [*spiritual darkness*], **and hath closed** [*"ye have closed," 2 Nephi 27:5*] **your eyes: the prophets and your rulers, the seers hath he covered** [*"because of your iniquity," 2 Nephi 27:5*].

Next, Isaiah begins a marvelous prophecy about the coming forth of the Book of Mormon in the last days. He gives an amazing amount of specific detail, which, as you will see, was fulfilled.

11 And **the vision of all** [*German: the vision of all the prophets, in other words, all of the scripture*] **is become unto you** [*Israelites who are spiritually dead*] **as the words of a book** [*Book of Mormon—see footnote 11a in your Bible*] **that is sealed** [*because you refuse to hearken to the scriptures, they might just as well be sealed and unreadable to you, like the copy of characters from the Book of Mormon plates*], **which men** [*Martin Harris, with the help of Joseph Smith*] **deliver to one that is learned** [*Professor Charles Anthon of Colombia College in New York City, February 1828*], **saying, Read this, I pray thee: and he** [*Charles Anthon*] **saith, I cannot; for it is sealed:**

You can read the account of Martin Harris and Charles

Anthon, referred to above, in the Pearl of Great Price, Joseph Smith—History 1:63–65.

12 **And the book** [*the gold plates*] **is delivered to him** [*Joseph Smith*] **that is not learned** [*educated, like Professor Anthon*], **saying, Read this, I pray thee: and he saith, I am not learned** [*I can't translate it without God's help*].

13 ¶ Wherefore the Lord said, **Forasmuch as this people draw near me with their mouth, and with their lips do honour me, but have removed their heart far from me** [*they are spiritually dead*], **and their fear toward me is taught by the precept** [*traditions*] **of men** [*people have gone far astray from truth*]:

14 **Therefore,** behold, **I will proceed to do a marvellous work** among this people, even **a marvellous** [*"astonishing" as used in Old Testament Hebrew*] **work and a wonder** [*the Restoration of the gospel*]: for **the wisdom of their wise men shall perish** [*revealed truth cuts through falsehood*], and the understanding of their prudent men shall be hid [*false philosophies and false scientific conclusions fade away in light of truth*].

15 **Woe unto them** [*the wicked*] **that seek deep to hide their counsel** [*plans*] **from the Lord,** and **their works are in the dark,** and **they say, Who seeth us? and who knoweth us?** [*We can get away with wickedness without getting exposed—typical thinking of wicked people.*]

16 **Surely your turning of things upside down** [*foolish perversion of the truth*] **shall be esteemed as** [*is the same as*] **the potter's clay**: for shall the work [*the pot*] say of him that made it [*the potter*], He made me not? or shall the thing framed say of him that framed it, He had no understanding? [*He doesn't know me; I have successfully hidden from God. In other words, you wicked are just as foolish as the potter's clay that claims it made itself into a pot and has no responsibility to its maker.*]

Next, beginning with verse 17, Isaiah tells us that the coming forth of the Book of Mormon will be the key event signaling the beginning of the Restoration of the gospel in the last days and the fulfilling of the many prophecies that will culminate with the Second Coming. Included in these prophecies is the gathering of the Jews and their establishment as a nation again in the Holy Land.

17 **Is it not yet a very little while** [*after the Book of Mormon comes forth*], **and Lebanon** [*the Holy Land*] **shall be turned into**

a fruitful field, and the fruitful field shall be esteemed as a forest? [*In other words, Israel will blossom with forests and in other ways (including eventual spiritual conversion) after the Restoration.*]

18 ¶ And in that day [*the time of the restoration of the Gospel, with the Book of Mormon leading the way*] shall the [*spiritually*] deaf hear the words of the book, and the eyes of the [*spiritually*] blind shall see out of obscurity, and out of darkness [*as a result of the Book of Mormon and Restoration, the spiritually deaf and blind will be healed*].

19 The meek also shall increase their joy in the Lord, and the poor among men shall rejoice in the Holy One of Israel [*the righteous will know the Savior again*].

20 For the terrible one [*tyrant*] is brought to nought, and the scorner [*scoffer*] is consumed, and all that watch for iniquity are cut off [*the restored truth will expose wickedness and eventually overthrow it*]:

In verse 21, next, Isaiah describes the crippling corruption in governments and judicial systems in the last days.

21 That make a man an offender for a word [*via unjust lawsuits, corrupt judicial system, and so forth*], and lay a snare for him that reproveth in the gate [*try to eliminate honest people in government, and those who try to expose corruption in government*], and turn aside the just for a thing of nought [*destroy the effectiveness of honest government and judicial leaders; replace truth and honesty with lies*].

Next, Isaiah uses his great skill as a writer to create in our minds a picture of a rather embarrassed Jacob (the father of the twelve sons who became the twelve tribes of Israel). In the past, he has been embarrassed by the behaviors of his posterity, rebellious Israel. However, because of the restoration of the gospel in the last days and the gathering of Israel, they will finally become a righteous people. He is no longer embarrassed to be their "father," rather; he is humbly proud of them.

22 Therefore thus saith the Lord, who redeemed Abraham, concerning the house of Jacob [*Israel; implies "I redeemed Abraham and I can and will redeem you."*], Jacob shall not now be ashamed, neither shall his face now wax pale [*Father Jacob, Israel, will no longer have to be embarrassed by the behavior of his posterity*].

23 But when he [*Jacob*] seeth his children [*his posterity*], the work of mine hands [*who are now finally righteous—"My people"*], in the midst of him, they shall

sanctify my name, and sanctify the Holy One of Jacob [*the Savior*], and shall fear [*respect*] the God of Israel. [*Isaiah here has said, in many ways, that in the last days Israel will return to God.*]

In concluding this vision, Isaiah summarizes the marvelous effects of the Book of Mormon and the restoration of the gospel through the Prophet Joseph Smith.

24 They also that erred in spirit shall come to understanding, and they that murmured shall learn doctrine [*through the Book of Mormon and the restoration of the Church of Jesus Christ*].

ISAIAH 30

Background
In this chapter, we will see the scattering of Israel because they rejected their prophets. Then we will see the gathering and eventual coming of the Savior and the destruction of the wicked.

The historical setting is 705–701 B.C. King Sargon II, of Assyria, has died. Judah joins the Philistines and Phoenicians in rebellion against Assyria. Judah makes a treaty for protection with Egypt (which sometimes is used to symbolize Satan's kingdom in Old Testament writings).

In verse 1, Isaiah points out that Judah has turned to political alliances for protection from her enemies, rather than repenting and turning to God for protection.

1 Woe to the rebellious children, saith the LORD, that take counsel [*make political plans*], but not of me; and that cover with a covering [*alliance*], but not of my spirit [*not approved by God*], that they may add sin to sin [*add insult to injury; make things worse*]:

2 That walk to go down into Egypt [*turn to Egypt for help*], and have not asked at my mouth [*haven't asked my permission*]; to strengthen themselves in the strength of Pharaoh, and to trust in the shadow [*protection*] of Egypt!

3 Therefore [*because you have done this*] shall the strength of Pharaoh be your shame [*downfall*], and the trust in the shadow [*protection*] of Egypt your confusion [*your pact with Egypt will lead to your ruin; you should have turned to God rather than man for help*].

4 For his [*Pharaoh's*] princes [*leaders*] were at Zoan [*Tanis*], and his ambassadors came to Hanes [*Leaders from one end of Egypt to the other worked out the treaty with Judah*].

5 They [*Judah*] were [*will be*] all ashamed of [*disappointed by*] a

people [*Egypt*] **that could not** [*can not*] **profit them**, nor be an help nor profit, but a shame, and also a reproach [*this deal with Egypt will bring shame and scorn to Judah*].

6 **The burden of** [*message of doom for those of Judah who travel with loads of gifts on animals toward Egypt, verses 2–7*] **the beasts of the south: into the land of trouble and anguish**, from whence come the young and old lion, the viper and fiery flying serpent, **they** [*Judah*] **will carry their riches upon the shoulders of young asses, and their treasures upon the bunches of camels, to a people** [*Egypt*] **that shall not profit them.**

7 **For the Egyptians shall help in vain, and to no purpose**: therefore have I cried concerning this, Their strength is to sit still [*Egypt won't help you at all!*].

Next, the Lord instructs Isaiah to be sure to write this prophecy and warning down as a written witness against these wicked people.

8 ¶ **Now go, write it before them in a table, and note it in a book** [*which will eventually become scripture*], **that it may be for the time to come for ever and ever** [*write this down as a witness against Judah*]:

9 **That this** [*Judah*] **is a rebellious people, lying children, children that will not hear the law of the LORD**:

10 **Which say to the seers, See not; and to the prophets, Prophesy not** unto us **right things, speak unto us smooth things** [*comfortable false doctrines*], **prophesy deceits**:

11 Get you out of the way, turn aside out of the path, **cause the Holy One of Israel to cease from before us** [*tell God to quit bothering us*].

12 **Wherefore thus saith the Holy One of Israel, Because ye despise** [*spurn, intentionally ignore*] **this word**, and trust in oppression [*German: wickedness*] and perverseness, and stay [*depend*] thereon:

13 **Therefore this iniquity shall be to you as a breach** [*broken section in a protective wall*] **ready to fall**, swelling [*bulging*] out in a high wall, whose breaking cometh suddenly at an instant [*you are living on borrowed time; you have broken the covenant that could protect you like a wall by making covenants with Egypt rather than God*].

14 **And he** [*Christ*] **shall break it as the breaking of the potters' vessel that is broken in pieces; he shall not spare**: so that there shall not be found in the bursting of it a sherd [*fragment*] to take fire from the hearth, or to take water

withal out of the pit [*there won't be a piece big enough left to take a fire start from the fireplace or to dip a little water from the well; nothing usable remains*].

Next, the Lord tells these rebellious people how they could be saved from the fate just described.

15 For **thus saith the Lord** GOD, the Holy One of Israel; **In returning** [*to God*] **and rest shall ye be saved** [*German: you could be saved*]; **in quietness** [peacefulness] **and in confidence** [*faith in God*] **shall be your strength**: and ye would not.

16 **But ye said** [*bragged*], **No**; for we will flee [*into battle against Assyria*] upon horses [*symbolize victory*]; therefore [*because of your rebellion*] shall ye flee [*from Assyria's armies*]: and, We will ride upon the swift [*Judah bragged*]; therefore shall they [*Assyrians*] that pursue you be swift [*it will be exactly opposite of what you brag, Judah*].

17 **One thousand** [*of Judah*] **shall flee at the rebuke of one** [*Assyrian*]; at the rebuke of five [*Assyrians*] shall [*German: all of you*] ye flee: till ye be left as a beacon upon the top of a mountain, and as an ensign on an hill [*lonely, nobody left, scattered*].

18 ¶ And **therefore will the LORD wait** [*because of your wickedness, the Lord will have to wait*], **that he may be gracious unto you** [*at a future time*], and therefore will he be exalted, that he may have mercy upon you: for the LORD is a God of judgment [*justice*]: **blessed are all they that wait for** [*German: trust in*] **him.**

Isaiah now describes the ultimate in paradisiacal conditions for those who do trust in the Lord.

19 For the people shall dwell in Zion at Jerusalem: **thou shalt weep no more: he will be very gracious unto thee at the voice of thy cry; when he shall hear it, he will answer thee.**

20 And **though the Lord give you the bread of adversity, and the water of affliction** [*even though you go through some trying times*], yet shall not thy teachers [*thy teacher, the Lord*] be removed into a corner any more, **but thine eyes shall see thy teachers:**

21 And **thine ears shall hear a word behind thee, saying, This is the way, walk ye in it**, when ye turn to the right hand, and when ye turn to the left [*you will be surrounded with guidance and truth*].

22 **Ye shall defile** [*cease to worship*] **also the covering of thy graven images of silver** [*your graven images covered with silver*],

and the ornament of thy molten images of gold: thou shalt cast them away as a menstruous cloth [*they will be totally repulsive to you*]; thou shalt say unto it, Get thee hence [*you will shudder at the thought of idol worship*].

23 **Then shall he give the rain of thy seed, that thou shalt sow the ground withal** [*you will prosper*]; and bread of the increase of the earth, and it shall be fat and plenteous: in that day shall thy cattle feed in large pastures [*things will go well when Israel repents and is gathered*].

24 **The oxen likewise and the young asses that ear the ground** [*work the ground in agriculture*] shall eat clean provender [*hay*], which hath been winnowed with the shovel and with the fan.

25 And **there shall be** upon every high mountain, and upon every high hill, **rivers and streams of waters** in the day of the great slaughter, when the towers fall [*when your enemies have been destroyed*].

26 **Moreover the light of the moon shall be as the light of the sun, and the light of the sun shall be sevenfold, as the light of seven days** [*everything will be better than you can imagine*], in the day that the LORD bindeth up the breach of his people, and healeth the stroke of their wound [*Christ heals when people repent*].

27 ¶ Behold, the name of **the LORD cometh from far, burning with his anger,** and the burden thereof is heavy: his lips are full of indignation, and his tongue as a devouring fire [*the wicked are destroyed*]:

28 And **his breath, as an overflowing stream** [*flood*], shall reach to the midst of the neck, **to sift** [*German: destroy*] **the nations** [*the wicked*] with the sieve of vanity [*German: until they are all filtered out, destroyed, gone*]: and there shall be a bridle in the jaws of the people, causing them to err [*they have allowed wickedness to take control of them; that's why they are destroyed*].

29 **Ye** [*the righteous survivors*] **shall have a song**, as in the night when a holy solemnity is kept; **and gladness of heart**, as when one goeth with a pipe [*German: flute*] to come into the mountain of the LORD, to the mighty One of Israel [*the Savior*].

30 **And the LORD shall cause his glorious voice to be heard, and shall shew the lighting down of his arm** [*will come crashing down upon the wicked*], with the indignation of his anger, and with the flame of a devouring fire, with scattering, and tempest, and hailstones.

31 For **through the voice** [*power*] **of the LORD shall the Assyrian** [*the*

enemy now threatening Judah] **be beaten down**, which smote [Israel] with a rod.

32 And in every place where the grounded staff shall pass [every stroke of the rod of punishment], which the LORD shall lay upon him [Assyria], it shall be with tabrets and harps: and in battles of shaking [several "waves" of battle] will he fight with it.

33 **For Tophet** [the "Place of Burning," hell] **is ordained of old** [was planned for in the beginning]; yea, **for the king** [of Assyria] **it is prepared**; he [God] hath made it deep and large [there is plenty of room in hell for the Assyrians and all other wicked]: the pile thereof is fire and much wood [plenty of fuel to burn them]; the breath of the LORD, like a stream of brimstone [fiery molten sulfur], doth kindle it [the Lord is prepared to destroy the wicked].

ISAIAH 31

Background
In chapter 30, we learned that the nation of Judah had determined to turn to Egypt for help against Assyria. In this chapter, Isaiah continues to warn them about this mistake.

1 **Woe to them** [Judah] **that go down to Egypt for help**; and stay [rely] on horses, and trust in chariots [the military might of Egypt], **because they** [Egyptian soldiers] **are many**; and in horsemen, because they are very strong; **but they look not unto the Holy One of Israel, neither seek the LORD** [Judah should turn to the Lord instead of Egypt for help]!

2 Yet **he** [the Lord] also **is wise, and will bring evil** [calamity upon the wicked], **and will not call back** [retract] **his words: but will arise against the house of the evildoers, and against the help** [helpers] **of them that work iniquity**.

3 **Now the Egyptians are men, and not God**; and their horses flesh, and not spirit. When the LORD shall stretch out his hand, both he that helpeth shall fall, and he that is holpen [helped] shall fall down, and they all shall fail together [Egypt and Judah will both fail].

Next, Isaiah reminds the Jews that the Lord does indeed have power to protect them against their enemies.

4 For **thus hath the LORD spoken unto me** [Isaiah], **Like as the lion** and the young lion roaring on his prey, **when a multitude of shepherds is called forth against him**, he will not be afraid of their voice, nor abase himself for the noise of them: **so**

shall the LORD of hosts come down to fight for mount Zion, and for the hill thereof [*the Lord will be as unstoppable among the wicked as a lion among sheep*].

5 **As birds flying** [*hovering over their young, protecting them*], **so will the LORD of hosts defend Jerusalem**; defending also he will deliver it; and passing over he will preserve it.

6 **Turn ye unto him** [*the Lord*] from whom the children of Israel have deeply revolted [*please repent*].

7 For **in that day** [*if and when you repent*] **every man shall cast away his idols of silver, and his idols of gold**, which your own hands have made unto you for a sin [*turn away from your sinful idol worship*].

8 ¶ **Then shall the Assyrian fall** with the sword, not of a mighty man; and the sword, not of a mean [*poor*] man, shall devour him: but he shall flee from the sword, and his young men shall be discomfited [*put in slavery; God, not men, will overthrow Assyria*].

9 **And he shall pass over to his strong hold for fear** [*will retreat in fear*], and his princes shall be afraid of the ensign, saith the LORD, whose fire is in Zion, and his furnace in Jerusalem [*the power of the Lord can protect Zion, Jerusalem*].

ISAIAH 32

Background

In this chapter, Isaiah prophesies that the day will come when Jesus Christ will rule and reign, but in the meantime, until the restoration of the gospel and the gathering of Israel, the land of Israel will be a wilderness.

1 Behold, **a king** [*Jesus*] **shall reign in righteousness, and princes** [*His leaders*] **shall rule in judgment** [*justice, fairness*].

2 **And a man** [*Jesus*] **shall be as an hiding place from the wind, and a covert** [*protection*] **from the tempest**; as rivers of water in a dry place, as the shadow of a great rock in a weary land [*Jesus will be our refuge and protection*].

Next, Isaiah teaches what the effects of the Savior and His gospel will be upon those who listen, who have previously been spiritually blind and deaf.

3 **And the eyes of them that see shall not be dim** [*the spiritual eyes of those who see the gospel, who were previously spiritually blind, shall no longer be dim*], **and the ears of them that hear shall hearken** [*people will be blessed with understanding and discernment*].

4 **The heart** [*mind*] also **of the rash** [*impulsive*] **shall understand** knowledge [*have good judgment*],

and the tongue of the stammerers shall be ready to speak plainly [*those who previously could not explain the purposes of life according to the gospel will now discuss the gospel plainly*].

5 The vile person [*villain*] shall be no more called liberal [*noble*], nor the churl [*miser; cruel financier*] said to be bountiful [*people will be recognized for what they really are, not what they appear to be*].

In verses 6–8, Isaiah describes what the motives of people alluded to in verse 5 really are like.

6 For the vile person will speak villany, and his heart will work iniquity, to practise hypocrisy, and to utter error against the LORD, to make empty the soul of the hungry [*oppress the poor and needy*], and he will cause the drink of the thirsty to fail.

7 The instruments [*devices*] also of the churl [*wicked moneylenders*] are evil: he deviseth wicked devices to destroy the poor with lying words [*trickery*], even when the needy speaketh right [*is in the right*].

8 But the liberal [*noble*] deviseth liberal [*honorable, righteous*] things; and by liberal things shall he stand [*German: he will hold to honorable thoughts and actions*].

Next, Isaiah warns the women against the spiritual dangers

that confront them.

9 ¶ Rise up, ye women [*German: proud women*] that are at ease [*overconfident about their safety; see 2 Nephi 28:24*]; hear my voice, ye careless daughters [*overconfident, complacent, too secure to change your ways*]; give ear unto my speech [*message*].

10 Many days and years shall ye be troubled, ye careless women: for the vintage [*vineyard*] shall fail [*not produce*], the gathering [*harvest*] shall not come [*famine*].

11 Tremble, ye women that are at ease; be troubled, ye careless ones: strip you [*of pride*], and make you bare, and gird sackcloth upon your loins [*humble yourselves*].

In verses 12–14, Isaiah tells of a long period of destruction soon to come upon unsuspecting Israelites.

12 They shall lament for the teats [*beat upon the breast in mourning*], for the pleasant fields, for the fruitful vine [*they will long for the good times*].

13 Upon the land of my people shall come up thorns and briers; yea, upon all the houses of joy in the joyous city [*rough times are coming because of wickedness*]:

14 Because the [*your*] palaces shall be forsaken; the multitude

of the city shall be left [*deserted*]; the forts and towers shall be for dens [*places of habitation for wild beasts*] for ever, a joy of wild asses, a pasture of flocks [*you will be scattered and your lands left lonely and desolate*];

Isaiah now mentions the peaceful conditions to come upon Israel in a future day of righteousness.

15 **Until the spirit be poured upon us from on high, and the wilderness be** [*become*] **a fruitful field, and the fruitful field be counted for a forest.**

16 **Then judgment** [*justice, fairness*] **shall dwell in the wilderness** [*in formerly apostate Israel*], **and righteousness remain in the fruitful field.**

17 **And the work** [*result*] **of righteousness shall be peace**; and the effect [*result*] of righteousness quietness [*lack of turmoil*] and assurance [*security*] for ever.

18 **And my people shall dwell in a peaceable habitation**, and in sure [*safe*] dwellings, and in quiet resting places [*German: splendid peace*];

19 **When it shall hail** [*destruction upon the wicked*], **coming down on the forest** [*wicked people?*]; **and the city** [*probably the proud and wicked*] **shall be low in a low place** [*brought down, humbled*].

20 **Blessed** [*happy*] **are ye** [*the righteous*] **that sow beside all waters** [*German: everywhere*], that send forth thither [*everywhere*] the feet of the ox and the ass [*perhaps saying that there will be peace everywhere for the righteous*].

ISAIAH 33

Background

Isaiah will now prophesy of great wickedness before the Second Coming of the Lord. Israel will be gathered. There will be great destruction among the wicked. The wicked will ultimately be destroyed by fire and the Savior will rule as our King during the Millennium.

The issue in verse 1 is that it seems as though the wicked often get away with sin without consequences. They don't.

1 **Woe to thee** [*probably Sennacherib, king of Assyria, Isaiah 36:1; symbolic of all wicked who seem to get away with wickedness*] **that spoilest, and thou wast not spoiled; and dealest treacherously, and they dealt not treacherously with thee!** when thou shalt cease to spoil, **thou shalt be spoiled**; and when thou shalt make an end to deal treacherously, they shall deal treacherously with thee [*after the*

Lord is through using you to punish other wicked nations, you will get your just reward].

2 O LORD, be gracious unto us [*Israel*]; **we have waited for thee: be thou their** [*our*] **arm** [*symbolic of power in biblical language*] every morning, our salvation also in the time of trouble.

3 At the noise of the tumult the people fled [*flee*]; at the lifting up of thyself [*Christ*] the nations were [*are*] scattered.

4 **And your spoil** [*Israel's remnants*] **shall be gathered** [*by missionaries*] like the gathering of the caterpiller: as the running to and fro of locusts [*perhaps describing missionaries going everywhere in the last days*] shall he [*they*] run [*collect*] upon them [*Israel*].

5 The LORD is exalted; for he dwelleth on high: he hath filled Zion with judgment and righteousness.

Next, Isaiah teaches that the restored gospel will provide stability in the lives of those who embrace it.

6 And **wisdom and knowledge shall be the stability of thy times, and strength of salvation**: the fear of the LORD is his treasure [*results of the Restoration*].

Verses 7–9 refer back to the Assyrian attack.

7 **Behold, their** [*wicked Israel's*] **valiant ones** [*wicked heroes*] **shall cry without** [*outside of Zion*]: **the ambassadors of peace shall weep bitterly.**

8 **The highways lie waste, the wayfaring man ceaseth** [*there are no more travelers*]: **he hath broken the covenant**, he hath despised the cities, he regardeth no man.

9 **The earth mourneth and languisheth: Lebanon is ashamed** [*the Holy Land is severely distressed*] **and hewn down**: Sharon is like a wilderness; and Bashan and Carmel shake off their fruits.

10 **Now will I rise, saith the LORD; now will I be exalted**; now will I lift up myself [*the time will come when God will take over from the wicked*].

11 **Ye shall conceive chaff, ye shall bring forth stubble** [*the end result of wicked lifestyles is nothing of value*]: **your breath, as fire, shall devour you** [*sow evil, harvest misery*].

12 **And the people shall be** as the burnings of lime: **as thorns cut up** [*as useless branches cut up for burning*] **shall they be burned in the fire.**

13 ¶ **Hear, ye that are far off** [*everybody in the whole world, listen up and acknowledge*], **what I have done**; and, ye that are

near, acknowledge my might [*in the future the whole world will know God*].

14 **The sinners in Zion are afraid; fearfulness hath surprised** [*seized*] **the hypocrites.** Who among us shall dwell with the devouring fire? who among us shall dwell with everlasting burnings [*who will not be burned, destroyed—who can survive the presence of God*]?

In verses 15–22, plus 24, next, Isaiah answers the question he posed in verse 14, above.

15 **He that walketh righteously, and speaketh uprightly**; he that despiseth the gain of oppressions [*unrighteous profit at the expense of others*], that shaketh his hands from holding of bribes [*refuses bribes*], that stoppeth his ears from hearing of blood, and shutteth his eyes from seeing evil [*does not participate in evils*];

16 **He** [*the righteous*] **shall dwell on high**: his place of defence shall be the munitions [*fortress*] of rocks: bread shall be given him; his waters shall be sure [*reward to the righteous*].

17 **Thine eyes shall see the king** [*the Savior*] in his beauty: they shall behold the land that is very far off [*heaven?*].

18 **Thine heart shall meditate** [*soften, put down*] **terror**. Where

is the scribe [*Assyrian tallyman, conqueror*]? where is the receiver? where is he that counted the towers [*Assyrian army? In other words, where are the wicked now?*]?

19 **Thou shalt not see a fierce people** [*foreign invaders*], a people of a deeper speech than thou canst perceive; of a stammering tongue, that thou canst not understand [*enemies who speak foreign languages*].

20 Look upon Zion, the city of our solemnities: **thine eyes shall see Jerusalem a quiet habitation**, a tabernacle that shall not be taken down; not one of the stakes thereof shall ever be removed, neither shall any of the cords thereof be broken [*the future has glorious things in store for the righteous*].

21 **But there the glorious LORD will be unto us a place of broad rivers and streams**; wherein shall go no galley [*enemy ships*] with oars, neither shall gallant ship pass thereby.

22 **For the LORD is our judge, the LORD is our lawgiver, the LORD is our king; he will save us.**

In verse 23, next, Isaiah describes the shutting down of the power of the wicked and compares it to the stopping of a ship.

23 Thy [*the wicked's*] **tacklings** [*ship's rigging*] **are loosed**; they

could not well strengthen their mast, they could not spread the sail [*the wicked will be shut down*]: then is the prey of a great spoil divided; **the lame** [*the righteous; the wicked have considered the righteous to be lame, weak*] **take the prey** [*the wicked*].

24 And the inhabitant shall not say, I am sick: **the people that dwell therein shall be forgiven their iniquity**.

ISAIAH 34

Background

This chapter speaks of the Second Coming and the destruction of the wicked. It contains Isaiah's harshest words against the wicked. It is a review of earlier chapters and is a companion chapter to chapter 35.

1 **Come near, ye nations** [*speaking to the whole world*], **to hear**; and hearken, ye people: let the earth hear, and all that is therein; the world, and all things that come forth of it.

Isaiah now speaks of the future as if it has already happened.

2 For **the indignation** [*righteous anger*] **of the LORD is upon all nations** [*all the wicked*], and his fury upon all their armies: **he hath utterly destroyed them**, he hath delivered them to the slaughter [*future; ultimate fate of the wicked*].

3 Their slain also shall be cast out, and their stink shall come up out of their carcases, and **the mountains shall be melted** [*soaked*] **with their blood**.

4 And all the host [*stars?*] of heaven shall be dissolved, and **the heavens shall be rolled together as a scroll** [*compare with D&C 88:95, which speaks of the Second Coming*]: and all their host [*starry host?*] shall fall down, as the leaf falleth off from the vine, and as a falling fig from the fig tree [*perhaps goes with D&C 133:49 and 88:95; Second Coming*].

5 For **my sword shall be bathed in heaven** [*bathed in blood*]: behold, **it shall come down upon Idumea** [*Edom; the world, see D&C 1:36; connotes the wicked world*], and **upon the people of my curse** [*upon the wicked*], to judgment.

6 **The sword of the LORD is filled with blood** [*bathed in blood*], it is made fat with fatness [*covered with fat like a knife used in animal sacrifices*], and with the blood of lambs and goats, with the fat of the kidneys of rams: for the LORD hath a sacrifice in Bozrah [*the capital of Edom, a kingdom south of the Dead Sea*], and a great slaughter in the land of Idumea [*the wicked world; the sword of the Lord is going to come crashing down on the wicked of the world*].

7 And the unicorns [*wild oxen*] shall come down with them, and the bullocks [*bull calves*] with the bulls; and **their land shall be soaked with blood**, and their dust [*land*] made fat with fatness [*covered with fat trimmed away by sword of justice*].

8 For **it is the day of the LORD's vengeance** [*it is time for the law of justice to take over*], and the year of recompences [*deserved rewards*] for the controversy [*German: avenging*] of Zion [*a day of avenging the wrongs done against Zion throughout the history of the world*].

9 **And the streams thereof** [*of Edom, the wicked*] **shall be turned into pitch** [*goes up in flames easily*], **and** the dust thereof into **brimstone** [*burning sulfur*], **and the land thereof shall become burning pitch** [*the wicked of the world will be destroyed by fire*].

10 **It shall not be quenched night nor day** [*no one can stop the destruction of the wicked*]; the smoke thereof shall go up for ever: from generation to generation it shall lie waste; none shall pass through it for ever and ever [*wickedness will be destroyed completely*].

Isaiah often uses the imagery that now follows to emphasize the theme that the wicked will all be gone.

11 **But the cormorant and the bittern** [*lonely desert creatures*] **shall possess it; the owl also** and the raven shall dwell in it: and he [*the Lord*] shall stretch out upon it the line [*measuring tape*] of confusion, and the stones [*plumb line*] of emptiness [*Edom, the wicked, will not "measure up."*].

12 **They shall call the nobles** [*leaders*] thereof to the kingdom, **but none shall be there**, and all her [*Edom's*] princes [*leaders*] shall be nothing [*German: they will be people without a kingdom, will have nothing to rule over*].

13 And **thorns shall come up in her palaces**, nettles and brambles in the fortresses thereof: and **it shall be an habitation of dragons** [*jackals*], **and a court** [*home*] **for owls** [*none of the wicked will remain*].

14 The wild beasts of the desert shall also meet with the wild beasts [*hyenas*] of the island [*in other words, the wicked will all be gone, and the ruins where they once lived will be inhabited by creatures that don't like to live around people*], and the satyr [*wild goat*] shall cry to his fellow; the screech owl also shall rest there, and find for herself a place of rest.

15 **There shall the great owl make her nest**, and lay, and hatch, and gather under her shadow: there shall the vultures also be gathered,

every one with her mate [*each of the animals mentioned above were considered unclean by the Israelites*].

16 ¶ **Seek ye out of the book of the LORD, and read** [*this is the word of God*]: **no one of these** [*unclean creatures*] **shall fail, none shall want** [*lack*] **her mate: for my mouth it hath commanded, and his spirit it hath gathered them.**

17 **And he hath cast the lot** [*voted*] **for them, and his hand hath divided it unto them by line: they shall possess it for ever, from generation to generation shall they dwell therein** [*If the Lord takes such good care of these "unclean" creatures, think how much more the righteous will get; a transition to chapter 35*].

ISAIAH 35

Background
This chapter is a continuation of the prophecy in chapter 34 (see background note for chapter 34). However, in this, we are given a prophetic picture of the beauty and peace that the righteous will receive.

1 **The wilderness and the solitary place shall be glad for them** [*the righteous who return*]; **and the desert shall rejoice, and blossom as the rose** [*a paradise awaits the righteous*].

2 **It shall blossom abundantly,** and rejoice even with joy and singing: the glory of Lebanon [*the Holy Land; symbolic of anywhere the righteous gather*] shall be given unto it, the excellency of Carmel and Sharon, **they shall see the glory of the LORD, and the excellency of our God.**

The Lord will strengthen the righteous, who have become weary in fighting evil.

3 ¶ **Strengthen ye the weak** [*German: tired*] **hands, and confirm** [*German: revive*] **the feeble** [*German: stumbling*] knees.

4 **Say to them** [*the righteous*] **that are of a fearful** [*German: discouraged*] **heart, Be strong, fear not: behold, your God will come with vengeance** [*upon the wicked*], even God with a recompence; he will come and save you [*the righteous*].

5 **Then the eyes of the** [*spiritually*] **blind shall be opened, and the ears of the** [*spiritually*] **deaf shall be unstopped** [*the restored gospel heals spiritual blindness and deafness*].

6 **Then shall the lame man leap as an hart** [*deer*], **and the tongue of the dumb** [*people who can't talk; symbolic of those who didn't know gospel previously*] **sing: for in the wilderness shall waters break out, and streams in the desert** [*literal; also symbolic of*

"living water," the gospel].

7 And the parched ground [*symbolic of apostate Israel; see Isaiah 53:2, Mosiah 14:2*] **shall become a pool, and the thirsty land springs of water** [*through the restoration of the gospel*]: in the habitation of dragons [*jackals; Isaiah has used this imagery before (see 13:22; 34:13–15) to depict the barrenness left when the wicked are destroyed. Here, he depicts the barrenness, apostate "wilderness," and so forth, being replaced with lush growth symbolizing the restoration of the gospel*] **where each lay, shall be grass with reeds and rushes** [*restored productivity*].

8 And an highway [*perhaps literal highways upon which various groups have returned or will return; symbolically, the path to God—the gospel, "straight and narrow" way, temple covenants, baptismal covenants, and so forth*] **shall be there**, and a way, and it shall be called **The way of holiness**; the unclean [*the wicked*] shall not pass over it; but it shall be for those: the wayfaring men, though fools [*JST (Joseph Smith Translation of the Bible): "though they are accounted fools"—though men might consider the righteous to be fools*], shall not err therein.

9 No lion shall be there, nor any ravenous beast [*enemies of Israel's return; forces of evil*] **shall go** up thereon, it shall not be found there [*perhaps looking ahead to millennial conditions*]; **but the redeemed shall walk there:**

10 And the ransomed of the LORD [*those who have been redeemed by the Lord's Atonement*] **shall return, and come to Zion** with songs and everlasting joy upon their heads: **they shall obtain joy and gladness, and sorrow and sighing shall flee away** [*see Revelation 21:4; 7:17; the final state of the righteous*].

ISAIAH 36

Background
Many of the chapters of Isaiah we have studied so far have dealt with the future. This chapter is an account of what happened when the Assyrians approached Judah with the goal of conquering Jerusalem and the cities of Judah. This took place near the end of Isaiah's service as a prophet.

1 Now it came to pass **in the fourteenth year** [*about 701 B.C.*] **of king Hezekiah** [*righteous king of Judah*], that **Sennacherib king of Assyria came up against all the defenced cities of Judah, and took them** [*perhaps as many as forty-six cities*].

Having conquered many cities

in Judah, the Assyrian king now sends one of his chief officers to the outskirts of Jerusalem to harass King Hezekiah and his people in preparation for conquering them.

2 And **the king of Assyria sent Rabshakeh** [*a title meaning "chief of the officers"—see footnote 2a in your Bible*] **to Jerusalem unto king Hezekiah with a great army.** And he [*Rabshakeh*] stood by the conduit of the upper pool in the highway of the fuller's field [*where fullers bleached cloth*].

Next, righteous King Hezekiah sends some trusted leaders to engage in talks with Rabshakeh.

3 **Then came forth unto him** [*Rabshakeh*] **Eliakim** [*prime minister of Judah*]**,** Hilkiah's son, which was over the house, **and Shebna** the scribe, **and Joah**, Asaph's son, the recorder.

4 ¶ **And Rabshakeh said unto them, Say ye now to Hezekiah, Thus saith the great king** [*sarcastically mimicking "Thus saith the Lord"*]**, the king of Assyria, What confidence is this wherein thou trustest** [*you are fools to trust Egypt for protection*]?

5 **I say, sayest thou,** [*but they are but vain words*] **I have counsel** [*plans with Egypt*] **and strength for war** [*Egypt is our ally*]: **now on whom dost thou** [*Hezekiah/Judah*] **trust, that thou rebellest against me** [*Assyria*]?

6 Lo, **thou trustest in the staff** [*"scepter," power*] **of this broken reed** [*"broken broom straw"*]**, on Egypt**; whereon if a man lean, it will go into his hand, and pierce it [*"Egypt is so weak, so thin that if you were to lean on it with your hand it would poke right through"*]: **so is Pharaoh king of Egypt to all that trust in him** [*Egypt never could protect anyone*].

Next, Rabshakeh takes a poke at the worship of God, which Hezekiah has centralized in Jerusalem.

7 **But if thou say to me, We trust in the LORD our God: is it not he** [*the Lord*]**, whose high places and whose altars** [*places of worship*] **Hezekiah hath taken away** [*King Hezekiah did away with local sites of worship and required the Jews to worship at the temple in Jerusalem*]**, and said to Judah and to Jerusalem, Ye shall worship before this altar** [*worship at the temple in Jerusalem*]?

8 **Now therefore give pledges** [*"Let's make a bet."*]**,** I pray thee, **to my master the king of Assyria, and I will give thee two thousand horses, if thou be able on thy part to set riders upon them** [*"if I give you two*

thousand horses, I'll bet you can't find two thousand able-bodied soldiers in all of Judah to ride them"].

9 How then wilt thou turn away the face of **one captain of the least of my master's servants**, and put thy trust on Egypt for chariots and for horsemen [*you'll get no help from puny Egypt!*]?

Next, in verse 10, Rabshakeh claims that the God of Israel, Jehovah, sent him to conquer Jerusalem.

10 And am I now come up without the LORD against this land to destroy it? **the LORD said unto me, Go up against this land, and destroy it** [*"your God told me to come up and destroy you!" A lie, but sometimes an effective intimidation strategy*].

Next, the emissaries sent by King Hezekiah timidly ask Rabshakeh to speak in a language all the public, who have gathered on the wall of Jerusalem to hear, can't understand.

11 **Then said Eliakim and Shebna and Joah unto Rabshakeh, Speak,** I [*we*] pray thee [*please*], **unto thy servants** [*us, King Hezekiah's representatives*] **in the Syrian language; for we understand it**: and **speak not to us in the Jews' language, in the ears of the people that are on the wall.** [*"Can't we discuss this in a language our*

citizens don't understand? This is too embarrassing."*]

12 **But Rabshakeh said**, Hath my master sent me to thy master and to thee to speak these words? hath he not sent me to the men that sit upon the wall, that they may eat their own dung, and drink their own piss with you [*Before Assyria is through with you, you'll be that bad off*]?

13 **Then Rabshakeh stood, and cried with a loud voice in the Jews' language** [*intentionally so the citizens could easily hear*], and said, **Hear ye the words of the great king, the king of Assyria.**

14 Thus saith the king, **Let not Hezekiah deceive you: for he shall not be able to deliver you.**

15 **Neither let Hezekiah make you trust in the LORD, saying, The LORD will surely deliver us**: this city shall not be delivered into the hand of the king of Assyria.

16 **Hearken not to Hezekiah: for thus saith the king of Assyria, Make an agreement with me** by a present [*via a payment*], and **come out to me** [*surrender*]: and eat ye every one of his vine, and every one of his fig tree, and drink ye every one the waters of his own cistern [*in effect, stay on your own land for a while in peace, until I make arrangements to transport you elsewhere—see verse 17, next*];

17 **Until I come and take you away to a land like your own land**, a land of corn [*grain*] and wine, a land of bread and vineyards [*you'll like where I take you*].

18 **Beware lest Hezekiah persuade you** [*don't let your foolish king fast-talk you into resisting us Assyrians*], **saying, The LORD will deliver us**. Hath any of the gods of the nations delivered his land out of the hand of the king of Assyria [*no other gods in other lands have been able to stop us and yours won't either!*]?

19 **Where are the gods of Hamath** [*part of modern Syria*] **and Arphad** [*part of modern Syria*]? where are the gods of **Sepharvaim** [*part of modern Syria*]? and have they delivered **Samaria** [*headquarters for the ten tribes, which the Assyrians conquered about twenty-one years earlier, in 722 B.C.*] out of my hand?

Next, Rabshakeh says, in effect, if the gods of all these other places could not hold us back from conquering them, what makes you think your Jehovah could possibly stop us?

20 **Who are they among all the gods of these lands, that have delivered their land out of my hand** [*which of their gods stopped us*], **that the LORD should deliver Jerusalem out of my hand?**

21 **But they** [*Hezekiah's three men*] **held their peace, and answered him not a word**: for the king's commandment was, saying, Answer him not.

22 **Then came Eliakim**, the son of Hilkiah, that was over the household, **and Shebna** the scribe, **and Joah**, the son of Asaph, the recorder, **to Hezekiah with their clothes rent** [*torn; a sign in their culture that they were very distraught*], **and told him the words of Rabshakeh.**

ISAIAH 37

Background
This chapter is a continuation of the tense situation reported in chapter 36. Righteous King Hezekiah will send to Isaiah the prophet, for counsel as to how to deal with the situation.

1 And it came to pass, **when king Hezekiah heard it** [*the report from his emissaries in Isaiah 36:22*], that **he rent** [*tore*] **his clothes** [*as a sign of extreme worry*], **and covered himself with sackcloth, and went into the house of the LORD** [*the temple*].

Have you noticed that the word "LORD" (end of verse 1, above, and elsewhere), as printed in your King James version of the Bible, is spelled with a large capital "L" and small caps "ORD"? This is the King James Version of the Bible's way of pointing out that it is "Jehovah" about whom they are speaking. We know from Isaiah 43:1–3, 11, 14, and elsewhere that Jehovah is the premortal Jesus Christ, who is the God of the Old Testament.

2 **And he sent Eliakim** [*his prime minister*], who was over the household, **and Shebna** the [*royal*] scribe, **and the elders** [*older priests*] of the priests covered with sackcloth [*a sign of deep distress and mourning in their culture*], **unto Isaiah** the prophet the son of Amoz.

3 **And they said unto him**, Thus saith Hezekiah, **This day is a day of trouble, and of rebuke** [*we're in big trouble*], **and of blasphemy** [*the Assyrians speak totally disrespectfully of the Lord*]: for the children are come to the birth, and there is not strength to bring forth [*we're doomed, like when a woman is in hard labor, but the baby doesn't come*].

4 **It may be the LORD thy God will hear** [*has heard*] **the words of Rabshakeh** [*Assyria's representative*], whom the king of Assyria his master hath sent to reproach [*blaspheme*] the living God, **and will reprove the words** [*of Rabshakeh*] which the LORD thy God hath heard [*we hope the Lord will not let them get away with such talk*]:

wherefore lift up thy prayer for the remnant that is left.

5 So the servants of king Hezekiah came to Isaiah.

6 ¶ And **Isaiah said** unto them, Thus shall ye **say unto your master**, Thus saith the LORD, **Be not afraid of the words that thou hast heard**, wherewith the servants of the king of Assyria have blasphemed me [*the Lord*].

7 **Behold, I** [*the Lord*] **will send a blast upon him** [*I will change his frame of mind, make him nervous*], and **he shall hear a rumour** [*bad news from home*], **and return to his own land; and I will cause him to fall by the sword in his own land.**

8 ¶ **So Rabshakeh returned, and found the king of Assyria warring against Libnah** [*southwest of Jerusalem*]: **for he** [*Rabshakeh*] **had heard that he** [*the King of Assyria*] **was departed from Lachish.**

9 **And he** [*the Assyrian King*] **heard** say **concerning Tirhakah king of Ethiopia** [*the Egyptian army*], He is come forth to make war with thee. **And when he** [*King of Assyria*] **heard it, he sent messengers to Hezekiah, saying** [*the King of Assyria, worried about approaching Egyptian armies, now presses King Hezekiah for quick surrender*],

10 Thus shall ye speak to Hezekiah king of Judah, saying, **Let not thy God, in whom thou trustest, deceive thee, saying, Jerusalem shall not be given into the hand of the king of Assyria** [*your God can't help you; you will be powerless before the Assyrians*].

11 Behold, **thou hast heard what the kings of Assyria have done to all lands by destroying them utterly; and shalt thou be delivered** [*what makes you think you'll be different*]?

12 **Have the gods of the nations delivered** them which my fathers have destroyed, as **Gozan** [*Iraq*], and **Haran** [*Turkey*], and **Rezeph** [*Iraq*], and the children of Eden which were in **Telassar** [*Iraq*]?

13 Where is the king of **Hamath** [*Syria*], and the king of Arphad [*Syria*], and the king of the city of **Sepharvaim** [*Syria*], **Hena** [*unknown*], and **Ivah** [*unknown*]?

14 And **Hezekiah received the letter** from the hand of the messengers, and read it: **and** Hezekiah **went up unto the house of the LORD, and spread it before the LORD.**

15 **And Hezekiah prayed unto the LORD, saying,**

16 **O LORD** of hosts, God of Israel, that dwellest between [*German: above*] the cherubims, **thou art the God, even thou alone**, of all the kingdoms of the earth: **thou hast made heaven and earth.**

17 **Incline thine ear, O LORD, and hear**; open thine eyes, O LORD, and see: and **hear all the words of Sennacherib** [*King of Assyria*], **which hath sent to reproach** [*blaspheme*] **the living God.**

18 **Of a truth** [*it is true*], LORD, **the kings of Assyria have laid waste all the nations, and their countries** [*just as the letter in verse 14 says*],

19 **And have cast their gods** [*idols*] **into the fire: for they were no gods** [*weren't real gods*], but the work of men's hands, wood and stone: **therefore they have destroyed them** [*that's why Assyria was able to conquer those cities and nations*].

20 **Now therefore, O LORD our God, save us from his hand, that all the kingdoms of the earth may know that thou art the LORD, even thou only.**

Next, the Lord answers Hezekiah's prayer through Isaiah, the prophet. This is often the case today, as the Lord answers many of our prayers through our living prophets.

21 ¶ **Then Isaiah the son of Amoz sent unto Hezekiah, saying, Thus saith the LORD** God of Israel,

Whereas thou hast prayed to me against Sennacherib king of Assyria:

22 **This is the word** which the LORD hath spoken concerning him [*this is the answer to Sennacherib*]; **The virgin, the daughter of Zion** [*the unconquered people of Jerusalem*], **hath despised thee, and laughed thee to scorn**; the daughter of Jerusalem hath shaken her head at thee [*not afraid of you Assyrians*].

23 **Whom hast thou reproached and blasphemed?** and against whom hast thou exalted thy voice, and lifted up thine eyes on high? even against the Holy One of Israel [*you chose the wrong one to offend this time; you have mocked the true God*].

24 **By thy servants** [*including Rabshakeh—see Isaiah 36:4*] **hast thou reproached** [*blasphemed*] **the Lord**, and hast said [*bragged*], By the multitude of my chariots am I come up to the height of the mountains, to the sides [*west*] of Lebanon; and I will [*have*] cut down the tall cedars thereof, and the choice fir trees thereof: and I will enter [*have entered*] into the height of his border, and the forest of his Carmel.

25 **I have digged** [*wells*], **and drunk water** [*in many a conquered land*]; and with the sole of my feet have I dried up all the rivers of the besieged places [*end of quoting the Assyrian King's boasts*].

26 Hast thou [*King of Assyria*] not heard long ago ["*Haven't you heard by now?*"], how I [*the Lord*] have done [*allowed*] it; and of ancient times, that I have formed it? now have I brought it to pass, that thou shouldest be to lay waste defenced cities into ruinous heaps [*I, the Lord, allowed you to do these things, otherwise you would never have had such power*].

27 **Therefore** [*that is why*] **their inhabitants were of small power** [*were weak before your armies*], they were dismayed and confounded: they were as the grass of the field, and as the green herb, as the grass on the housetops, and as corn [*grain*] blasted before it be grown up.

28 **But I** [*the Lord*] **know thy abode** [*I know you well*], **and thy going out, and thy coming in, and thy rage against me.**

29 Because thy rage against me, and thy tumult, is come up into mine ears, **therefore will I put my hook in thy nose** [*such as a ring in the nose of a wild animal with which to control it*], **and my bridle in thy lips** [*I will control you, King of Assyria*], and I will turn thee back by the way [*road*] by which thou camest [*I will stop you cold*].

The topic now turns to the word

of the Lord to Hezekiah and his people, who have been worrying because of the siege against them by the Assyrians.

30 **And this shall be a sign unto thee** [*Hezekiah and his people*], Ye shall eat this year such as groweth of itself [*because of the Assyrian siege, you have not had time to plant crops normally, yet you will harvest some "volunteer" crops from plants that grew from seeds spilled during last year's harvest; in other words, you'll be okay food wise*]; and the second year that which springeth of the same: and in the third year sow ye, and reap, and plant vineyards, and eat the fruit thereof [*you'll be back to normal planting and harvesting by the third year from now*].

31 And **the remnant that is escaped of the house of Judah shall again take root downward, and bear fruit upward** [*a remnant of Judah will flourish again*]:

32 For **out of Jerusalem shall go forth a remnant**, and they that escape out of mount Zion: the zeal of the LORD of hosts shall do this [*a remnant will flourish again via God's intervention*].

Verse 33 is a specific prophecy and most comforting to King Hezekiah. The Assyrians, despite their boasting, will not shoot so much as one arrow into Jerusalem!

33 **Therefore thus saith the LORD**

concerning the king of Assyria, **He shall not come into this city, nor shoot an arrow there, nor come before it with shields, nor cast a bank** [*a mound of dirt around it thrown up from trenches dug in order to lay siege*] **against it.**

34 **By the way** [*road*] **that he** [*the Assyrian king and his armies*] **came, by the same shall he return** [*he will retreat*], **and shall not come into this city, saith the LORD.**

35 For **I will defend this city** to save it for mine own sake, and for my servant David's sake.

Next, we see how the Lord stopped the Assyrian armies dead in their tracks.

36 **Then** [*after the Assyrian armies had come to the outskirts of Jerusalem and were ready to attack*] **the angel of the LORD went forth, and smote in the camp of the Assyrians a hundred and fourscore and five thousand**: and when they [*the few survivors*] arose early in the morning, behold, **they were all dead corpses** [*185,000 Assyrians were dead the following morning*].

37 ¶ **So Sennacherib king of Assyria departed, and went and returned, and dwelt at Nineveh** [*went home to his headquarters*].

38 **And** it came to pass, as he was worshipping in the house of Nisroch his god, that **Adrammelech**

and **Sharezer his sons smote** [*killed*] **him with the sword;** and they escaped into the land of Armenia: and Esar-haddon his son reigned in his stead [*this happened about twenty years after his retreat from Jerusalem*].

ISAIAH 38

Background
Chapters 38 and 39 fit historically before chapters 36 and 37 and could be considered "flashbacks" to 705–703 B.C.

Isaiah was the prophet during Hezekiah's reign. At one point, righteous King Hezekiah was sick and on his deathbed. We will quote Isaiah to see what happened.

1 **In those days** [*about 705–703 B.C.*] **was Hezekiah sick unto death**. And **Isaiah** the prophet the son of Amoz **came unto him, and said** unto him, Thus saith the LORD, **Set thine house in order** [*get ready*]: **for thou shalt die, and not live**.

2 **Then Hezekiah** turned his face toward the wall, and **prayed unto the LORD**,

3 And said, **Remember** now, O LORD, I beseech thee, **how I have walked before thee in truth and with a perfect heart, and have done that which is good** in thy sight [*in other words, I have lived a good life*]. And Hezekiah wept sore [*bitterly*].

4 ¶ **Then came the word of the LORD to Isaiah, saying,**

5 **Go, and say to Hezekiah**, Thus saith the LORD, the God of David thy father [*ancestor*], **I have heard thy prayer, I have seen thy tears: behold, I will add unto thy days fifteen years** [*I will add fifteen years to your life*].

Major Message

When it is in harmony with the will of the Lord, the mighty prayers of the faithful can change the plan temporarily.

6 And **I will deliver thee and this city out of the hand of the king of Assyria**: and I will defend this city [*this would seem to place Hezekiah's illness sometime during the Assyrian threats to Jerusalem as described in chapters 36 and 37*].

7 And this **shall be a sign unto thee** from the LORD, that the LORD will do this thing that he hath spoken;

8 Behold, **I will bring again the shadow of the degrees** [*the shadow on the sundial*], which is gone down in the sun dial of Ahaz, **ten degrees backward**. So the sun returned ten degrees, by which degrees it was

gone down [*the sun came back up ten degrees; in other words, time was turned backward*].

Hezekiah was healed and now gives thanks and praise to the Lord for his miraculous recovery.

9 ¶ **The writing** [*psalm*] **of Hezekiah** king of Judah, **when he had been sick, and was recovered** of his sickness [*after he had been sick and had recovered*]:

Righteous King Hezekiah now tells us what he said, expressing the thoughts of his heart, when he was blessed with another fifteen years of life by the Lord.

First, he tells us what was going through his mind when he knew he was going to die.

10 **I** [*Hezekiah*] **said** in the cutting off of my days [*when I was on my deathbed*], I shall go to the gates of the grave [*I am doomed*]: I am deprived of the residue [*remainder*] of my years [*I am too young to die*].

11 I said, I shall not see the LORD, even the LORD, in the land of the living [*I am about to leave this mortal life*]: I shall behold man no more with the inhabitants of the world [*I won't be around anymore to associate with my fellow men*].

12 Mine age is departed [*German Bible: my time is up*], and is removed

from me as a shepherd's tent [*they are taking down my tent*]: I have [*Thou hast*] cut off like a weaver my life [*Thou hast "clipped my threads" like a weaver does when the rug is finished*]: he will cut me off with pining sickness [*fatal illness is how the Lord is sending me out of this life*]: from day even to night wilt thou make an end of me [*I will die shortly*].

13 I reckoned till morning [*German: I thought, If I could just live until morning*], that, as a lion, so will he break all my bones [*I can't stop the Lord if he wants me to die any more than I could stop a lion*]: from day even to night wilt thou make an end of me [*I'm doomed; my time is short*].

14 Like a crane or a swallow, so did I chatter [*German: whimper*]: I did mourn as a dove: mine eyes fail with looking upward [*falter as I look up to heaven*]: O LORD, I am oppressed [*German: suffering*]; undertake [*German: soothe, moderate my condition*] for me [*be Thou my help, security*].

Next, Hezekiah tells us how he felt when he found out he was not going to die.

The Joseph Smith Translation of the Bible helps us considerably with verses 15–17, next.

15 **What shall I say** [*how can I express my gratitude*]? he hath both

spoken unto me, and himself hath done it [*JST: healed me*]: I shall go softly [*German: in humility*] all my years [*JST: that I may not walk*] in the bitterness of my soul.

16 O Lord, by these things men live, and in all these things is the life of my spirit [*JST: "thou who art the life of my spirit, in whom I live"*]: so wilt thou recover [*heal*] me, and make me to live [*JST: "and in all these things I will praise thee"*].

17 Behold, for peace I had great bitterness [*JST: "Behold, I had great bitterness instead of peace"*]: but thou hast in love to my soul delivered it [*JST: "saved me"*] from the pit of corruption [*from rotting in the grave*]: for thou hast cast all my sins behind thy back [*the effect of the Atonement*].

18 For the grave cannot praise [*German: Hell does not praise*] thee, death can not celebrate thee: they [*people in spirit prison*] that go down into the pit [*hell; see Isaiah 14:15*] cannot hope for thy truth [*see Alma 34:32–34*].

19 The living, the living, he shall praise thee, as I do this day [*I am very happy to still be alive*]: the father to the children shall make known thy truth [*I will testify to my family and others of Thy kindness to me*].

20 The LORD was ready to save me: therefore we [*I and my family*] will sing my songs to the stringed instruments [*we will put my words of praise to music*] all the days of our life in the house of the LORD.

Next, Hezekiah refers to something Isaiah instructed him to do in order to be healed.

21 **For Isaiah had said, Let them take a lump of figs, and lay it for a plaister [*plaster*] upon the boil, and he shall recover** [*perhaps the lump of figs served the same purpose as the lump of clay to heal the blind man in John 9:6–7; faith obedience*].

22 Hezekiah also had said, What is the sign that I shall go up to the house of the LORD? [*This verse fits after verse 6. See 2 Kings 20:8.*]

ISAIAH 39

Background

As you have perhaps noticed, these chapters are not particularly in chronological order. This chapter records events that took place before chapters 36–37. It appears that King Hezekiah, King of Judah with headquarters in Jerusalem, as a gesture of good faith, showed emissaries from Babylon the great treasures in the temple and in the palace at Jerusalem (verse 2). In about one hundred years, Babylon will be an enemy to Judah and will carry them away into captivity.

1 **At that time** [*about 705–703*]

B.C.] **Merodach-baladan,** the son of Baladan, **king of Babylon, sent letters and a present to Hezekiah: for he had heard that he had been sick,** and was recovered.

2 **And Hezekiah** was glad of them, and **shewed them** [*the Babylonian delegation who brought the letters and present*] **the house of his precious things,** the silver, and the gold, and the spices, and the precious ointment, and all the house of his armour, and all that was found in his treasures: **there was nothing in his house, nor in all his dominion, that Hezekiah shewed them not.**

Next, Isaiah comes to Hezekiah and expresses concern about what he has shown to the delegation from Babylon. It sets the stage for a prophecy about the future Babylonian captivity of the Jews.

3 ¶ **Then came Isaiah the prophet unto king Hezekiah, and said** unto him, **What said these men? and from whence came they** unto thee? **And Hezekiah said, They are come from a far country unto me, even from Babylon.**

4 **Then said he** [*Isaiah*], **What have they seen in thine house? And Hezekiah answered, All that is in mine house have they seen:** there is nothing among my treasures that I have not shewed them.

5 **Then said Isaiah to Hezekiah, Hear the word of the LORD** of hosts:

6 Behold, **the days come, that all that is in thine house,** and that which thy fathers [*ancestors*] have laid up in store until this day, **shall be carried to Babylon:** nothing shall be left, saith the LORD [*prophecy regarding Babylonian captivity, which will take place in about a hundred years*].

7 **And of thy sons** that shall issue from thee, which thou shalt beget, **shall they take away; and they shall be eunuchs** [*servants; they will be made unable to father children—see Bible Dictionary, under "Eunuch"*] **in the palace of the king of Babylon.**

8 **Then said Hezekiah to Isaiah, Good is the word of the LORD which thou hast spoken. He said moreover, For there shall be peace and truth in my days.**

Some scholars are critical of Hezekiah's response in verse 8, above, but he remained loyal to God and did much good for his people during his reign. Perhaps he did mourn for his people in the future and it is just not recorded here. See 2 Kings 20:19–20. It is possible to be happy and at peace with God despite others' wickedness. For instance, see Mormon in Mormon 2:19 and Lehi in 2 Nephi 1:15.

ISAIAH 40

Background

This chapter contains a number of prophecies about the Messiah, and includes a description of the role of John the Baptist. Chronologically, it seems to move around quite a bit, including prophecies of the Savior's mortal mission as well as of His Second Coming. It is a chapter of comfort and witness about the Savior, and teaches beautifully that none on earth can compare to Him.

Isaiah will also point out the absurdity of idol worship, in view of the true power of the true God.

1 **Comfort ye, comfort ye my people**, saith your God.

Verse 2, next, seems to refer to the last days and on into the Millennium.

2 **Speak ye comfortably** [*German: in a friendly manner; Hebrew: tenderly*] **to Jerusalem, and cry unto her, that her warfare** [*time of service*] **is accomplished, that her iniquity is pardoned** [*through repentance and the Atonement*]: **for she hath received of the LORD's hand double for all her sins** [*has paid a heavy penalty for wickedness*].

3 ¶ **The voice of him that crieth in the wilderness, Prepare ye the way of the LORD**, make straight in the desert a highway for our God. [*This fits John the Baptist as described in Matthew 3:1–3. Other "Eliases," or "preparers" and prophets, also fit this passage in the last days as they prepare us for the Second Coming.*]

4 **Every valley shall be exalted** [*raised*], **and every mountain and hill shall be made low**: and the crooked shall be made straight, and the rough places [*mountains*] plain [*changes in the earth at the Second Coming; also can be symbolic of wickedness, being "straightened out" at the Second Coming*]:

5 **And the glory of the LORD shall be revealed, and all flesh shall see it together** [*at the same time at the Second Coming*]: for the mouth of the LORD hath spoken it.

Verse 6, next, is a course in perspective. Man's power is insignificant compared to that of God. See also verse 18.

6 **The voice said, Cry** [*preach*]. **And he said, What shall I cry** [*preach*]? [*Answer:*] **All flesh** [*people*] **is** [*are like*] **grass, and all the goodliness thereof is as the flower of the field:** [*Mortality is temporary; not that we are not significant and important—Christ gave His life for us—but just a*

reminder that God is way ahead of us and we would be wise to follow and obey Him completely. We are nothing, at this point, compared to Him.]:

7 **The grass withereth, the flower fadeth**: because the spirit of the LORD bloweth upon it: surely the people is grass [*man's power and wisdom pale against the Lord's*].

8 **The grass withereth, the flower fadeth: but the word of our God shall stand for ever** [*trust in God, not in the "arm of flesh"*].

9 O Zion, that bringest good tidings [*the gospel*], get thee up into the high mountain; O Jerusalem, that bringest good tidings, lift up thy voice with strength; lift it up, be not afraid; say unto the cities of Judah, Behold your God!

Next, Isaiah bears witness of the Second Coming.

10 **Behold, the Lord GOD will come with strong hand** [*German: with power*], **and his arm** [*symbolic of power*] **shall rule** for him [*He will rule on earth; Second Coming and Millennium*]: **behold, his reward is with him** [*He will reward the righteous and the wicked, according to what they have earned*], and his work before him [*German: reward precedes Him; that is, Second Coming, Revelation 22:12*].

11 **He shall feed his flock like a shepherd** [*He knows each of us by name; Millennial reign*]: **he shall gather the lambs with his arm, and carry them in his bosom, and shall gently lead those that are with young** [*peaceful conditions during the Millennium*].

The "course in perspective" concerning the greatness of God continues, leading to verse 18.

12 ¶ **Who hath measured the waters** in the hollow of his hand, **and meted out heaven** with the span, and comprehended the dust of the earth in a measure, and weighed the mountains in scales, and the hills in a balance? [*Who else do you know who can create worlds and design oceans, continents, mountains, heavens, and so forth?*]

13 **Who hath directed** [*taught*] **the Spirit of the LORD** [*the Holy Ghost*], or being his counsellor hath taught him [*what mortal could teach God anything!*]?

14 **With whom took he** [*God*] **counsel** [*from whom does God seek counsel, advice*], and **who instructed him**, and taught him in the path of judgment, **and taught him knowledge**, and shewed to him the way of understanding [*the answer "no one" is implied*]?

15 **Behold, the nations** [*of this earth*] **are as a drop of** [*in*] **a bucket**

[*compared to God's domain*], and are counted as [*like*] the small dust of the balance [*are about as significant as a small speck of dust on a scale*]: behold, he taketh up the isles as a very little thing [*German: the continents are like the tiniest speck of dust to Him*].

16 **And Lebanon** [*sometimes used to represent all of Palestine*] **is not sufficient to burn, nor the beasts thereof sufficient for a burnt offering** [*all the wood and all the animals in Lebanon wouldn't even begin to make a sacrifice worthy of who God really is*].

17 **All nations** before [*compared to*] him **are as nothing;** and **they are counted** [*compared*] **to him less than nothing,** and vanity.

Verse 18, next, serves as a transition to the topic of how absurd and foolish it is to use idols as substitutes for God.

18 ¶ **To whom then will ye liken** [*compare*] **God? or what likeness** [*idol*] **will ye compare unto him?**

19 **The workman** [*craftsman*] **melteth** [*uses molten metal to form*] **a graven image, and the goldsmith spreadeth** [*covers*] **it over with gold,** and casteth [*makes*] silver chains [*foolish people make idols and then compare them to God*].

20 **He that is so impoverished that**

he hath no oblation [*German: so poor that he can give only the smallest offering*] **chooseth a tree that will not rot** [*selects wood for an idol*]; **he seeketh unto him a cunning workman** [*he hires a skilled craftsman*] **to prepare a graven image** [*idol*], that shall not be moved [*German: becomes a permanent fixture*].

21 **Have ye not known** [*German: Do you not know?*]? **have ye not heard?** hath it not been told you from the beginning? **have ye not understood from the foundations of the earth** [*don't you understand!*]?

22 **It is he** [*the Lord*] **that sitteth upon the circle of the earth** [*is above all*], **and the inhabitants thereof are as grasshoppers** [*compared to God; continues the theme of verse 17*]; **that stretcheth out** [*creates*] **the heavens** as a curtain, and spreadeth them out as a tent to dwell in [*the Lord is the Creator*]:

23 That bringeth the princes [*leaders*] to nothing; he maketh the judges [*rulers*] of the earth as vanity [*nothing*].

24 **Yea, they** [*the wicked rulers and leaders*] **shall not be planted** [*German: shall be as if they hadn't even been planted*]; yea, they shall not be sown: yea, their stock shall not take root in the earth: and **he** [*the Lord*] **shall also blow upon them, and they shall wither,** and the whirlwind shall take them away as

stubble [*they are nothing compared to God*].

25 **To whom then will ye liken me, or shall I be equal?** saith the Holy One [*Jehovah: Jesus Christ; same question as in verse 18*].

26 **Lift up your eyes on high** [*look all around you*], **and behold** [*see*] **who hath created these things** [*God's creations*], that bringeth out their host by number: **he calleth them all by names** [*He knows every one of them*] by [*because of*] the greatness of his might [*German: ability*], for that he is strong in power; not one faileth [*His creations all obey him*].

27 **Why sayest thou, O Jacob** [*you Israelites*], and speakest, O Israel, **My way is hid from the LORD** [*why do you think that you can hide your wickedness from God*], and my judgment [*cause*] is passed over from [*is unknown by*] my God?

28 ¶ **Hast thou not known? hast thou not heard** [*haven't you heard by now*], **that the everlasting God**, the LORD, the Creator of the ends of the earth, **fainteth not** [*German: is not weak*], **neither is weary?** there is no searching of his understanding [*you can't comprehend His understanding*].

29 **He giveth power to the faint**; and to them that have no might he increaseth strength [*Ether 12:27*].

30 **Even the youths** [*with lots of energy*] **shall** [*may grow*] **faint and be weary**, and the young men shall utterly fall [*all mortals have their limitations*]:

31 **But they that wait** [*base their hopes*] **upon the LORD shall renew their strength**; they shall mount up with wings as eagles [*be renewed like molting eagles are as they lose their old feathers each year, then get new ones*]; they shall run, and not be weary; and they shall walk, and not faint [*in pursuing exaltation. See context of D&C 89:20–21; the righteous receive extra strength on earth, have a glorious resurrection, and receive the strength of the Lord as joint heirs with Christ*].

ISAIAH 41

Background
Chapters 41–44 refer mainly to the last days.

There are many different opinions among scholars concerning the meaning of some verses in this chapter. In such cases, I have used the *Old Testament Student Manual* (Institute of Religion, Religion 302), as the authority for interpretive notes in brackets. I have also made considerable use of the Martin Luther version of the German Bible for clarifications.

1 **Keep silence before me** [*hush, and let me teach you*], **O islands** [*all

land masses where scattered Israel live]; **and let the people renew their strength** [as mentioned in 40:31]: let them come near; then let them speak: let us come near together to judgment. [German: dispute, see who is right—see who is more powerful, God or your idols; similar to Elijah and priests of Baal in I Kings 18];

In verse 2, next, Isaiah asks the question, "Who is more powerful, your idols or our God?"

2 **Who raised up the righteous man from the east** [the Savior Himself fits this description, coming in from the east wilderness at age thirty to begin His ministry; could also refer to many prophets, including Abraham, who have come from the "East"—on assignment from the Lord, and assisted in "calling the generations from the beginning," verse 4], **called him to his foot** [German: to go forth], **gave** [him power over] **the nations before him, and made him rule over kings?** he gave them [kings] as the dust to his sword [they couldn't stop his sword (power) anymore than dust particles could], and as driven stubble to his bow [nations and kings couldn't stop him].

3 **He pursued them, and passed safely; even by the way that he had not gone with his feet** [German: without wearying of his errand, assignment; perhaps ties back to 40:31].

4 **Who hath wrought and done it** [the things referred to above], **calling the generations** [German: calling all people] **from the beginning?** [Answer to the question put in verse 2:] **I the LORD, the first, and with the last; I am he.**

5 **The isles** [scattered Israel] **saw it, and feared** [respected it, responded positively]; **the ends of the earth were afraid, drew near, and came** [people from all parts of the earth responded; the gathering of Israel].

6 **They helped every one his neighbour; and every one said to his brother, Be of good courage.**

7 **So** [yet, nevertheless] **the carpenter encouraged the goldsmith, and he that smootheth with the hammer him that smote the anvil, saying,** It [an idol] is ready for the sodering: and he fastened it with nails, that it should not be moved [yet, many foolishly continued with their making and worshipping of idols].

Next, those who want to be the faithful covenant people of the Lord are encouraged to remember who they are and to remain loyal to God.

8 **But thou, Israel, art my servant, Jacob whom I have chosen, the seed of Abraham my friend.**

9 **Thou whom I have taken**

[*gathered*] **from the ends of the earth**, and called thee from the chief men thereof, and said unto thee, Thou art my servant; I have chosen thee, and not cast thee away [*I have not left you*].

Verse 10, next, reminds us of the third verse of our hymn, "How Firm a Foundation" (*Hymns,* 85).

10 **Fear thou not**; for **I am with thee: be not dismayed; for I am thy God: I will strengthen thee**; yea, I will **help thee**; yea, I will **uphold thee with the right hand of my righteousness.**

Verse 11, next, reminds us that the wicked will someday face the consequences of their fighting against the Saints.

11 **Behold, all they that were incensed** [*German: prejudiced; angry*] **against thee shall be ashamed** [*shamed*] and confounded [*German: humiliated*]: they shall be as nothing; and they that strive with [*fight against*] thee shall perish [*ultimately, your enemies will not succeed against you*].

12 **Thou shalt seek them** [*your enemies*], **and shalt not find them**, even them that contended with thee: they that war against thee shall be as nothing, and as a thing of nought [*eventually, the wicked will all be gone*].

13 **For I the LORD thy God**

will **hold thy right hand** [*covenant hand; in other words, I will strengthen you with covenants*], **saying unto thee, Fear not; I will help thee.**

Have you noticed that most Christians do not believe that Jesus is the God of the Old Testament (under the Father's direction)? Verse 14, next, teaches correct doctrine on this matter. It uses the word "redeemer" in reference to the Lord (the premortal Christ) who is directing Israel in Old Testament times. We will see additional strong evidence in chapter 43 of this doctrine.

14 **Fear not, thou worm** [*meek, humble*] **Jacob**, and ye men of Israel; **I will help thee, saith the LORD, and thy redeemer, the Holy One of Israel** [*Jesus*].

15 Behold, **I will make thee** [*German: into*] **a new sharp threshing instrument having teeth** [*capable of much destruction*]: **thou shalt thresh the mountains** [*your former strong enemies*], **and beat them small**, and shalt make the hills as chaff. [*Israel will triumph over her enemies. Perhaps this verse could also remind us that Israel, as a "sharp threshing instrument," will help gather the wheat—scattered Israel—and separate it from the "chaff," or the wicked.*]

16 **Thou shalt fan** [*German: scatter; as in the threshing process*

of throwing wheat up into the wind so the chaff is blown away while the wheat drops back to the threshing floor] **them, and the wind shall carry them away**, and the whirlwind shall scatter them: **and thou shalt rejoice in the LORD**, and shalt glory in the Holy One of Israel [*Israel will once again become righteous and give glory to God*].

17 When the poor and needy seek water, and there is none, and their tongue faileth for thirst, **I the LORD will hear them, I the God of Israel will not forsake them** [*I will help you. I have not left you; see verse 9*].

18 **I will open rivers in high places, and fountains in the midst of the valleys: I will make the wilderness a pool of water, and the dry land springs of water** [*geographical changes will help Israel; could also be symbolic of "living water" (John 4:10), or the gospel, bringing forth new life in an apostate wilderness and satisfying the thirst mentioned in verse 17*].

19 I will plant in the wilderness the cedar, the shittah [*acacia*] tree, and the myrtle, and the oil tree; I will set in the desert the fir [*cypress*] tree, and the pine [*ash*], and the box tree together [*Hebrew prophets often use trees to represent people, for example, Isaiah 2:13; Ezekiel 31:3; thus various types of trees*

in this verse could be symbolic of the gospel's going to all races of people in the last days*]:

20 **That they may see, and know, and consider, and understand together, that the hand of the LORD hath done this**, and the Holy One of Israel hath created it.

21 **Produce your cause** [*present your case*], saith the LORD; **bring forth your strong reasons** [*arguments against the Lord*], **saith the King of Jacob** [*Christ, Jehovah, the King of Israel*].

22 **Let them** [*idol worshippers*] **bring them** [*their idols*] **forth, and shew us what shall happen** [*predict the future*]: let them [*idols*] shew the former things [*the past*], what they be, that we may consider them, and know the latter end [*the final outcome*] of them; or declare us things for to come [*predict the future*].

23 **Shew the things that are to come hereafter, that we may know that ye are gods** [*let's see if your idols can predict the future like God can; in other words, prove that your idols are gods*]: **yea, do good, or do evil, that we may be dismayed** [*surprised, startled*], and behold it together [*just do anything, good or bad, to demonstrate your power to us*].

24 **Behold, ye** [*idols*] **are of nothing, and your work of nought**

[*you are worthless and do absolutely nothing*]: **an abomination is he** [*the wicked who worship idols*] **that chooseth you** [*idols*].

25 **I have raised up one** [*perhaps meaning Christ, referring back to verse 2*] from the north [*possibly meaning coming from Nazareth, north of Jerusalem*], **and he shall come: from the rising of the sun** shall he call upon my name: **and he shall come upon** [*descend upon, destroy*] **princes** [*wicked leaders of nations*] as upon morter, and as the potter treadeth clay [*He will tread upon the wicked and none will stop Him; D&C 133:50–51*].

26 **Who** [*which of your idols*] **hath declared** [*prophesied this*] **from the beginning, that we may know?** and beforetime, that we may say, He is righteous? yea, there is none that sheweth, yea, there is none that declareth, yea, there is none that heareth your words [*none of your idols do a thing!*].

27 The first shall say to Zion [*the Lord will prophesy it*], Behold, behold them: and I [*the Lord*] will give to Jerusalem one that bringeth good tidings.

28 For I beheld, and there was no man; even among them, and **there was no counsellor, that, when I asked of them, could answer a word** [*idol worship has reduced them to a completely confused people*].

29 **Behold, they are all vanity** [*false*]; their works are nothing: their molten images [*idols*] are wind and confusion.

ISAIAH 42

Background

In this chapter, Isaiah continues to prophesy about the Messiah. Considerable emphasis is given to the Restoration of the gospel in the last days and the taking of the gospel to all the world.

1 **Behold my servant** [*Christ— see Matthew 12:18; perhaps in a dual sense could also include the whole house of Israel—see Isaiah 41:8*], **whom I uphold; mine elect** [*Christ; those set apart as a chosen people; Israelites*], **in whom my soul delighteth**; I have put my spirit upon him: he shall bring forth judgment to the Gentiles.

2 **He shall not cry, nor lift up, nor cause his voice to be heard in the street** [*Christ was low-key, designed His preaching to not make great disturbances, often said to those healed, "tell no one"*].

The tenderness of the Savior is described beautifully by Isaiah in verse 3, next.

3 **A bruised reed shall he not break** [*he came to help the weak, the "bruised," not to crush them*

more], **and the smoking flax** [*the glowing candle wick that still has a tiny spark of light in it*] **shall he not quench** [*he came to gently fan the spark within into a flame of belief and testimony, not to snuff it out*]: he shall bring forth judgment unto truth [*victory, see Matthew 12:20*].

4 **He shall not fail** [*falter, stop, quit; see D&C 19:19*] **nor be discouraged** [*German: unable to finish*], till he have set judgment in the earth: and the isles [*all continents, nations*] shall wait for [*trust in*] his law.

5 ¶ **Thus saith God the LORD,** he that created the heavens, and stretched them out; he that spread forth the earth, and that which cometh out of it; he that giveth breath unto the people upon it, and spirit to them that walk therein [*the Creator of all*]:

Verse 6, next, seems to apply mainly to Israel. See Israel's responsibility and mission in Abraham 2:9–11.

6 **I the LORD have called thee in righteousness, and will hold thine hand,** and will keep thee, **and give thee for a covenant of the people, for a light of** [*German: unto*] **the Gentiles;**

7 **To open the blind eyes, to bring out the prisoners from the prison, and them that sit in darkness out of the prison house** [*what Christ

and his righteous servants can do*].

8 **I am the LORD: that is my name: and my glory will I not give to another** [*you are still my chosen people*], neither my praise to graven images [*idols*].

9 **Behold, the former things** [*truth and keys from former days—restoration of the gospel*] **are come to pass, and new things** [*new knowledge in dispensation of fulness of times*] **do I declare**: before they spring forth I tell you of them [*they have been prophesied*].

10 **Sing unto the LORD a new song,** and his praise from the end of the earth [*to all the world*], ye that go down to the sea, and all that is therein; the isles, and the inhabitants thereof [*restored gospel will be preached to all the world*].

11 **Let the wilderness** [*dual meaning: literal wilderness; apostate Israel*] **and the cities thereof lift up their voice,** the villages that Kedar [*nomadic tribe in the wilderness east of Sea of Galilee; Kedar was a grandson of Abraham through Ishmael, see Genesis 25:13*] doth inhabit: let the inhabitants of the rock [*Sela, a desert town south of the Dead Sea*] sing, let them shout from the top of the mountains [*even remote places like Kedar and Sela will receive the gospel and be able to rejoice in it*].

12 **Let them give glory unto the LORD**, and declare his praise in the islands [*everybody will hear the gospel in the last days*].

13 **The LORD shall go forth as a mighty man**, he shall stir up jealousy [*with zeal*] like a man of war: he shall cry, yea, roar; **he shall prevail against his enemies** [*the Lord will ultimately triumph*].

14 **I** [*the Lord*] **have long time holden my peace** [*I have been patient*]; I have been still, and refrained myself [*I have been patient and not shown forth great power*]: now will I cry like a travailing woman [*woman in labor; in other words, delivery time for Israel has come; the restored gospel will go forth with great power that none can stop*]; I will destroy and devour at once.

15 **I will make waste mountains and hills, and dry up all their herbs; and I will make the rivers islands, and I will dry up the pools** [*after the gospel is restored, there will be great destruction, drought, and so forth as the Lord preaches "sermons" via the forces of nature as a way of getting people's attention in the last days—see D&C 88:87–90*].

16 **And I will bring the blind** [*the spiritually blind scattered of Israel*] **by a way** [*the restored gospel*] **that they knew not; I will lead them in**

paths [*truths and covenants of the restored gospel*] **that they have not known: I will make darkness light before them**, and crooked things straight [*effects of the Restoration*]. **These things will I do unto them, and not forsake them**.

17 ¶ They shall be turned back, **they shall be greatly ashamed, that trust in graven images**, that say to the molten images, Ye are our gods [*idol worship will not pay off*].

18 **Hear, ye deaf; and look, ye blind, that ye may see** [*open your eyes and ears to the truth*].

The Joseph Smith Translation makes many changes in verses 19 through 25. We will first examine these verses as they stand in our Bible, and then provide the JST—with explanatory notes added to the JST.

19 Who *is* blind, but my servant? or deaf, as my messenger *that* I sent? who *is* blind as *he that is* perfect, and blind as the LORD's servant?

20 Seeing many things, but thou observest not; opening the ears, but he heareth not.

21 The LORD is well pleased for his righteousness' sake; he will magnify the law, and make *it* honourable.

22 But this *is* a people robbed and

spoiled; *they are* all of them snared in holes, and they are hid in prison houses: they are for a prey, and none delivereth; for a spoil, and none saith, Restore.

23 Who among you will give ear to this? *who* will hearken and hear for the time to come?

24 Who gave Jacob for a spoil, and Israel to the robbers? did not the LORD, he against whom we have sinned? for they would not walk in his ways, neither were they obedient unto his law.

25 Therefore he hath poured upon him the fury of his anger, and the strength of battle: and it hath set him on fire round about, yet he knew not; and it burned him, yet he laid *it* not to heart.

JST Isaiah 42:19–25

19 For I will send my servant unto you who are blind; yea, a messenger to open the eyes of the blind, and unstop the ears of the deaf;

20 And they [*those who listen and repent*] shall be made perfect [*the power of the Atonement; 2 Nephi 25:23*] notwithstanding their blindness, if they will hearken unto the messenger, the Lord's servant.

21 Thou [*Israel*] art a people, seeing many things, but thou observest not [*you don't obey*];

opening the ears to hear, but thou hearest not [*you don't want to hear the truth*].

22 The Lord is not well pleased with such a people, but for his righteousness' sake he will magnify the law and make it honorable.

23 Thou art a people robbed and spoiled; thine enemies, all of them, have snared thee in holes, and they have hid thee in prison houses; they have taken thee for a prey, and none delivereth; for a spoil, and none saith, Restore [*consequences of Israel's wickedness*].

24 Who among them [*Israel's enemies in verse 23*] will give ear unto thee [*Israel*], or hearken and hear thee for the time to come? and who gave Jacob for a spoil, and Israel to the robbers [*who turned Israel over to her enemies*]? did not the Lord, he against whom they have sinned [*the Lord did, because of Israel's wickedness*]?

25 For they [*Israel*] would not walk in his ways, neither were they obedient unto his law; therefore [*that is why*] he [*the Lord*] hath poured upon them the fury of his anger, and the strength of battle; and they [*Israel's enemies*] have set them [*Israel*] on fire round about [*have caused terrible destruction*], yet they [*Israel*] know not [*won't*

acknowledge that they are being punished], and it burned them, yet they laid it not to heart [refused to repent].

ISAIAH 43

Background
This chapter contains clear doctrine that Jesus Christ, our Savior and Redeemer, is the God of the Old Testament—see, for example, verses 3, 11 and 14.

Having pointed out the foolishness of idol worship and the wisdom of being loyal to the true God, the Savior now reaches out to covenant Israel, inviting them to be gathered to Him. Everyone on earth can become a member of covenant Israel, through being baptized, living the gospel, and making and keeping the additional covenants available to faithful members of the Church.

1 But now **thus saith the LORD that created thee, O Jacob**, and he that formed thee, **O Israel** [emphasis on the words "created" and "formed" as used in Genesis 1:27 and 2:7; in other words, the true God is your Creator as described by Moses; these words will again be repeated for emphasis in verse 7], Fear not: for **I have redeemed thee**, I have called thee by thy name; thou art mine [the Savior will succeed in redeeming a remnant of Israel despite their coming problems as described in 42:22–25].

2 **When thou passest through the waters, I will be with thee; and through the rivers, they shall not overflow thee** [referring to the parting of the Red Sea and Jordan River; in other words, I helped you then and the same power and help is still available to you]: **when thou walkest through the fire, thou shalt not be burned**; neither shall the flame kindle upon thee. [Remember how I helped Shadrach, Meshach, and Abed-nego survive the fiery furnace (Daniel 3). I want to protect and bless you too.]

3 For **I am** the LORD thy God, the Holy One of Israel, **thy Saviour**: I gave Egypt for thy ransom, Ethiopia and Seba [a people in southern Arabia] for thee [I will ransom you from your enemies, sin, Satan, represented by Egypt—I will pay the price that you might go free. Applies literally also, in terms of protection from physical enemy nations, see Isaiah 45:14].

4 **Since thou wast** [art, are] **precious in my sight**, thou hast been honourable [honored by me], and **I have loved thee: therefore will I give men for thee** [prophets' lives have been sacrificed for us, for our benefit], **and people for thy life** [many have given their lives for the benefit of others. Most especially, Christ's Atonement works for us].

5 **Fear not: for I am with thee**: I will bring thy [*Israel's*] seed from the east, and gather thee from the west [*the gathering of Israel*];

6 **I will say to the north**, Give up [*give up the Israelites you're holding back from the Lord*]; and to the **south**, Keep not back: bring my sons from far, and my daughters from the ends of the earth [*the gathering of Israel is worldwide*];

7 **Even every one that is called by my name** [*that is willing to make and keep covenants*]: for **I have created him for my glory, I have formed him; yea, I have made him** [*carries the connotation of redemption through the Atonement via repentance—being "born again" as discussed in Alma 5. That is how the Savior "creates" us as new people spiritually*].

8 ¶ **Bring forth the blind people that have eyes, and the deaf that have ears** [*spiritually blind and deaf who have ignored prophets' messages and turned to other gods—see verse 9*].

9 Let all the nations be gathered together, and let the people be assembled: who among them can declare this [*the true gospel*], and shew us former things [*such as premortal life details*]? **let them bring forth their witnesses** [*their false gods, sorcerers, and so forth*], **that they may be justified** [*let's*

see their false gods, sorcerers, etc., do the kinds of things the true God of Israel can do]: **or let them hear, and say, It** [*Israel's message as given in verses 11–13*] **is truth.**

10 **Ye** [*Israel*] **are my witnesses, saith the LORD, and my servant whom I have chosen** [*to carry the gospel to all the world, see Abraham 2:9*]: that ye may know and believe me, and understand that I am he: **before me there was no God formed, neither shall there be after me** [*no idols ever have nor ever will take My place*].

11 I [*Jesus*], even **I, am the LORD; and beside me there is no saviour.** [*This is* the *message!*]

12 **I have declared, and have saved, and I have shewed, when there was no strange god** [*idol*] **among you** [*I have greatly blessed you when you were not worshiping idols*]: **therefore ye** [*Israel*] **are my witnesses** [*our calling, responsibility*], saith the LORD, **that I am God.**

13 Yea, **before the day was I am he** [*I was God before time began for you and will continue to be God*]; **and there is none that can deliver out of my hand: I will work** [*perform the Atonement and bless you with the gospel*], **and who shall let** [*JST: "hinder"*] **it?**

14 ¶ Thus saith the LORD, **your redeemer**, the Holy One of Israel; **For your sake I have sent to** [*I*

will triumph over] **Babylon** [*dual meaning: Symbolically Satan's kingdom; literally Israel's enemies in the nation of Babylon*], **and have brought** [*will bring*] **down all their nobles, and the Chaldeans** [*inhabitants of southern Babylon; symbolic of the wicked in all nations*], **whose cry is in the ships** [*German: whose shouting will turn to lamenting as I hunt them in their ships; in other words, freedom from your enemies comes through the Savior*].

Verse 15, next, summarizes the main point of this chapter.

15 **I am the LORD, your Holy One, the creator of Israel, your King.**

16 **Thus saith the LORD, which maketh a way in the sea** [*parted the Red Sea*], **and a path in the** mighty waters;

17 **Which bringeth forth** [*German: puts down, dismantles*] **the chariot and horse, the army and the power; they** [*your enemies*] **shall lie down** [*die*] together, they shall not rise: they are extinct, **they are quenched as tow** [*snuffed out like a smoldering candle*].

In verse 18, next, we see, among other things, that the gospel of Jesus Christ allows us to leave the past behind us and put all our energy into the present in order to have a glorious future. This is the essence of the Atonement of Christ.

18 **Remember ye not the former things, neither consider the things of old** [*forget the past troubles and oppressions; they are now behind you*].

19 **Behold, I will do a new thing** [*the restoration of the gospel; the gathering of Israel*]; now it shall spring forth; **shall ye not know it** [*you will see it plainly*]? I will even make a way in the wilderness, and rivers in the desert [*perhaps dual meaning, referring to physical changes in the earth to help Israel's gathering, and also symbolic of effects of "living water," gospel, bringing life to apostate Israel (referred to as "dry ground" in 53:2; 44:3) as water does to the wilderness, desert*].

20 **The beast of the field shall honour me,** the dragons and the owls [*jackals and ostriches—see footnote 20a in your Bible; in other words, even "unclean" animals and fowls will honor Me*]: **because I give waters in the wilderness**, and rivers in the desert, to give drink [*"living water" also; John 7:37–38*] to my people, my chosen.

21 **This people have I formed** [*German: prepared*] **for myself**; they shall shew forth my praise [*definite, strong prophecy that Israel will return to the Lord and be gathered*].

Next, the topic turns to Israel's

past performance, which has not been good.

22 ¶ **But thou hast not called upon me, O Jacob; but thou hast been weary of me, O Israel** [*you have a poor "track record," a history of disloyalty to Me*].

23 **Thou hast not brought me** the small cattle [*lambs or young goats*] of thy **burnt offerings**; neither hast thou honoured me with thy **sacrifices**. I have not caused thee to serve with an offering [*German: I have not been pleased with your offerings of the first fruits, Numbers 18:12*], nor wearied thee with incense [*German: nor taken pleasure in your incense*].

24 **Thou hast bought me no sweet cane** [*spices used in making anointing oil for use in the tabernacle; Exodus 30:23–25*] **with money, neither hast thou filled** [*satisfied*] **me with the fat of thy sacrifices** [*your sacrifices are empty ritual*]: **but thou hast made me to serve** [*burdened me; German: made work for me*] **with thy sins,** thou hast wearied me [*German: caused me trouble and pains*] with thine iniquities.

Next, in verse 25, we see another clear statement that Jesus Christ is the God of the Old Testament, in other words, the one who is speaking and teaching in the Old Testament. Here He teaches about His Atonement.

25 I [*the Savior*], even **I, am he**

that blotteth out thy transgressions for mine own sake [*I desire very much to forgive you and save you; Moses 1:39, Isaiah 1:18*], **and will not remember thy sins** [*if you truly repent; D&C 58:42–43*].

26 **Put me in remembrance** [*remember me*]: **let us plead together** [*German: debate as in a court of law; in other words, let us look at the facts*]: **declare thou** [*state your point of view*], **that thou mayest be justified** [*go ahead, try to justify your wicked behavior*].

27 **Thy first father** [*ancestors; early Israel, the children of Israel under Moses—see footnote 27a in your Bible*] **hath sinned, and thy teachers** [*priests and ministers*] **have transgressed against me.**

28 **Therefore** [*for this reason*] **I have profaned the princes** [*priests and ministers; considered them to be worldly, not acceptable to Me*] of the sanctuary [*probably meaning the tabernacle or the temple in Jerusalem*], **and have given Jacob** [*Israel*] **to the curse** [*German: excommunication, cut off*], **and Israel to reproaches** [*German: become the object of scorn*].

ISAIAH 44

Background

Verses 1–8 deal mostly with Christ's role in redeeming Israel. Verses 9–20 deal mainly with pagan idol worship.

1 Yet **now hear, O Jacob** [*another word for Israel*] **my servant; and Israel, whom I have chosen** [*in other words, Israel constitutes the Lord's "chosen people"*]:

There are many things one could say about the word "chosen" in verse 1, above. For example, Israel is chosen to carry the gospel and blessings of the priesthood to all the world (see Abraham 2:9–11). Israel is chosen to carry heavy burdens of persecution and scorn, from time to time. Israel (which can include anyone who is willing to join the Church through baptism and afterwards keep the commandments) is chosen to be exalted. Israel is chosen "to stand as witnesses of God at all times and in all things, and in all places" (Mosiah 18:9). And the list of meanings for the word "chosen" goes on and on.

The thing that "chosen" does not imply is that God arbitrarily chooses some people over others to be saved.

Notice that "Jacob" and "Israel" are often used interchangeably in the scriptures. That is because they are both names of the father of the twelve sons who became the heads of the twelve tribes of Israel.

2 **Thus saith the LORD** that made thee, and formed thee from the womb, which will help thee [*I have been helping you from the beginning and will continue to do so*]; **Fear not, O Jacob, my servant; and thou, Jesurun** [*those who are righteous, Deuteronomy 33:26, footnote 26a*], **whom I have chosen.**

3 **For I will pour water** [*dual meaning: literal; also "living water" (the gospel of Jesus Christ), 2 Nephi 9:50*] **upon him that is thirsty, and floods upon the dry ground** [*apostate Israel; Isaiah 53:2*]: **I will pour my spirit upon thy seed** [*descendants*], and my blessing upon thine offspring [*the "blessings of Abraham, Isaac, and Jacob;" Abraham 2:9–11*]:

4 **And they shall spring up as among the grass, as willows by the water courses** [*there will be righteous Israelites all over the place; Isaiah 49:21, 1 Nephi 21–21*]

5 **One shall say, I am the LORD's; and another shall call himself by the name of Jacob** [*they have both converted to the Lord and are loyal to Him; compare with 19:25*]; **and another shall subscribe with his hand** [*make covenants*] **unto the** LORD, **and surname himself by the name of Israel** [*take upon himself the name of Christ and become part of righteous covenant Israel*].

6 **Thus saith the LORD** the King of Israel, and **his** [*Israel's*] **redeemer**

the LORD of [*heavenly*] hosts; **I am the first, and I am the last** [*Jesus was chosen at the first, in the premortal existence, to be our Redeemer, and He will be around at the last, to be our Judge—see John 5:22*]; **and beside me there is no God** [*there are no idols that are actually gods*].

7 **And who** [*what idols; compare with 40:25*], **as I, shall call, and shall declare it, and set it in order for me, since I appointed** [*established*] **the ancient people** [*my people*]? and the things that are coming [*future events*], and shall come, **let them** [*your idols, false gods*] **shew unto them** [*foretell for you; in other words, this whole verse is a challenge for apostate Israel to have their idols do as well as the Lord in leading them and prophesying the future*].

8 **Fear ye not, neither be afraid** [*trust in me*]: have not I told thee from that time [*from the ancient times from the beginning; see verse 7*], and have declared it? ye are even my witnesses [*Israel's calling, stewardship*]. **Is there a God beside me** [*is there an idol that is a God like Me*]? **yea, there is no God; I know not any.**

Verses 9–20 will now deal primarily with the apostate practice of worshiping idols.

9 **They that make a graven image**

[*an idol*] **are all of them vanity** [*German: vain, conceited, won't take counsel from God*]; **and their delectable** [*German: precious*] **things shall not profit** [*will do them no good*]; **and they are their own witnesses; they see not, nor know** [*those who worship idols are as blind and empty-headed as the idols they worship*]; **that they may be ashamed** [*may be put to shame*].

10 **Who hath formed a god, or molten a graven image that is profitable for nothing** [*good for nothing; in other words, who would do such a foolish thing*]?

11 Behold, **all his fellows** [*fellow idol worshipers*] **shall be ashamed**: and the workmen, they are of men [*are mere mortals*]: let them all be gathered together, let them stand up; yet they shall fear, and they shall be ashamed together [*no matter how many worship idols, it does no good; they will all be put to shame*].

12 **The smith** [*blacksmith*] with the tongs both worketh in the coals, and fashioneth it [*an idol*] with hammers, and worketh it with the strength of his arms: yea, **he is hungry** [*the craftsman is a mere mortal*], and **his strength faileth**: he **drinketh no water, and is faint** [*the craftsmen who make idols for you are mere mortals themselves*].

13 The carpenter stretcheth out his rule; he marketh it [*the idol he is making*] out with a line; he fitteth it with planes, and he marketh it out with the compass [*your craftsmen exercise great care and skill in manufacturing your idols*], and maketh it after the figure of a man, according to the beauty of a man; that it may remain in the house [*your craftsmen put great care into making your idols; implication: if you were as careful worshipping God as you are in making idols . . .*].

14 He heweth him down cedars, and taketh the cypress and the oak, which he strengtheneth [*cultivates and grows*] for himself among the trees of the forest: he planteth an ash [*tree*], and the rain doth nourish it.

15 Then shall it be for a man to burn: for he will take thereof, and warm himself; yea, he kindleth it, and baketh bread; yea, he maketh a god, and worshippeth it [*you use most of the tree's wood for normal daily needs; how can you possibly turn around and worship wood from the same tree in the form of idols!*]; he maketh it a graven image, and falleth down thereto.

16 He burneth part thereof in the fire; with part thereof he eateth flesh; he roasteth roast, and is satisfied: yea, he warmeth himself, and saith, Aha, I am warm, I have seen the fire [*normal uses*]:

17 And **the residue thereof** [*with the rest of the tree*] **he maketh a god**, even his graven image: **he falleth down unto it, and worshippeth it**, and prayeth unto it, and saith, Deliver [*save*] me; for thou art my god [*Isaiah is saying how utterly ridiculous it is to assign part of a tree to have powers over yourselves*].

18 **They** [*idol worshipers; see 45:20*] **have not known** [*German: know nothing*] **nor understood** [*German: understand nothing*]: for he hath shut their eyes [*German: they are blind*], that **they cannot see** [*are spiritually blind*]; and **their hearts, that they cannot understand** [*they are as blind and unfeeling, insensitive, as the idols they make and worship*].

19 And **none considereth in his heart** [*if idol worshipers would just stop and think*], **neither is there knowledge nor understanding** [*they don't have enough common sense*] **to say, I have burned part of it** [*the tree spoken of in verse 44*] **in the fire**; yea, also **I have baked bread upon the coals thereof**; I have **roasted flesh, and eaten it**: and **shall I make the residue thereof an abomination** [*is it reasonable to make the leftover portion into an abominable idol*]? **shall I fall down to the stock of a tree** [*is it rational to worship a chunk of wood*]?

20 **He** [*the idol worshiper*] **feedeth**

on ashes [*German: takes pleasure in ashes, perhaps referring to ashes left over from some forms of idol worship*]: a [*German: his own*] **deceived heart hath turned him aside** [*German: leads him astray*], **that he cannot deliver** [*save*] **his soul, nor say** [*wake up and think*], **Is there not a lie in my right hand** [*covenant hand—am I not making covenants with false gods*]?

21 ¶ Remember these, O Jacob and Israel; for thou art my servant: **I have formed thee** [*the exact opposite of idol worshipers who form their gods*]; **thou art my servant: O Israel, thou shalt not be forgotten of me.**

> Next, in verse 22, the Savior assures Israel that their sins can be blotted out completely by His Atonement.

22 **I have blotted out, as a thick cloud, thy transgressions**, and, as a cloud, thy sins [*the Atonement can still work for you*]: **return unto me**; for **I have redeemed thee** [*I have paid the price of your sins; therefore, please repent*].

> In verse 23, next, all things in nature are invited to praise the Lord for what He has done for Israel.

23 **Sing, O ye heavens**; for the LORD hath done it: **shout, ye lower parts of the earth** [*German: O earth below*]: break forth into singing, ye **mountains, O forest**, and every tree therein: **for the LORD hath redeemed Jacob, and glorified himself in Israel** [*speaking of the future*].

24 Thus saith the LORD, **thy redeemer**, and he that formed [*German: prepared*] thee from the womb, I am the LORD **that maketh all things**; that stretcheth forth the heavens alone; that spreadeth abroad the earth by myself [*I created heaven and earth; no idols helped Me!*];

> One of the evil things rebellious Israelites had done was to go to fortune-tellers, witches, sorcerers, and so forth for "revelation," rather than repenting and going to God for revelation. Verse 25, next, addresses this issue.

25 **That frustrateth** [*causeth to fail*] **the tokens** [*signs*] **of the liars** [*German: fortune tellers*], **and maketh diviners** [*people who deal in the occult*] **mad** [*German: absurd*]; **that turneth** [*so-called*] **wise men backward, and maketh their knowledge** [*German: business of fortune-telling*] **foolish**;

26 [*I am the Lord*] **That confirmeth the word of his servant, and performeth the counsel of his messengers** [*I support My servants, whereas idols don't support theirs*]; **that saith to Jerusalem, Thou shalt be inhabited; and**

to the cities of Judah, Ye shall be built, and I will raise up the decayed places thereof [*when I command, things obey; idols can't command and aren't obeyed*]:

27 [*I am the Lord*] **That saith to the deep** [*the sea, such as the Red Sea when the Israelites crossed through it*], **Be dry, and I will dry up thy rivers** [*as in the case of the Jordan River when the Israelites crossed through it into the promised land; see Joshua 3:17*]:

28 **That saith of Cyrus** [*the Persian*], **He is my shepherd** [*a tool in my hand*]**, and shall perform all my pleasure**: even saying to Jerusalem, Thou shalt be built; and to the temple, Thy foundation shall be laid. [*A specific prophecy! Cyrus conquered Babylon about 538 B.C., who had conquered Jerusalem about fifty years earlier in 588 B.C. In 537 B.C., Cyrus issued a decree to let the Jews return home to Palestine to rebuild Jerusalem and the temple. See 538 B.C. on the chronology chart in the Bible Dictionary at the back of your LDS Bible*].

ISAIAH 45

Background

This chapter contains a prophecy about Cyrus the Persian, who conquered Babylon in about 538 B.C. and subsequently (about 537 B.C.)

allowed the Jews to return to Jerusalem to build up the city again and rebuild the temple. One of the lessons we learn here is that the Lord often uses "nonmember" leaders and individuals to accomplish His purposes. For example, the British helped the Jews return to their homeland in 1948 and establish their own nation.

1 **Thus saith the LORD** to his anointed, **to Cyrus**, whose right hand I have holden [*strengthened*], to subdue nations before him; and I will loose the loins of kings [*German: take the sword of kings away from them*], to open before him the two leaved gates [*main city gates*]; and the gates shall not be shut [*the Lord will open the way for Cyrus and none will stop him*];

2 **I will go before thee**, and make the crooked places straight [*German: will take out the bumps*]: I will break in pieces the gates of brass, and cut in sunder [*cut through*] the bars of iron:

3 And **I will give thee** the **treasures** of darkness, and hidden riches of secret places [*hidden treasures, probably referring to Babylon*], that thou mayest know that I, the LORD, which call thee [*Cyrus*] by thy name, am the God of Israel.

Remember, "Jacob" and "Israel," as used in verse 4, next, are the same thing. In "the manner of prophesying among the Jews" (2 Nephi 25:1), it is common for prophets such as Isaiah to say the same thing in succession, for emphasis. If you don't understand this, you might think that Jacob and Israel are two separate groups in this verse.

4 For Jacob my servant's sake, and Israel mine elect, I have even called thee [*Cyrus*] by thy name: I have surnamed thee, though thou hast not known me [*although you don't know Me and do not realize that I am using you to fulfill My purposes, I will use you to free the Jews*].

5 I am the LORD, and there is none else, there is no God beside me: I girded thee [*dressed you for war and strengthened you*], though thou hast not known me:

6 That they may know from the rising of the sun, and from the west [*from east to west—everywhere*], that there is none beside me [*that I am the only true God; in other words, idols and man-made deities are not gods*]. I am the LORD, and there is none else.

7 I form the light, and create darkness: I make peace, and create evil [*cause calamity, as in 3 Nephi 9:3–12*]: I the LORD do all these things.

8 Drop [*drip; rain*] down, ye heavens, from above, and let the skies pour down righteousness: let the earth open [*produce*], and let them [*heaven and earth*] bring forth salvation [*the main purpose of creating the earth*], and let righteousness spring up together [*with it*]; I the LORD have created it [*let the purposes of creating heaven and earth be wonderfully fulfilled*].

9 Woe unto him that striveth with [*fights against*] his Maker! Let the potsherd [*vessel of clay; shard, broken piece of pottery*] strive with the potsherds of the earth [*German: a shard like other mortal shards—how foolish of a mere mortal to quarrel with his Creator*]. Shall the clay say to him that fashioneth it, What makest thou? or thy work, He hath no hands [*an insolent question, asking, in effect, "Who do you think you are, God?"; compare with Isaiah 29:16*]?

10 Woe unto him that saith unto his father, What begettest thou? or to the woman [*his mother*], What hast thou brought forth [*what do you think you're doing; being sassy*]?

11 Thus saith the LORD, the Holy One of Israel [*Jehovah, Jesus Christ*], and his [*Israel's*] Maker, Ask me of things to come [*about the future*] concerning my sons, and concerning the work of my hands command [*German: acknowledge me as the Creator*] ye me [*ask Me, I'll tell you*].

12 **I have made the earth, and created man upon it**: I, even my hands, have stretched out [*created*] the heavens, and all their host have I commanded [*I am the Creator*].

Having borne strong witness of the fact that none of the pagan gods are real gods, the Lord returns now to the prophecy that He will use a leader named Cyrus (verse 1) to free the Jews from Babylon so that they can return to Jerusalem. Since Isaiah served as a prophet from about 740 B.C. to 701 B.C., and since Cyrus the Persian conquered Babylon in about 538 B.C. and decreed the Jews' freedom about 537 B.C., this prophecy is given by Isaiah over 160 years before it takes place!

13 **I have raised him** [*Cyrus—see verse 1*] **up** in righteousness [*I will use him to fulfill My righteous purposes*], and I will direct all his ways: **he shall build my city** [*rebuild Jerusalem*], **and he shall let go my captives** [*the Jews*], not for price nor reward [*the hand of the Lord is in it*], saith the LORD of hosts.

14 Thus saith the LORD, The labour of **Egypt**, and merchandise of **Ethiopia** and of **the Sabeans** [*a people in southeastern Arabia*], men of stature, shall come over unto thee, and they **shall be thine**: they shall come after thee [*behind you*]; in chains they shall come

over, and they shall fall down unto thee, they shall make supplication unto thee, saying, Surely God is in thee; and there is none else, there is no God [*all nations will recognize that the Lord is with Cyrus and Israel*].

15 Verily **thou art a God that hidest thyself** [*in other words, can't be seen physically on a daily basis like idols can*], O God of Israel, the Saviour.

16 **They** [*nations of the world*] **shall be ashamed** [*put to shame because of their wickedness and corruption*], and also confounded, all of them: they shall go to confusion together **that are makers of idols** [*results of idol worship*].

17 **But Israel shall be saved in the LORD with an everlasting salvation**: ye shall not be ashamed nor confounded world without end [*throughout eternity; results of righteousness*].

18 **For thus saith the LORD** [*in answer to the insolent question in verses 9 and 10*] **that created the heavens**; God himself that formed **the earth** and made it; he hath established it, he created it not in vain, he formed it to be inhabited: **I am the LORD; and there is none else**.

19 **I have not spoken in secret, in a dark place of the earth** [*I have not hidden from you, played "hard to get." I have been open and direct*

with you.]: **I said not unto the seed of Jacob** [*the covenant people, Israel*]**, Seek ye me in vain**: I the LORD speak righteousness, I declare things that are right.

20 **Assemble yourselves and come**; draw near together, **ye that are escaped** [*survivors*] of the nations: **they** [*idol worshippers, 44:18*] **have no knowledge** [*see notes for 44:18*] that set up the wood of their graven image, and pray unto a god [*idol*] that cannot save.

21 **Tell ye** [*spread the word*], and **bring them** [*idol worshippers*] **near**; yea, **let them take counsel** [*plot*] together: **who hath declared** [*explained*] **this from ancient time** [*since time began*]? who hath told it from that time? **have not I the LORD? and there is no God else beside me**; a just God and **a Saviour**; there is none beside me [*there is no comparison between idols and the true God!*].

Next, the Lord invites all people everywhere to repent.

22 **Look unto me** [*German: turn to me; in other words, repent*], **and be ye saved**, all the ends of the earth [*the Atonement applies to all*]: for I am God, and there is none else.

Next, in verse 23, we are taught that every person who has ever been born or who will be born, will someday acknowledge that Jesus is the Christ.

23 **I have sworn** [*covenanted, promised*] **by myself** [*in My own name*], the word is gone out of my mouth in righteousness, and shall not return [see *D&C 1:38*], **That unto me every knee shall bow, every tongue shall swear** [*acknowledge Christ; does not mean that everyone will repent and be righteous; for example this phrase refers to inhabitants of the telestial glory as used in D&C 76:110*].

24 **Surely, shall one say, in the LORD have I righteousness and strength**: even to him shall men come; **and all that are incensed** [*angry*] **against him shall be ashamed** [*put to shame; disappointed, disconcerted*].

25 **In the LORD** [*Christ*] **shall** [*can*] **all the seed of Israel be justified** [*brought into harmony with God's ways, thus be approved to dwell with God*]**, and shall glory** [*in the Lord, 1 Corinthians 1:31*].

It is interesting to note that the word "justified," seen in verse 25 above, is used in current word processing terminology to mean "lined up," as in "justify the margins." In scriptural language, "justified" likewise means "lined up"—in other words, "lined up with God's will," or in harmony with God's commandments and thus worthy to be ratified and approved by the Holy Ghost, the

Holy Spirit of Promise, to live with God forever.

ISAIAH 46

Background

This chapter continues the comparison of Jehovah with the false gods and idols worshiped by so many people in Isaiah's day. The point is that there is no comparison!

Verse 1 introduces us to two prominent false gods in Isaiah's day. Bel and Nebo were chief gods in Babylon. Ancient cultures such as Babylon believed that each "god" had a territory, and when a city or country was defeated in battle by enemies, it meant that their gods (such as Bel and Nebo) had been defeated by the enemy's gods. Chapter 46 ties in with chapters 13 and 14 concerning Babylon's downfall, and with chapters 40–45 concerning Jehovah's power as compared to the lack of power of idols.

1 **Bel boweth down** [*German: has been defeated*], **Nebo stoopeth, their idols were upon the beasts, and upon the cattle** [*the idols are powerless; they can't move by themselves and have to be transported upon beasts of burden*]: your carriages were heavy loaden; they [*the idols*] are a burden to the weary beast [*the message, by implication, is that Bel and Nebo are burdens to those who "created" them, in contrast to the true God of Israel, who*

lightens the burdens of those He created, who worship Him].

2 **They** [*Bel and Nebo*] **stoop, they bow down together** [*German: they are both defeated*]; **they could not deliver** [*German: remove*] **the burden** [*they couldn't do the job*], **but themselves are gone into captivity** [*they have failed their worshippers and couldn't even save themselves*].

3 **Hearken unto me, O house of Jacob, and all the remnant of the house of Israel, which are borne by me** [*note that I the Lord carry you, help you, am not a burden*] from the belly [*from the womb, or from the beginning*], which are carried from the womb [*I have carried you from the beginning, contrasted to idol worshipers who have to transport their "gods"*]:

4 **And even to your old age** [*throughout your entire life*] **I am he** [*the true God*]; **and even to hoar** [*gray*] **hairs will I carry you: I have made** [*German: I want to do it*], **and I will** [*German: desire to*] **bear**; **even I will carry**, and will **deliver** you [*I want to help, support and bless you throughout your entire life; I want to be your Redeemer!*].

5 **To whom will ye liken me, and make me equal**, and compare me, that we may be like [*who among your false gods can compare to Me*]? [*Same question as in 40:18, 25.*]

Next, in verses 6–7, Isaiah again points out how ridiculous it is to make and then worship idols.

6 **They** [*idol worshippers*] **lavish gold** out of the bag, **and weigh silver** in the balance [*on the scales; in other words, you pay out much money for your worthless idols*], **and hire a goldsmith; and he maketh it a god** [*turns it into an idol*]: **they fall down, yea, they worship.**

7 **They** [*idol worshippers*] **bear him** [*their idol*] **upon the shoulder, they carry him, and set him in his place** [*put the idol in the room or place they want it to stay*], **and he standeth; from his place shall he not remove** [*the idol can't even move from the place the people put it*]: yea, **one shall cry** [*pray*] **unto him** [*the idol*], **yet can he** [*the idol*] **not answer, nor save him** [*the idol worshiper*] out of his trouble [*idols are totally worthless!*].

8 Remember this, and shew your-selves men [*think about this and prove that you are man enough to face the truth*]: **bring it again to mind, O ye transgressors** [*face the issue, you sinners!*].

9 Remember the former things of old [*the many miracles I performed for you in the past*]: **for I am God, and there is none else; I am God, and there is none like me,**

10 **Declaring the end from the beginning** [*prophesying the future*], **and from ancient times the things that are not yet done** [*things prophesied anciently that are yet in the future*], saying, **My counsel shall stand, and I will do all my pleasure** [*everything I have said will happen; this message is also given in D&C 1:38*]:

11 **Calling a ravenous bird from the east** [*a bird of prey; in other words, Cyrus from Persia—see 45:1*], **the man that executeth** [*carries out*] **my counsel** [*plans*] from a far country [*Persia*]: yea, **I have spoken it, I will also bring it to pass**; I have purposed [*planned*] it, I will also do it.

12 **Hearken unto me, ye stout-hearted** [*hardhearted*], **that are far from righteousness** [*as mentioned in verse 8*]:

13 I bring near my righteousness [*victory, triumph*]; it shall not be [*German: is not*] far off, and my salvation shall not tarry [*will not be late*]: and **I will place salvation in Zion for Israel my glory** [*I will succeed in bringing salvation and glory to Israel, and you can be a part of it if you repent*].

ISAIAH 47

Background

This chapter is a prophecy about the downfall of Babylon. Remember that Babylon was an actual large city (56 miles around with walls 335 feet high and 85 feet wide—see Bible Dictionary, under "Babylon"), but that Babylon is also used often in the scriptures to symbolize Satan's kingdom.

1 **Come down** [*be humbled*], **and sit in the dust** [*a sign of humiliation in eastern cultures; see Isaiah 3:26, Lamentations 2:10*], **O virgin** [*unconquered*] **daughter of Babylon** [*the Babylonian Empire*], sit on the ground [*humiliation*]: **there is no throne** [*Babylon was to be conquered, overthrown; this prophecy was fulfilled literally by Cyrus the Persian in 538 B.C. and will be fulfilled symbolically as Christ overthrows Satan's kingdom*], **O daughter of the Chaldeans** [*inhabitants of southern Babylonia, part of the Babylonian Empire*]: **for thou shalt no more be called tender and delicate** [*German: desirable*].

Using imagery to illustrate a conquered Babylon, Isaiah now describes conditions and tasks of slaves, according to the culture of his day.

2 **Take the millstones, and grind meal** [*flour*]: **uncover thy locks** [*take off your veil, like slaves do*], **make bare the leg, uncover the thigh** [*tie up your skirts and expose your legs so you can get around easily to do the work required of slaves*], **pass over the rivers** [*you'll have to wade through canals to get from one field to another as you do the work of slaves*].

3 **Thy nakedness shall be uncovered** [*dual meaning: sexual abuse suffered by slaves; also the "true colors"—in other words, the wickedness of Babylon will be uncovered, exposed*], **yea, thy shame shall be seen: I** [*the Lord*] **will take vengeance, and I will not meet thee** [*Babylon and all things represented by Babylon*] **as a man** [*you won't be able to stop Me because I'm not a mortal man*].

4 **As for** [*German: thus doeth*] **our redeemer**, the LORD of hosts is his name, the Holy One of Israel.

5 **Sit thou** [*Babylon*] **silent**, and get thee into darkness, O daughter of the Chaldeans [*Babylon*]: for **thou shalt no more be called, The lady of kingdoms** [*you've been conquered*].

Next, in verse 6, the Lord explains why He allowed Babylon to conquer the Jews (the main portion of Israel affected by this prophecy). Remember that Isaiah is prophesying of the future as if it had already happened. The events foretold here didn't actually take place until over one hundred years later.

6 **I** [*God*] **was wroth** [*angry*] **with my people, I have polluted** [*German: disowned*] **mine inheritance** [*wicked Israel*], **and given**

them [*prophecy of future*] **into thine** [*Babylon's*] **hand: thou didst shew them** [*Israel, especially the Jews*] **no mercy; upon the ancient hast thou very heavily laid thy yoke** [*in other words, you abused the power I allowed you to have over Israel*].

7 **And thou** [*Babylon*] **saidst** [*boasted*], **I shall be a lady** [*German: a queen*] **for ever**: so that **thou didst not lay these things to thy heart** [*you didn't take my warnings seriously*], **neither didst remember the latter end of it** [*you didn't stop to consider the consequences of your behavior*].

8 **Therefore hear now this**, thou [*Babylon*] **that art given to pleasures** [*lustful and riotous living*], **that dwellest carelessly** [*NIV: "lounging in your security"*], **that sayest in thine heart, I am, and none else beside me** [*I am the most powerful of all!*]; **I shall not sit as a widow** [*have my kingdom taken away from me*], **neither shall I know the loss of children** [*Babylon boasts she will never be conquered; however, she will be depopulated and her king destroyed*]:

9 **But these two things** [*the loss of your king and your inhabitants*] **shall come to thee in a moment** [*suddenly*] **in one day**, the **loss of children**, and **widowhood**: they shall come upon thee in their perfection [*in full measure*] for [*despite*] the multitude of thy sorceries, and

for [*despite*] the great abundance of thine enchantments [*the so-called "magic" of your false religions will not save you*].

10 **For thou hast trusted in** [*relied on*] **thy wickedness**: thou hast said, None seeth me [*I can get away with it*]. Thy wisdom and thy knowledge, it hath perverted thee [*German: has led you astray*]; and thou hast said in thine heart, I am, and none else beside me [*I am all-powerful*].

11 **Therefore** [*because of the things mentioned above*] **shall evil come upon thee**; thou shalt not know [*German: expect it*] from whence it riseth [*the source of your demise will surprise you*]: and mischief [*ruin*] shall fall upon thee; thou shalt not be able to put it off [*German: atone for it via sacrifices to false gods; see verse 12*]: and **desolation shall come upon thee suddenly**, which thou shalt not know [*foresee*].

12 **Stand now with thine enchantments**, and with the multitude of thy sorceries, wherein thou hast laboured from thy youth [*like you've done all your lives*]; if so be thou shalt be able to profit, if so be thou mayest prevail [*go ahead, try to stop this destruction with your false gods and enchantments; see if they help or not*].

13 **Thou art wearied in the multitude of thy counsels** [*you have*

spent many boring hours with your counselors, stargazers, and so forth]. **Let now the astrologers, the stargazers**, the monthly **prognosticators** [those who predict the future], **stand up, and save thee from these things that shall come upon thee** [call their bluff].

14 **Behold, they** [your religious leaders, soothsayers, wizards, and so forth, as mentioned in verse 13] **shall be as stubble; the fire shall burn them**; they shall not deliver themselves from the power of the flame: there shall not be a coal to warm at, nor fire to sit before it [your soothsayers are utterly powerless to save themselves, let alone you].

The whole message of this chapter, that no one can save Babylon, is summarized in verse 15, next.

15 **Thus** [like straw in a fire] **shall they be unto thee** with whom thou hast laboured, even thy merchants [religious leaders], from thy youth: they shall wander every one to his quarter; **none shall save**.

ISAIAH 48

Background

In this chapter, "Babylon" is used in the symbolic sense. It means wickedness and evil, in other words, Satan's kingdom. This is one of the two chapters of Isaiah that Nephi

read to his people in First Nephi, including his rebellious brothers, Laman and Lemuel (1 Nephi 20 and 21). Nephi explained to us why he chose to read these words of Isaiah. He said (**bold** added for emphasis):

1 Nephi 19:23–24

23 And I did read many things unto them which were written in the books of Moses; but **that I might more fully persuade them to believe in the Lord their Redeemer I did read unto them that which was written by the prophet Isaiah**; for I did liken all scriptures unto us, that it might be for our profit and learning.

24 Wherefore I spake unto them, saying: Hear ye the words of the prophet, ye who are a remnant of the house of Israel, a branch who have been broken off; hear ye the words of the prophet, which were written unto all the house of Israel, and liken them unto yourselves, **that ye may have hope** as well as your brethren from whom ye have been broken off; for after this manner has the prophet written.

Every verse of 1 Nephi, chapter 20, has at least one thing that is different than what we will read here in Isaiah, chapter 48. This is a reminder that the Book of Mormon text of Isaiah was translated from the Brass Plates of Laban, which Lehi and his family had obtained. The Isaiah passages found in the Book of Mormon come from records much closer to the original source (Isaiah only lived about one hundred years before Lehi's departure from Jerusalem). In contrast, Isaiah in the Bible is derived from sources much further removed from the original. Therefore, we will use 1 Nephi chapter 20 often for clarification as we study this chapter.

As we begin, we see that Isaiah is pointing out the empty worship and hypocrisy of Israel. After doing so, he issues an invitation from the Lord for these people to repent, to flee from Babylon (wickedness), and come unto Him. He finishes with a stern warning that there is no peace for the wicked.

1 **Hear ye this, O house of Jacob** [*the twelve tribes of Israel*]**, which are called by the name of Israel** [*who are known as the Lord's covenant people*]**, and are come forth out of the waters of Judah** [*waters of baptism, 1 Nephi 20:1*]**, which swear by the name of the LORD** [*who make covenants in the name of Jesus Christ*]**, and make mention of the God of Israel, but not in truth, nor in righteousness** [*you make covenants but don't live the gospel; empty worship is the problem*].

2 **For they call themselves of the**

holy city [*they claim to be the Lord's people*]**, and stay themselves upon** [*pretend to rely upon*] **the God of Israel; The LORD of** hosts [*Jehovah*] is his name.

In the next several verses, the Lord reminds Israel that there is no lack of evidence that He exists.

3 **I have declared the former things from the beginning** [*I've had prophets prophesy*]**; and they** [*their prophecies*] **went forth out of my mouth, and I shewed them** [*fulfilled them, so you would have solid evidence that I exist*]**; I did them suddenly, and they came to pass** [*so you can know I am God; 42:9*].

4 **Because I knew that thou art obstinate, and thy neck is an iron sinew** [*your necks won't bend; you are not humble*]**, and thy brow brass** [*you are thickheaded; can't get things through your skulls*]**;**

5 **I have even from the beginning declared it** [*prophecies*] **to thee; before it** [*prophesied events*] **came to pass I shewed it thee:** lest thou shouldest say, Mine idol hath done them, and my graven image, and my molten image, hath commanded them [*so you couldn't claim your idols, false gods, did it*].

6 **Thou hast heard, see all this; and will not ye declare it**

[*acknowledge it*]? **I have shewed thee new things** from this time, even hidden things, and **thou didst not know them** [*German: that thou hadst no way of knowing*].

7 **They** [*the prophesied events*] **are created** [*happening*] **now**, and not from the beginning; even before the day when thou heardest them not [*without my prophecies, you couldn't have known in advance*]; lest thou shouldest say, Behold, I knew them [*I did it this way so you would have obvious evidence that I exist*].

8 Yea, **thou heardest not**; yea, thou knewest not; yea, from that time that **thine ear was not opened** [*you wouldn't listen*]: for **I knew that thou wouldest deal very treacherously** [*the Lord knew right from the start that it would be hard to "raise" us. Great potential for good inherently has great potential for evil, but it was worth the risk!*], **and wast called a transgressor from the womb** [*I've had trouble with you Israelites right from the start*].

9 **For my name's sake** [*because I have a reputation to uphold—mercy, patience, love, and so forth*] **will I defer mine anger**, and for my praise will I refrain for thee, that I cut thee not off [*I will not cut you off completely*].

In verse 10, next, the Lord is speaking of the future as if it has already happened. The message is that He will yet have a people who are righteous and worthy of celestial glory. They will have gone through the refiner's fire to get there, just as pure gold must go through the refiner's fire in order to be set free from the impurities of the ore in which it is found.

10 **Behold, I have refined thee**, but not with [*German: "as"*] silver [*"but not with silver" is deleted in 1 Nephi 20:10. Perhaps this phrase in the Bible implies that we are not being refined to be "second-best"—in other words, silver—but rather to be gold, the best, celestial. See Revelation 4:4*]; **I have chosen thee** [*German: I will make you*] **in the furnace of affliction**.

11 **For mine own sake, even for mine own sake, will I do it**: for how should my name be polluted [*German: lest My name be slandered for not keeping My promise*]? and I will not give my glory unto another [*the Lord will stick with Israel*].

12 **Hearken unto me, O Jacob** and Israel, my called [*chosen people*]; **I am he; I am the first, I also am the last** [*I am the Savior*].

13 **Mine hand also hath laid the foundation of the earth** [*I am the Creator*], **and my right hand** [*the covenant hand; the hand of power*] **hath spanned** [*spread out; created*] **the heavens**: when I call unto

them, they stand up together.

14 All ye, assemble yourselves, and hear; which among them hath declared these things? **The LORD hath loved him** [*Israel*]: **he** [*God*] **will do his pleasure on** [*will punish*] **Babylon**, and his arm shall be on the Chaldeans [*southern Babylon*].

15 I, even I, have spoken; yea, **I** [*Jesus speaking for Heavenly Father?*] **have called him** [*Jesus?*]: **I have brought him, and he shall make his way prosperous.**

16 **Come ye near unto me, hear ye this; I have not spoken in secret** [*I have been open about the gospel*] **from the beginning; from the time that it was** [*declared, 1 Nephi 20:16*], **there am I** [*from the time anything existed, I have spoken*]: and now the Lord GOD, and his Spirit, hath sent me.

17 **Thus saith the LORD, thy Redeemer**, the Holy One of Israel [*Jesus*]; **I am the LORD thy God** which teacheth thee to profit [*German: for your profit, benefit*], **which leadeth thee by the way that thou shouldest go.**

18 **O that thou** [*Israel*] **hadst hearkened** [*if you had just listened and been obedient*] **to my commandments! then had thy peace been as a river** [*you would have had peace constantly flowing unto you*], **and thy righteousness as the waves of the sea** [*you would have been steady, constant*]:

19 **Thy seed also had been as the sand** [*your posterity could have been innumerable; exaltation*], and the offspring of thy bowels like the gravel thereof [*like the sand of the seashore*]; his name should not have been cut off nor destroyed from before me [*Israel could have had it very good and would not have been conquered*].

Next, in verse 20, the Lord invites all people to flee from wickedness. Remember, Babylon is often used in the scriptures to mean wickedness.

20 **Go ye forth of Babylon** [*quit wickedness*], **flee ye from the Chaldeans** [*Babylonians*], **with a voice of singing** [*be happy in your righteousness*] declare ye, tell this, utter it even to the end of the earth; **say ye, The LORD hath redeemed his servant Jacob** [*spread the word everywhere you go that the Atonement of Christ works*].

Next, the Savior reminds Israel that just as He brought forth water for the children of Israel in the desert, so also He can provide the refreshing living water of the gospel for all who are willing to partake.

21 And **they thirsted not when he led them through the deserts**

[*perhaps symbolic of the results of drinking "living water" (the gospel) as you follow the Savior through the barren world of the wicked*]: **he caused the waters to flow out of the rock** [*Exodus 17:6; symbolic of the Savior*] for them: he clave the rock also, and the waters gushed out.

One of the major messages of Isaiah's writings is summarized in verse 22, next.

22 **There is no peace, saith the LORD, unto the wicked**.

ISAIAH 49

Background

1 Nephi 21 is the Book of Mormon version of this chapter of Isaiah. As was the case with Isaiah 48, we will draw heavily from the Book of Mormon as we study Isaiah 49, here.

Isaiah continues his prophecy about the Messiah, and of the gathering of Israel in the last days. The prophecy includes the fact that the governments of many nations will assist in this gathering. In the last days, Israel will finally do the work she was originally called to do but failed to accomplish.

This particular chapter contains one of my personal favorite verses, verse 16, which contains beautiful Atonement symbolism. Beginning with verse 1, we will be taught

about the foreordination of covenant Israel and the responsibilities we have as the Lord's chosen people. Remember that "chosen" includes the concept that we are chosen to carry whatever burdens are necessary in order to spread the gospel and the priesthood throughout the earth.

Isaiah sets the stage for this prophecy by having us think of Israel as a person who is thinking about her past and feels like she has been a failure as far as her calling and mission from the Lord is concerned. Then she is startled by her success in the last days. Note that Isaiah says the same thing twice in a row, using different words, several times in this chapter. In verse 1, for example, he says "**Listen**, O isles unto me; and **hearken** . . ." As previously mentioned in this study guide, this was typical repetition for emphasis in Biblical culture.

1 **Listen, O isles** [*"isles" means "continents and nations throughout the world;" symbolic of scattered remnants of Israel throughout the world—see 1 Nephi 21:1*], **unto me**; and hearken, ye people, from far; **The LORD hath called me** [*Israel; see verse 3*] **from the womb** [*before I was born; foreordination*]; from the bowels of my mother [*from my mother's womb*] hath he made mention of my name [*Israel was foreordained in*

premortality to assist the Lord in His work].

2 And **he hath made my mouth like a sharp sword** [Israel is to be an effective instrument in preaching the gospel; the imagery of a sharp sword implies that the gospel is hard on the wicked but helps the righteous by cutting through falsehood]; in the shadow [protection] of his hand hath he hid me, and made me a polished shaft; in his quiver hath he hid me [Israel has been refined and prepared by the Lord to fulfill its calling];

3 And said unto me, **Thou art my servant, O Israel, in whom I will be glorified** [a prophecy that Israel will yet fulfill its stewardship].

In verses 4–12, Isaiah portrays Israel's loneliness and regrets because of rebellion and apostasy in times past. The prophecy also shows us the glorious blessings and responsibilities that await her as she repents.

In order to better appreciate what Isaiah is doing to portray Israel to us, you might picture an actor, representing Israel, dressed in black, sitting all alone on stage, with a single spotlight on her, speaking to the audience as she discusses her past failure to fulfill the mission the Lord gave her.

4 **Then I** [Israel] **said** [to myself],

I have laboured in vain, I have spent my strength for nought, and in vain [uselessly, in apostasy, false religions, and so on]: **yet surely my judgment is with the LORD** [German: the case against me is in God's hands], **and my work** [German: my office, my calling] **with my God** [German: is from God].

5 **And now, saith the LORD that formed** [foreordained] **me** [Israel, Abraham's posterity through Isaac] **from the womb to be his servant, to bring Jacob** [Israel] **again to him**, Though Israel be not gathered, yet shall I be glorious in the eyes of the LORD, and my God shall be my strength [those who try valiantly to convert and gather Israel will be blessed, whether or not Israel responds; similar to Nephi with respect to Laman and Lemuel in 1 Nephi 2:18–21].

Next, in verse 6, Israel tells us that the Lord not only wants her to bring the gospel to the scattered remnants of Israel, but to the whole world also.

6 **And he said, It is a light thing** [German: not enough of a load] **that thou shouldest be my servant** to raise up the tribes of Jacob [Israel], and **to restore the preserved** [remnants or survivors] **of Israel: I will also give thee for a light to the Gentiles** [you must also bring the gospel to everyone else; quite

a prophecy in Isaiah's day when almost any enemy nation could walk all over Israel], **that thou mayest be my salvation unto the end of the earth** [*the responsibility of members of the Church today; compare with Abraham 2:9–11*].

7 **Thus saith the LORD, the Redeemer of Israel**, and [*"and" is deleted in 1 Nephi 21:7*] his [*Israel's*] Holy One, **to him** [*Israel*] **whom man despiseth, to him whom the nation abhorreth** [*German: to the people despised by others*], **to a servant of rulers** [*you have been servants and slaves to many nations*], **Kings shall see** [*the true gospel as you fulfill your stewardship*] **and arise** [*out of respect for God*], **princes** [*leaders of nations*] **also shall worship** [*German: fall down and worship*], **because of the LORD** that is faithful, and the Holy One of Israel, **and he shall choose thee** [*German: who chose you*].

Next, Isaiah speaks prophetically of the future as though it had already happened. We are watching this prophecy being fulfilled.

8 **Thus saith the LORD, In an acceptable time** [*when the time is right, beginning with Joseph Smith and the Restoration*] **have I heard thee, and in a day of salvation have I helped thee**: and I will preserve thee, and give thee for a covenant of the people, **to establish the earth** [*to establish the gospel on the earth again*], **to cause to inherit the desolate heritages** [*the spiritual wildernesses caused by apostasy, in other words, the Lord will gather Israel and help Israel fulfill its stewardship as described in verse 6 above*];

9 **That thou mayest say to the prisoners** [*including the living and the dead in spiritual darkness*], **Go forth** [*Go free*]; to them that are in darkness, Shew yourselves [*German: Come out!*]. They shall feed in the ways, and their pastures shall be in all high places [*they will have it good when they repent and follow the true God*].

10 They shall not hunger nor thirst; neither shall the heat nor sun smite them: **for he** [*Christ*] that hath mercy on them **shall lead them**, even by the springs of water shall he guide them [*benefits of accepting and living the gospel*].

11 And **I will make all my mountains a way, and my highways shall be exalted** [*the high road of the gospel will be available to all; "mountains" could symbolize temples in the last days and during the Millennium, where the Lord teaches us the plan of salvation and provides ordinances of exaltation*].

12 Behold, **these** [*remnants of scattered Israel*] **shall come from far**: and, lo, these from the north and

from the west [*the gathering will be from all parts of the world*]; and these from the land of Sinim [*perhaps China but not certain; see Bible Dictionary, under "Sinim"*].

13 Sing, O heavens; and be joyful, O earth; and break forth into singing, O mountains: for **the LORD hath comforted his people, and will have mercy upon his afflicted** [*the Lord will eventually redeem Israel*].

With verse 14, next, Isaiah takes us back to Israel, who says, in effect, "Don't waste your effort trying to comfort me. I have failed and the Lord has given up on me."

14 **But Zion said** [*Israel hath said*], **The LORD hath forsaken me, and my Lord hath forgotten me** [*wicked Israel's complaint; 1 Nephi 21:14 adds "but he will show that he hath not" to this verse*].

Next, Isaiah says, in effect, "You think that a mother's bond to her nursing child is strong, but that is nothing compared to how much the Lord cares for Israel."

15 **Can a woman forget her sucking** [*nursing*] **child**, that she should not have compassion on the son of her womb? yea, **they** [*Israel*] **may forget, yet will I** [*the Lord*] **not forget thee** [*Israel*].

Verse 16, next, contains beautiful Atonement symbolism and demonstrates how much the Savior cares for all of us.

16 Behold, **I have graven thee upon the palms of my hands** [*In effect, I will be crucified for you. Just as a workman's hands bear witness of his profession, his type of work, so shall nail prints in My hands bear witness of My love for you.*]; **thy walls are continually before me** [*I know where you live, see you continuously, and I will not forget you*].

17 **Thy children** [*descendants*] **shall make haste;** [*"haste against," 1 Nephi 21:17*] **thy destroyers and they that made thee waste shall go forth of** [*flee from*] **thee** [*the tables will be turned in the last days*].

18 **Lift up thine eyes round about, and behold** [*look into the future*]: **all these** [*Israelites*] **gather themselves together, and come to thee** [*you thought you had no family left, but look at all your descendants in the future*]. **As I live** [*the strongest Hebrew oath or promise possible was to promise by the Living God*], saith the LORD, **thou shalt surely clothe thee with them all, as with an ornament, and bind them on thee, as a bride doeth** [*a bride puts on her finest clothing for the occasion; in other words, Israel will have many of her finest descendants in the last days*].

19 **For thy waste and thy desolate**

places, and the land of thy destruction [*where you've been trodden down for centuries*], **shall even now be too narrow by reason of the inhabitants** [*you will have so many Israelites, you'll seem to be running out of room for them all; latter-day gathering of Israel*], **and they** [*your former enemies*] **that swallowed thee up shall be far away.**

20 **The children** [*converts to the true gospel*] **which thou shalt have, after thou hast lost the other** [*child; through apostasy, war and so on*], **shall say again in thine ears, The place is too strait for me: give place to me that I may dwell** [*there is not enough room for us all*].

We see evidence of the rapid growth of the Church, as prophesied in these verses, in the ever expanding need for new chapels and temples for the Saints in our day.

21 **Then shalt thou** [*Israel*] **say in thine heart, Who hath begotten me these, seeing I have lost my children** [*where in the world did all these Israelites come from*], **and am desolate, a captive, and removing to and fro** [*scattered all over*]? **and who hath brought up these? Behold, I was left alone** [*I thought I was done for*]; **these, where had** [*have*] **they been?**

In verses 22–26, next, the Lord answers the question asked in verse 21, above, as to where all these future faithful Israelites will come from. The answer is simple and powerful. The Lord will use His power to gather them.

22 **Thus saith the Lord GOD, Behold, I will lift up mine hand to the Gentiles, and set up my standard** [*the true Church, gospel*] **to the people: and they** [*the Gentiles or non-Jews*] **shall bring thy sons in their arms, and thy daughters shall be carried upon their shoulders** [*the Lord will open the way and inspire people everywhere to help in gathering Israel*].

23 **And kings shall be thy nursing fathers, and their queens thy nursing mothers** [*leaders of nations will help gather Israel; for instance, as mentioned previously, Great Britain sponsored the return of the Jews to Palestine in 1948*]: **they shall bow down to thee with their face toward the earth, and lick up the dust of thy feet** [*the tables will be turned and they will show respect for you*]; **and thou shalt know that I am the LORD: for they shall not be ashamed** [*disappointed*] **that wait for** [*trust in*] **me.**

24 **Shall the prey be taken from the mighty, or the lawful** [*the Lord's covenant people*] **captive delivered** [*Israel asks how they can be freed from such powerful enemies*]?

25 **But thus saith the LORD,** Even **the captives** [*Israel*] **of the mighty** [*Israel's powerful enemies*] **shall be taken away** [*from the enemy*], **and the prey** [*victims*] **of the terrible** [*tyrants*] **shall be delivered** [*set free*]: **for I** [*the Lord*] **will contend with him that contendeth with thee, and I will save thy children** [*the covenant people; see 2 Nephi 6:17*].

26 **And I will feed them that oppress thee with their own flesh** [*your enemies will turn on each other and destroy themselves*]; and they shall be drunken with their own blood, as with sweet wine: and **all flesh shall know that I the LORD am thy Saviour and thy Redeemer,** the mighty One of Jacob.

ISAIAH 50

Background

This chapter can be compared with 2 Nephi 7. As with many other portions of Isaiah, this chapter speaks of the future as if it had already taken place. A major question here is who has left whom when people apostatize and find themselves far away from God spiritually. Another question that Isaiah asks is, essentially, "Why don't you come unto Christ? Has He lost His power to save you?"

It is in this chapter that we learn that one of the terrible tortures inflicted upon the Savior during His trial and crucifixion was the pulling out of His whiskers (see verse 6).

At the beginning of verse 1, the Lord asks, in effect, "Did I leave you, or did you leave me?"

1 Thus saith the LORD, **Where is the bill of your mother's divorcement, whom I have put away** [*where are the divorce papers, decreeing that I left you; in other words, do you think I would divorce you (break My covenants with you) and send you away from me like a man who divorces his wife*]? **or which of my creditors is it to whom I have sold you** [*was it I who sold you into slavery*]? Behold, for your iniquities have **ye sold yourselves** [*the real cause*], **and for your transgressions is your mother put away** [*you brought it upon yourselves*].

2 **Wherefore** [*why*], **when I** [*Jesus*] **came** [*to save my people*], **was there no man** [*who accepted me as Messiah; in other words, why did My people reject me*]? **when I called** [*"Come unto me"*], **was there none to answer** [*German: no one answered*]? **Is my hand shortened at all, that it cannot redeem? or have I no power to deliver** [*have I lost My power*]? **behold, at my rebuke** [*command*] **I dry up the sea** [*as with the*

parting of the Red Sea], **I make the rivers a wilderness**: their fish stinketh, because there is no water, and dieth for thirst [*no, I have not lost My power!*].

3 I clothe the heavens with blackness, and I make sackcloth [*a sign of mourning*] **their covering** [*I can cause the sky to be dark during the day, as if it were mourning the dead (which it will do at Christ's death; see Matthew 27:45)*].

4 The Lord GOD [*the Father*] **hath given me** [*Jesus*] **the tongue of the learned** [*Father taught Me well*], **that I should know how to speak a** [*strengthening*] **word in season to him** [*Israel; see 2 Nephi 7:4*] **that is weary**: he wakeneth morning by morning, he wakeneth mine ear to hear as the learned [*German: the Father is constantly communicating with Me and I hear as His disciple*].

5 The Lord GOD [*the Father*] **hath opened mine ear, and I was not rebellious, neither turned away back** [*I was obedient and did not turn away from accomplishing the Atonement*].

In verses 6–7, next, Isaiah prophesies some details surrounding Christ's crucifixion. In verse 6, especially, He speaks of the future as if it is past.

6 I gave my back to the smiters [*allowed Himself to be flogged; see Matthew 27:26*], **and my cheeks to them that plucked off the hair** [*pulled out the whiskers of My beard*]: **I hid not my face from shame and spitting** [*see Matthew 26:67*].

Here is a quote from Bible scholar Edward J. Young, (not a member of the Church) concerning the plucking of the beard, in verse 6, above:

"In addition the servant [*Christ, in Isaiah 50:6*] gave his cheeks to those who pluck out the hair. The reference is to those who deliberately give the most heinous and degrading of insults. The Oriental regarded the beard as a sign of freedom and respect, and to pluck out the hair of the beard (for *cheek* in effect would refer to a beard) is to show utter contempt." (*Book of Isaiah*, vol. 3, page 300.)

7 For the Lord GOD [*the Father*] **will help me; therefore shall I not be confounded** [*I will not be stopped*]: **therefore have I set my face like a flint** [*I brace Myself for the task*], **and I know that I shall not be ashamed** [*I know I will not fail*].

8 He [*the Father*] **is near that justifieth me** [*approves of everything I do*]; **who will** [*dares to*] **contend with me? let us** [*Me and those who would dare contend against Me*] stand together [*go to court, as in a court of law—go ahead and present your arguments against Me*]: **who is mine adversary? let him come near to me** [*face Me*].

9 **Behold, the Lord GOD** [*the Father*] **will help me** [*the Savior*]; **who is he that shall condemn me? lo, they** [*those who contend against Me*] **all shall wax old as a garment; the moth shall eat them up** [*the wicked will have their day and then fade away and reap the punishment*].

Next, in verse 10, the question is asked, in effect, "Who is loyal to the Lord and is not supported by Him?" The answer, as you will see, is no one.

10 **Who is among you that feareth** [*respects*] **the LORD**, **that obeyeth the voice of his servant, that walketh in darkness, and hath no light?** [*Answer: No one, because the Lord blesses His true followers with light.*] **let him trust in the name of the LORD, and stay upon** [*be supported by*] **his God.**

Verse 11, next, addresses all who decide that they can get along fine without God.

11 **Behold, all ye that kindle a fire, that compass** [*surround*] **yourselves about with sparks: walk in the light of your fire** [*try to live without God, according to your own philosophies*], **and in the sparks that ye have kindled** [*rather than Christ's gospel light*]. **This shall ye have of mine hand** [*German: you will get what you deserve*]; **ye shall lie down in sorrow** [*misery awaits those who try to live without God*].

ISAIAH 51

Background

The Lord now speaks to the righteous in Israel. Compare with 2 Nephi 8.

One of Satan's goals is to get people to believe that they have no basic worth, that they are simply a biological accident that has somehow developed an ability to think and move about. He teaches that there is no God and that when people die, that is the absolute end of them. In this chapter, Isaiah begins with an invitation for us to consider our origins, the marvelous heritage we have from Abraham and Sarah, and the reality of the hand of the Lord in our lives.

1 **Hearken to me, ye that follow after righteousness**, **ye that seek the LORD: look unto the rock whence** [*from whence; 2 Nephi 8:1*] **ye are hewn** [*look at the top-quality stone from which you originate*], **and to the hole of the pit** [*the rock quarry*] **whence ye are digged** [*consider your origins; you come from the finest stock*].

2 **Look unto Abraham your father, and unto Sarah** [*note that Abraham and Sarah are of equal importance*] **that bare you** [*your ancestors; in other words, your heritage is the finest*]: **for I called him alone** [*of his family, to renew the covenant line*], **and blessed him** [*see Abraham 2:9–11*], **and increased him**.

3 For **the LORD shall comfort Zion: he will comfort all her waste places; and he will make her wilderness like Eden, and her desert like the garden of the LORD** [*the Garden of Eden*]; **joy and gladness shall be found therein, thanksgiving, and the voice of melody** [*wonderful reward for the righteous*].

4 Hearken unto me, my people; and give ear unto me, O my nation: for a law shall proceed from me, and **I will make my judgment to rest for a light of the people** [*My laws will bring light to the nations*].

5 **My righteousness** [*triumph; ability to save*] **is near** [*is available to you*]; my salvation is gone forth, and mine arms shall judge the people [*I will personally rule over the nations*]; the isles [*nations of the world*] shall wait [*trust; rely*] upon me, and on mine arm [*My power*] shall they trust.

6 **Lift up your eyes to the heavens, and look upon the earth beneath**: for the heavens shall vanish away like smoke, and the earth shall wax old like a garment, and they that dwell therein shall die in like manner: but **my salvation** [*the salvation I bring*] **shall be for ever** [*will last forever*], and my righteousness [*triumph*] shall not be abolished [*compare D&C 1:38*].

7 **Hearken unto me, ye that know righteousness** [*you who are righteous*], the people **in whose heart is my law** [*you who have taken My gospel to heart*]; **fear ye not the reproach** [*insults*] **of men, neither be ye afraid of their revilings** [*stinging criticism*].

8 For **the moth shall eat them** [*the wicked who revile against the righteous*] **up like a garment, and the worm shall eat them like wool** [*they are just like moth-eaten clothing that will disintegrate and disappear*]: **but my righteousness** [*salvation and deliverance*] **shall be** [*will last*] **for ever**, and my salvation from generation to generation [*throughout eternity*].

The righteous now reply and invite the Lord's blessings and help in their lives, leading to salvation.

9 **Awake, awake** [*German: Now then, come, Lord*], **put on strength, O arm** [*symbolic of power*] **of the**

LORD; awake, as in the ancient days, in the generations of old [*please, Lord, use Thy power to save us like You did in olden days*]. Art thou not it that hath cut Rahab [*German: the proud; hath trimmed the proud down to size. Rahab can refer to the sea monster, Leviathan, in 27:1, which represents Satan and any who serve him, such as Egypt when the Israelites escaped them via the Red Sea.*], **and wounded the dragon** [*in other words, defeated Satan, see Revelation 12:7–9*]?

10 **Art thou not it which hath dried the sea** [*the Red Sea*], the waters of the great deep; **that hath made the depths of the sea a way** [*a path*] **for the ransomed** [*the children of Israel, whom the Lord ransomed from Egypt*] **to pass over**?

Next, Isaiah prophesies about the gathering of Israel in the last days.

11 **Therefore** [*because of the Lord's power*] **the redeemed of the LORD** [*Israel; those who will be saved*] **shall return** [*the gathering of Israel in the last days*], **and come with singing unto Zion**; and **everlasting joy shall be upon their head**: they shall obtain gladness and joy; and sorrow and mourning shall flee away [*the results of righteousness*].

Now the Lord speaks to righteous Israel, responding to their plea for help and reminding them again that He is their God and the One who will help them return.

12 **I, even I, am he that comforteth you: who art thou, that thou shouldest be afraid of a man that shall die** [*mortal men*], **and of the son of man** [*mortal men*] which shall be made as grass [*short-lived glory of evil mortal men; fear God, not man*];

13 **And forgettest the LORD thy maker**, that hath stretched forth the heavens, and laid the foundations of the earth [*how could you forget Me, your Creator!*]; and hast feared continually every day because of the fury of the oppressor, as if he were ready to destroy [*why should you live in fear of mortal men*]? and where is the fury of the oppressor [*the day will come when their fury won't be able to touch you*]?

14 **The captive exile hasteneth that he may be loosed, and that he should not die in the pit, nor that his bread should fail** [*the day will come when Israel will be set free, no more to die in captivity, and will have plenty*].

15 But **I am the LORD thy God, that divided the sea** [*parted the Red Sea*], whose waves roared: The LORD of hosts is his name [*is My name, 2 Nephi 8:15*].

16 And **I have put my words in thy mouth** [*I have given you My*

teachings], and **I have covered thee in the shadow** [*protection*] **of mine hand**, that I may plant the heavens, and lay the foundations of the earth [*I created heaven and earth for you*], **and say unto Zion, Thou art my people** [*you are My covenant people*].

17 **Awake, awake, stand up, O Jerusalem**, which hast drunk at the hand of the LORD the cup of his fury; thou hast drunken the dregs [*the bitter, coarse stuff that settles in the bottom of the cup*] of the cup of trembling, and wrung them out [*you have "paid through the nose" for your wickedness*].

Next, we are reminded that in times of apostasy, the people lose direction.

18 **There is none to guide her** among all the sons whom she [*Israel*] hath brought forth [*you have spent many years without prophets*]; neither is there any that taketh her by the hand of all the sons that she hath brought up.

The Book of Mormon provides much-needed help for understanding verse 19, next.

19 **These two things are come unto thee; who shall be sorry for thee** [*2 Nephi 8:19 changes this line considerably: "These two sons are come unto thee, who shall be sorry for thee"*]? **desolation, and destruction, and the famine, and**

the sword: by whom shall I comfort thee? [*This verse in the Book of Mormon seems to refer to the two prophets in the last days who will keep the enemies of the Jews from totally destroying them. See Revelation 11.*]

20 **Thy sons** [*your people*] **have fainted** [*German: are on their last leg, save these two, 2 Nephi 8:20*], **they lie at the head of all the streets, as a wild bull in a net** [*your wicked people are being brought down like a wild animal by a net of wickedness*]: **they are full of the fury of the LORD** [*they are catching the full fury of the Lord*], **the rebuke of thy God** [*the consequences of sin have caught up with them*].

21 **Therefore hear now this, thou afflicted, and drunken** [*out of control*], **but not with wine** [*rather with wickedness*]:

22 **Thus saith thy Lord the LORD, and thy God that pleadeth the cause of his people** [*I have not deserted you*], **Behold, I have taken out of thine hand the cup of trembling** [*I suffered the Atonement for you; see D&C 19:15–19*], **even the dregs of the cup of my fury; thou shalt no more drink it again** [*Christ will save the Jews in the last days, see 2 Nephi 9:1–2*]:

23 **But I will put it** [*the cup of his fury in verse 22*] **into the hand of**

them [*your enemies*] **that afflict thee**; which have said to thy soul [*have said to you*], Bow down, that we may go over [*lie down so we can walk on you*]: and thou hast laid thy body as the ground [*you did*], and as the street, to them that went over [*you have been walked all over, treated like dirt*].

ISAIAH 52

Background

Most of this chapter is essentially contained in 3 Nephi 20:30–44, although in different order. It is an invitation to come unto Christ and be gathered to Him with His covenant people, Zion. It begins with a focus on the gathering of the Jews to Jerusalem. The imagery is that of clothing oneself in the gospel of Jesus Christ.

1 **Awake, awake; put on thy strength** [*repent and take Christ's name upon you*], **O Zion; put on thy beautiful garments** [*return to proper use of the priesthood; see D&C 113:7–8*], **O Jerusalem**, the holy city: for henceforth there shall no more come into thee the uncircumcised and the unclean [*the wicked*].

2 **Shake thyself from the dust; arise** [*from being walked on, 51:23*], **and sit down** [*in dignity, redeemed at last*], **O Jerusalem: loose thyself from the bands of thy neck** [*come forth out of spiritual bondage*], O captive daughter of Zion.

Next, we get a brief review of why Israel has had troubles in the past.

3 For thus saith the LORD, **Ye have sold yourselves for nought** [*for nothing of value; in other words, apostatized*]; **and ye shall be redeemed without money** [*the hand of the Lord is in it*].

4 For thus saith the Lord GOD [*Jehovah*], **My people went down aforetime** [*a long time ago*] **into Egypt to sojourn** [*live*] there; **and the Assyrian oppressed them without cause** [*were not justified in how they treated Israel; they abused their power as did Babylon; see 47:6*].

Verse 5, next, emphasizes the need for redemption.

5 Now therefore, **what have I here,** saith the LORD, **that my people is taken away for nought** [*why have My people sold themselves into spiritual bondage for such worthless things (such as pride, wickedness, worshiping false gods, materialism)*]? **they that rule over them make them to howl,** saith the LORD; and **my name continually every day is blasphemed.**

Verse 6, next, foretells the day when Israel, including the Jews, will return to the Lord.

6 Therefore **my people shall know my name**: therefore they shall know in that day [*in the last days*] that I am he that doth speak: behold, it is I.

7 [*"And then shall they say,"* 3 Nephi 20:40, referring to the last days] **How beautiful upon the mountains are the feet of him that bringeth good tidings**, that publisheth peace; that bringeth good tidings of good, that publisheth salvation; that saith unto Zion, Thy God reigneth [*missionary work, gathering, etc.*]!

8 [*Compare with 3 Nephi 20:32*] **Thy watchmen** [*prophets, leaders*] **shall lift up the voice; with the voice together shall they sing: for they shall see eye to eye,** <u>when the LORD shall bring again Zion</u>. [*The underlined phrase is replaced in 3 Nephi 20:33 with "Then will the Father gather them together again and give unto them Jerusalem for the land of their inheritance."*]

9 [*"Then shall they,"* 3 Nephi 20:34] **Break forth into joy**, sing together, ye waste places of Jerusalem: **for the LORD** hath comforted his people, he **hath redeemed Jerusalem** [*will likely occur in the last days, near or at the beginning of the Millennium*].

10 The LORD [*the Father*, 3 Nephi 20:35] **hath made bare his holy arm** [*shown forth His power*] **in the eyes of all the nations**; and **all the ends of the earth shall see the salvation** [*the power to save and redeem*] of our God [*"of the Father; and the Father and I are one." 3 Nephi 20:35*].

Verse 11, next, provides direction for being among those who are gathered to the Father through the Savior.

11 [*And then shall a cry go forth*, 3 Nephi 20:41; referring to the last days] **Depart ye, depart ye, go ye out from thence** [*from among the wicked, D&C 38:42*], **touch no unclean thing; go ye out of the midst of her** [*Babylon, or wickedness*]; **be ye clean, that bear the vessels of the LORD** [*a major message of Isaiah*].

12 For **ye shall not go out with haste, nor go by flight** [*the gospel brings calmness*]: for **the LORD will go before you; and the God of Israel will be your rereward** [*rearward, protection; see D&C 49:27*].

13 Behold, **my servant** [*could be Joseph Smith Jr., 3 Nephi 21:10–11; page 428 of* Religion 121 Book of Mormon Student Manual*; or Christ; or modern servants, prophets of God; or all of the above working together to fulfill verse 15*] **shall deal prudently**, he shall be exalted and extolled, and be very high.

14 **As many were astonied** [*astonished*] **at thee; his visage was so**

marred more than any man [*the Savior as well as most prophets are highly praised by some, see verse 13, and much maligned by others*], and his form more than the sons of men:

15 **So shall he sprinkle** [*JST: gather*] **many nations; the kings shall shut their mouths at him**: for that which had not been told them shall they see; and that which they had not heard shall they consider [*see 3 Nephi 21:8; kings (powerful leaders) will not be able to stop the Lord's work in the last days*].

ISAIAH 53

Background

This chapter compares with Mosiah 14 in the Book of Mormon. It is a wonderful chapter, showing that a dominant part of the work of Old Testament prophets was teaching and prophesying about Christ.

Isaiah gives specific details about the Savior's mortal mission and gives a beautiful description of the blessings of the Atonement for each one of us. Among other insights, he teaches us that Jesus Himself derived great personal satisfaction in having performed the Atonement for us (verse 11).

Isaiah starts out with a bit of frustration over how few people take him and his fellow prophets seriously.

1 **Who hath believed our report** [*German: Who listens to us prophets anyway*]? and **to whom is the arm of the LORD revealed** [*who sees God's hand in things*]?

Beginning with the last part of verse 2, next, Isaiah speaks prophetically about the future, as if it has already taken place.

2 **For he** [*Jesus*] **shall grow up before him** [*possibly referring to the Father but could also refer to mankind as implied in the last phrase of verse 1*] **as a tender plant** [*a new plant, a restoration of truth*], **and as a root out of a dry ground** ["*dry ground*" *symbolizes apostate Judaism*]: **he** [*Jesus*] **hath no form nor comeliness** [*no special, eye-catching attractiveness*]; **and when we shall see him, there is no beauty that we should desire him** [*normal people couldn't tell He was the Son of God just by looking at Him*].

3 **He** [Jesus] **is despised and rejected of men; a man of sorrows** [*sensitive to people's troubles and pain*], **and acquainted with grief** [*He endured much suffering and pain*]: **and we hid as it were our faces from him** [*wouldn't even look at Him*]; **he was despised, and we** [*people in general*] **esteemed him not** [*German: paid no attention to him; even his own brothers rejected him at first; see John 7:5*].

4 **Surely he hath borne our**

griefs, and carried our sorrows [*the Atonement*]: **yet we did esteem him stricken, smitten of God, and afflicted** [*we didn't recognize Him as the Great Atoner; we rather thought He was just another criminal receiving just punishment from God*].

5 But **he was wounded for our transgressions** [*He suffered for our sins; see 2 Nephi 9:21*], **he was bruised for our iniquities** [*He suffered for our sins (double emphasis)*]: **the chastisement of** [*required for*] **our peace was upon him** [*He was punished so that we could have peace*]; and **with his stripes** [*wounds and punishments*] **we are healed** [*from our sins, upon repentance*].

6 **All we** like sheep **have gone astray; we have turned every one to his own way** [*every one of us has sinned; we all need the Atonement*]; **and the LORD** [*the Father*] **hath laid on him** [*the Savior*] **the iniquity of us all** [*2 Nephi 9:21*].

Isaiah continues to speak prophetically as if the future events he is foretelling have already taken place, thus emphasizing the fact that they will take place.

7 **He** [*Christ*] **was oppressed, and he was afflicted, yet he opened not his mouth** [*for instance, He wouldn't even speak to Pilate; see Mark 15:3*]: **he is brought as a lamb to the slaughter, and as a**

sheep before her shearers is dumb [*doesn't speak*], **so he openeth not his mouth**.

8 **He was taken from prison and from judgment** [*He was refused fair treatment*]: **and who shall declare his generation?** for **he was cut off out of the land of the living: for the transgression of my people was he stricken** [*He was punished for our sins*].

9 And **he made his grave with the wicked** [*He died with convicted criminals*], **and with the rich in his death** [*a rich man (Joseph of Arimathaea) donated his tomb; see John 19:38–42*]; **because he had done no violence** [*German: no wrong*], **neither was any deceit in his mouth** [*Christ was perfect*].

10 **Yet it pleased the LORD to bruise him** [*it was the Father's will to allow the Atonement to be performed by His Son*]; he hath put him to grief: **when thou** [*He, Christ*] **shalt make** [*makes*] **his soul** [*German: life*] **an offering for sin, he shall see his seed** [*His loyal followers, success; see Mosiah 15:10–12*], he shall prolong his days, and **the pleasure of the LORD** [*the Father's plan*] **shall prosper in his hand** [*will succeed through Christ's mission and Atonement*].

11 **He** [*Jesus*] **shall see** [*the results*] **of the travail** [*suffering*] **of his soul, and shall be satisfied** [*shall*]

have joy—*the Savior will have personal joy because of having performed the Atonement for us*]: **by his knowledge** [*by the knowledge He brings*] **shall my righteous servant** [*Christ*] **justify** [*save; prepare them to be approved by the Holy Ghost, sealed by the Holy Spirit of Promise*] **many; for he shall bear their iniquities.**

12 **Therefore will I divide him a portion with the great** [*He will receive His reward*], and **he shall divide the spoil** [*share the reward, in other words, we can be joint heirs with Him; see Romans 8:17*] **with the strong** [*the righteous*]; **because he hath poured out his soul unto death** [*laid down His life*]: and he was numbered with the transgressors; and he bare the sin of many, and made intercession for the transgressors.

ISAIAH 54

Background

This chapter deals with the last days and compares with 3 Nephi 22. A major message of this chapter is that in the last days, Israel will finally be righteous and successful.

1 **Sing, O barren** [*one who has not produced children; Israel, who has not produced righteous children*], thou that didst not bear; **break forth into singing, and cry aloud, thou that didst not travail** [*go into*

labor] **with child** [*in former days, you did not succeed in bringing forth righteous children, loyal to Christ*]: **for more are the children** [*righteous converts*] **of the desolate** [*perhaps meaning scattered Israel*] **than the children of the married wife** [*perhaps meaning Israelites who remained in the Holy Land; in other words, now in the last days, you've got more righteous Israelites than you ever thought possible, with almost all the converts coming from outside the land of Israel*], saith the LORD.

2 **Enlarge the place of thy tent** [*make more room*], and let them stretch forth the curtains of thine habitations: spare not, **lengthen thy cords, and strengthen thy stakes** [*the Church will greatly expand in the last days as righteous Israel is gathered*];

3 **For thou shalt break forth on the right hand and on the left** [*righteous Israel will show up everywhere*]; and **thy seed shall inherit the Gentiles, and make the desolate cities** [*cities without the true gospel*] **to be inhabited** [*Church membership will grow throughout the world*].

4 Fear not; for **thou shalt not be ashamed** [*you will not fail in the last days*]: neither be thou confounded; for thou shalt not be put to shame: for **thou shalt forget the shame of thy youth, and shalt**

not remember the reproach of thy widowhood any more [*you can forget the failures of the past when Israel was apostate; the once "barren" Church is going to bear much fruit in the last days*].

5 For **thy Maker is thine husband** [*you have returned to your Creator in the last days*]; the LORD of hosts is his name; and **thy Redeemer** the Holy One of Israel; The God of the whole earth shall he be called.

6 For **the LORD hath called thee as a woman forsaken and grieved in spirit** [*Israel has been through some very rough times*], **and a wife of youth, when thou wast refused** [*when you didn't bear righteous children*], saith thy God.

7 **For a small moment have I forsaken thee** [*because you apostatized*]; **but with great mercies will I gather thee** [*in the last days*].

8 In a little wrath I hid my face from thee for a moment [*when you rejected me*]; but **with everlasting kindness will I have mercy on thee**, saith the LORD thy Redeemer.

9 For **this** [*your situation*] **is as the waters of Noah** unto me: **for as I have sworn** [*promised*] **that the waters of Noah should no more go over the earth; so have I sworn that I would not be wroth with thee, nor rebuke thee** [*just as I promised not to flood the earth again, so I have promised to accept*

you back as you return to Me in the last days].

10 For the mountains shall depart, and the hills be removed; but **my kindness shall not depart from thee**, neither shall the covenant of my peace be removed, saith the LORD that hath mercy on thee. [*Isaiah reminds us here of the true nature of God, a very kind and merciful God indeed! Unfortunately, many people have not been correctly taught this truth.*]

Next, the Lord promises to prepare fine accommodations for righteous Israel in the last days, as well as in the celestial kingdom.

11 **O thou** [*Israel*] **afflicted, tossed with tempest, and not comforted** [*you have been through some very rough times*], behold, **I will lay thy stones with fair colours** [*I will use the finest "materials" for the restoration of the gospel in the last days and to build your "celestial homes"*], and lay thy foundations with sapphires [*precious gemstones*].

12 And I will make thy windows [*German: battlements*] of agates [*gemstones*], and thy gates of carbuncles [*bright, glittering gemstones*], and all thy borders of pleasant stones [*similar to the description of the celestial city in Revelation 21; you Israelites will have it very good, even better than*

you can imagine, when you repent and return unto Me to dwell].

13 And **all thy children shall be taught of the LORD; and great shall be the peace of thy children** [*likely referring to the Millennium; see D&C 45:58–59*].

14 **In righteousness shalt thou be established**: thou shalt be far from oppression; for thou shalt not fear: and from terror; for it shall not come near thee [*seems to refer to millennial conditions*].

15 Behold, they [*enemies of righteousness*] shall surely gather together, but not by me: **whosoever shall gather together against thee shall fall for thy sake** [*I will protect you, you will finally have peace*].

16 Behold, **I have created the smith** that bloweth the coals in the fire, and that bringeth forth an instrument for his work; **and I have created the waster** [*German: the Destroyer*] to destroy [*I created all things and have power over Satan. I can control all things; you are safe with Me*].

17 **No weapon that is formed against thee shall prosper**; and every tongue that shall rise against thee in judgment thou shalt condemn. **This is the heritage of the servants of the LORD**, and their righteousness is of me, saith the LORD [*there is safety for the righteous with Me*].

ISAIAH 55

Background

The Lord here invites all to come partake of the bounties of the gospel (which are equally available to all, either here on earth or afterward in the spirit world), and to enjoy eternity with Him.

1 **Ho** [*German: come now!*], **every one that thirsteth, come ye to the waters** [*the "living water"; in other words, Christ; see John 4:14, 7:37–38*], **and he that hath no money; come ye, buy** [*with your good works, keeping the commandments, and so forth*], **and eat; yea, come, buy wine and milk without money and without price** [*the gospel is available to all without regard to economic status*].

2 **Wherefore** [*why*] **do ye spend money for that which is not bread** [*not of true value*]? **and your labour for *that which* satisfieth not** [*why are you so materialistic*]? **hearken diligently unto me** [*the Lord*], **and eat ye that which is good** [*that which comes of Christ*], and **let your soul delight itself in fatness** [*the best; in other words, the richness of the gospel*].

3 **Incline your ear** [*listen carefully*], and **come unto me** [*Christ*]: hear, and your soul shall live [*you will receive salvation*]; and **I will make an everlasting covenant**

[the fulness of the gospel; see D&C 66:2] **with you,** even **the sure mercies of David** [German: the mercies and pardons of Christ spoken of by David; "David" is often used symbolically for Christ—see Isaiah 22:22; hence, "sure mercies of David" can mean the "sure mercies of Christ"].

4 **Behold, I have given him** [Christ] **for a witness to the people,** a leader and commander to the people.

There could be many different interpretations of verse 5, next. One possibility is presented here.

5 Behold, **thou** [Christ] **shalt call a nation that thou** [Israel] **knowest not, and nations** [the true Church in the last days] **that knew not thee** [weren't personally acquainted with ancient Israel] **shall run unto thee** [shall gather Israel] **because of the LORD** thy God [under the direction of the Lord], and for the Holy One of Israel; **for he** [Israel] **hath glorified thee** [God]. [In the last days, Israel will be gathered, will return to God, and be saved.]

Verses 6–7, next, are an invitation to repent and return to a kind, merciful God.

6 **Seek ye the LORD while he may be found,** call ye upon him while he is near:

7 Let the wicked forsake his way, and the unrighteous man his thoughts:

and let him return unto the LORD, and he [the Lord] will have mercy upon him; and to our God, for he will abundantly pardon.

Next, in verses 8–9, Isaiah again uses chiasmus in order to make a point. You may wish to read the background notes accompanying Isaiah chapter 3 in this study guide for some insights about chiasmus. In this case, the chiastic structure is brief, consisting of **A, B, C, C,' B,' A.'** You'll notice that **C** and **C'** are not the same; rather, they are related ideas, and thus still work in a chiasmus.

8 For my **thoughts (A)** are not your thoughts, neither are your **ways (B)** my ways, saith the LORD.

9 For as the **heavens (C)** are higher than the **earth (C'),** so are my **ways (B')** higher than your ways, and my **thoughts (A')** than your thoughts [come unto Me and live as I do, which way of life is much more satisfying than you can possibly comprehend].

10 For **as the rain cometh down, and the snow from heaven, and returneth not thither, but watereth the earth, and maketh it bring forth and bud, that it may give seed to the sower, and bread to the eater:**

11 **So shall my word be** [designed to bring forth exaltation] **that**

goeth forth out of my mouth: it shall not return unto me void, but **it shall accomplish that which I please**, and it shall prosper in the thing whereto I sent it [*My gospel will ultimately succeed; can also mean that those who receive the gospel into their lives will be greatly blessed*].

12 **For ye shall go out** [*from premortality to earth*] **with joy, and be led forth** [*to return home to God*] with peace: **the mountains and the hills shall break forth** before you **into singing, and all the trees of the field shall clap their hands** [*God's creations rejoice as their role in helping man achieve exaltation is fulfilled*].

13 **Instead of the thorn shall come up the fir tree, and instead of the brier shall come up the myrtle tree** [*the earth will eventually be celestialized; see D&C 130:9*]: **and it** [*the earth and many of its inhabitants' achieving celestial glory*] **shall be to the LORD for a name** [*will increase God's glory and dominion*], **for an everlasting sign** [*that God's promises are fulfilled and that man can achieve exaltation*] **that shall not be cut off** [*that will never end*].

ISAIAH 56

Background

Verses 1–8 extend the invitation (given in chapter 55) to exaltation to all, including Gentiles.

1 Thus saith the LORD, **Keep ye judgment, and do justice** [*be righteous*]: for my salvation is near to come, and my righteousness to be revealed.

2 **Blessed is the man that doeth this** [*the good mentioned in verse 1*], and the son of man that layeth hold on it [*who follows My counsel to live righteously*]; **that keepeth the Sabbath from polluting it, and keepeth his hand from doing any evil.**

3 **Neither let the son of the stranger** [*the Gentiles*], **that hath joined himself to the LORD** [*that has joined the Church, accepted and follows Christ*], **speak, saying, The LORD hath utterly separated me from his people** [*the Lord has made me a second-class citizen forever*]: **neither let the eunuch** [*see Bible Dictionary, under "eunuch"*] **say, Behold, I am a dry tree** [*I will never have children; eunuchs were not allowed into the congregation of Israel; see Deuteronomy 23:1*].

4 **For thus saith the LORD unto the eunuchs** [*symbolically represent a class of people that the Israelites despised and would never consider to be potential citizens of heaven*] **that keep my sabbaths, and choose the things that please me** [*keep my commandments*], **and take hold of my covenant** [*make*

and keep covenants of exaltation with Me];

5 Even unto them will I give in mine house *[temple; celestial kingdom]* **and within my walls** *[perhaps dual, meaning temples or heavenly home]* **a place and a name** *[King Benjamin promised his people a "name" in Mosiah 1:11; in other words, the name of Christ, Mosiah 5:8]* **better than of sons and of daughters** *[they will have more honor and glory in exaltation than they would have had from having sons and daughters on earth]*: **I will give them an everlasting name** *[a new name (see Revelation 2:17, D&C 130:11), symbolic of covenants of exaltation]*, **that shall not be cut off** *[eunuchs and all "outcasts" can be exalted too!]*.

6 Also the sons of the stranger *[Gentiles]*, **that join themselves to the LORD** *[make covenants]*, **to serve him, and to love the name of the LORD, to be his servants, every one that keepeth the Sabbath from polluting it, and taketh hold of my covenant** *[all Gentiles can receive exaltation if they keep the commandments]*;

7 Even them will I bring to my holy mountain *[God's kingdom]*, **and make them joyful in my house** of prayer: their burnt offerings and their sacrifices shall be accepted upon mine altar; for mine

house shall be called an house of prayer for all people *[celestial exaltation is available for all people who make covenants with the Lord and keep His commandments]*.

8 The Lord GOD which gathereth the outcasts of Israel *[the gathering of scattered Israel]* **saith, Yet will I gather others** *[Gentiles]* **to him** *[Israel]*, **beside those** *[Israelites]* **that are gathered unto him** *[Israel]*.

Isaiah switches topics now to the Gentile "beasts" who will come to "devour" (destroy) the wicked of Israel.

9 All ye beasts *[Gentile armies]* **of the field, come to devour** *[come to devour Israel]*, **yea, all ye beasts in the forest.**

10 His watchmen *[Israel's wicked leaders]* **are blind: they are all ignorant** *[of the dangers of wickedness]*, **they are all dumb dogs** *[not doing their job of warning the people of danger]*, **they cannot bark** *[they won't sound the alarm]*; **sleeping, lying down, loving to slumber** *[they are asleep on the job]*.

11 Yea, they are greedy dogs which can never have enough *[are never satisfied]*, **and they are shepherds that cannot understand** *[leaders who don't understand the seriousness of the situation]*: **they all look to their own way** *[look only after* *their own interests*], **every one for his gain**, from his quarter.

12 **Come ye, say they, I will fetch wine, and we will fill ourselves with strong drink** [*"Let's party!"*]; and to morrow shall be as this day, and much more abundant [*"And tomorrow we will have even a bigger and better party!"*].

ISAIAH 57

Background

In this chapter, Isaiah gives comfort to the righteous and a warning to the wicked. In verse 1, he addresses the issue that the righteous often suffer and no one seems to care. In verse 2, Isaiah gives counsel and comfort to the righteous.

1 **The righteous perisheth** [*the righteous suffer when the wicked rule; see D&C 98:7*], **and no man layeth it to heart** [*no one seems to care*]: and merciful men are taken away, none considering that the righteous is taken away from the evil to come.

2 **He** [*the righteous*] **shall enter into peace**: they shall rest in their beds [*or on their couches*], each one walking in his uprightness [*personal righteousness leads to inner peace here and peace in eternity*].

Beginning with verse 3, next,

Isaiah addresses the wicked.

3 **But draw near hither, ye sons of** [*followers of*] **the sorceress** [*people who live wickedly*], **the seed of** [*followers of*] **the adulterer and the whore** [*gross wickedness; used in 1 Nephi 22:14 to represent Satan's kingdoms*].

4 **Against whom do ye sport yourselves** [*whom are you mocking*]? **against whom make ye a wide mouth** [*making faces*], **and draw out the tongue** [*sticking your tongues out*]? **are ye not children of transgression** [*totally caught up in sin*], **a seed of falsehood** [*a bunch of liars*],

5 **Enflaming yourselves** [*sexually arousing yourselves*] **with idols under every green tree** [*German: You run to your gods with sexual arousal, referring to the use of prostitutes as part of pagan worship*], slaying the [*your*] **children in the valleys under the clifts of the rocks** [*killing your children as human sacrifices*]?

6 **Among the smooth stones of the stream** [*used for building altars for idol worship*] **is thy portion** [*German: you base your whole existence on your false gods, idols*]; they, **they are thy lot** [*you have chosen them over Me, therefore, you will have to depend on them for your reward*]: **even to them hast thou poured a drink**

offering [*part of idol worship that was originally revealed for worship of the true God—see Exodus 29:40; they have perverted proper worship ceremonies over to their idol worship*], **thou hast offered a meat offering** [*to your idols; see Exodus 29:41*]. Should I receive comfort in these [*do you expect Me to be happy about such perversions of true worship*]?

In verses 7 and 8, the Lord chastises Israel for breaking the seventh commandment literally by having sexual intercourse with temple prostitutes as part of pagan worship services. Symbolically, the Lord is the husband and Israel is the bride in the covenant relationship, symbolized by marriage. In these next verses, Isaiah uses the imagery of a wife being unfaithful to her husband and committing adultery.

7 **Upon a lofty and high mountain hast thou set thy bed**: even thither wentest thou up to offer sacrifice.

8 **Behind the doors also and the posts hast thou set up thy remembrance** [*German: statue*]: for **thou hast discovered** [*uncovered, exposed, undressed*] **thyself to another than me** [*you have "stepped out on Me," been unfaithful to Me*], and art gone up; **thou hast enlarged thy bed** [*made room*

for many false gods in your life*], **and made thee a covenant with them** [*you have given your loyalty to many false gods*]; thou lovedst their bed where thou sawest it.

9 **And thou wentest to the king** [*Molech, a large, brass idol with a hollow fire-pit stomach, used for sacrificing children*] **with ointment, and didst increase thy perfumes** [*you have worshipped the idol, Molech, with ointment and perfumes*], and didst send thy messengers far off, **and didst debase thyself even unto hell.** [*"You have traveled all the way to hell to find new and worse ways to commit sin!"; the Lord implies that they have made covenants with Satan himself.*]

10 **Thou art wearied in the greatness of thy way** [*you got tired trying to find worse ways to sin*]; **yet saidst thou not, There is no hope** [*but you didn't give up; rather, you said to yourself, "There has got to be something more wicked we can do!"*]: **thou hast found the life of thine hand** [*renewal of strength*]; **therefore thou wast not grieved** [*you kept striving for worse wickedness against all odds*].

11 **And of whom hast thou been afraid or feared, that thou hast lied** [*why have you respected false gods instead of Me*], **and hast not remembered me, nor laid it to thy heart** [*you don't even seem to be aware of Me*]? **have not I held**

my peace even of old, and thou fearest me not [*have I been too kind and gentle with you*]?

12 **I will declare** [*German: point out*] **thy** [*so-called*] **righteousness, and thy works; for they shall not profit thee** [I *will expose your so-called righteousness and good works; they won't save you*].

13 **When thou criest** [*cry out for help when you are in trouble*], **let thy companies** [*of idols*] **deliver** [*save*] **thee**; but the wind shall carry them all away [*your idols and false gods are no more secure and stable than a tumbleweed in the wind*]; vanity shall take them [*a puff of breath will blow them away*]: **but he that putteth his trust in me shall possess the land, and shall inherit my holy mountain** [*I do have power to save you and can give you great blessings*];

14 **And** [*I, the Lord*] **shall say**, Cast ye up, cast ye up [*German: make a highway, make a highway*], prepare the way [*clear the way*], take up the stumbling block out of the way of my people [*prepare the way for the return of My people—certainly foreshadowing the Restoration*].

15 For thus saith the high and lofty One [*the Lord*] that inhabiteth eternity, whose name is Holy; **I dwell in the high and holy place, with him also that is of a contrite and humble spirit** [*the contrite and humble will find safety and security with Me*], **to revive** [*German: refresh*] **the spirit of the humble, and to revive the heart of** [*give new courage to*] **the contrite ones.**

The word "contrite," used at the end of verse 15, above, not only means "humble," but also carries with it the connotation of "desiring to be corrected as needed."

16 For **I will not contend** [*against you*] **for ever**, neither will I be always wroth [*angry*]: for the spirit should fail before me [*if I did, all mankind would perish*], and the souls [*people*] which I have made [*no one would survive*].

17 **For the iniquity** [*because of the wickedness*] **of his** [*Israel's*] **covetousness** [*wicked greediness*] **was I wroth, and smote him**: I hid me [*I withdrew My spirit*], and was wroth, and he [*Israel*] went on frowardly in the way of his heart [*kept right on in his wicked ways*].

18 **I have seen his ways** [*probably referring to Israelites who repent with a contrite and humble spirit as mentioned in verse 15*], **and will heal him**: I will lead him also, and restore comforts [*comfort him*] unto him and to his mourners [*those Israelites who mourn for their sins, who repent*].

19 **I create the fruit of the lips** [*speech; German: I will create fruit*

of the lips that preaches:]; **Peace, peace to him** [*the righteous*] that is far off, and to him that is near, saith the LORD; and I will heal him [*the repentant, anywhere he is found*].

20 **But the wicked are like the troubled sea, when it cannot rest, whose waters cast up mire and dirt.**

21 **There is no peace, saith my God, to the wicked** [*a major message from the Lord through Isaiah*].

ISAIAH 58

Background

Verses 1–3 imply that the people have been complaining about not getting the blessings they want from the Lord, even though they keep the letter-of-the-law ordinances. The Lord responds in verses 4–5.

Verses 6–12 are some of the most beautiful found anywhere in scripture regarding the purposes of fasting and detailing some of the blessings of fasting as the Lord intends it to be.

Verses 13–14, likewise, describe the desired attitude about keeping the Sabbath holy.

1 **Cry aloud, spare not, lift up thy voice like a trumpet, and shew my people their transgression,** and the house of Jacob their sins

[*go ahead, Isaiah, tell the people why they aren't getting the desired blessings; tell them of their sins*].

2 **Yet they seek me daily** [*are going through the motions, doing all the rituals*], **and** [*appear to*] **delight to know my ways, as a nation that did righteousness, and forsook not the ordinance of their God** [*German: as if they were a nation who had not forsaken the ordinances of their God*]: **they ask of me the ordinances of justice** [*German: they demand their rights*]; **they take delight in approaching to God** [*German: want to debate with God and demand their rightful blessings*].

3 **Wherefore** [*why*] **have we fasted, say they, and thou seest not** [*You don't seem to notice*]? **wherefore have we afflicted our soul** [*why do we put our bodies through this pain*], **and thou takest no knowledge** [*You ignore it*]? [*God now answers their question:*] **Behold, in the day of your fast ye find pleasure** [*German: you do what you desire*], **and exact all your labours** [*German: make your employees work*].

4 Behold, **ye fast for strife and debate** [*your way of fasting causes contention*], and to smite with the fist of wickedness: **ye shall not fast as ye do this day, to make your voice to be heard on high** [*you*

cannot expect the Lord to bless you for such hypocritical fasting].

5 **Is it such a fast that I have chosen** [*do you really think such fasting pleases Me*]? a day **for a man to afflict his soul** [*German: do evil to his body*]? is it to bow down his head as a bulrush, and to spread sackcloth and ashes under him? **wilt thou call this a fast, and an acceptable day to the LORD** [*do you really think outward appearance is everything*]?

Next, in verses 6–12, we are taught principles of true fasting.

6 **Is not this the fast that I have chosen** [*let Me tell you the real purpose of the fast*]? **to loose the bands of wickedness** [*to help you grow in righteousness*], **to undo the heavy burdens** [*including those that are brought on by sin*], **and to let the oppressed** [*by sin*] **go free, and that ye break every yoke** [*break loose from every burden*]?

7 **Is it not to deal thy bread to the hungry** [*to feed the hungry*], **and that thou bring the poor that are cast out to thy house** [*to take care of the homeless*]? **when thou seest the naked, that thou cover him** [*to clothe the naked*]; **and that thou hide not thyself from thine own flesh** [*to help your own family and relatives*]?

8 **Then** [*when you do the above*] **shall thy light break forth as the morning,** and **thine health shall spring forth speedily:** and **thy righteousness shall go before thee; the glory of the LORD shall be thy rereward** [*rear guard; protection*].

9 **Then shalt thou call, and the LORD shall answer;** thou shalt cry [*pray*], and he shall say, Here I am. **If thou take away from the midst of thee the yoke** [*root out the evils from among you*], **the putting forth of the finger** [*pointing in a gesture of scorn*], **and speaking vanity** [*maliciously*];

10 **And if thou draw out thy soul** [*German: heart*] **to the hungry** [*help the hungry*], **and satisfy the afflicted soul** [*help the afflicted*]; **then shall thy light rise in obscurity** [*shine in the darkness*], and thy darkness be as the noonday [*instead of darkness, you will have light*]:

11 **And the LORD shall guide thee continually,** and satisfy thy soul in drought, and make fat thy bones [*strengthen you*]: and **thou shalt be like a watered garden, and like a spring of water, whose waters fail not** [*never cease*].

12 And they that shall be of thee shall build the old waste places [*German: and through you shall the old waste places be built*]: **thou shalt raise up the foundations of many generations; and thou**

shalt be called, **The repairer of the breach, The restorer of paths to dwell in** [*perhaps indicating that as Israel returns to the Lord and does the things prescribed in verses 6 and 7, then they will be the means of restoring the Church*].

Next we are taught the proper attitude about keeping the Sabbath day holy.

13 **If thou turn away** thy foot from the Sabbath, **from doing thy pleasure on my holy day** [*if you will do My will rather than your will on the Sabbath*]; **and call the Sabbath a delight** [*have a good attitude about the Sabbath*], the holy of the LORD, honourable; **and shalt honour him** [*the Lord*], **not doing thine own ways, nor finding thine own pleasure, nor speaking thine own words:**

14 **Then shalt thou delight thyself in the LORD** [*then you will have joy in the Lord*]; **and I will cause thee to ride upon the high places of the earth, and feed thee with the heritage of Jacob thy father** [*you will receive the Lord's choicest blessings, the blessings of Abraham, Isaac, and Jacob*]: for the mouth of the LORD hath spoken it [*this is a promise!*].

ISAIAH 59

Background

In this chapter Isaiah teaches us a lesson on the behaviors of the wicked and the motives and thought processes found in their minds and hearts. Then he teaches us about the Messiah and His role in intervening for our sins, if we choose to repent. Isaiah concludes by strongly emphasizing that the Lord will indeed save those who repent from their sins (verse 20).

Verse 1 explains that the Lord has not lost His power to save, and verses 2–8 explain that the Israelites have put distance between themselves and the Lord by their wicked behaviors.

1 Behold, **the LORD's hand is not shortened, that it cannot save**; neither his ear heavy [*deaf*], that it cannot hear [*the Lord has not lost His power to save, perhaps referring back to the people's questions in 58:3*]:

2 But **your iniquities have separated between you and your God**, and your sins have hid his face from you, that he will not hear [*your wickedness has separated you from God*].

3 For **your hands are defiled with blood** [*perhaps referring to their killing the prophets and others as implied in verse 7*], **and your fingers with iniquity** [*you've got your hands in all kinds of wickedness*]; **your lips have spoken lies** [*you are dishonest*], **your tongue hath muttered perverseness** [*German:*

unrighteousness; you are wicked through and through].

4 None calleth [seeks] for justice, nor any pleadeth for [desires; advocates] truth: they trust in vanity [man rather than God], and speak lies [are dishonest]; they conceive mischief [they are constantly dreaming up more ways to sin], and bring forth iniquity [their desires are to do evil continually].

5 They hatch cockatrice' eggs [they "hatch" all kinds of wickedness, like hatching poisonous snake eggs in their minds], and weave the spider's web [design entanglements in sin]: he that eateth of their eggs dieth, and that which is crushed breaketh out [hatches] into a viper [they are creating a menu for spiritual death and going from bad to worse].

6 Their webs [the things they've surrounded themselves with] shall not become garments [they cannot clothe themselves comfortably in wickedness], neither shall they cover themselves ["insulate" themselves] with their works [they will not "insulate" themselves from consequences of wickedness; they can't get completely comfortable in wickedness; see 28:20]: their works are works of iniquity, and the act of violence is in their hands.

7 Their feet run to evil [they are anxious to sin], and they make haste to shed innocent blood [they are anxious to kill their true prophets and others of the righteous]: their thoughts are thoughts of iniquity [evil desires are constantly on their minds]; wasting and destruction are in their paths [they are wasting away their lives, heading for disaster].

8 The way of peace they know not; and there is no judgment [justice] in their goings: they have made them [for themselves] crooked paths [they have created a very wicked and perverse lifestyle for themselves]: whosoever goeth therein shall not know peace [there is no peace for the wicked; compare with 57:21].

In verses 9–15, Israel admits guilt and faces the issue that they are behaving wickedly, like Alma the Younger did as described in Alma 36:13–14. This paves the way for the Atonement to work in their lives.

9 Therefore [for this reason] is judgment [fairness, integrity in our dealings with others] far from us, neither doth justice [charity, righteousness] overtake us: we wait for [look forward to] light, but behold obscurity [darkness]; for brightness, but we walk in darkness [because of our wickedness].

10 **We grope for the wall like the blind, and we grope as if we had no eyes** [*we are stumbling around in the dark (spiritual darkness)*]: **we stumble at noonday** as in the night; we are in desolate places as dead men [*we are as good as dead, we've about had it*].

11 **We roar all like bears** [*we are fierce*], **and mourn sore** [*plaintively*] **like doves** [*and have our sorrows*]: **we look for judgment** [*pleasant treatment*], **but there is none; for salvation, but it is far off from us** [*we are a long way away from God*].

12 For [*because we are so wicked*] **our transgressions are multiplied before thee, and our sins testify against us**: for our transgressions are with us [*we are dragging our sins around with us*]; **and as for our iniquities, we know** [*German: feel*] **them** [*we are aware of and acknowledge our sins*];

13 In **transgressing** and **lying** against the LORD [*making and then breaking covenants*], and **departing** away from our God, **speaking oppression** and **revolt, conceiving and uttering from the heart words of falsehood** [*our hearts have not been right before God*].

14 And **judgment is turned** away backward, and **justice standeth afar off**: for truth is fallen in the street [*our lifestyle is completely out of line*], and **equity** [*honesty*] **cannot enter** [*into our lives the way we are living them now*].

15 Yea, **truth faileth** [*is lacking*]; and **he that departeth from evil maketh himself a prey** [*When a person repents and turns from evil, he is mocked and becomes a victim in a wicked society. From here to the end of verse 21, Isaiah says that the Lord can now start redeeming Israel, because they have faced guilt, verses 9–15, and are turning from transgression, verse 20.*]: **and the LORD saw it, and it displeased him that there was no judgment.**

16 And **he saw that there was no man** [*no one besides Christ could do the job of redeeming Israel; similar to Revelation 5:3–4*], **and wondered that there was no intercessor: therefore his** [*the Lord's*] **arm brought salvation unto him** [*German: himself; Christ had the power within Himself; see 63:5*]; **and his** [*Christ's personal*] **righteousness, it sustained him** [*Christ*].

17 **For he** [*Christ*] **put on righteousness** as a breastplate, and an helmet of salvation upon his head [*breastplate and helmet are armor and imply intense attacks by the enemies of righteousness*]; and he put on the garments of vengeance for clothing [*Christ can save us through His righteousness and power of salvation (the law*

of mercy), or punish us (according to the law of justice, sometimes referred to as "vengeance"), depending on our deeds as stated in verse 18], and was clad with zeal as a cloke [Christ is completely able to be the Intercessor desired in verse 16].

18 **According to their deeds, accordingly he will repay** [the law of the harvest], fury to his [Christ's] adversaries, recompence [Alma 41:4] to his enemies; to the islands [all continents, nations] he will repay recompence [emphasis is on "recompence," or giving them what they have earned].

19 **So shall they fear** [includes the idea of respect, reverence] **the name of the LORD** from the west, and his glory from the rising of the sun [from east to west, everywhere]. When the enemy [German: the Lord] shall come in like a flood [the judgments of God will come quickly to the whole earth, "islands" in verse 18], the Spirit of the LORD shall lift up a standard against him [the enemies; the wicked in verse 18].

20 And **the Redeemer shall come to Zion, and unto them that turn from** [repent from] **transgression** in Jacob [among the house of Israel], saith the LORD [the righteous will live with Christ; implies Millennium].

21 **As for me** [the Lord], **this is my covenant with them** [those who have turned away from sin, verse 20], saith the LORD; **My spirit** that **is upon thee**, and **my words** [the fulness of the gospel] which I have put in thy mouth, **shall not depart out of thy mouth**, nor out of the mouth of thy seed, nor out of the mouth of thy seed's seed, saith the LORD, from henceforth and for ever [an everlasting covenant which will see ultimate fulfillment with those who attain exaltation in the celestial kingdom].

ISAIAH 60

Background

Isaiah now prophesies that in the last days the Church of Jesus Christ will arise, shine forth, and be a light to the nations as taught in Isaiah 5:26, as well as other places. Ultimately, all those who have chosen to join with the Lord and become part of covenant Israel will enjoy celestial glory with Him forever.

1 **Arise, shine; for thy light is come** [the time for the restoration of the gospel through the Prophet Joseph Smith has come], **and the glory of the LORD is risen upon thee.**

2 **For, behold, the darkness** [spiritual darkness in the last days, see Teachings of the Prophet Joseph Smith, page 47] **shall cover the**

earth, and gross darkness the people: **but the LORD shall arise upon thee, and his glory shall be seen upon thee** [*the restored Church; Zion in the last days*].

3 And **the Gentiles shall come to** [*German Bible: walk in*] **thy light, and kings to the brightness of thy rising** [*German: to the brightness that has come upon you*].

4 Lift up thine eyes round about, and see: **all they gather themselves together, they come to thee** [*Israel, Zion*]: **thy sons** [*converts*] **shall come from far, and thy daughters** [*converts*] **shall be nursed at thy side** [*people will gathered to Zion from far and near, and will be nourished by the true gospel of Jesus Christ*].

5 **Then thou shalt see, and flow together** [*be radiant, be happy*], **and thine heart shall fear** [*German: be surprised, thrill*], **and be enlarged** [*swell; rejoice*]; because the abundance of the sea [*multitude*] shall be converted unto thee [*Zion*], the forces [*wealth*] of the Gentiles shall come unto thee.

In these verses, we see, among other things, that the restored Church will become prosperous in the last days.

6 The multitude of camels shall cover thee, the dromedaries [*young camels*] of Midian and Ephah [*parts of Jordan and Saudi Arabia*]; all

they from Sheba [*part of Saudi Arabia*] shall come: **they shall bring gold and incense** [*similar to when the Wise Men came to Christ; perhaps symbolic of when people come to Christ*]; **and they shall shew forth the praises of the LORD** [*people from these Arabic countries will come unto Christ; symbolic of people from all nations coming to Christ in the last days*].

7 All the flocks [*perhaps symbolic of converts*] of Kedar [*Syria*] shall be gathered together unto thee, the rams [*strong men, leaders, chiefs*] of Nebaioth shall minister unto thee [*Israel in the last days*]: **they** [*people out of all nations*] **shall come up with acceptance on mine altar** [*shall become acceptable to Me*], and I will glorify the house of my glory.

8 **Who are these that fly as a cloud**, and as the doves to their windows [*who are these people who flock into the Church from over the sea (the gathering)*]?

9 Surely **the isles** [*nations*] **shall wait** [*German: trust in; look forward eagerly*] **for me**, and the ships of Tarshish first, to bring thy sons [*converts*] from far, **their silver and their gold with them**, unto the name of the LORD thy God, and **to the Holy One of Israel**, because he hath glorified thee [*Israel; the true Church*].

10 **And the sons of strangers** [*foreigners*] **shall build up thy walls** [*will help build up Zion*], and **their kings shall minister unto thee** [*leaders of foreign governments will help the spread of the Church in the last days*]: for in my wrath I smote thee [*in times past, I've had to severely discipline you*], but in my favour have I had mercy on thee [*but in the last days as you (Israel) return to Me, you will partake of My mercy*].

11 **Therefore thy gates** [*as in city gates, closed as needed for defense*] **shall be open continually** [*you will not fear attack by enemies*]; they shall not be shut day nor night; that men may bring unto thee the forces [*wealth*] of the Gentiles, and that their kings may be brought [*German: that their kings may be brought to you also*].

12 For **the nation and kingdom that will not serve thee** [*Zion, in the last days, and as the Millennium begins*] **shall perish**; yea, those nations shall be utterly wasted.

Remembering that Isaiah often uses trees to symbolize people is helpful in understanding verse 13, next.

13 **The glory** [*the best of*] **of Lebanon** [*the Holy Land*] **shall come unto thee**, the fir tree, the pine tree, and the box together, to beautify the place of my sanctuary [*temple*]; and I will make the place of my feet [*footstool, earth, temple*] glorious.

14 **The sons also of them** [*your former enemies*] **that afflicted thee shall come bending unto thee**; and all they that despised thee shall bow themselves down at the soles of thy feet [*your former enemies and oppressors will humbly respect you*]; **and they shall call** [*acknowledge*] **thee, The city of the LORD, The Zion of the Holy One of Israel.**

15 **Whereas thou hast been forsaken and hated** [*in the past*], so that no man went through thee [*people hated you and avoided you*], **I will make thee an eternal excellency, a joy of many generations.**

16 **Thou shalt also suck the milk of** [*be nourished and assisted by*] **the Gentiles, and** shalt suck the breast of [*be nourished and assisted by*] **kings**: and **thou shalt know that I the LORD am thy Saviour and thy Redeemer**, the mighty One of Jacob [*in other words, the God of Abraham, Isaac, and Jacob*].

The basic message of verse 17, next, is that the gospel of Jesus Christ brings the very best into our lives.

17 **For** [*instead of*] **brass I will bring gold**, and **for** [*instead of*] **iron** I will bring **silver**, and for

[*instead of*] wood brass, and for [*instead of*] stones iron [*you will prosper*]: **I will also make thy officers** [*leaders*] **peace, and thine exactors** [*rulers*] **righteousness** [*righteous leaders will bless our lives in the Church in the last days; also, during the Millennium, Christ will be assisted by the righteous Saints as leaders and rulers; see Revelation 20:4*].

18 **Violence shall no more be** heard in thy land, wasting nor destruction within thy borders [*wonderful peace awaits the righteous*]; but thou shalt call thy walls Salvation [*you will be surrounded with peace and salvation*], and thy gates Praise.

19 The sun shall be no more thy light by day; neither for brightness shall the moon give light unto thee: but **the LORD shall be unto thee an everlasting light**, and thy God thy glory [*some conditions in New Jerusalem will be similar to conditions in the celestial glory as described in Revelation 21:23 and 22:5*].

20 Thy sun shall no more go down; neither shall thy moon withdraw itself: for the LORD shall be thine everlasting light, and **the days of thy mourning shall be ended** [*your earthly sorrows will be over*].

Next, we are taught that the righteous will inherit the earth forever. We know that this earth will be celestialized and become the celestial kingdom for those from our world who are worthy of it (see D&C 130:9).

21 Thy people also shall be all righteous: they shall inherit the land [*earth*] **for ever** [*D&C 88:17–20; 130:9*], the branch of my planting, the work of my hands [*the righteous*], that I may be glorified.

22 **A little one** [*a seemingly unimportant, insignificant person*] **shall become a thousand**, and a small [*insignificant*] one **a strong nation** [*perhaps referring to "a continuation of the seeds (children) forever," D&C 132:19; eternal posterity for those who gain exaltation*]: I the LORD will hasten it [*act quickly*] in his [*My*] time [*the Lord will act quickly to bestow these blessings when the time is right*].

ISAIAH 61

Background

Isaiah here describes Christ's authority, power, and the purposes of His earthly ministry. The Savior quoted verse 1 and the first phrase of verse 2 in Luke 4:18–19 as He stood and read from Isaiah, identifying Himself as the Messiah to those assembled in the synagogue at Nazareth. They were incensed and attempted to throw Him off a cliff.

1 **The Spirit of the Lord GOD** [*Jehovah—see footnote 1b in your*]

Bible] **is upon me;** because **the LORD hath anointed me** [*My mission, calling, is*] **to preach good tidings** [*the gospel*] **unto the meek; he hath sent me to bind up** [*apply first aid; to heal*] **the brokenhearted, to proclaim liberty to the captives** [*those in spiritual bondage here and in spirit prison*], **and the opening of the prison** [*spirit prison; spiritual blindness*] **to them that are bound;**

2 **To proclaim the acceptable year** [*the time designated by the Father for Me to perform My earthly missions—see Bruce R. McConkie,* Doctrinal New Testament Commentary, *vol. 1, page 161*] **of the LORD, and the day of vengeance of our God;** [*this phrase refers to the destruction of the wicked at the Second Coming*] **to comfort all that mourn;**

3 **To appoint** [*extend compassion*] **unto them that mourn in Zion,** to give unto them **beauty for** [*in place of*] **ashes,** the **oil of joy for** [*in place of*] **mourning,** the garment of **praise for** [*in the place of*] **the spirit of heaviness** [*depression*]**; that they might be called trees of righteousness,** [*righteous people in the Lord's garden*] **the planting** [*people, work*] of the LORD, **that he might be glorified** [*that He might bring people to live in exaltation with Him eternally; compare with Moses 1:39*].

4 And they [*the righteous in the last days*] shall build the old wastes,

they shall raise up the former desolations, and **they shall repair the waste cities, the desolations of many generations** [*in last days Zion will be built up again*].

5 **And strangers** [*foreigners, your former enemies*] **shall stand and feed your flocks,** and the sons of the alien [*foreigner*] shall be your plowmen and your vinedressers [*the tables are turned, former enemies will be your servants now*].

6 **But ye shall be named the Priests of the LORD:** [*make covenants leading to exaltation*] men shall call you **the Ministers of our God:** [*you will have priesthood authority*] ye shall eat the riches of the Gentiles, and in their glory [*wealth*] shall ye boast [*German: enjoy*] yourselves.

7 **For** [*in place of*] **your shame** [*German: humiliation in times past*]**; ye shall have double** [*a reference to the birthright blessing; in other words, exaltation; see D&C 132:20*]**; and for** [*in place of*] **confusion they** [*righteous Israel in the last days and beyond*] **shall rejoice in their portion** [*reward*]**:** therefore in their land they shall possess the double [*birthright blessing; see Deuteronomy 21:17*]**: everlasting joy shall be unto them.**

8 **For I the LORD love judgment** [*justice, righteousness*]**, I hate robbery** [*plundering*] **for** [*in place*

of] **burnt offering** [*I hate hypocrisy, evil lifestyles, combined with empty worship rituals with which people try to look righteous*]; and **I will direct their work in truth, and I will make an everlasting covenant with them.**

9 And their seed [*the righteous*] **shall be known among the Gentiles** [*the gospel will spread to all nations*], **and their offspring among the people: all that see them shall acknowledge** [*recognize*] **them, that they are the seed which the LORD hath blessed** [*they are the people of the Lord, those who receive the blessings of Abraham as promised in Abraham 2:8–11*].

Next, in verses 10–11, we see rejoicing and singing songs of praise to the Lord. This can have dual or triple or quadruple meaning, which is typical of Isaiah's words. For example, it can be Isaiah who is rejoicing, or Zion, or any of the righteous in the last days, or anyone who attains exaltation. And, no doubt, you can come up with additional possibilities.

10 I [*Isaiah or Zion or other*] **will greatly rejoice in the Lord, my soul shall be joyful in my God; for he hath clothed me with the garments of salvation** [*2 Nephi 4:33–35, similar to Nephi's rejoicing in the Lord*], **he hath covered me with the robe of righteousness, as a bridegroom decketh himself with ornaments**

[*German: priestly clothing; Hebrew: mitre or cap; see Exodus 39:28 footnote b*], **and as a bride adorneth herself with her jewels.**

Reference to garments, robes, priestly "ornaments" or cap, in verse 10, above, points one's mind to ordinances of exaltation in temples today.

11 For as the earth bringeth forth her bud, and as the garden causeth the things that are sown in it to spring forth; so the Lord GOD will cause righteousness [*victory of Zion*] **and praise** [*of Zion, Israel*] **to spring forth before** [*among*] **all the nations** [*the Lord will restore Israel and will again make the blessings of exaltation available in the last days*].

ISAIAH 62

Background
This chapter deals with the gathering of Israel in the last days, and the fact that earth will have true prophets of God again. The gathering will be the result of the preaching of the gospel throughout the world. People will once again become part of the covenant people of the Lord, which is another way of saying that they will be saved.

1 For Zion's sake will I not hold my peace [*remain silent*], **and for Jerusalem's sake I will not rest** [*remain silent*], **until the righteousness thereof** [*victory of*

Zion] **go forth as brightness** [*very noticeable, beautifully conspicuous*], **and the salvation thereof as a lamp that burneth** [*flaming torch; in other words, the restored gospel will be a light for all who chose to come unto Christ*].

2 **And the Gentiles shall see thy** [*Zion's*] **righteousness, and all kings** [*world leaders*] **thy glory**: and **thou shalt be called by a new name** [*symbolic of having made covenants with God, which, when kept, lead to life in celestial glory; see D&C 130:11; Revelation 2:17*], which the mouth of the LORD shall name.

3 **Thou shalt also be a crown of glory** [*symbolic of exaltation; see Revelation 4:4; 2 Timothy 4:8*] **in the hand of the LORD**, and a royal diadem [*crown, symbolic of royal power and authority*] in the hand of thy God.

4 **Thou shalt no more be termed Forsaken** [*you will never again be forsaken*]; neither shall thy land any more be termed Desolate: **but thou shalt be called Hephzi-bah** [*JST: delightful*], **and** thy land **Beulah** [*the married wife; you will belong to the Lord and the Lord to you*]: for the LORD delighteth in thee, and **thy land shall be married** [*you will belong to the Lord; you will be His covenant people*].

5 **For as a young man marrieth a virgin, so shall thy sons** [*JST: God*] **marry thee**: and as the bridegroom rejoiceth over the bride, so shall thy God rejoice over thee.

Remember that Isaiah is speaking prophetically of the future as if it has already happened.

6 **I have set watchmen** [*latter-day prophets*] **upon thy walls, O Jerusalem, which shall never hold their peace** [*remain silent*] **day nor night** [*in other words, there will again be continuous revelation*]: **ye that make mention of the LORD** [*you who pray and worship the Lord*], **keep not silence,**

7 And **give him** [*the Lord*] **no rest** [*don't stop praying*], **till he** [*the Lord*] **establish, and till he** [*the Lord*] **make Jerusalem** [*Zion, the Lord's covenant people in the last days*] **a praise in the earth** [*highly respected throughout the earth*].

Verses 8–9, next, appear to describe conditions during the Millennium.

8 **The LORD hath sworn by his right hand** [*has covenanted*], and by the arm of his strength, **Surely I will no more give thy corn** [*crops*] **to be meat** [*food*] **for thine enemies**; and the sons of the stranger [*foreigners, Gentiles*] shall not drink thy wine, for the which thou hast laboured [*in other words, you will live in peace with Me*]:

9 **But they that have gathered** [*harvested*] **it shall eat it, and praise** [*give thanks to*] **the LORD**; and they that have brought it [*made it*] together shall drink it in the courts of my holiness [*you will enjoy the fruits of your labors in peace in My holy kingdom*].

10 **Go through, go through the gates** [*come to Zion, via the gates—baptism and other gospel ordinances, coupled with righteous living*]; **prepare ye the way of the people; cast up, cast up the highway** [*the highway to Zion, the way to God, will be built up*]; **gather out the stones** [*remove the stumbling blocks*]; **lift up a standard** [*ensign, or the restored gospel of Jesus Christ*] **for the people.**

11 **Behold, the LORD hath proclaimed unto the end of the** [*all of the*] **world, Say ye to the daughter of Zion** [*Jerusalem, the righteous*], **Behold, thy salvation** [*your Deliverer*] **cometh; behold, his** [*Christ's*] **reward** [*He brings your reward with Him when He comes*] **is with him, and his work before him.**

12 **And they shall call them** [*the righteous will be referred to as*], **The holy people, The redeemed of the LORD**: and thou [*righteous Israel*] shalt be called, Sought out, A city not forsaken

[*chosen by the Lord to be blessed and enjoy His help*].

ISAIAH 63

Background

This is one of the better-known chapters of Isaiah, particularly because it informs us that the Savior will wear red (either literally or symbolically) when He comes at the time of the Second Coming (see verses 1–2). The red represents the blood of the wicked, who are destroyed at His coming. Verses 3–6 continue the theme of the destruction of the wicked at that time.

Isaiah is a master at using comparison and contrast for teaching purposes. Thus, beginning with verse 7, he compares the horror of the wicked, depicted in the first six verses, with the blessed state of the righteous, who will receive the promised blessings of peace and safety when the Lord returns.

1 **Who is this** [*Christ*] **that cometh** [*the Second Coming*] **from Edom** [*from the east; travelers from the east to Jerusalem usually came north past the Dead Sea and then west to Jerusalem. From Edom could also mean from the east, or heaven; see D&C 133:46*], **with dyed** [*red—see verse 2*] **garments** [*clothing*] from Bozrah [*the capital city of Edom*]? this **that is glorious in his apparel** [*Christ comes in*

glory], **travelling in the greatness of his strength** [*Christ comes in great power at the Second Coming*]? **I** [*Christ; "It is I," the Savior*] **that speak in righteousness, mighty to save** [*the repentant*].

2 **Wherefore** [*why*] **art thou red in thine apparel** [*what is the red spattered all over Your clothing; see D&C 133:51*], **and thy garments like him that treadeth in the winefat** [*Hebrew: press, in other words, the wine press and the vat for collecting the juice of the grapes or olives*]?

Next, the Savior answers the question posed in verses 1–2, above, as to who He is.

3 **I have trodden the winepress alone** [*I was the only one capable of doing the Atonement*]; **and of** the people **there was none with me** [*I had to do it alone*]: **for** [*the reason that My clothing is red is that*] **I will tread them** [*the wicked*] **in mine anger, and trample them in my fury; and their blood** [*the blood of the wicked—see D&C 133:51*] **shall be sprinkled upon my garments, and I will stain all my raiment** [*judgment will be thorough*].

4 **For the day of vengeance is in mine heart** [*German: is part of My task, My responsibility*], **and the year of my redeemed is come** [*the time has come for the righteous*

to be set free from the cares of a wicked world, perhaps referring to the Millennium*].

Another way to look at the phrase "the day of vengeance is in mine heart," in verse 4, above, is to say "the law of justice is also in My heart"; in other words, the law of justice is a vital part of the plan of salvation (see Alma 42:25).

5 **And I looked, and there was none to help** [*no mortal; no one could help Me do the Atonement*]; **and I wondered that there was none to uphold** [*I had to do it alone—see Matthew 27:46*]: **therefore mine own arm** [*the power was within Me*] **brought salvation unto me**; and my fury [*My own divine strength*], it upheld me.

6 **And I will tread down the people** [*the wicked*] **in mine anger, and make them drunk in my fury** [*judgment, the law of justice, will fall upon the wicked*], **and I will bring down their strength to the earth** [*I will humble the wicked*].

Isaiah now switches topics and turns to the kindness and blessings of the Lord to the righteous. In so doing, he will review some of Israel's rebellious past.

7 **I will mention the lovingkindnesses of the LORD**, and the praises of the LORD, according to all that the LORD hath bestowed on

us, and the great goodness toward the house of Israel, which he hath bestowed on them according to his mercies, and according to the multitude of his lovingkindnesses.

8 For he said, **Surely they are my people**, children that will not lie [*German: people of integrity*]: **so he was their Saviour.**

9 **In all their affliction he was afflicted** [*He suffered and paid for their sins*], **and the angel of his presence saved them** [*the Lord rescued the children of Israel from Egypt*]: **in his love and in his pity he redeemed them; and he bare them, and carried them all the days of old** [*see D&C 133:53–55, referring to righteous*].

10 **But they** [*the children of Israel*] **rebelled, and vexed his holy Spirit: therefore he was turned to be their enemy, and he fought against them.** [*He had to discipline them severely*]

11 **Then he remembered,** [*His people remembered—see footnote 11a in your Bible*] **the days of old, Moses, and his people, saying, Where is he that brought them** [*us*] **up out of the sea** [*the parting of the Red Sea*] **with the shepherd** [*leaders—see footnote 11c in your Bible*] **of his flock? where is he that put his holy Spirit within him?** [*within them—see footnote 11e in your Bible*];

Isaiah is reminding the people that they had been greatly blessed by the Lord in times past (verses 11–14), in contrast to wicked Israel's punishments in Isaiah's day and for centuries since then.

12 **That led them by the right hand of Moses** with his glorious arm, dividing the water [*parting the Red Sea*] before them, to make himself an everlasting name?

13 **That led them** [*children of Israel*] **through the deep** [*Red Sea*], as [*easily as a*] an horse in the wilderness [*walks along in the desert*], **that they should not stumble** [*be stopped*]?

14 **As a beast goeth** [*as cattle walk easily*] **down into the valley, the Spirit of the LORD caused him** [*them, the Israelites*] **to rest:** so didst thou lead thy people, to make thyself a glorious name [*You led Your people and became famous among surrounding nations as a result*].

Next, Isaiah pleads with the Lord to bless Israel.

15 **Look down from heaven, and behold from the habitation of thy holiness** [*German: from Your heavenly home*] **and of thy glory: where is thy zeal and thy strength, the sounding of thy bowels** [*Thy tenderness*] **and of**

thy mercies toward me? are they restrained?

16 **Doubtless thou art our father, though Abraham be ignorant of us, and Israel acknowledge us not** [*Abraham is long since dead, can't help us. Jacob is long since dead, can't help us*]: **thou, O LORD, art our father, our redeemer**; thy name is from everlasting [*German: You have been our Redeemer since the beginning*].

17 **O LORD, why hast thou made** [*JST: "suffered," (allowed)*] **us to err from thy ways, and hardened** [*allowed us to harden*] **our heart from thy fear** [*German: to the point that we no longer feared You*]? **Return for thy servants' sake, the tribes of thine inheritance** [*let us be Thy people again*].

18 **The people of thy holiness** [*covenant Israel*] **have possessed it** [*the temple*] **but a little while**: our adversaries have trodden down thy sanctuary [*the temple, D&C 64:11; in other words, enemies have possessed the temple more than we have through the ages*].

19 **We are thine: thou never barest rule over them** [*German: we have become just like people over whom You have never ruled*]; **they were not called by thy name** [*like people who are not*

Your covenant people, not bearing Your name.].

ISAIAH 64

Background

Isaiah continues the theme of 63:15, desiring that the Lord would come down now and rule over Israel. Isaiah, in effect, has Israel pleading with the Lord to come again, as promised (the Second Coming— see heading to this chapter in your Bible).

1 **Oh that thou wouldest** rend the heavens, that thou wouldest **come down**, that the mountains might flow down at thy presence [*the Second Coming*],

2 As when the **melting fire burneth**, the fire causeth the waters to boil, **to make thy name known to thine adversaries** [*the wicked*], that the nations may tremble at thy presence!

3 **When thou didst terrible things** [*German: because of the miracles you do*] which we looked not for [*German: which we didn't expect*], **thou camest down, the mountains flowed down at thy presence.**

4 For since the beginning of the world **men have not heard, nor perceived by the ear, neither hath the eye seen**, O God, beside thee, **what he hath prepared for him that waiteth for him** [*trusts in*

Him; no one can even imagine the blessings the Lord has in store for the righteous].

The JST makes significant changes in verse 5, next. We will give it as it stands in the King James Version of the Bible and then give it from the Joseph Smith Translation of the Bible.

5 Thou meetest [*guidest*] him that rejoiceth and worketh righteousness, those that remember thee in thy ways: behold, thou art wroth; for we have sinned: in those is continuance, and we shall be saved.

JST Isaiah 64:5

5 Thou meetest him that worketh righteousness, and rejoiceth him that remembereth thee in thy ways; in righteousness there is continuance, and such shall be saved.

6 But [*JST: "we have sinned"*] **we are all as an unclean thing**, and all our righteousnesses are as filthy rags [*the few things we do right are of little value because of our gross wickedness*]; **and we all do fade as a leaf** [*we are fading away as a covenant people because of wickedness*]; and **our iniquities**, like the wind, **have taken us away** [*our wickedness has separated us from Thee*].

7 And **there is none that calleth**

upon thy name [*no one turns to the Lord*], that stirreth up himself to take hold of thee: for **thou hast hid thy face from us, and hast consumed us, because of our iniquities** [*we have separated ourselves from You*].

8 **But now** [*and yet*], **O LORD, thou art our father; we are the clay, and thou our potter** [*our Maker*]; **and we all are the work of thy hand.**

9 **Be not wroth very sore** [*please don't be too angry with us*], O LORD, **neither remember** [*our*] **iniquity for ever** [*please forgive us*]: behold, see, we beseech thee, we are all thy people.

10 **Thy holy cities are a wilderness, Zion is a wilderness, Jerusalem a desolation** [*much destruction has come to us already because of our wickedness*].

11 **Our holy and our beautiful house** [*the temple in Jerusalem*], where our fathers praised thee, **is burned up with fire**: and **all our pleasant** [*German: beautiful-to-look-at*] **things are laid waste.**

12 **Wilt thou refrain thyself for these things** [*will You continue to withhold blessings despite our pleas*], **O LORD? wilt thou hold thy peace** [*keep silent*], **and afflict us very sore** [*continue to punish us severely—please have mercy on us!*]?

ISAIAH 65

Background

This chapter summarizes the reasons the Lord rejected ancient Israel and explains in some detail the consequences of rejecting the Lord. In contrast, it also gives some details about the Millennium and the blessings for the righteous at that time, including the fact that mortals then living will live to be one hundred years old (verse 20).

The JST makes several changes in verses 1, 2, 4, and 20. We will point these out as we go along.

Verse 1 in the JST seems to answer the question in Isaiah 64:12, namely, how long the Lord will remain silent and keep punishing rebellious Israel.

1 I am sought of them that asked not for me [*JST: "I am found of them who seek after me. I give unto all them that ask of me"*]; I am [*JST: "I am not"*] found of them that sought me not [*JST: "or that inquireth not after me"*]: I said [*JST: "unto my servant" (probably meaning Isaiah)*], Behold me, behold me [*JST: "look upon me; I will send you"*], unto a nation that was not called by my name [*JST: "is not called after my name"*]; [*that has not taken upon them My name*].

2 I have spread out my hands [*invited them to come unto me—compare with Jacob 6:4–5*] all the day [*constantly*] unto a rebellious people, which walketh in a way that was not good, after their own thoughts [*they are rebellious and wicked*];

JST Isaiah 65:2

2 For I have spread out my hands all the day to a people who walketh not in my ways, and their works are evil and not good, and they walk after their own thoughts.

3 A people that provoketh me to anger continually to my face [*in other words, blatantly disobey God*]; that sacrificeth in gardens, and burneth incense upon altars of brick [*the Israelites were commanded in Exodus 20:25 to use unhewn (uncut) stones in making altars; in other words, they just won't obey God*];

4 Which remain [*German: sit*] among the graves [*implies that they were breaking the commandment in Leviticus 19:31: they were attempting to commune with spirits of the dead*], and lodge in the monuments [*German: hang around the graveyards overnight*], which eat swine's flesh [*strictly forbidden by Mosaic law*], and broth of abominable [*unclean*] things is in their vessels [*they are breaking every rule in the book*];

JST Isaiah 65:4

4 Which remain among the graves, and lodge in the monuments; which eat swine's flesh, **and broth of abominable beasts, and pollute their vessels**;

5 **Which say, Stand by thyself** [*stay away from me*], **come not near to me; for I am holier than thou. These are a smoke in my nose** [*such hypocrites are a constant source of irritation*], a fire that burneth all the day.

6 **Behold, it is written** before me [*it is written in the scriptures*]: **I will not keep silence, but will recompense** [*pay back, reward*], even recompense **into their bosom** [*drop their sins right back into their own laps; they will be held accountable for their wickedness*],

7 **Your iniquities, and the iniquities of your fathers** [*ancestors*] together [*along with yours*], saith the LORD, **which have burned incense upon the mountains** [*worshiped idols*]**, and blasphemed me upon the hills** [*worshiped false gods*]**: therefore will I measure their former work into their bosom** [*I will drop their sins right back into their laps*].

8 Thus saith the LORD, **As the new wine** [*fresh grape juice*] **is found in the cluster** [*of grapes; there is still potential for good in*

Israel], **and one saith, Destroy it not; for a blessing is in it** [*Israel still has potential*]**: so will I do for my servants' sakes, that I may not destroy them all** [*a remnant of Israel will remain*].

9 **And I will bring forth a seed** [*descendants; a remnant*] **out of Jacob** [*Israel*]**, and out of Judah** [*the Jews*] **an inheritor of my mountains** [*God's kingdom and blessings*]**: and mine elect shall inherit it, and my servants shall dwell there.

10 **And Sharon** [*part of the Holy Land*] **shall be a fold of flocks** [*a peaceful place*]**, and the valley of Achor** [*a part of the Holy Land, near Jericho*] **a place for the herds to lie down in, for my people that have sought me** [*the righteous will receive wonderful peace and blessings*].

11 **But ye are they that forsake the LORD, that forget my holy mountain** [*the gospel*], that prepare a table for that troop [*Gad, an idol of fortune—see footnote 11a in your Bible*], and that furnish the drink offering unto that number [*Meni, an idol of fate or destiny—see footnote 11b in your Bible*].

12 **Therefore** [*because of your wickedness*] **will I number you** [*turn you over*] **to the sword, and ye shall all bow down to the slaughter** [*great destruction will*

come upon you]: **because when I
called, ye did not answer**; when
I spake, ye did not hear; **but did
evil** before mine eyes, and did
choose that [*wickedness*] wherein I
delighted not.

Isaiah now contrasts rewards for
the righteous with punishments
for the wicked.

13 **Therefore thus saith the Lord
GOD, Behold, my servants** [*the
righteous*] **shall eat, but ye** [*the
wicked*] **shall be hungry**: behold,
**my servants shall drink, but ye
shall be thirsty**: behold, **my servants shall rejoice, but ye shall
be ashamed** [*put to shame, devastated*]:

14 Behold, **my servants shall sing
for joy** of heart, **but ye shall cry
for sorrow** of heart, and shall howl
for vexation of spirit.

15 **And ye** [*the wicked*] **shall leave
your name for a curse unto my
chosen** [*it is you, the wicked, who
will be cursed*]: **for the Lord
GOD shall slay thee** [*you will be
destroyed*], **and call his servants
by another name** [*a new name; see
Isaiah 62:2, D&C 130:11, Revelation
2:17; symbolic of celestial glory*]:

16 That **he who blesseth himself**
[*asks for blessings from the Lord*]
in the earth **shall bless himself in
the God of truth** [*will pray to God,
not idols*]; and **he that sweareth**
[*makes covenants*] in the earth

shall swear by the God of truth
[*rather than idols*]; because **the
former** [*past*] **troubles are forgotten** [*over*], and because they are hid
from mine eyes [*your troubles will
then be over, gone*].

17 For, behold, **I create new
heavens and a new earth** [*paradisiacal conditions during the Millennium—see footnote 17c in your
Bible*]: and the former shall not be
remembered, nor come into mind
[*because past troubles will be completely overshadowed by the beau-
ties of millennial life*].

18 But be ye glad and rejoice
for ever in that which I create:
for, behold, **I create Jerusalem a
rejoicing, and her people a joy**
[*the Jews in Jerusalem will become
a righteous covenant people of the
Lord during the Millennium*].

19 And **I will rejoice in Jerusalem, and joy in my people**: and
**the voice of weeping shall be no
more heard in her**, nor the voice
of crying [*millennial conditions*].

20 **There shall be no more thence**
[*during the Millennium*] an infant
of days [*German: an infant who
lives just a few days*], **nor an old
man that hath not filled his days**
[*lived out his years completely*]:
for **the child shall die an hundred years old**; but the sinner
being an hundred years old shall
be accursed.

JST Isaiah 65:20

20 In those days there shall be no more thence an infant of days, nor an old man that hath not filled his days; for **the child shall not die, but shall live to be an hundred years old; but the sinner, living to be an hundred years old, shall be accursed**.

Elder Joseph Fielding Smith taught the following about the age of mortals during the Millennium (**bold** added for emphasis):

"When Christ comes the Saints who are on the earth will be quickened and caught up to meet him. This does not mean that those who are living in mortality at that time will be changed and pass through the resurrection, for mortals must remain on the earth until after the thousand years are ended. A change, nevertheless, will come over all who remain on the earth; they will be quickened so that they will not be subject unto death until they are old. **Men shall die when they are one hundred years of age**, and the change shall be made suddenly to the immortal state. Graves will not be made during this thousand years, and Satan shall have no power to tempt any man. Children shall grow up 'as calves of the stall' unto righteous-

ness, that is, without sin or the temptations that are so prevalent today. Even the animal kingdom shall experience a great change, for the enmity of beasts shall disappear, as we have already stated, 'and they shall not hurt nor destroy in all my holy mountain: for the earth shall be full of the knowledge of the Lord, as the waters cover the sea.'—Isaiah 11:9." (*The Way to Perfection*, pages 298–99)

21 **And they shall build houses, and inhabit them; and they shall plant vineyards, and eat the fruit of them** [*no one will attack and take things away during the Millennium*].

22 **They shall not build, and another inhabit; they shall not plant, and another eat: for as the days** [*age; see D&C 101:30*] **of a tree** [*one hundred years, Isaiah; see 65:20*] **are the days of my people, and mine elect shall long enjoy the work of their hands.**

23 **They shall not labour in vain, nor bring forth** [*German: bear children*] **for trouble** [*into a world of trouble*]; **for they** [*the children you bring forth during the Millennium*] **are the seed** [*children*] **of the blessed** [*you, the righteous*] **of the LORD, and their offspring** [*descendants*] **with them.**

24 And it shall come to pass, that

before they call, I will answer; and while they are yet speaking, I will hear [*conditions during the Millennium will be even better than you can imagine*].

25 The **wolf and the lamb shall feed together, and the lion shall eat straw like the bullock:** and dust shall be the serpent's meat [*food*]. **They shall not hurt nor destroy in all my holy mountain, saith the LORD** [*peace will abound during the Millennium*].

ISAIAH 66

Background
The Lord now says that everything He has created is designed for the purpose of developing humble, righteous people.

1 Thus saith the LORD, **The heaven is my throne, and the earth is my footstool**: where is the house that ye build unto me? and where is the place of my rest?

2 For **all those things hath mine hand made**, and those things [*everything I have created*] have been [*created*], saith the LORD: but **to this man** [*the humble, righteous person*] **will I look** [*with this type of person I am pleased*], even **to him that is poor** [*humble*] **and of a contrite spirit, and trembleth at my word** [*takes God's word seriously*].

Isaiah now switches topics and speaks of hypocrites.

3 **He** [*the type of person who wants to look good by offering sacrifices to God, yet intentionally lives in sin*] **that killeth an ox is as if he slew a man** [*is like a murderer*]; **he that sacrificeth a lamb, as if he cut off** [*German: broke*] **a dog's neck** [see *Exodus 13:13; his efforts are useless, just as an animal with a broken neck is useless*]; **he that offereth an oblation** [*a grain offering*], **as if he offered swine's blood; he that burneth incense, as if he blessed** [*worshipped*] **an idol.** Yea, **they have chosen** [*they have their agency*] **their own ways, and their soul delighteth in their abominations** [*they are wicked and like to be so*].

4 **I also will choose** [*they have "chosen" to have the Lord "choose" to punish them*] **their delusions** [*punishments*], **and will bring their fears** [*German: that which they dread*] **upon them; because when I called, none did answer; when I spake, they did not hear** [*they have been intentionally disobedient*]: but **they did evil before mine eyes, and chose that in which I delighted not** [*they chose wickedness*].

5 **Hear the word of the LORD, ye** [*the righteous*] **that tremble at his word** [*that take His word seriously*]; **your brethren** [*your*

own people] **that hated you, that cast you out for my name's sake** [*that persecuted you because you obeyed Me*], **said, Let the LORD be glorified** [*let the Lord come and show His power—we're not afraid; the haughty attitude of the wicked*]: **but he** [*the Lord*] **shall appear to your joy** [*to the joy of the righteous*], **and they** [*the wicked*] **shall be ashamed** [*put to shame, devastated*].

6 A voice of noise from the city, a voice from the temple, a voice of **the LORD** that **rendereth recompence to his enemies** [*the punishments spoken of will surely come upon the wicked*].

> Verses 7 and 8 seem to parallel Isaiah 49:21, "Who hath begotten me these . . .?" In other words, "Where in the world did all these Israelites come from?" Isaiah is describing the rapid growth of Zion as the earth is prepared for the Millennium (see verse 22, near the end of this chapter).

7 **Before she travailed** [*went into labor*], **she brought forth** [*her child was born*]; **before her pain** [*labor pains*] **came, she** [*perhaps the Church of God; see JST Revelation 12:7; in other words, the Church brings forth the kingdom of God very rapidly upon the earth in the last days and on into the Millennium*] **was delivered of a man child** [*the kingdom of God; see JST*

Revelation 12:7; in other words, the kingdom of God will grow much faster than expected].

8 **Who hath heard such a thing?** who hath seen such things? **Shall the earth be made to bring forth in one day** [*it will seem to happen overnight!*]? or **shall a nation** [*righteous Israel*] **be born at once?** for as soon as Zion travailed, she brought forth her children [*can refer to rapid progress of the work of the Lord in the last days, or the righteousness brought suddenly by the Second Coming, or both*].

9 **Shall I bring to the birth, and not cause to bring forth** [*would the Lord get everything ready and then not follow through with what He has revealed*]? saith the LORD: shall I cause to bring forth, and shut the womb [*stop it at the last moment*]? saith thy God.

10 **Rejoice ye with Jerusalem** [*the Lord's people*], **and be glad with her, all ye that love her** [*the Lord's kingdom*]: **rejoice for joy with her,** all ye that mourn for her [*the day will come when joy and peace will reign supreme*]:

> Isaiah now describes wonderful blessings that will come to those who join Zion and seek nourishment from the Lord therein.

11 **That ye may** suck, and be satisfied with the breasts of her consolations; that ye may milk out, and

be delighted with the abundance of her glory.

12 **For thus saith the LORD, Behold, I will extend peace to her** [*Zion, the righteous*] **like a river** [*a constant supply*], and the glory [*wealth*] of the Gentiles like a flowing stream: **then shall ye suck** [*the righteous will be nourished*], ye shall be borne upon her sides [*German: in her arms*], **and be dandled** [*German: held happily*] **upon her knees.**

13 **As one whom his mother comforteth, so will I comfort you** [*the righteous will feel right at home with the Savior; millennial conditions*]; and ye shall be comforted in Jerusalem [*God's kingdom*].

14 **And when ye** [*the righteous*] **see this, your heart shall rejoice, and your bones shall flourish like an herb** [*German: you will green up like lush grass*]: and the hand of the LORD shall be known toward his servants [*great blessings will come to the righteous*], and his indignation toward his enemies [*but the wicked will be punished*].

15 For, behold, **the LORD will come with fire**, and with his chariots like a whirlwind, **to render his anger with fury, and his rebuke with flames of fire** [*the destruction of the wicked at the Second Coming*].

16 **For by fire and by his sword**

will the LORD plead with all flesh [*judge all people*]: and the slain of the LORD shall be many [*there will be large numbers of wicked in the last days, and they will be destroyed at His coming*].

Isaiah now refers again to forbidden practices among the wicked of Israel, as already mentioned in verse 3.

17 **They** [*the wicked*] **that sanctify themselves, and purify themselves in the gardens** behind one tree in the midst [*attempting to make themselves holy via false gods, idol worship located in groves of trees, and so on*], **eating swine's flesh** [*strictly forbidden*], and the abomination, **and the mouse** [*a forbidden food; see Leviticus 11:29*], **shall be consumed together** [*suddenly, at the same time, at the Second Coming*], saith the LORD.

18 **For I know their** [*the wicked*] **works and their thoughts** [*and that is why they will be destroyed*]: [*Isaiah begins a new topic now, namely the gathering of Israel in the last days and on into the Millennium*] **it shall come, that I will gather all nations and tongues; and they shall come, and see my glory.**

19 **And I will set a sign** [*ensign; see Isaiah 5:26—the true gospel, certainly including the Book of Mormon as explained in 3 Nephi*]

21:1–7] **among them** [*the remnant of Israel*], **and I will send those that escape of them** [*a righteous remnant of Israel; see Isaiah 37:32; missionary work*] **unto the nations**, to Tarshish [*Spain?*], Pul [*Lybia*], and Lud, that draw the bow [*famous for skilled archers*], to Tubal [*Turkey*], and Javan [*Greece; Isaiah has thus described basically all the commonly known world in his day*], **to the isles** [*continents*] **afar off** [*to all nations*], that have not heard my fame, neither have seen my glory; **and they shall declare my glory among the Gentiles** [*the gospel will be preached to all nations*].

20 **And they** [*the missionaries; the true Church*] **shall bring all your brethren** [*Israelites; the gathering*] **for an offering** [*righteous lives; see 1 Samuel 15:22*] **unto the LORD out of all nations** upon horses, and in chariots [*with great power—compare with Jeremiah 23:3*], and in litters, and upon mules, and upon swift beasts, **to my holy mountain** Jerusalem [*to the true gospel*], saith the LORD, as the children of Israel bring an offering in a clean vessel into the house of the LORD.

21 **And I will also take of them for priests and for Levites**, saith the LORD [*the priesthood will be restored to men in the last days*].

22 **For as the new heavens and the new earth** [*can refer to millennial earth, D&C 101:25; and celestial earth, D&C 130:9; 88:18, 19, 25, 26*], which I will make, **shall remain** [*will be eternal*] before me, saith the LORD, **so shall your seed** [*families*] **and your name** [*symbolic of celestial glory, D&C 130:11*] **remain** [*you and your families can be with Me forever*].

23 **And it shall come to pass, that from one new moon** [*special Sabbath ritual among the Israelites at the beginning of the month; see Bible Dictionary, under "New Moon"*] **to another, and from one Sabbath to another, shall all flesh come to worship before me, saith the LORD** [*the righteous are those who will be completely consistent and faithful during the Millennium and beyond*].

24 **And they** [*the righteous*] **shall go forth, and look upon the carcases of the men that have transgressed against me** [*they will be aware that the judgments of God did finally come upon the wicked*]: **for their worm shall not die** [*"Worm" refers to a scarlet dye that was made from the dried body of a certain type of female worm* (Coccus ilicis). *Scarlet was considered a "colorfast" dye— permanent, lasting. Hence, "their worm shall not die" implies that, even though their dead bodies*

can be seen, the "permanent" part of them (spirit up until the resurrection of the wicked, then their resurrected bodies) will live forever and they will thus face the consequences of their wicked *choices.]* **neither shall their fire be quenched; and they shall be an abhorring unto all flesh** [*a final warning from Isaiah that wickedness does not pay at all*].

ISAIAH
IN THE BOOK OF MORMON

The Book of Mormon contains approximately 35 percent of the writings of Isaiah in the Bible. Many changes are contained in the Book of Mormon, and thus we are greatly blessed in our study of Isaiah by what is found in it. Nephi helps us understand the basic messages of Isaiah and explains much for us. An example of this is found in 2 Nephi 25, where Nephi explains the writings of Isaiah that are found in 2 Nephi 12–24.

We will now set the stage for studying the Isaiah chapters in the Book of Mormon contained in this study guide by quoting Nephi as he explains the main messages of Isaiah to his people and especially to his brothers. We will use **bold** for emphasis.

1 Nephi 19

23 And I did read many things unto them which were written in the books of Moses (the first five books of the Old Testament, written by Moses, namely, Genesis, Exodus, Leviticus, Numbers, and Deuteronomy); but **that I might more fully persuade them to believe in the Lord their Redeemer** I did read unto them that which was written by the prophet Isaiah; for I did liken all scriptures unto us, that it might be for our profit and learning.

24 Wherefore I spake unto them, saying: Hear ye the words of the prophet, ye who are a remnant of the house of Israel, a branch who have been broken off; hear ye the words of the prophet, which were written unto all the house of Israel, and liken them unto yourselves, **that ye may have hope** as well as your brethren from whom ye have been broken off; for after this manner has the prophet written.

Just a few more thoughts and comments about understanding Isaiah before we continue with our study of the Isaiah chapters in the Book of Mormon. For many members of the Church, Isaiah is difficult to understand. Just knowing what Nephi said in verses 23 and 24, above, is motivation for a renewed effort at understanding Isaiah's writings. If we succeed, even to a small extent, we will have a stronger understanding and testimony of Christ as our Redeemer. This, in turn, will give us wonderful "hope" that we will succeed in attaining exaltation, which includes having a pleasant judgment day (see 2 Nephi 9:14, last half of verse). The word "hope," as used in the Book of Mormon, is not the same as in common English usage today. In the Book of Mormon, "hope" means "assurance" (see Alma 57:11.) Thus, in 2 Nephi 31:20, Nephi speaks of "steadfastness in Christ" which brings "a perfect brightness of hope" which leads to eternal life (exaltation.) There is nothing "wishy-washy" or "maybe-ish" about this type of hope.

If you will pay the price to study the Book of Mormon Isaiah chapters and accompanying notes carefully and prayerfully, you will begin to understand Isaiah. You will see that he uses rich symbolism. You will see that he paints pictures with words. We will use many notes within the verses as well as between verses to help you get the feel for Isaiah's writing style and messages. Be aware that the Savior quoted Isaiah more than He quoted any other prophet. In fact, in 3 Nephi 23:1, Jesus commanded His people to study Isaiah. He said: "Ye ought to search these things [*Isaiah's writings*], Yea, a commandment I give unto you that ye search these things diligently; for great are the words of Isaiah."

One last suggestion before continuing. Nephi said that his people had difficulty understanding Isaiah because **"they know not concerning the manner of prophesying among the Jews."** (See 2 Nephi 25:1.) This can make it difficult for us also. It may help to note a few characteristics of Isaiah's "manner of prophesying." For example:

Isaiah uses much of symbolism.
He uses many phrases peculiar to his time and people. These are known as "idioms."

Example:
"Thy neck is an iron sinew, and thy brow brass"; (1 Nephi 20:4.) This is, in effect, saying, "You have iron in your neck and you are thick-skulled." In other words, "You are not humble; you won't bow your heads in humility before God, and it is hard to get anything into your heads."

Isaiah deliberately repeats for emphasis.

Because of this writing and teaching technique, some people begin to think they have missed something, because they don't believe that Isaiah would constantly repeat things.

Example:

"Go ye forth of Babylon, flee ye from the Chaldeans (the inhabitants of southern Babylon)." (1 Nephi 20:20) In other words, "flee evil!"

Example:

Isaiah repeats the same concept in two different ways in the following:

"The Lord hath called me from the womb; from the bowels of my mother hath he made mention of my name." (1 Nephi 21:1)

In other words, Israel was foreordained to be God's covenant people.

Many of the things Isaiah teaches can have more than one meaning and more than one fulfillment.

Therefore, it is usually unwise to limit what he teaches to only one specific meaning, unless the context warrants it.

Example:

"And they thirsted not; he led them through the deserts; he caused the waters to flow out of the rock for them; he clave the rock also and the waters gushed out." (1 Nephi 20:21)

While the Lord literally led the children of Israel through the wilderness, and literally caused water to flow out of the rock to quench their thirst and save their lives, there is much symbolic meaning also. For instance, He leads us through the wilderness of sin and wickedness. He provides "living water" (John 4:10) and quenches our spiritual thirst eternally.

1 NEPHI 20

Background

Every verse in this chapter reads differently than in Isaiah, chapter 48, in the Bible. Nephi lived just 100 years after Isaiah, which puts him much closer to the original records containing Isaiah's writings, including the brass plates. Nephi was also a prophet of God and thus could be inspired to make certain that his rendition of Isaiah's writings was correct. Also remember that Nephi's main reason for teaching Isaiah to his people as well as Laman, Lemuel, and the others, is to give them hope, not to condemn them (see 1 Nephi 19:23–24). We would do well to keep this major message of Isaiah in mind also, rather than seeing him only as a dismal prophet of doom as so many people do.

1 Hearken and hear this, O house of Jacob [*Jacob's children; in other words, the 12 Tribes of Israel*], who are called by the name of Israel [*Jacob*], and are come forth out of the waters of Judah, or out of the waters of baptism [*who are my covenant people*], who swear [*make covenants*] by the name of the Lord [*just as we, today, make covenants in the name of Jesus Christ*], and make mention of [*pray to and talk about*] the God of Israel, yet they swear [*make covenants*] not in truth nor in righteousness [*the problem is that they claim to be the Lord's people but break covenants, don't live the gospel*].

2 Nevertheless, they call themselves of the holy city [*claim to be the Lord's people*], but they do not stay themselves [*do not rely*] upon the God of Israel, who is the Lord of Hosts [*the God of all*]; yea, the Lord of Hosts is his name.

In the next several verses, Isaiah reminds Israel that there is no lack of obvious evidence that the true God exists.

3 Behold, I [*the Lord*] have declared the former things [*prophecies*] from the beginning [*so you would have plenty of evidence that I exist*]; and they [*prophecies*] went forth out of my mouth [*through the prophets*], and I showed [*fulfilled*] them. I did show them suddenly [*when you did not expect them to take place, so you can know I really am your God, and your idols are false; see Isaiah 42:9*].

Next, the Lord tells His covenant people that they are prideful and stubborn.

4 And I [*the Lord*] did it [*gave and fulfilled prophecies*] because I knew that thou art obstinate [*prideful, stubborn*], and thy neck is an iron sinew [*your necks are as if they have iron in them; you are not humble, won't bend your neck in humility*], and thy brow brass [*thick-headed; it is hard to get anything through your thick skulls*];

Next, through Isaiah, the Lord tells covenant Israel that from the very beginning he has placed obvious evidence that He exists in the form of prophecies of the future. He has then fulfilled these prophecies so that His people have every chance of gaining and keeping testimonies of His existence and love and concern for them. This is similar to the prophecies of the last days, or signs of the times, which are being fulfilled all around us now.

5 And I have even from the beginning declared to thee [*prophesied things*]; before it [*the prophesied events*] came to pass I showed them thee [*I prophesied them to you*]; and I showed them for fear lest thou shouldst say—mine idol hath done them, and my graven image, and my molten image hath commanded them [*I have shown you my power via prophecies so you couldn't claim your idols have power*].

6 Thou hast seen and heard all this [*all this obvious evidence that I exist*]; and will ye not declare [*acknowledge*] them? And that I have showed thee new things [*things you couldn't possibly have known in advance*] from this time, even hidden things, and thou didst not know them [*didn't pay attention; didn't acknowledge them*].

7 They are created now [*the prophesied events are taking place now*], and not from the beginning [*you couldn't have guessed they were going to happen back then when the prophecies were given*], even before the day when thou heardest them not [*back then when there was no clue that the prophesied events would take place*] they were declared unto thee [*I told you in advance*], lest thou shouldst say—Behold I knew them.

8 Yea, and thou heardest not [*you ignored the prophecies*]; yea, thou knewest not [*you would not acknowledge them*]; yea, from that time thine ear was not opened [*you refused to listen*]; for I knew that thou wouldst deal very treacherously, and wast called a transgressor from the womb [*I've had trouble with you Israelites right from the start!*].

Next, the Lord reminds all of us that if it were not for His mercy, Israel would have been cut off long ago.

9 Nevertheless, for my name's sake [*I, the Lord, have a reputation of being merciful to uphold*] will I defer mine anger, and for my praise [*In the German Bible, Martin Luther edition: glory, honor; reputation*] will I refrain from thee, that I cut thee not off [*I'll not destroy you completely*].

10 For, behold, I [*the Lord*] have refined thee [*Israel*], I have chosen thee [*German: I will make you*] in the furnace of affliction [*I will*]

purify you in the refiner's fire].

"The refiner's fire" calls up the image of a skillful craftsman carefully applying fire to the ore in order to remove all the impurities and thus produce pure gold.

Next, in verse 11, we are reminded that the Lord doesn't help us only because it is His calling as the Redeemer and Savior. Rather, He helps us and works patiently with us because He loves us.

11 For mine own sake [*because I love you; see verse 14*], yea, for mine own sake [*because I want to*] will I do this [*refine and purify you in the furnace of affliction*], for I will not suffer [*allow*] my name to be polluted [*German: lest my name be slandered for not keeping my promises to Israel*], and I will not give my glory unto another [*I will remain true to you; see Jeremiah 3:14. By the way, this can be good advice for marriage partners*].

The main theme of verses 12–17 is that Israel is called and foreordained to serve.

12 Hearken unto me, O Jacob, and Israel my called [*you have a calling; see Abr. 2:9–11*], for I am he [*Christ*]; I am the first, and I am also the last [*I am your Savior; Jesus was there at the creation and will be there at final judgment*].

13 Mine hand hath also laid the foundation of the earth [*I am the Creator*], and my right hand

[*covenant hand; hand of power*] hath spanned the heavens [*spread out; created, the skies*]. I call unto them [*Israel in verses 12 and 14*] and they stand up together [*let them, Israel, all stand up and listen; this goes with the first part of verse 14*].

14 All ye, assemble yourselves, and hear; who among them [*perhaps referring to Israel's idols; see verse 5*]. hath declared these things [*prophecies; see verses 3, 6 etc.*] unto them [*Israel*]? The Lord hath loved him [*Israel*]; yea, and he [*the Lord*] will fulfill his word which he hath declared by them [*the prophets*]; and he will do his pleasure on Babylon, and his arm [*symbolic of power*] shall come upon the Chaldeans [*Southern Babylon; Babylon will eventually be destroyed, just as has been prophesied*].

15 Also, saith the Lord; I the Lord, yea, I have spoken; yea, I have called him [*Israel*] to declare [*Israel has a job to do*], I have brought him, and he shall make his way prosperous [*God will help; could also mean that Heavenly Father called Christ to prophesy; also that Christ called Isaiah to prophesy*].

Verse 15, above, is an example of where Isaiah's writing can have more than one meaning.

16 Come ye [*Israel*] near unto me; I have not spoken in secret [*I have been very open about the gospel, etc.*]; from the beginning, from

the time that it was declared have I spoken; and the Lord God, and his Spirit, hath sent me [*the Father sent Christ; or perhaps this means that Christ sent Isaiah*].

17 And thus saith the Lord, thy Redeemer [*Christ*], the Holy One of Israel; I have sent him [*Israel; see verses 12 and 19; or, dualistically, this could refer to Isaiah*], the Lord thy God who teacheth thee to profit [*German: for your profit, benefit*], who leadeth thee by the way thou shouldst go, hath done it.

18 O that thou hadst hearkened to my commandments [*can apply directly to Laman and Lemuel; no doubt this is one reason Nephi is quoting Isaiah to them*]—then had thy peace been as a river [*you could have had peace flowing constantly into your lives*], and thy righteousness as the waves of the sea [*steady, constant*].

Next, Isaiah says, in effect, that Israel has the potential to become a truly large and great nation, if they would just make and keep covenants with God. As it is, though, Isaiah goes into what can be termed "future perfect tense" wherein he treats the future as if it has already happened and prophetically tells the Israelites that they could have become a great nation, if only. . . .

19 Thy [*Israel's*] seed [*posterity*] also had been [*would have been*] as the sand; the offspring of thy bowels [*your descendants*] like the gravel [*grains of sand*] thereof; his [*Israel's*] name should not [*would not*] have been cut off nor destroyed from before me [*Israel could have had it very good, and could have avoided such great destruction*].

20 Go ye forth of Babylon [*flee wickedness; stop being wicked*], flee ye from the Chaldeans [*wickedness; Chaldeans were residents of southern Babylon*], with a voice of singing [*be happy about being righteous*] declare ye, tell this, utter to the end of the earth; say ye: The Lord hath redeemed his servant Jacob [*Israel can be saved—including Laman and Lemuel—if they will repent*].

"Babylon," as used in verse 20, above, is very symbolic. Anciently, it was an actual country and city, basically where Iraq is today. Isaiah as well as many other prophets use "Babylon" to symbolize wickedness, and to represent Satan's kingdom. The imagery is fascinating, because Babylon was a fearsome enemy of Israel.

The huge city of Babylon was so enormous that it took 56 miles of walls to surround and protect it. The walls were 335 feet high and 85 feet wide [see Bible Dictionary, page 618]. It was a center of wickedness, and thus came to symbolize general wickedness and the devil's domain in many scriptures.

In fact, part of the imagery

of Babylon is that it seemed indestructible, just as Satan's kingdom and domain on earth seems powerful and indestructible. However, Babylon fell in 538 B.C. and was never rebuilt, just as Satan's kingdom will eventually fall, and never be rebuilt as he and his evil followers are cast into outer darkness (see D&C 1:16; 88: 111–15).

21 And they thirsted not; he led them through the deserts; he caused the waters to flow out of the rock for them; he clave the rock also and the waters gushed out [*just look what the Lord can do for those who trust in him!*].

22 And notwithstanding [*even though*] he hath done all this, and greater also, there is no peace, saith the Lord, unto the wicked [*a major message for Laman and Lemuel and all of us*].

1 NEPHI 21

Background
Isaiah continues his prophecy about the Messiah, and of the gathering of Israel in the last days. The prophecy includes the fact that the governments of many nations will assist in this gathering. In the last days, Israel will finally do the work she was originally called to do but failed to accomplish.

This particular chapter contains one of my personal favorite verses, verse 16, which contains beautiful

Atonement symbolism.

Beginning with verse 1, we will be taught about the foreordination of covenant Israel and the responsibilities we have as the Lord's chosen people. Remember that "chosen" includes the concept that we are chosen to carry whatever burdens are necessary in order to spread the gospel and the priesthood throughout the earth.

Isaiah sets the stage for this prophecy by having us think of Israel as a person who is thinking about her past and feels like she has been a failure as far as her calling and mission from the Lord is concerned. Then she is startled by her success in the last days. Note that Isaiah says the same thing twice in a row, using different words, several times in this chapter. In verse 1, for example, he says "**Listen**, O isles unto me; and **hearken** . . ." As previously mentioned in this study guide, this was typical repetition for emphasis in Biblical culture.

1 And again: Hearken, O ye house of Israel, all ye that are broken off and are driven out [*scattered; Isaiah is speaking prophetically to scattered Israel*] because of the wickedness of the pastors [*leaders and teachers*] of my people; yea, all ye that are broken off, that are scattered abroad, who are of my people, O house of Israel. Listen, O isles [*far away nations and lands, including those across the sea*], unto me [*Israel; see verse 3*], and

hearken ye people from far; the Lord hath called me [*Israel*] from the womb [*foreordination*]; from the bowels of my mother hath he [*the Lord*] made mention of my name [*Israel has had a job to do since the beginning*].

2 And he hath made my mouth like a sharp sword [*Israel is to spread the gospel, which is hard on the wicked, but enables the righteous to cut through falsehood*]; in the shadow [*shade; protection*] of his hand hath he hid me, and made me a polished shaft [*an effective servant of the Lord, such as Joseph Smith, Isaiah or any faithful Israelite*]; in his quiver hath he hid me;

3 And said unto me [*Israel*]: Thou art my servant, O Israel, in whom I will be glorified [*Israel will yet fulfill its stewardship*].

In verses 4–12 and beyond, Isaiah portrays the loneliness of Israel waiting for the restoration. It is almost as if Isaiah were writing a stage play with one lone character on the stage, representing Israel, speaking in a sad, lonely, remorseful voice and recounting the missed and seemingly lost opportunities to fulfill her mission and God-given destiny.

4 Then I [*Israel*] said, I have labored in vain [*I haven't been a very good servant; I have wasted my efforts*], I have spent my strength for naught [*for nothing*] and in vain [*in false religions and riotous living*]; surely my judgment is with the Lord, and my work with my God [*in other words, my fate rests with the Lord; it is up to God what He wants to do with me now that I have failed Him*].

5 And now, saith the Lord—that formed me from the womb [*who foreordained me*] that I [*especially Ephraim*] should be his servant, to bring Jacob again to him—though Israel be not gathered, yet shall I be glorious in the eyes of the Lord [*if I do my best, I'll be OK, even if people reject my message*], and my God shall be my strength.

Next, in this "drama," the Lord, in effect, tells Israel that it is too easy of a calling to merely work at bringing scattered Israel back to God. Israel needs to have something more challenging to do, namely, to bring the gospel to all peoples of the earth.

6 And he [*the Lord*] said: It is a light thing [*German: not enough*] that thou [*Israel*] shouldst be my servant to raise up [*restore the gospel to*] the tribes of Jacob, and to restore the preserved [*remnant*] of Israel [*the job of the Church today*]. I will also give thee for [*another assignment, namely to be*] a light to the Gentiles [*quite a prophecy in Isaiah's day when almost any nation that wanted to could walk all over Israel*], that thou mayest be my salvation unto the ends of the earth [*bring the gospel to everyone on earth*].

Abraham 2:9–11 clearly teaches this responsibility which Israel has, to bring the gospel and the priesthood blessings to all the earth. In fact, in your patriarchal blessing, your lineage is declared. This is a most important part of your blessing because it reminds you of your sacred duty to help bring the gospel to all the world throughout your life.

Next, Isaiah prophesies that the day will come when Israel will become a powerful force in the world, whereas, in the past, Israel was walked on almost at will by nation after nation.

7 Thus saith the Lord, the Redeemer of Israel [*Christ*], his [*Israel's*] Holy One, to him [*Israel*] whom man despiseth, to him whom the nation abhorreth [*German: to the nation abhorred by others*], to servant of rulers [*for much of past history, Israel has been servants and slaves to many nations*]: Kings shall see and arise [*out of respect for Israel*], princes [*leaders of nations*] also shall worship, because of the Lord that is faithful [*because the Lord will keep His promises to you*].

8 Thus saith the Lord: In an acceptable time [*when the time is right, beginning with the restoration and Joseph Smith*] have I heard thee [*I will have answered your cries for help*], O isles of the sea [*far continents beyond Asia and Africa, such as America, etc.*], and in a day of salvation have I helped thee; and I will preserve thee, and give thee

my servant [*prophets, including Joseph Smith*] for a covenant of the people, to establish the earth [*to reestablish the gospel upon the earth*], to cause to inherit the desolate heritages [*to restore Israel to the lands of her inheritance. In other words, the gathering will take place; see verse 19*];

9 That thou mayest say to the prisoners [*the living and the dead in spiritual darkness*]: Go forth [*go free from spiritual bondage*]; to them that sit in darkness: Show yourselves [*come out of prison*]. They shall feed in the ways [*their "Shepherd," Christ, will lead them to the gospel path*], and their pastures shall be in all high places [*they will partake of the best, the highest, the gospel of Christ*].

10 They shall not hunger nor thirst [*for the true gospel any more, because they will have it*], neither shall the heat nor the sun smite them; for he that hath mercy on them shall lead them, even by the springs of water [*symbolic of living water; see John 4:10*] shall he guide them [*benefits of accepting and living the gospel*].

As mentioned at the beginning of chapter 20, Isaiah is very thorough. He repeats, then repeats the message, and then repeats it again, and yet again. In these verses, we are seeing this method employed by Isaiah to emphasize the wonderful benefits of the restored gospel and following Christ to the "high places" where the best "pasture" is to be found, namely, eternal exaltation.

11 And I will make all my mountains *["mountains" are often symbolic of temples] a way [a means of arriving at a destination]*, and my highways shall be exalted *[I will prepare "gospel highways" in all parts of the world, through the restoration of the gospel and the gathering in the last days, which will lead the faithful saints to exaltation].*

12 And then *[in the days of gathering]*, O house of Israel, behold, these *[Israel]* shall come from far; and lo, these from the north and from the west; and these from the land of Sinim *[Strong's Exhaustive Bible Concordance says this might refer to inhabitants of southern China; see also Smith's Bible Dictionary, under "Sinim"].*

13 Sing, O heavens; and be joyful, O earth; for the feet of those who are in the east shall be established; and break forth into singing, O mountains; for they shall be smitten no more; for the Lord hath comforted his people *[speaking prophetically of the future, as if it has already happened]*, and will have mercy upon his afflicted *[the Lord will eventually redeem Israel].*

Remember, after verse 3, above, we suggested that verses 4–12 (and beyond) could be like a stage play, with Israel as the sole actor or actress, lamenting her failure to do what the Lord called her to do. In verse 14, next, Israel in effect brushes off the prophetic encouragement given in verse 13.

14 But, behold, Zion *[Israel]* hath said: The Lord hath forsaken me, and my Lord hath forgotten me *[wicked Israel's complaint]*—but he will show that he hath not.

15 For can a woman forget her sucking *[nursing]* child, that she should not have compassion on the son of her womb? Yea, they may forget *[yes, even that happens among mortals]*, yet will I not forget thee, O house of Israel *[a promise! I will keep my promise to restore the gospel and to gather Israel again].*

Verse 16, next, contains some of the most beautiful Atonement symbolism in scripture. Just as a workman's hands bear witness of his work, such as a carpenter with callouses and blisters, so shall the nail prints in the Savior's hands bear witness of His work for us.

16 Behold, I have graven thee upon the palms of my hands *[each of us is "engraved" upon the Savior's hands where the nails pierced His flesh; in other words, the wounds on the palms of His hands bear witness of His work for us]*; thy walls are continually before me *["walls" would represent a person's house; in other words, I know where you live and always know what help you need].*

Next, Isaiah prophesies that things will be turned around in the last days such that the enemies of Israel, who once distressed her, will now flee from her.

17 Thy children shall make haste against thy destroyers [*your descendants will finally gain the upper hand against your enemies*]; and they that made thee waste shall go forth of thee [*will flee from you, the tables will be turned in the last days*].

18 Lift up thine eyes [*let me show you—complaining Israel in verse 14—the future*] round about and behold; all these [righteous, faithful descendants in the last days] gather themselves together [*You thought you were going to be wiped out completely, but look at all your descendants in the future!*], and they shall come to thee. And as I live [*the most serious and solemn promise in Hebrew culture*], saith the Lord, thou shalt surely clothe thee with them all, as with an ornament, and bind them on even as a bride [*a bride puts on her finest clothing for the occasion; Israel will have her finest descendants in the last days*].

19 For thy waste and thy desolate places, and the land of thy destruction [*you've been trodden down for centuries*], shall even now be too narrow by reason of the inhabitants [*you will have so many descendants you'll seem to be running out of room; latter-day gathering of Israel*]; and they [*your*

former enemies] that swallowed thee up shall be far away.

20 The children [*converts to the true gospel*] whom thou shalt have, after thou hast lost the first [*via apostasy, war, etc.*], shall again in thine ears say: The place is too strait for me [*there's not enough room for us all*]; give place to me that I may dwell.

The fulfillment of the above prophecy, that, in the last days, there will be a great increase in faithful members of the Church, is very apparent in our day. Just consider the vast building program of the Church as we build temples and chapels to try to keep up with the increase.

21 Then [*in the last days*] shalt thou [*Israel*] say in thine heart: Who hath begotten me these [*where in the world did all these Israelites come from!*], seeing I have lost my children, and am desolate, a captive, and removing to and fro [*scattered*]? And who hath brought up these? Behold, I was left alone [*I thought I was finished off, done for*]; these, where have they been?

I hope that you are beginning to appreciate Isaiah's inspired ability to create pictures and feelings, indeed drama, with words, as he teaches. Perhaps you have now felt Israel's discouragement and maybe even caught a slight touch of self-pity on her part as Isaiah has portrayed her in this chapter. Isaiah thus skillfully set the stage for her astonishment at the fulfillment of the Lord's promises to her in the last days. This could be symbolic of skeptics in all ages of the world who are bound to be caught off guard as the prophesied miracles of gathering take place.

Next, the Lord answers Israel's question, "Where did all these come from?" He tells us how He will accomplish this great gathering of Israel in the last days.

22 Thus saith the Lord God: Behold, I will lift up mine hand [*I will signal*] to the Gentiles, and set up my standard [*the Church, true gospel of Christ*] to the people; and they [*the Gentiles*] shall bring thy sons in their arms, and thy daughters shall be carried upon their shoulders [*Gentile nations will help gather Israel*].

23 And kings shall be thy nursing fathers, and their queens thy nursing mothers [*example: Great Britain was very influential in establishing a homeland for the Jews in Palestine, after World War I, and helped sponsor the establishment of the Nation of Israel, in the United Nations in 1948*]; they [*the leaders of nations*] shall bow down to thee with their face towards the earth, and lick up the dust of thy feet [*the tables will be turned in the last days*]; and thou shalt know that I am the Lord; for they shall not be ashamed that wait for [*trust in*] me.

Just a bit more about the fulfillment

of the marvelous prophecy in verse 23, above. In 1830, when the Church was officially organized, the Jewish population in the Holy Land was about seven thousand. Now, it is over three million! Next, in verse 24, Isaiah portrays Israel as asking, in effect, "How could we, who have virtually always been victims (prey) of such powerful enemies, ever be rescued from them and set free?" The Lord will answer their question in verse 25.

24 For shall the prey [*Israel*] be taken from the mighty [*powerful enemies*], or the lawful [*the Lord's covenant people*] captives delivered [*be set free*]?

25 But thus saith the Lord, even the captives [*Israel*] of the mighty [*powerful enemies*] shall be taken away [*rescued*], and the prey [*victims*] of the terrible [*tyrants*] shall be delivered [*set free*]; for I [*the Lord*] will contend with him that contendeth with thee [*Israel*], and I will save thy children [*the answer to Israel's question in verse 24 is that the Lord will rescue them and set them free*].

26 And I will feed them [*Israel's enemies*] that oppress thee with their own flesh; they shall be drunken [*out of control*] with their own blood as with sweet wine [*your enemies will turn against each other and destroy themselves; compare with Mormon 4:5*]; and all flesh shall know that I, the Lord, am thy Savior and thy Redeemer, the Mighty One of Jacob.

2 NEPHI 7

Background

Since Isaiah uses much symbolism, and since the Lord uses symbolism in many settings, including the temple, to teach us, we will include here a list of several items of symbolism commonly used in the scriptures.

SYMBOLISM OFTEN USED IN SCRIPTURES

Colors

white	purity; righteousness; exaltation (Example: Rev. 3:4–5)
black	evil; famine; darkness (Example: Rev. 6:5–6)
red	sins; bloodshed (Example: Rev. 6:4; D&C 133:51)
blue	heaven; godliness; remembering and keeping God's commandments (Example: Numbers 15:37–40)
green	life; nature (Example: Rev. 8:7)
amber	sun; light; divine glory (Example: D&C 110:2, Rev. 1:15, Ezek. 1:4, 27; 8:2)
scarlet	royalty (Example: Dan. 5:29; Matt. 27:28–29)
silver	worth, but less than gold (Example: Ridges, *Isaiah Made Easier*, Isa. 48:10 notes)
gold	the best; exaltation (Example: Rev. 4:4)

Body parts

eye	perception; light and knowledge
head	governing
ears	obedience; hearing
mouth	speaking
hair	modesty; covering
members	offices and callings
heart	inner man; courage
hands	action, acting

right hand	covenant hand; making covenants
bowels	center of emotion; whole being
loins	posterity; preparing for action (gird up your loins)
liver	center of feeling
reins	kidneys; center of desires, thoughts
arm	power
foot	mobility; foundation
toe	associated with cleansing rites (Example: Lev. 14:17)
nose	anger (Example: 2 Sam. 22:16; Job 4:9)
tongue	speaking
blood	life of the body
knee	humility; submission
shoulder	strength; effort
forehead	total dedication, loyalty (Example: Rev. 14:1—loyalty to God); Rev. 13:16 (loyalty to wickedness, Satan)

Numbers

1	unity; God
3	God; Godhead; A word repeated 3 times means superlative, "the most" or "the best" (See Isaiah 6:3).
4	mankind; earth (see Smith's Bible Dictionary, p. 456). (Example: Rev. 7:1. Four angels over four parts of the earth)
7	completeness; perfection. When man lets God help, it leads to perfection. (man + God = perfection) 4 + 3 = 7
10	numerical perfection; well-organized (Example: Ten Commandments, tithing) (Example: Satan is well-organized, Rev. 13:1)
12	divine government; God's organization (Example: JST Rev. 5:6)
40 days	literal; sometimes means "a long time" as in 1 Samuel 17:16
forever endless	can sometimes be a specific period or age, not endless (see *BYU Religious Studies Center Newsletter*, Vol. 8, No. 3, May 1994)

Other

horse   victory; power to conquer (Example: Rev. 19:11; Jer. 8:16)

donkey   peace (Example: Christ came in peace at the Triumphal Entry)

palms   joy; triumph, victory (Example: John 12:13; Rev. 7:9)

wings   power to move, act, etc. (Example: Rev. 4:8; D&C 77:4)

crown   power; dominion; exaltation (Example: Rev. 2:10; 4:4)

robes   royalty; kings, queens; exaltation (Example: Rev. 6:11, 7:14; 2 Ne. 9:14; D&C 109:76; 3 Ne. 11:8)

As we continue with 2 Nephi 7, Jacob now quotes what is basically known as Isaiah, chapter 50, in the Bible. A major question here is who has left whom when people find themselves far away from God spiritually? Another question that Isaiah asks is essentially "Why don't you come unto Christ? Has He lost His power to save you?"

It is in this chapter that we learn that one of the terrible tortures inflicted upon the Savior during His trial and crucifixion was the pulling out of His whiskers. In this chapter, Isaiah speaks of the future as if it had already happened.

1 [*The Lord asks the question, "Did I divorce you or did you divorce me?" "Did I leave you or did you leave me? Did I break My covenants with you or did you break your covenants with Me?"*] Yea, for thus saith the Lord: Have I put thee away [*divorced you*], or have I cast thee off forever? For thus saith the Lord: Where is the bill of your

mother's divorcement? To whom have I put thee away, or to which of my creditors have I sold you [*Was it I who sold you*]? Yea, to whom have I sold you? Behold, for your iniquities have ye sold yourselves [*you brought it upon yourselves!*], and for your transgressions is your mother [*your apostate nation; Hosea 2:2*] put away [*scattered and smitten*].

2 Wherefore [*this is why*], when I [*Jesus*] came, there was no man [*who received me as the Messiah*]; when I called, yea, there was none to answer [*nobody responded*]. O house of Israel, is my hand shortened at all that it cannot redeem, or have I no power to deliver [*have I lost my power*]? Behold, at my rebuke [*command*] I dry up the sea, I make their rivers a wilderness and their fish to stink because the waters are dried up, and they die because of thirst [*I haven't lost my power*].

3 I clothe the heavens with blackness, and I make sackcloth their

covering [*I can cause the sky to be dark during the day as if it were mourning the dead. In fact it will at Jesus' crucifixion; see Matt 27:45*].

4 The Lord God [*the Father*] hath given me [*Jesus; see verse 6*] the tongue of the learned [*Father taught me well*], that I should know how to speak a word [*a strengthening and comforting word*] in season unto thee, O house of Israel. When ye are weary he waketh morning by morning. He waketh mine ear to hear as the learned [*German Bible, Luther edition: "He, the Father, is constantly communicating with me and I hear as his disciple"*].

5 The Lord God [*the Father*] hath opened mine ear, and I was not rebellious [*hint, hint, Israel*], neither turned away back [*I accomplished my calling, the atonement; you should do yours as given in 1 Nephi 21:6*].

Isaiah now prophesies some very specific details surrounding Christ's crucifixion.

6 I gave my back to the smiter [*scourging; see Matt. 27:26*], and my cheeks to them that plucked off the hair [*pulled out whiskers of my beard*]. I hid not my face from shame and spitting [*as my time for crucifixion came*].

7 For the Lord God [*Father*] will help me, therefore shall I not be confounded [*I'll not be stopped*]. Therefore have I set my face like a flint [*I have braced myself for the*

ordeal], and I know that I shall not be ashamed [*will not fail*].

8 And the Lord [*the Father; see verse 9; could refer to Isaiah too*] is near, and he justifieth me [*approves of everything I do*]. Who will contend with me [*who is willing to go against such odds*]? Let us stand together [*go to court as in a court of law*]. Who is mine adversary? Let him come near me [*face me*], and I will smite him with the strength of my mouth [*the truth from My mouth will ultimately win*].

The phrase, "and I will smite him with the strength of my mouth" in verse 8, above, is not in our Bible, thus showing us that the Brass Plates contained a more accurate record of Isaiah's teachings.

9 For the Lord God [*the Father*] will help me. And all they who shall condemn me, behold, all they shall wax old as a garment, and the moth shall eat them up [*the wicked will have their day, then reap the punishment*].

10 Who is among you that feareth [*respects*] the Lord, that obeyeth the voice of his servant [*prophets*], that walketh in darkness and hath no light? [*Answer. No one because the Lord blesses his followers with light.*]

11 Behold all ye [*the wicked*] that kindle fire, that compass [*surround*] yourselves about with sparks, walk in the light of your

fire and in the sparks which ye have kindled [*trying to live without God, according to your own "light" and philosophies*]. This shall ye have of mine hand—ye shall lie down in sorrow [*misery awaits those who try to live without God*].

2 NEPHI 8

Background

Next, Isaiah first speaks to the righteous and teaches a course in perspective. He reminds all of us not to sell ourselves short. Rather, remember who we are and live to fulfill our potential.

1 Hearken unto me, ye that follow after righteousness [*the Lord is now speaking to the righteous*]. Look unto the rock [*the good, solid rock—Abraham and Sarah*] from whence ye are hewn, and to the hole of the pit [*the rock quarry*] from whence ye are digged [*consider your origins; you are really somebody!*].

2 Look unto Abraham, your father, and unto Sarah, she that bare you [*Sarah is side by side with Abraham in importance*]; for I called him alone [*when he was childless*], and blessed him [*see Abraham 2:9–11*].

3 For the Lord shall comfort Zion, he will comfort all her waste places; and he will make her wilderness like Eden, and her desert like the garden of the Lord [*the Garden of Eden*]. Joy and gladness shall be found therein, thanksgiving and

the voice of melody [*wonderful reward for the righteous*].

4 Hearken unto me [*Christ*], my people; and give ear unto me, O my nation; for a law shall proceed from me [*teachings, doctrines; see Isaiah 51:4, footnote a*], and I will make my judgment to rest for a light for the people [*my laws will bring light to the nations*].

The Lord reminds the righteous that His Atonement and His gospel are always closely available to them.

5 My righteousness [*my ability to save you; triumph*] is near [*is close to you; is available to you*]; my salvation is gone forth, and mine arm shall judge the people. The isles [*nations of the world*] shall wait [*trust, rely*] upon me, and on mine arm [*my power*] shall they trust.

Next, Isaiah reminds us that the salvation that comes through the Lord is completely and totally reliable. No matter what else happens, it will always come through.

6 Lift up your eyes to the heavens, and look upon the earth beneath; for the heavens shall vanish away like smoke [*D&C 29:23–24*], and the earth shall wax [*grow*] old like a garment; and they that dwell therein shall die in like manner. But my salvation [*the salvation I bring*] shall be forever, and my righteousness [*triumph, victory*] shall not be abolished [*glad*

message of hope; see D&C 1:38].

7 Hearken unto me, ye that know righteousness [*you who are righteous*], the people in whose heart I have written my law [*you who have taken my gospel to heart*], fear ye not the reproach [*insults*] of men, neither be ye afraid of their revilings [*stinging criticisms*].

8 For the moth shall eat them [*the wicked who revile against the righteous*] up like a garment [*they will vanish like moth-eaten clothing*], and the worm shall eat them like wool. But my righteousness [*salvation and deliverance*] shall be [*last*] forever, and my salvation from generation to generation [*throughout eternity*].

Isaiah now depicts Israel as replying to the Lord's assurances in the previous verses. Righteous Israel now invites the Lord to exercise his power in their behalf like he did in ancient times.

9 Awake, awake! Put on strength, O arm [*symbolic of power*] of the Lord; awake as in the ancient days [*help us like you did in days gone by*]. Art thou not he that hath cut Rahab [*trimmed Egypt down to size. Rahab is a mythical sea monster and symbolically represents Satan and nations who serve him*], and wounded the dragon [*Satan; see Rev. 12:7–9*]?

10 Art thou not he who hath dried the sea [*Red Sea*], the waters of the great deep; that hath made the

depths of the sea a way [*pathway*] for the ransomed [*redeemed, you redeemed the Children of Israel from Egypt; symbolic of the Atonement's redeeming us from our sins*] to pass over [*parting of the Red Sea*]?

11 Therefore [*because of your power*], the redeemed of the Lord shall return [*the gathering*], and come with singing unto Zion; and everlasting joy and holiness shall be upon their heads; and they shall obtain gladness and joy; sorrow and mourning shall flee away [*ultimate results of righteousness*].

The Lord now replies to righteous Israel's request in verse 9, above.

12 I am he; yea, I am he that comforteth you. Behold, who art thou, that thou shouldst be afraid of man [*mortal man*], who shall die [*trust in God, not man*], and of the son of man [*mortal men*], who shall be made like unto grass [*short-lived glory*]?

13 And forgettest the Lord thy maker, that hath stretched forth the heavens, and laid the foundations of the earth [*how could you forget me, your Creator, after all I've done for you?*], and hast feared continually every day, because of the fury of the oppressor [*Israel's captors who have oppressed them; see 2 Nephi 8, footnote 13c*], as if he were ready to destroy [*German Bible: whose intent is to destroy, why should you live in fear of mortal men*]? And

where is the fury of the oppressor? [*If you live righteously, the day will come when enemies won't be able to hurt you anymore.*]

14 The captive exile hasteneth, that he may be loosed [*the day will come when Israel will be set free; see Isaiah 52:1–2*], and that he should not die in the pit [*not die in captivity*], nor that his bread should fail [*run out; famine, etc.*]

15 But I am the Lord thy God, whose waves roared [*as they drowned Pharaoh's armies in the Red Sea; see 1 Nephi 4:2*]; the Lord of Hosts is my name.

16 And I have put my words in thy mouth [*have given you my gospel*], and have covered [*protected*] thee in the shadow of mine hand, that I may plant the heavens and lay the foundations of the earth [*I created the heavens and the earth*], and say unto Zion: Behold, thou art my people [*I haven't deserted you*].

17 Awake, awake, stand up, O Jerusalem, which hast drunk at the hand of the Lord the cup of his fury—thou hast drunken the dregs [*bitter residue at the bottom of a cup*] of the cup of trembling wrung out [*you have paid a terrible price for your wickedness*]—

18 And none to guide her [*Israel*] among all the sons she hath brought forth [*you have spent many years without prophets*]; neither that taketh her by the hand, of all the sons she hath brought up [*You have spent many years without prophets*].

19 These two sons [*two prophets in the last days who will help keep enemies of the Jews from totally destroying them; see Rev. 11*] are come unto thee, who shall be sorry for thee [*who will care about you*]—thy desolation and destruction, and the famine and the sword—and by whom shall I comfort thee?

20 Thy sons [*your people*] have fainted [*German Bible: are on their last leg*], save these two [*the two prophets in Rev. 11*]; they [*your people*] lie at the head of all the streets [*German Bible: are being destroyed right and left*]; as a wild bull in a net [*implies that they are trapped in a net woven by their own wickedness*], they are full of the fury of the Lord [*they are catching the full fury of the Lord*], the rebuke of thy God [*the punishments of God*].

21 Therefore hear now this, thou [*Israel*] afflicted, and drunken [*out of control*], and not with wine [*rather, with wickedness*]:

22 Thus saith thy Lord, the Lord and thy God pleadeth the cause of his people [*I have not deserted you*]; behold, I have taken out of thine hand the cup of trembling, the dregs of the cup of my fury; thou shalt no more drink it again [*Christ will save the Jews in the last days; see 2 Nephi 9:1–2*].

23 But I will put it [*the cup in*

verse 22] into the hand of them that afflict thee [*your enemies will get what they gave you*]; who have said to thy soul: Bow down, that we may go over [*lie down while we walk all over you!*]—and thou hast laid thy body as the ground and as the street to them that went over [*you have been walked on by your enemies*].

24 Awake, awake, put on thy strength, O Zion [*return to the proper use of the priesthood; see D&C 113:7,8*]; put on thy beautiful garments [*dress in your finest and prepare to be with the Savior; see Rev. 21:2–3*], O Jerusalem, the holy city; for henceforth there shall no more come into thee the uncircumcised and the unclean [*the wicked*].

25 Shake thyself from the dust [*from being walked on, verse 23; see also 2 Nephi 13:26*]; arise [*from being walked on, verse 23*], sit down [*in dignity, redeemed at last*], O Jerusalem; loose thyself [*free yourself*] from the bands of thy neck [*from captivity, bondage, wickedness*], O captive daughter of Zion.

2 NEPHI 12

Background
Chapters 12, 13 and 14 go together. Also note that of the 433 verses of Isaiah quoted in the Book of Mormon, over half of them are given differently than in the King James Bible, while about 200 of

them are the same; see 2 Nephi 12, footnote 2a. Thus, the Book of Mormon is a major source of clarification and help for understanding Isaiah. This chapter, 2 Nephi 12, is similar to Isaiah 2 in the Bible. It deals with the gathering of Israel to the true Church in the last days, the Millennium, and the destruction of the proud and the wicked at the Second Coming.

1 The word that Isaiah, the son of Amoz, saw concerning Judah [*the Jews as a political kingdom as well as the Jews as Israelites*] and Jerusalem:

As you know, because Isaiah uses so much symbolism, his writings can have many different meanings and applications. Next, in verse 2 for instance, the phrase "mountain of the Lord's house" can mean the headquarters of the Church in Salt Lake City in the Rocky Mountains in the last days. Also, since "mountains" are often symbolic of temples ("high places" where we can draw closer to God), "mountain of the Lord's house" can have a dual meaning referring to temples.

2 And it shall come to pass in the last days, when the mountain of the Lord's house [*"high place," or Church headquarters in the last days; also temples will be established*] shall be established in the top of the mountains, and shall be exalted above the hills [*you can get "higher," or closer to God in the temples through covenant-making*

than on the highest mountains], and all nations [*the gathering involves people from every nation*] shall flow unto it [*the true Church in the last days*].

LeGrand Richards, an Apostle and scholar, explained how "mountain" can refer to temples as follows:

The word mountain is used in the scriptures in different allegorical or figurative senses. In 2 Nephi 12:1–4 the word mountain refers to a high place of God, a place of revelation, even the temple of the Lord.

This temple [*Salt Lake Temple*] on this temple block is that house of the God of Jacob that our pioneer fathers started to build when they were a thousand miles from transportation, and it took them forty years to build it. (LeGrand Richards, in Conference Report, Oct. 1975, p. 77; or *Ensign*, Nov. 1975, p. 51)

3 And many people shall go and say, Come ye, and let us go up to the mountain [*to the true Church; temple*] of the Lord, to the house [*temples*] of the God of Jacob [*Israel*]; and he will teach us of his ways, and we will walk in his paths [*we will be obedient*]; for out of Zion shall go forth the law, and the word of the Lord from Jerusalem [*"law" and "word" are synonyms*].

There will be two "headquarters" of the Church during the Millennium, one in "Zion" (Jackson County, Missouri) and one in Old Jerusalem.

4 And he [*Christ*] shall judge among the nations, and shall rebuke many people: and they shall beat their swords into plow-shares [*the promised millennial peace will come*], and their spears into pruning-hooks [*there will be peace*]—nation shall not lift up sword against nation, neither shall they learn war any more [*the Millennium*].

Isaiah now switches from the future back to his own time and people who have become very wicked, inviting them to repent and return to the Lord.

5 O house of Jacob [*Israel*], come ye and let us walk in the light of the Lord; yea, come, for **ye have all gone astray**, every one to his wicked ways.

Next, Isaiah explains why the blessings of the Lord are not coming upon the Israelites of his day. Remember that the phrase "house of Jacob" means "family of Jacob" or in other words, "descendants of Abraham, Isaac, and Jacob" who are the covenant people of the Lord. Remember also that all people are invited by the gospel of Jesus Christ to join with the "covenant people of the Lord" through baptism, whether or not they are bloodline descendants of Jacob. Thus all can become covenant people and ultimately enter into celestial exaltation.

6 Therefore [*this is the reason why*], O Lord, thou hast forsaken thy people, the house of Jacob [*the Israelites*], because they be replenished from the east [*they are adopting false eastern religions*], and hearken unto soothsayers like the Philistines [*are into witchcraft, sorcery etc.; see 3 Nephi 21:16*], and they please themselves in the children of strangers [*they are mixing and marrying with foreigners, people not of covenant Israel; they are "marrying" themselves right out of the Church, so to speak*].

The word "strangers," as used in Isaiah's writings (see verse 6, above), almost always means "foreigners" or in other words, non-Israelites.

7 Their land also is full of silver and gold, neither is there any end of their treasures [*they have become materialistic*]; their land is also full of horses, neither is there any end of their chariots.

Horses and chariots are symbolic of military equipment and preparations for war in Isaiah's writings. They can also represent military might and ability to conquer.

8 Their land is also full of idols [*they are in a condition of deep apostasy; they have left God*]; they worship the work of their own hands, that which their own fingers have made [*an absurd thing to do;*

emphasizing that wickedness does not promote rational thought, a theme Isaiah pursues throughout his writings].

9 And the mean man [*poor, low in social status*] boweth not down [*is not humble*], and the great [*wealthy, powerful, high in social status*] man humbleth himself not, therefore, forgive him not [*nobody is humble, therefore, no forgiveness!*].

Verse 9, above, is a great example of the value of the Book of Mormon Isaiah verses. In the Bible, the equivalent of verse 9 reads as follows:

Isaiah 2:9

9 And the mean man boweth down, and the great man humbleth himself: therefore forgive them not.

When you compare 2 Nephi 12:9 with Isaiah 2:9, you see that the word "not" is left out twice in the Bible version and makes all the difference! If you were reading Isaiah in the Bible and trying to understand God's mercy and His dealings with people based on Isaiah 2:9, you would be in trouble. This is an example of the meaning of the 8th Article of Faith which says: "We believe the Bible to be the word of God as far as it is translated correctly; we also believe the Book of Mormon to be the word of God" (Pearl of Great Price, Articles of Faith 1:8).

10 O ye wicked ones, enter into the rock [*caves; see verse 19*], and hide thee in the dust, for the fear of the Lord and **the glory of his majesty shall smite thee** [*you will not be able to stand the brightness of his glory at the Second Coming and will thus be consumed; see D&C 5:19*].

Many people wonder how the wicked will be burned at the time of the actual Second Coming. We learned the answer in verse 10, above. As stated, they will be burned by his glory. This is stated again in verses 19 and 21.

Some years ago, a student asked me how the temples would survive the burning at the Second Coming. Verses 10, 19, 21, plus D&C 5:19 provide a simple answer. Temples can stand the glory of the Lord. Therefore, they will not be burned.

11 And it shall come to pass that the lofty looks [*pride*] of man shall be humbled, and the haughtiness [*pride*] of men shall be bowed down [*put down*], and the Lord alone shall be exalted in that day [*the Lord will demonstrate that He has power over all things at the Second Coming*].

Verse 11, above, is a good example of the fact that Isaiah repeats important concepts as he writes and teaches. The phrases "lofty looks" and "haughtiness of men" both mean pride. If people do not understand that Isaiah uses repetition as a technique for emphasizing important points, they could spend a lot of time and fruitless effort in trying to figure out the difference in message between these two phrases. In fact, in verse 12, next, Isaiah says "pride" three different ways. They are in **bold**. This emphasis against pride continues in succeeding verses. We will **bold** some of them too.

12 For the day of the Lord of Hosts [*the Second Coming*] soon cometh upon [*Hebrew: "against"*] all nations, yea, upon every one [*who is wicked*]; yea, upon the **proud** and **lofty**, and upon every one who is **lifted up** [*prideful*], and he shall be brought low [*humbled*].

13 Yea, and the day of the Lord shall come upon all the **cedars** [*symbolic of high and mighty people; can also mean groves of trees which idol worshipers often used for seclusion when they participated in sexual immorality with temple prostitutes as a part of their idol worship*] **of Lebanon**, for they are **high and lifted up** [*full of pride*]; and upon all the **oaks** [*people*] **of Bashan**;

As mentioned in verse 13, above, sexual immorality was often a part of idol worship among apostate Israelites as they joined in the false religions of their pagan neighbors. The Bible Dictionary confirms this abominable practice on page 706, under the topic "Idol." It describes various aspects of idol worship in practice in ancient times and, among other things, says, "Such idolatry being some form of nature worship, **which encouraged** as a rule **immoral practices**."

Perhaps you have wondered why conquering Israelite armies were often commanded to cut down groves of trees as part of their conquering of their enemies. Most of us are environmentally conscientious and would prefer that they leave these trees standing. But, when we understand that the groves represented sexual immorality associated with apostasy, we understand. An example of such a command to destroy the groves is found in Exodus 34:13, as follows:

"But ye shall destroy their altars, break their images, and cut down their groves."

14 And upon all the high mountains [*where people worship idols*], and upon all the hills [*where they worship idols*], and upon all the nations which are **lifted up** [*in pride etc.*], and upon every people;

15 And upon every high tower, and upon every fenced wall [*symbolic of the pride and "trusting in the arm of flesh" which can go along with man-made defenses*];

16 And upon all the ships of the sea, and upon all the ships of Tarshish [*noted for ability to travel long distances, carry large cargos and*

strength as warships; apparently symbolic of pride and materialism], and upon all pleasant pictures [*pleasure ships upon which the wealthy traveled*].

17 And the **loftiness** [*pride*] of man shall be bowed down [*shall be brought down*], and the **haughtiness** of men shall be made low [*brought down*]; and the Lord alone shall be exalted in that day.

18 And the idols he [*Christ*] shall utterly abolish [*at the Second Coming*].

In verse 19, next, Isaiah paints a picture with words of the terror of the wicked as the Savior actually comes at the time of His Second Coming.

19 And they [*the wicked*] shall go into the holes of the rocks [*caves*], and into the caves of the earth, for the fear of the Lord shall come upon them **and the glory of his majesty shall smite them** [*D&C 5:19*], when he ariseth [*becomes active*] to shake terribly the earth.

20 In that day [*the Second Coming*] a man shall cast his idols of silver, and his idols of gold, which he hath made for himself to worship [*an absurd thing to do*], to the moles and to the bats [*creatures who live in darkness; symbolical of wicked people who live in spiritual darkness*];

21 To go into the clefts of the rocks, and into the tops of the ragged rocks [*to try to hide from God*],

for the fear of the Lord shall come upon them and **the majesty of his glory shall smite them** [*D&C 5:19*], when he ariseth to shake terribly the earth.

22 Cease ye from man, whose breath is in his nostrils; for wherein is he to be accounted of [*why trust in man, why trust in the arm of flesh when God is truly powerful and can save you*]?

2 NEPHI 13

Background

This chapter is to be compared with Isaiah 3 in the Bible. In this chapter as well as others, Isaiah uses a literary technique known as "chiasmus," a writing form in which the author says certain things and then repeats them in reverse order for emphasis. Usually, the middle element or elements of the chiasmus are the main point being emphasized. An example of a simple "chiasmus" is found in Isaiah 6:10 as follows. We will use **bold** to point it out.

Chiastic structure in Isaiah 6:10:

"Make the **heart** of this people fat, and make their **ears** heavy, and shut their **eyes**; lest they see with their **eyes**, and hear with their **ears**, and understand with their **heart**, and convert, and be healed."

A way of showing the flow of the above chiasmus would be:

A, B, C, C', B', A'

The ancient use of chiasmus as a literary technique was not discovered until after the coming forth of the Book of Mormon. Therefore, the fact that chiasmus is found in other places in the Book of Mormon is a very strong internal evidence of its authenticity as an ancient document. Two examples of chiasmus in the Book of Mormon, other than in the Isaiah passages, follow. We will again use **bold** to point out the ancient chiastic writing form.

Example 1: Mosiah 3:18–19

18 For behold he judgeth, and his judgment is just; and the infant perisheth not that dieth in his infancy; but men drink damnation to their own souls except they **humble [A]** themselves and become as **little children [B]**, and believe that salvation was, and is, and is to come, in and through the **atoning blood of Christ [C]**, the Lord Omnipotent.

19 For **the natural man [D]** is an enemy to God, and has been from the fall of Adam, and will be, forever and ever, unless he yields to the enticings of the Holy Spirit, and putteth off **the natural man [D']** and becometh a saint through the **atonement of Christ [C']** the Lord, and becometh as a **child [B']**, submissive, meek, **humble [A']**, patient, full of love, willing to submit to all things which the Lord seeth fit to inflict upon him, even as a child doth submit to his father.

In the case of the above chiasmus,

we could show the flow of concepts as follows:

A, B, C, D, D', C', B', A'

<u>**Example 2: Alma 36**</u>

1 My son, give ear to my **words** [A]; for I swear unto you, that inasmuch as ye shall **keep the commandments** [B] of God ye shall prosper in the land.

2 I would that ye should do as I have done, in remembering the captivity of our fathers; for they were **in bondage** [C], and none could deliver them except it was the God of Abraham, and the God of Isaac, and the God of Jacob; and he surely did deliver them in their afflictions.

3 And now, O my son Helaman, behold, thou art in thy youth, and therefore, I beseech of thee that thou wilt hear my words and learn of me; for I do know that whosoever shall put their trust in God shall be **supported in their trials** [D], and their troubles, and their afflictions, and shall be lifted up at the last day.

4 And I would not that ye think that I know of myself—not of the temporal but of the spiritual, not of the carnal mind but of God.

5 Now, behold, I say unto you, if I had not been **born of God** [E] I should not have known these things; but God has, by the mouth of his holy angel, made these things known unto me, not of any worthiness of myself;

6 For I went about with the sons of Mosiah, seeking to destroy the church of God; but behold, God sent his holy angel to stop us by the way.

7 And behold, he spake unto us, as it were the voice of thunder, and the whole earth did tremble beneath our feet; and we all fell to the earth, for the fear of the Lord came upon us.

8 But behold, the voice said unto me: Arise. And I arose and stood up, and beheld the angel.

9 And he said unto me: If thou wilt of thyself be destroyed, seek no more to destroy the church of God.

10 And it came to pass that I fell to the earth; and it was for the space of three days and three nights that I could not open my mouth, neither had I the use of my limbs.

11 And the angel spake more things unto me, which were heard by my brethren, but I did not hear them; for when I heard the words—If thou wilt be destroyed of thyself, seek no more to destroy the church of God—I was struck with such great fear and amazement lest perhaps I should be destroyed, that I fell to the earth and I did hear no more.

12 But I was racked with eternal torment, for my soul was harrowed up to the greatest degree and racked with all my sins.

13 Yea, I did remember all my sins and iniquities, for which I was tormented with the pains of hell; yea, I saw that I had rebelled against my God, and that I had not kept his holy commandments.

14 Yea, and I had murdered many of his children, or rather led them away unto destruction; yea, and in fine so great had been my iniquities, that the very thought of coming into the presence of my God did rack my soul with inexpressible horror.

15 Oh, thought I, that I could be banished and become extinct both soul and body, that I might not be brought to stand in the presence of my God, to be judged of my deeds.

16 And now, for three days and for three nights was I racked, even with the pains of a damned soul.

17 And it came to pass that as I was thus racked with torment, while I was harrowed up by **the memory of my many sins** (F), behold, I remembered also to have heard my father prophesy unto the people concerning the coming of one Jesus Christ, a Son of God, to atone for the sins of the world.

18 Now, as my mind caught hold upon this thought, I cried within my heart: O Jesus, thou Son of God, have mercy on me, who am in the gall of bitterness, and am encircled about by the everlasting chains of death.

19 And now, behold, when I thought this, I could remember my pains no more; yea, I was harrowed up by **the memory of my sins [F']** no more.

20 And oh, what joy, and what marvelous light I did behold; yea, my soul was filled with joy as exceeding as was my pain!

21 Yea, I say unto you, my son, that there could be nothing so exquisite and so bitter as were my pains. Yea, and again I say unto you, my son, that on the other hand, there can be nothing so exquisite and sweet as was my joy.

22 Yea, methought I saw, even as our father Lehi saw, God sitting upon his throne, surrounded with numberless concourses of angels, in the attitude of singing and praising their God; yea, and my soul did long to be there.

23 But behold, my limbs did receive their strength again, and I stood upon my feet, and did manifest unto the people that I had been born of God.

24 Yea, and from that time even until now, I have labored without ceasing, that I might bring souls unto repentance; that I might bring them to taste of the exceeding joy of which I did taste; that they might also be born of God, and be filled with the Holy Ghost.

25 Yea, and now behold, O my son, the Lord doth give me exceedingly great joy in the fruit of my labors;

26 For because of the word which he has imparted unto me, behold, many have been **born of God [E']**, and have tasted as I have tasted, and have seen eye to eye as I have seen; therefore they do know of these things of which I have spoken, as I do know; and the knowledge which I have is of God.

27 And I have been **supported under trials [D']** and troubles of every kind, yea, and in all manner of afflictions; yea, God has delivered me from prison, and from bonds, and from death; yea, and I do put my trust in him, and he will still deliver me.

28 And I know that he will raise me up at the last day, to dwell with him in glory; yea, and I will praise him forever, for he has brought our fathers out of Egypt, and he has swallowed up the Egyptians in the Red Sea; and he led them by his power into the promised land; yea, and he has delivered them out of bondage and captivity from time to time.

29 Yea, and he has also brought our fathers out of the land of Jerusalem; and he has also, by his everlasting power, delivered them **out of bondage [C']** and captivity, from time to time even down to the present day; and I have always retained in remembrance their captivity; yea, and ye also ought to retain in remembrance, as I have done, their captivity.

30 But behold, my son, this is not

all; for ye ought to know as I do know, that inasmuch as ye shall **keep the commandments [B']** of God ye shall prosper in the land; and ye ought to know also, that inasmuch as ye will not keep the commandments of God ye shall be cut off from his presence. Now this is according to his **word [A']**.

By the way, did you notice the center of the "chiasmus"? It deals with "memory of sins" and teaches very strongly that memory of sins need not devastate members for the rest of their lives if they repent and are cleansed by the Atonement. Also, if you look closely, there is much more of chiasmus in Alma 36. In fact, there is a chiasmus containing 34 elements, 17 going forward and 17 going backward.

We will now go ahead with 2 Nephi 13, which contains a chiastic structure also. Isaiah uses chiasmus to show the destruction of stability within a society which smiles upon gross sin and wickedness.

1 For behold, the Lord, **the Lord of Hosts, doth take away from Jerusalem [A]**, and from Judah, the stay [*supply*] and the staff [*support*], **the whole staff of bread, [B]** and the whole stay of water [*the Lord is going to pull the props out and the whole kingdom of the Jews will collapse*]—

2 **The mighty man, [C] and the man of war**, the judge, and the

prophet, and the prudent, and the ancient [*all the stable, capable leaders will be gone*];

3 **The captain of fifty, and the honorable man, and the counselor** [**D**], **and the cunning artificer** [*skilled craftsman*], **and the eloquent orator** [*all capable leaders and craftsman will be gone*].

4 And I will give **children unto them to be their princes** [*leaders*], **and babes** [**E**] **shall rule over them** [*immature, irresponsible leaders will take over*].

5 And **the people shall be oppressed,** [**F**] **every one by another** [*anarchy, gangs, citizens against citizens, etc.*], and every one by his neighbor; the **child shall behave himself proudly against the ancient,** [**E'**] and the base [*crude, rude*] against the honorable [*no respect for authority*].

Next, Isaiah describes how bad things will get when stable society crumbles.

6 When a man shall take hold of his brother of the house of his father, and shall say: Thou hast clothing, **be thou our ruler** [**D'**], **and let not this ruin come under thy hand** [*don't let this happen to us, you've got half decent clothing, you be our leader*]—

7 In that day shall he swear [*protest*], saying: [**C'**] **I will not be a healer** [*I can't lead you nor defend and protect you!*]; for in my house there is neither **bread** [**B'**] nor

clothing [*I've got my own problems*]; make me not a ruler of the people.

Next, Isaiah describes the end result of a society that allows open evil and wickedness.

8 **For Jerusalem is ruined,** [**A'**] **and Judah is fallen,** because their tongues and their doings have been against the Lord, to provoke the eyes of his glory [*in word and actions, the people are completely against the Lord*].

9 The show of their countenance doth witness against them [*they even look wicked*], and doth declare their sin to be even as Sodom [*wicked through and through, including homosexuality; see Gen. 19, footnote 5a*], and they cannot hide it [*blatant sin, can't be rationalized away or hidden from God*]. Wo unto their souls, for they have rewarded evil unto themselves [*they are getting what they deserve*]!

So far, this chapter is pretty dismal. In order to make sure that the righteous do not despair, who are trying to survive spiritually and otherwise in such a society, the Lord assures them that they will ultimately be rewarded for their righteousness.

10 Say unto the righteous that it is well with them; for they shall eat the fruit of their doings.

11 Wo unto the wicked, for they shall perish; for the reward of their hands shall be upon them!

[*As ye sow, so shall ye reap.*]

Isaiah continues to describe the end results of such uncontrolled wickedness among the Jews. This of course applies to any nation, any time in history, anywhere.

12 And my people, children [*immature leaders*] are their oppressors, and women rule over them [*breakdown of traditional family; men are weak leaders*]. O my people, they who lead thee cause thee to err and destroy the way of thy paths [*leadership without basic gospel values causes terrible damage*].

Next, Isaiah will take the wicked leaders of the Jews to task for selfishly taking all they possibly can from the very people they are supposed to protect as leaders.

13 The Lord standeth up to plead [*Hebrew: contend, or, you are in big trouble*], and standeth to judge the people.

14 The Lord will enter into judgment with the ancients [*the wicked elders and leaders*] of his people and the princes [*leaders*] thereof; for ye have eaten up the vineyard [*you have ruined, destroyed the country*] and the spoil of the poor in your houses [*you have all kinds of loot in your houses which you have taken from the poor; you were supposed to protect them, but, instead, you ruin them*].

15 What mean ye [*what have you got to say for yourselves*]? Ye beat my people to pieces, and grind the faces of the poor [*push the poor farther into poverty*], saith the Lord God of Hosts.

Isaiah now shows what happens when women get as wicked as men, and points out that when this happens, society is doomed as pointed out in verses 25 and 26.

16 Moreover, the Lord saith: Because the daughters of Zion are haughty [*full of wicked pride*], and walk with stretched-forth necks [*pride*] and wanton [*lustful*] eyes, walking and mincing [*short, rapid steps; see Isaiah 3, footnote 16e*] as they go, and making a tinkling with their feet [*German Bible: wearing expensive shoes so people will notice them*]—

17 Therefore [*for these reasons*] the Lord will smite with a scab the crown of the head [*German Bible: make them bald; perhaps the "scab" is a result of being shaved as slaves*] of the daughters of Zion, and the Lord will discover their secret parts [*expose their evil deeds*].

In verse 17, above, Isaiah prophesied that the Lord's covenant people would go into captivity because of their wickedness. Below, he describes the taking away of all that has been precious in the hearts and minds of the women who have become wicked in Isaiah's day. This same scene is typical of any society whose morals and values decay.

18 In that day the Lord will take away the bravery [German Bible: decoration, beauty] of their tinkling ornaments [German Bible: expensive shoes], and cauls, and round tires like the moon [female ornamentations representing high status in materialistic society];

19 The chains [necklaces] and the bracelets, and the mufflers [veils];

20 The bonnets, and the ornaments of the legs, and the headbands, and the tablets [German Bible: musk boxes, perfume boxes], and the ear-rings;

21 The rings, and nose jewels;

22 The changeable suits of apparel [German Bible: party clothes], and the mantles [German Bible: gowns, robes], and the wimples [medieval women's head coverings], and the crisping-pins [German Bible: money purses];

23 The glasses [German Bible: mirrors; Hebrew: see-through clothing; see Isaiah 3, footnote 23a], and the fine linen, and hoods [turbans], and the veils.

As indicated above, Isaiah has described female high-society fashions, arrogance, sexual immorality and materialism in terms of such things in his day. Next, he prophetically describes the end results of such wickedness for these women, and

literally and symbolically for Jerusalem and the kingdom of Judah.

24 And it shall come to pass, instead of sweet smell [perfume] there shall be stink [from corpses of people killed by invading armies; also the stench associated with miserable slavery conditions]; and instead of a girdle [German Bible: nice waistband], a rent [rags]; and instead of well set hair, baldness [slaves had shaved heads]; and instead of a stomacher [a nice robe], a girding of sackcloth; burning [branding, a mark of slavery; see Isaiah 3, footnote 24d] instead of beauty.

In the above verses, Isaiah spoke of "shaved" heads. Symbolically, this represents slavery or bondage. Literally, conquering armies often kept the best captives who would bring a good price in the slave markets back home. They shaved the hair off of these slaves for three basic reasons:

1. Humiliation

2. Identification (makes it easier to spot a runaway slave)

3. Sanitation

25 Thy men shall fall by the sword and thy mighty in the war [wars will deplete your male population].

26 And her [Jerusalem's; see verse 8] gates shall lament and mourn; and she shall be desolate [empty, cleaned out; see Isa. 3, footnote

26d], and shall sit upon the ground [*Jerusalem, symbolic of the wicked, will be brought down completely and conquered—one fulfillment of this prophecy was the Babylonian captivity which ended about 587 B.C.*].

2 NEPHI 14

Background

The Joseph Smith Translation, the Hebrew Bible and the German Bible put this next verse at the end of Isaiah, chapter 3 in the Bible. Thus, 2 Nephi 14:1 fits in the context of Jerusalem's destruction and the scarcity of men resulting from that invasion [see Isaiah 4, footnote 1a]. Verses 2–6 refer to the Millennium.

1 And in that day [*referred to in chapter 13:25–26*], seven women shall take hold of one man, saying: We will eat our own bread, and wear our own apparel [*we will pay our own way*]; only let us be called by thy name [*please marry us*] to take away our reproach [*the stigma of being unmarried and childless*].

Verse 2, below, starts a new topic, namely conditions during the Millennium.

2 In that day shall the branch of the Lord [*The "branch" can have dual meaning. In Jer. 23:5 and footnote 5 b, this "branch" refers to Christ. In Isa. 60:21; 61:3, it refers to righteous people during the Millennium*] be beautiful and glorious; the fruit of the earth excellent and

comely [*pleasant to look at*] to them that are escaped of Israel [*the righteous who have escaped the destruction of the wicked*].

3 And it shall come to pass, they [*the righteous remnant of Israel*] that are left in Zion and remain in Jerusalem shall be called holy [*will be righteous*], every one that is written among the living [*those saved by approval of the Messiah*] in Jerusalem—

4 When the Lord shall have washed away the filth of the daughters of Zion [*when the Lord has cleansed the earth*], and shall have purged the blood of Jerusalem from the midst thereof by the spirit of judgment [*Hebrew: carrying out a sentence; punishment*] and by the spirit of burning [*the earth will be cleansed by fire*].

The Angel Moroni quoted verses 5 and 6 to Joseph Smith in reference to the last days (see *Messenger and Advocate*, April, 1835, p. 110). Next, Isaiah depicts the peace and security that will prevail for the righteous during the Millennium as a result of having the presence of the Savior here on earth.

5 And the Lord will create upon every dwelling-place of mount Zion [*Jerusalem; the earth during the Millennium*], and upon her assemblies, a cloud and smoke by day [*represents the presence of the Lord as in Exodus 19:16–19 when He spoke from Mount Sinai and the Children of Israel heard Him*]

and the shining of a flaming fire by night [*presence of God*]; for upon all [*everyone*] the glory of Zion shall be a defence.

6 And there shall be a tabernacle [*shelter; can symbolize Hebrew marriage canopy, thus representing the remarriage of Christ and his people who were worthy to meet Him when He came at the time of the Second Coming; see Jeremiah 3:1*] for a shadow [*protection*] in the daytime from the heat, and for a place of refuge, and a covert [*protection*] from storm and from rain [*millennial peace and protection; verses 5 and 6 could be dual, referring also to the stakes of Zion as protection, defense, refuge in the last days—see D&C 115:6*].

2 NEPHI 15

Background

Isaiah is a master at creating intrigue and interest among his students such that they become motivated to find out the "end of the story." Here, he will compose a "song" or poetic parable of a vineyard, showing God's mercy and Israel's unresponsiveness to His invitations to come unto Him and have peace and security. It causes the reader to become quite exasperated with the people of Judah. But we would do well to look into the mirror and make sure the person we see does not fall into similar foolishness and wickedness.

1 And then will I sing to my well-beloved a song of my beloved [*Christ*], touching his vineyard [*Israel*]. My well-beloved [*the Lord of Hosts; see verse 7*] hath a vineyard [*Israel; see verse 7*] in a very fruitful hill [*in Israel*].

2 And he fenced it [*protected it*], and gathered out the stones thereof [*removed stumbling blocks or gave it every chance to succeed*], and planted it with the choicest vine [*the men of Judah; see verse 7*], and built a tower [*put prophets*] in the midst of it, and also made a wine-press therein [*indicates potential for a good harvest*]; and he looked that it should bring forth grapes [*the desired product, such as faithful people*], and it brought forth wild grapes [*apostasy, wickedness*].

3 And now, O inhabitants of Jerusalem, and men of Judah, judge, I pray you, betwixt me [*Christ*] and my vineyard [*apostate Israel; I'll give you the facts and you be the judge*].

4 What could have been done more to my vineyard that I have not done in it [*the main question: have I not done my job? Is that why you are wicked*]? Wherefore [*Why*], when I looked [*planned*] that it should bring forth grapes [*righteous people*] it brought forth wild grapes [*apostasy*].

5 And now go to [*German Bible: All right. That's settled*]; I will tell you what I will do to my vineyard [*Israel*]—I will take away the

hedge thereof [*I will take away divine protection*], and it [*Israel*] shall be eaten up [*destroyed*]; and I will break down the wall [*withdraw my protection*] thereof, and it shall be trodden down;

6 And I will lay it waste; it shall not be pruned nor digged [*the Spirit will withdraw; no prophets to "prune" out false doctrines and warn against evil*]; but there shall come up briers and thorns [*apostate doctrines and behaviors*]; I will also command the clouds that they rain no rain upon it [*drought, famine*].

Isaiah now explains what the elements in his parable represent.

7 For the vineyard of the Lord of Hosts [*Christ*] is the house of Israel, and the men of Judah his pleasant plant; and he looked for judgment [*expected justice, fairness, kindness etc. from them*], and behold, oppression [*instead, He found them oppressing one another*]; for righteousness, but behold, a cry [*in place of righteousness, He found riotous living*].

On occasions, people have been known to use the phrase "join house to house" verse 8, next, to condemn builders and contractors who construct and sell apartment buildings and condominiums. While this is perhaps amusing, it also shows how badly Isaiah can be misinterpreted.

8 Wo unto them [*the powerful, wealthy*] that join house to house [*who grab up house after house*], till there can be no place, that they [*the poor*] may be placed alone in the midst of the earth [*those in power cheat and push the poor farmers off their land, taking their houses from them in the process*]!

9 In mine ears [*German Bible: Isaiah's ears*], said the Lord of Hosts, of a truth many houses shall be desolate, and great and fair cities without inhabitant [*great troubles are coming because of your wickedness; many of you will be captured and taken far away and your cities will be deserted*].

As we have said many times, Isaiah is a master at painting mental images with words. Watch now as he describes the abject poverty that awaits rebellious Israel when He withdraws His help and protection from them.

10 Yea, ten acres of vineyard [*fields where grapes are grown*] shall yield [*produce*] one bath [*about 8 1/4 U.S. gallons*], and the seed of a homer [*6 1/2 bushel of seed*] shall yield an ephah [*1/2 bushel of harvest, a terrible famine is coming!*].

Next, Isaiah condemns the riotous lifestyle of the wicked, which includes drunkenness.

11 Wo unto them that rise up early in the morning, that they may follow strong drink, that continue until night, and wine inflame them!

Isaiah now describes the hypocritical religious worship services among the apostate Israelites. They go through the motions of true religious worship, having all the elements of that proper worship as prescribed by past prophets, but their lives make a mockery of it. As he "paints" this picture with words, he will describe musical instruments that were properly a part of their religious services in his day. It would be like describing the proper components of our worship services today by saying "You have your music, your prayers, your meetings, your sacrament, pay your tithing and fast offering, hold temple recommends, attend the temple, etc., but then cheat, lie, steal at work, take unfair advantage of your neighbors, view pornography, break the Sabbath, get involved in sexual immorality, gossip, etc." In other words, your worship and ritual are hollow and empty. You are hypocrites.

12 And the harp, and the viol [*Hebrew: lyre; a small stringed instrument of the harp family*], the tabret [*drums or tambourines*], and pipe [*Hebrew: flute, or musical instruments associated with worship of the Lord*], and wine are in their feasts; but they regard not [*don't pay attention to*] the work of the Lord, neither consider the operation of his hands [*their worship is empty, hypocritical; they do not actually acknowledge God nor do they hardly even think about Him*].

13 Therefore [*this is why*], my people are gone into captivity [*prophecy about Israel's future captivity*], because they have no knowledge [*they have become ignorant of the true gospel; see D&C 131:6*]; and their honorable men are famished [*they have lost their righteous leaders*], and their multitude dried up with thirst [*dual: fits with Amos 8:11–12 about a famine of hearing the words of the Lord; also, literal results of famine*].

Next, Isaiah uses very interesting language and imagery to describe where Israel is going because of her wickedness.

14 Therefore [*this is why*], hell hath enlarged herself [*they've had to add on to hell to make room for you!*], and opened her mouth without measure [*seemingly without limit because there are so many of you heading for it*]; and their [*the wicked*] glory, and their multitude, and their pomp, and he that rejoiceth [*in wicked, riotous living*], shall descend into it [*hell*].

Next, Isaiah explains that the whole society is riddled with pride. In other words, no one is humble. Isaiah's writing here demonstrates his use of repetition for emphasis.

15 And the mean [*poor*] man shall be brought down [*humbled*], and the mighty [*wealthy, powerful*] man shall be humbled, and the eyes of the lofty [*proud*] shall be humbled [*everyone needs humbling*].

16 But the Lord of Hosts shall be exalted [*will be victorious*] in judgment, and God that is holy shall be sanctified in righteousness [*the Lord will triumph*]. [*This verse is another example of how Isaiah says the same thing two different ways.*]

Next, Isaiah describes the completeness of the devastation that will come upon wicked Israel unless they repent.

17 Then shall the lambs feed [*graze where the Lord's vineyard, Israel, once stood; the destruction will be so complete that animals will graze where wicked Israelites once lived*] after their manner [*German: where the city once stood*], and the waste places of the fat ones [*the former wealthy, wicked*] shall strangers [*foreigners*] eat.

18 Wo unto them that draw [*pull*] iniquity with cords of vanity [*pride*], and sin as it were with a cart rope [*you are tethered to your sins; they follow you around like a cart follows the animal pulling it!*];

In verse 19, next, we see the arrogance which wickedness can bring upon individuals and societies. We see the wicked challenging God to be more obvious about His existence if He actually expects people to pay any attention to Him. This reminds us of some of the antichrists such as Sherem, Nehor, and Korihor in the Book of Mormon who demanded a sign from God to prove His existence.

19 That say: Let him [*the Lord*] make speed, hasten his work, that we may see it [*it is up to God to prove to us that he exists*]; and let the counsel [*plans*] of the Holy One of Israel draw nigh and come, that we may know it [*we are "calling his bluff"; tell him to follow through with his threats so we can know he really exists!*].

Next comes one of the most famous of all the writings and teachings of Isaiah. We are witnessing this problem on every side today in our world. It seems that one of Satan's most effective tools is getting people to think and act just the opposite of what God says.

20 Wo unto them that call evil good, and good evil, that put darkness for light, and light for darkness, that put bitter for sweet, and sweet for bitter!

21 Wo unto the wise in their own eyes [*full of evil pride*] and prudent in their own sight [*the wicked, who make their own rules*]!

22 Wo unto the mighty to drink wine, and men of strength to mingle strong drink [*drunkenness and riotous living*];

Next, Isaiah reminds us that corrupt judicial systems and processes go along with the downfall of a society.

23 Who justify the wicked for reward [*take bribes, corrupt judicial system etc.*], and take away the righteousness of the righteous from him [*deprive the innocent of his rights*]!

Next, Isaiah describes the downfall and destruction of the wicked. Watch as he masterfully says the same thing in many different ways.

24 Therefore [*because of such wickedness*], as the fire devoureth the stubble [*just as fire burns dry grain stocks*], and the flame consumeth the chaff [*highly flammable byproduct of harvesting grain*], their root shall be rottenness [*the wicked lose their roots, anchor, stability; family ties*], and their blossoms [*potential to bear fruit; families*] shall go up as dust [*in summary: the wicked will not bear fruit; no posterity in the next life and destruction of many in this life*]; because they have cast away the law of the Lord of Hosts, and despised the word of the Holy One of Israel.

You've noticed by now that Isaiah always explains the "why" of what is going to happen. This reminds us that the Lord wants us to have understanding, so we can make wise and advantageous agency choices.

25 Therefore [*for these reasons*], is the anger of the Lord kindled against his people, and he hath stretched forth his hand against them, and hath smitten them; and the hills did tremble, and their carcasses were torn in the midst of the streets [*terrible destruction resulting from Israel's wickedness*]. For [*because of*] all this his anger is not turned away, but his hand is stretched out still [*inviting you to repent; in other words, despite all this, you can still repent; compare with 2 Nephi 28:32 and Jacob 6:4 and 5*].

The end of verse 25, above, is a strong and very comforting reminder that the Lord is very desirous that we use His Atonement and be freed from the burden of sin, even if we have a long history of not living the gospel. Elder Neal A. Maxwell of the Quorum of the Twelve Apostles taught the following:

Our long-suffering and merciful Lord is ever ready to help. His "arm is lengthened out all the day long." (October 1996 General Conference of the Church, 2 Nephi 28:32)

It appears that Isaiah was shown our day in vision and that he saw modern forms of transportation involved in the gathering process. It is interesting to consider his dilemma as far as how to describe trains, airplanes, etc. when such things did not exist in his day. Watch as he uses terminology and objects of his time and day to describe objects of our time and day.

26 And he will lift up an ensign [*flag, rallying point; the true gospel*] to the nations from far, and will hiss [*whistle; a signal to gather*] unto them from the end of the earth; and behold, they [*the righteous*] shall come with speed swiftly [*because of modern transportation?*]; none shall be weary nor stumble among them. [*They will travel so fast and arrive so soon that they won't even hardly get tired.*]

27 None shall slumber nor sleep; neither shall the girdle of their loins be loosed, nor the latchet of their shoes be broken [*perhaps meaning that they will travel so fast via modern transportation that they won't need to change clothes; get pajamas on, or even take their shoes off*];

28 Whose arrows shall be sharp [*airplane fuselages perhaps looked to Isaiah like arrows poised in a bow?*], and all their bows bent [*like airplane wings?*], and their horses' hoofs shall be counted like flint [*making sparks like train wheels do?*], and their wheels like a whirlwind [*going around extremely fast?*], their roaring like a lion [*the deafening roar of trains, airplanes?*].

29 They shall roar [*airplanes, etc.?*] like young lions; yea, they shall roar, and lay hold of the prey [*passengers, converts will board them?*], and shall carry away safe [*will transport them safely, securely*], and none shall deliver

[*no enemies can stop them or prevent the gathering*].

Elder LeGrand Richards of the Quorum of Twelve Apostles commented on verses 26–29, above, as follows:

In fixing the time of the great gathering, Isaiah seemed to indicate that it would take place in the day of the railroad train and the airplane [*Isaiah 5:26–29*]:

Since there were neither trains nor airplanes in that day, Isaiah could hardly have mentioned them by name. However, he seems to have described them in unmistakable words. How better could "their horses" hoofs be counted like flint, and their wheels like "a whirlwind" than in the modern train? How better could "their roaring? be like a lion" than in the roar of the airplane? Trains and airplanes do not stop for night. Therefore, was not Isaiah justified in saying: "none shall slumber nor sleep; neither shall the girdle of their loins be loosed, nor the latchet of their shoes be broken"? With this manner of transportation the Lord can really "hiss unto them from the end of the earth," that "they shall come with speed swiftly." Indicating that Isaiah must have foreseen the airplane, he stated: "Who are these that fly as a cloud, and as the doves to their windows?" [*Isaiah 60:8*] (LeGrand Richards, *Israel! Do You Know?*, p. 182).

30 And in that day [*the last days*] they shall roar against them like the roaring of the sea; and if they look unto the land, behold, darkness and sorrow, and the light is darkened in the heavens thereof [*perhaps referring to conditions in the last days, war, smoke, pollutions, etc. while the righteous are gathering to Zion and the gospel in various locations throughout the world*].

2 NEPHI 16

Background

Since this chapter is relatively short and has beautiful Atonement symbolism, it is perhaps one of the very best chapters of Isaiah to study to get a feel for the power and majesty of Isaiah's inspired writings. This chapter deals with Isaiah's call, either his initial call or a subsequent call to major responsibility.

1 In the year that king Uzziah [*king of Judah*] died [*about 750–740 B.C.*], I [*Isaiah*] saw also the Lord [*Jesus; see verse 5*] sitting upon a throne, high and lifted up [*exalted*], and his train [*skirts of his robe; Hebrew: wake, light; can also mean His power and authority*] filled the temple.

2 Above it [*the Savior's throne*] stood the seraphim [*angelic beings*]; each one had six wings [*wings are symbolic of power to move, act etc. in God's work; see D&C 77:4*]; with twain [*two*] he covered his face, and with twain he covered his feet, and with twain he did fly.

To cover one's face (verse 2, above) is a way of showing respect and humility before God in many cultures.

3 And one cried unto another, and said: Holy, holy, holy [*repeated three times means the very best in Hebrew, or, superlative*], is the Lord of Hosts; the whole earth is full of his glory.

4 And the posts of the door moved [*shook*] at the voice of him that cried, and the house was filled with smoke [*symbolic of God's presence, as with the shaking of the mountain at Sinai, Exodus 19:18, when the Lord was there*].

Next, Isaiah expresses profound feelings of inadequacy and unworthiness to be in the presence of the Lord. Watch as the Atonement takes away his shortcomings and feelings of falling short and gives him confidence to do the work to which the Lord is calling him. The same principle applies to each of us as we realize our dependence on the Lord as we strive to do His work.

5 Then said I [*Isaiah*]: Wo is unto me! for I am undone [*feel completely overwhelmed*]; because I

am a man of unclean lips [*I am so imperfect, inadequate!*]; and I dwell in the midst of a people of unclean lips [*none of us mortals is worthy to be in the presence of God*]; for mine eyes have seen the King, the Lord of Hosts [*I am feeling completely overwhelmed because I have just seen the Savior*].

Watch the beautiful symbolism now, in verses 6 and 7, as the Atonement is represented and its power to cleanse and heal is taught.

6 Then flew one of the seraphim [*symbolic of a being with authority*] unto me, having a live coal [*symbolic of the Holy Ghost's power to cleanse "by fire"*] in his hand, which he had taken with the tongs from off the altar [*symbolic of the Atonement; Christ was sacrificed for us on the "altar" cross*];

7 And he laid it upon my mouth [*applied the Atonement to me*], and said: Lo, this [*the Atonement*] has touched thy lips [*symbolic of his shortcomings, imperfections and feelings of inadequacy*]; and thine iniquity is taken away, and thy sin purged [*cleansed; the results of the Atonement; compare with Isaiah 1:18*].

Next, watch what the application of the Atonement did to Isaiah's confidence to embark in the service of the Lord. We will use bold for emphasis.

8 Also I heard the voice of the Lord, saying: Whom shall I send, and who will go for us [*plural deity*]? Then I [*Isaiah*] said: **Here am I; send me** [*the cleansing power of the Atonement gave Isaiah the needed confidence to accept the call*].

Now, the Lord will give Isaiah a brief description of the people to whom he will be preaching as a prophet. You will note that the people are going to be extremely difficult to reach. Perhaps this is a bit of an "MTC" experience for Isaiah to help him brace for the difficulties ahead.

9 And he [*the Lord*] said: Go and tell this people—Hear ye indeed, but they understood not; and see ye indeed, but they perceived not [*Isaiah's task is not going to be easy with these kinds of people*].

As discussed in notes at the beginning of 2 Nephi, chapter 13, Isaiah often uses a literary technique known as "chiasmus" as he teaches. It involves an intentional listing of key elements of the teaching in reverse order for emphasis, after having given them in regular order.

10 Make [*picture in your mind*] the **heart** [A] of this people fat [*insulated against truth*], and make their **ears** [B] heavy [*picture them as being spiritually deaf*], and shut their **eyes** [C] [*picture them as being spiritually blind*]—lest they see with their **eyes** [C'], and hear with **their ears** [B'], and

understand with their **heart** [A'], and be converted and be healed.

It may be that verse 11, next, can be viewed as a reminder that the Lord has a sense of humor.

11 Then said I [*Isaiah*]: Lord, how long [*will people be like this*]? And he said: Until the cities be wasted without inhabitant, and the houses without man, and the land be utterly desolate [*empty; in other words, when you go to preach some morning and no one is left in the city, you will not be confronted with such people; as long as people are around, you will run into such people*];

12 And the Lord have removed men far away, for there shall be a great forsaking [*many deserted cities*] in the midst of the land.

Verse 13, next, is a great example of Isaiah's use of symbolism understood by people in his time and culture. It is also an example of a verse that is virtually impossible for us in our time and culture to understand without help.

13 But yet there shall be a tenth [*remnant of Israel*], and they [*Israel*] shall return, and shall be eaten [*pruned, as by animals eating the limbs, leaves and branches; the Lord "prunes" his vineyard, cuts out old false doctrines and apostates etc., destroys old unrighteous generations so new may have a chance*], as a teil-tree [*like pruning a lime tree? See*

Bible Dictionary, p. 780], and as an oak whose substance [*sap*] is in them when they cast their leaves [*shed the old, non-functioning leaves and look dead in winter*]; so the holy seed shall be the substance thereof [*Israel may look dead, but there is still life in it*].

In summary, verse 13, above, explains that although various Israelites will be carried away into captivity and thus be scattered and seemingly die out as a people, yet the Lord will eventually "prune" them, shape them and guide them to become a righteous covenant people again. They will look dead, as a people, like a fruit tree does in winter, but Israel will be gathered again and become powerful in the last days. We are watching the fulfillment of this prophecy as we see the great gathering now taking place.

2 NEPHI 17

Background
This next chapter compares with Isaiah chapter 7 in the Bible. It deals with literal historical events, including the virgin birth of the Savior.

King Ahaz is a wicked, idol-worshiping king of Judah [the nation of the Jews and part of the tribe of Benjamin, who are in the southern part of the Holy Land at this time]. His nation is being threatened from the north by both Israel (the ten tribes who have their own nation called "Israel") and by Syria. Israel and Syria are plotting to take over Judah and Jerusalem and to set up a puppet regime in Jerusalem controlled by themselves. Watch Ahaz's reaction as the Lord tells Isaiah to bring him the news that if he will trust in the Lord, he has no need to fear these two enemy nations. It is a reminder, among other things, that the wicked live in fear, despite the availability of help and safety with the Lord.

1 And it came to pass in the days of Ahaz [*a wicked, idol-worshipping king of Judah about 734 B.C.*] the son of Jotham, the son of Uzziah, king of Judah [*the Jews*], that Rezin, king of Syria, and Pekah the son of Remaliah, king of Israel [*the ten tribes or northern Israel*], went up toward Jerusalem to war against it, but could not prevail against it [*didn't win, but they did kill 120,000 men of Judah and take 200,000 captives in one day; see 2 Chr. 28:6–15*].

2 And it was told the house of David [*Jerusalem*], saying: Syria is confederate [*has joined*] with Ephraim [*the ten tribes; northern Israel*]. And his [*Ahaz's*] heart was moved [*shaken*], and the heart of his people, as the trees of the wood are moved with the wind [*the people of Judah were trembling with fear, "shaking in their boots"*].

3 Then said the Lord unto Isaiah: Go forth now to meet Ahaz [*king of Judah living in Jerusalem*], thou and Shear-jashub [*Hebrew,*

meaning "the remnant shall return"] thy son, at the end of the conduit of the upper pool in the highway of the fuller's field [*Ahaz is hiding where the women do their laundry, or, he is hiding behind the women's skirts; a coward*];

4 And say unto him [*King Ahaz*]: Take heed, and be quiet [*Relax!*]; fear not, neither be faint-hearted for [*because of*] the two tails of these smoking firebrands [*don't worry because of the threats from Syria and Israel*], for the fierce anger of Rezin with Syria, and of the son of Remaliah [*don't worry about continued threats from Syria and Israel; they think they are "hot stuff" but are nothing but smoldering stubs of firewood; they are "have beens"*].

5 Because Syria, Ephraim [*Syria and northern Israel*], and the son of Remaliah [*northern Israel's king*], have taken evil counsel [*are plotting*] against thee, saying:

6 Let us go up against Judah and vex it [*cause trouble for Judah*], and let us make a breach [*an opening*] therein for us, and set a king in the midst of it [*let's set up our own king in Jerusalem*], yea, the son of Tabeal.

7 Thus saith the Lord God: It shall not stand, neither shall it come to pass [*the plot will fail, so don't worry about it, Ahaz*].

8 For the head [*capital city*] of Syria is Damascus, and the head

[*leader*] of Damascus, Rezin; and within three score and five years [*65 years*] shall Ephraim [*the ten tribes*] be broken that it be not a people [*within 65 years the ten tribes will be lost*].

9 And the head [*capital city*] of Ephraim is Samaria [*about 35 miles north of Jerusalem*], and the head [*leader*] of Samaria is Remaliah's son. If ye [*Ahaz and his people, the tribe of Judah plus some of Benjamin*] will not believe surely ye shall not be established [*not be saved by the Lord's power; see Isa. 7, footnote 9b*].

10 Moreover, the Lord spake again unto Ahaz, saying:

11 Ask thee a sign [*to assure you that the Lord is speaking to you*] of the Lord thy God; ask it either in the depths, or in the heights above [*ask anything you want*].

12 But Ahaz said: I will not ask, neither will I tempt [*test*] the Lord [*refuses to follow prophet's counsel; is deliberately evasive because he is already secretly depending on Assyria for help*].

13 And he [*Isaiah*] said: Hear ye now, O house of David [*Ahaz and his people, Judah*]; is it a small thing for you to weary men, but will ye weary my God also [*try the patience of God*]?

14 Therefore [*because of your disobedience*], the Lord himself shall give you a sign—Behold, a virgin shall conceive, and shall bear a son, and shall call his name Immanuel [*the day will come when the Savior will be born*].

15 Butter and honey [*curd and honey, the only foods available to the poor at times; see Isa. 7, footnote 15a*] shall he eat [*Jesus will eat what the poor people eat; in other words, He will not be considered high in social status*], that he may know to refuse the evil and to choose the good.

16 For before the child shall know to refuse the evil and choose the good [*in as many years as it takes for the child to be old enough to know good from evil, or in just a few years*], the land [*northern Israel*] that thou [*Judah*] abhorrest [*are afraid of*] shall be forsaken of both her kings [*both Syria and the northern ten tribes will be taken by Assyria; see Isa. 8:4, 2 Nephi 17:17*].

17 The Lord shall bring upon thee [*Ahaz*], and upon thy people [*Judah*], and upon thy father's house, days that have not come from the day that Ephraim departed [*northern ten tribes split*] from Judah, the king of Assyria [*the king of Assyria will bring troubles like you have not seen since the twelve tribes of Israel split apart, about 975 B.C., into the northern kingdom under Jeroboam I, and the tribe of Judah under Rehoboam*].

18 And it shall come to pass in that day that the Lord shall hiss [*signal, call for*] for the fly [*associated with*

plagues, troubles; this will remind you of the plagues in Egypt] that is in the uttermost part of Egypt, and for the bee [*sting*] that is in the land of Assyria [*the Assyrians will come like flies and bees*].

19 And they shall come, and shall rest all of them in the desolate valleys, and in the holes of the rocks, and upon all thorns, and upon all bushes [*your enemies will be everywhere, will over-run your land*].

20 In the same day [*when this terrible day comes upon you because you refuse to turn to the Lord*] shall the Lord shave with a razor [*fate of captives, slaves—for humiliation, sanitation, identification*] that is hired [*Assyria will be "hired" to do this to Judah*], by them beyond the river, by the king of Assyria, the head, and the hair of the feet; and it shall also consume the beard [*they will shave you completely; will conquer you completely*].

21 And it shall come to pass in that day [*after the above-mentioned devastation*], a man shall nourish a young cow and two sheep;

22 And it shall come to pass, for the abundance of milk they [*the few remaining domestic animals*] shall give he shall eat butter; for butter and honey shall every one eat that is left in the land [*not many people left, so a few animals can supply them well*].

23 And it shall come to pass in that day, every place shall be, where there were [*used to be*] a thousand vines at a thousand silverlings [*worth a thousand pieces of silver*], which shall be for briers and thorns [*formerly valuable, cultivated land will become overgrown with weeds; this can be symbolic of apostasy*].

Isaiah continues emphasizing that Judah will be conquered and her inhabitants scattered to the point that relatively few of them will remain. The Babylonian captivity in about 587 B.C. was one fulfillment of this prophecy. Other devastations and scatterings of the Jews have also occurred.

24 With arrows and with bows shall men come thither, because all the land shall become briers and thorns [*previously cultivated land will become wild and overgrown such that hunters will hunt wild beasts there where you used to live*].

25 And all hills that shall be digged with the mattock [*that were once cultivated with the hoe*], there [*you*] shall not come thither [*because of*] the fear of briers and thorns; but it shall be for the sending forth [*pasturing*] of oxen, and the treading of lesser cattle [*sheep or goats; your once cultivated lands will revert to wilds; symbolic of apostasy*].

2 NEPHI 18

Background
The Lord has Isaiah continue spreading the unpopular word that an attack by the Assyrians [a

large, wicked, powerful nation in approximately the region occupied by Iraq today] is coming unless the people and their political leaders repent and return to their God. He will be asked by the Lord to use a large scroll on which he can write a warning in large letters for all to see. He was also asked to give his son a name, the meaning of which is that the Assyrians will be quick to ruin the country.

In contrast to the cruel devastation coming at the hands of the Assyrians, Isaiah invites the people to enjoy the gentle "waters of Shiloah" [verse 6], symbolic of the mercy and kindness of the Savior. If they turn to Christ, He will protect them. The choice is theirs. There is much symbolism in this for us.

1 Moreover, the word of the Lord said unto me [*Isaiah*]: Take thee a great [*large*] roll [*scroll*], and write in it with a man's pen, concerning Maher-shalal-hash-baz [*a Hebrew saying, meaning "destruction is imminent" or "to speed to the spoil, he hasteneth the prey"; in other words, Assyria will be here soon and destruction will overtake you soon*].

2 And I [*Isaiah*] took unto me faithful witnesses to record, Uriah the priest, and Zechariah the son of Jeberechiah [*these were required witnesses and legal authorities for a proper Hebrew wedding*].

3 And I went unto the prophetess [*Isaiah's wife*]; and she conceived and bare a son. Then said the Lord to me: Call his name, Maher-shalal-hash-baz [*meaning "destruction" is imminent"*].

Next, Isaiah indicates that the Assyrians will be upon Syria and the northern ten tribes in about as much time as it takes his baby boy to learn to say "Daddy" or "Mommy."

4 For behold, the child shall not have knowledge to cry, My father, and my mother, before the riches of Damascus [*Syria*] and the spoil [*wealth*] of Samaria [*northern Israel*] shall be taken away before [*by*] the king of Assyria [*before my son is old enough to say "Daddy," "Mommy," Assyria will attack northern Israel and Syria*].

5 The Lord spake also unto me [*Isaiah*] again, saying:

6 Forasmuch as this people [*Judah, Jerusalem*] refuseth the waters of Shiloah [*the gentle help of Christ, John 4:14*] that go softly [*mercifully*], and rejoice in [*place more trust in*] Rezin and Remaliah's son [*Syria and northern Israel instead of the Lord*];

7 Now therefore, behold, the Lord bringeth up upon them [*Judah*] the waters of the river [*you'll be flooded with Assyrians*], strong and many, even the king of Assyria and all his glory [*his pomp and armies*]; and he shall come up over all his channels, and go over all

his banks [*you will have a flood of Assyrians*].

8 And he [*Assyria*] shall pass through Judah; he shall overflow and go over, he shall reach even to the neck [*you will be up to your neck in Assyrians; can also mean "will reach clear to Jerusalem, the head or capital city", which Assyria did before being stopped via the death by plague of 185,000 soldiers; see 2 Kings 19:32–36*]; and the stretching out of his wings [*Assyria*] shall fill the breadth of thy land [*Judah*], O Immanuel [*the land of the future birth and ministry of Christ*].

9 Associate yourselves [*if you form political alliances with other nations for protection rather than turning to God*], O ye people [*of Judah*], and ye shall be broken in pieces; and give ear all ye of far countries [*foreign nations who might rise against Judah*]; gird yourselves [*prepare for war*], and ye [*foreign nations who attack Judah*] shall be broken in pieces; gird yourselves, and ye shall be broken in pieces [*note that "broken in pieces" is repeated three times for emphasis; 3 times in Hebrew is a form of superlative*].

10 Take counsel together [*go ahead, plot against Judah, you foreign nations*], and it shall come to naught [*won't succeed*]; speak the word, and it shall not stand [*and it will still not happen*]; for God is with us [*Judah won't be destroyed completely*].

The Lord has asked Isaiah, His prophet, to give some very unpopular messages to the citizens and political leaders of wicked Judah. This must have been extremely hard on Brother and Sister Isaiah and their little family. Next, the Lord gives Isaiah strong instructions not to give in to peer pressure and tell the Jews what they want to hear concerning making treaties with other nations for protection from their enemies, rather than turning to righteousness for God's protection. He then counsels Isaiah to stick with the Lord no matter what.

11 For the Lord spake thus to me [*Isaiah*] with a strong hand [*firmly*], and instructed me that I should not walk in the way of this people [*Judah*], saying:

12 Say ye not, A confederacy [*a treaty*], to all to whom this people shall say, A confederacy; neither fear ye their fear, nor be afraid [*"Isaiah, don't endorse Judah's plan for confederacy with Assyria. Don't tell them what they want to hear."*].

13 Sanctify the Lord of Hosts himself, and let him be your fear, and let him be your dread [*"Isaiah, you rely on the Lord, not public approval."*].

14 And he [*the Lord*] shall be for a sanctuary [*for you, Isaiah*]; but for a stone of stumbling, and for a rock of offense [*a rock that makes them fall rather than the Rock of their salvation*] to both the houses of [*wicked*] Israel [*Judah*

and Ephraim—the ten tribes], for a gin [*a trap*] and a snare to the inhabitants of Jerusalem.

Notice how simple but powerful Isaiah's wording is in the next verse.

15 And many among them shall **stumble** and **fall**, and be **broken**, and be **snared**, and be **taken**.

16 Bind up the testimony [*record your testimony, Isaiah*], seal the law among my disciples [*righteous followers*].

We discover from verse 16, above, that there were other faithful saints among the people of Judah, in addition to Isaiah and his family.

Next, Isaiah responds to the Lord's admonition to him to remain faithful at all costs.

17 And I [*Isaiah*] will wait upon [*trust*] the Lord, that hideth his face [*is holding His blessings back*] from the house of Jacob [*Israel*], and I will look for him.

18 Behold, I and the children whom the Lord hath given me are for signs and for wonders in Israel from the Lord of Hosts, which dwelleth in Mount Zion. [*My family and I are a reminder to Israel that the Lord lives.*]

It seems that too often, the wicked just can't get the obvious! They are so blind that they can't see that the only way to preserve

their freedom is to follow the commandments and guidelines of the gospel of Christ. In this case, rather than repenting and returning to the God of Israel, which would restore civil peace and security to them, they turn to witchcraft and sorcery which are controlled by forces other than and alien to God. Wickedness certainly does not promote rational thought!

19 And when they [*the wicked*] shall say unto you: Seek unto them [*spiritualists, mediums, fortune tellers, and so forth*] that have familiar spirits [*who contact dead relatives and friends*], and unto wizards that peep and mutter [*into their "crystal balls"*]—should not a people seek unto their God for the living to hear from the dead? [*In other words, wouldn't it be wise for them to turn to God for help?*]

Next, Isaiah wisely counsels his people to compare any advice, counsel, etc. they receive from any source, to the scriptures. We often refer to our scriptures as the "standard works" which means "the standard by which all things should be measured."

20 To the law and to the testimony [*to the scriptures*]; and if they [*the spiritualists and their media*] speak not according to this word [*the scriptures*], it is because there is no light in them [*the fortune tellers, mediums, and so forth*].

21 And they [*the wicked of Judah*]

shall pass through it [*the land; the trouble described in verses 7 and 8*] hardly bestead [*severely distressed*] and hungry; and it shall come to pass that when they shall be hungry, they shall fret themselves [*become enraged*], and curse their king and their God, and look upward [*proud, defiant*].

22 And they shall look unto the earth [*will look around them*] and behold [*see only*] trouble, and darkness, dimness of anguish [*gloom; Hebrew: dark affliction*], and shall be driven to darkness [*thrust into utter despair; results of wickedness*].

2 NEPHI 19

Background

This is a continuation of the topic in chapter 18. King Ahaz of Judah ignored the Lord's counsel and made an alliance with Assyria anyway. Symbolism here can include that Assyria would represent the devil and his evil, prideful ways. King Ahaz could symbolize foolish and wicked people who make alliances with the devil or his evil ways and naively think that they are thus protected from destruction spiritually and often physically.

In this next chapter, which can be compared to Isaiah 9, Isaiah gives one of the most famous and beautiful of all his messianic prophecies. He prophesies that Christ will come. Handel's Messiah puts some of this chapter to magnificent music.

1 [*This verse is the last verse of chapter 8 in the Hebrew Bible and in the German Bible. It serves as a natural transition from chapter 18 to verse 2.*] Nevertheless, the dimness [*affliction referred to in 18:22*] shall not be such as was in her vexation, when at first [*the first Assyrian attacks in Isaiah's day*] he lightly [*German: strictly*] afflicted the land of Zebulun [*the Nazareth area, part of northern Israel; see maps 5 & 14 in the first editions of the new LDS Bible*], and the land of Naphtali [*in northern Israel*], and afterwards did more grievously afflict [*Hebrew: gloriously bless, German: brought honor to*] by the way of the Red Sea beyond Jordan in Galilee of the nations [*Jesus grew up in Galilee and righteous Israel has been gloriously blessed through him, whereas wicked Israel has been grievously afflicted as a result of rejecting him*].

2 The people that walked in darkness [*spiritual darkness; apostasy and captivity*] have seen a great light [*the Savior and his teachings*]; they that dwell in the land of the shadow of death, upon them hath the light shined [*the gospel of Christ is made available to them*].

3 Thou [*the Savior*] hast multiplied the nation, and increased the joy—they joy before thee according to the joy in harvest, and as men rejoice when they divide the spoil [*Christ and his faithful followers will ultimately triumph and divide the spoils; reap the rewards*]

of righteous living as they enjoy celestial exaltation].

Next, Isaiah continues prophesying about the future and the redemption made available by the Savior.

4 For thou [*Christ*] hast broken the yoke of his burden [*Israel's captivity, bondage*], and the staff of his shoulder, the rod [*power*] of his [*Israel's*] oppressor.

5 For every battle of the warrior is with confused noise, and garments rolled in blood; but this shall be with burning [*the burning at the Second Coming, according to Joseph Smith; see Isa. 9, footnote 5b*] and fuel of fire.

6 **For unto us a child [*Christ*] is born, unto us a son is given; and the government shall be upon his shoulder; and his name shall be called, Wonderful, Counselor, The Mighty God, The Everlasting Father, The Prince of Peace.**

7 Of the increase of government and peace there is no end [*for the righteous*], upon the throne of David, and upon his kingdom to order it, and to establish it with judgment [*fairness*] and with justice from henceforth, even forever. The zeal of the Lord of Hosts will perform this [*God will do this*].

The Lord now continues his message of warning to the northern ten tribes, [known at this point in history as Israel]. He addresses their arrogance and prideful claims that they can get along well without Him or His help.

8 The Lord sent his word unto Jacob [*Israel*] and it [*the message from the Lord*] hath lighted upon Israel.

9 And all the people shall know, even Ephraim [*the northern ten tribes, Israel*] and the inhabitants of Samaria [*the northern ten tribes, Israel*], that say [*boast*] in the pride and stoutness of heart:

10 The bricks are fallen down, but we will build with hewn stones [*boastful Israel claims they can't be destroyed successfully, but would simply rebuild with better materials than before*]; the sycamores [*trees*] are cut down, but we will change them into cedars [*more valuable trees*].

11 Therefore [*this is why, or, because of wicked pride*] the Lord shall set up the adversaries of Rezin [*Syria*] against him [*Israel*], and join his enemies together;

A very important theme is repeated over and over in Isaiah's writings. It is, "but his hand is stretched out still." We will see it in verse 12 and again in verses 17, and 21. The message is that no matter what mistakes you have made in the past, the mercy of the Atonement is still being offered to you by the outstretched hand of the Savior. We will **bold** this in these three verses for teaching emphasis.

Remember too that when something is repeated three times in Hebrew culture, it means it is the very best, the very most important, etc. The message, **"but his hand is stretched out still"** is repeated three times in this chapter!

12 The Syrians before [*on the East*] and the Philistines behind [*on the West*]; and they shall devour Israel with open mouth. For all this his anger is not turned away, **but his hand is stretched out still** [*the Lord will still let you repent if you will turn to him; see Jacob 6:4 and 5; see also Isa. 9, footnote 12d. Laman and Lemuel need to hear this message of mercy, as do we in our day*].

13 For the [*wicked*] people turneth not unto him [*the Lord*] that smiteth [*punishes*] them, neither do they seek the Lord of Hosts [*the people won't repent; they are going through the pain without learning the lesson*].

14 Therefore [*for this reason*] will the Lord cut off from Israel head [*leaders*] and tail [*false prophets*], branch [*Hebrew: palm branch, triumph and victory; see John 12:13*] and rush [*reed; people low in social status*] in one day.

Isaiah now explains some of the imagery above.

15 The ancient [*elders, leaders*], he is the head; and the prophet that teacheth lies, he is the tail.

16 For the leaders of this people cause them to err; and they that are led of them are destroyed.

17 Therefore the Lord shall have no joy in their young men, neither shall have mercy on their fatherless and widows [*all levels of society have gone bad; no one qualifies for mercy*]; for every one of them is a hypocrite and an evildoer, and every mouth speaketh folly [*foolishness*]. For all this his anger is not turned away, **but his hand is stretched out still** [*you can still repent; please do*].

18 For wickedness burneth as the fire [*wickedness destroys like wildfire*]; it shall devour the briers and thorns [*symbolic of wicked people and apostate philosophies and doctrines*], and shall kindle in the thickets of the forests, and they shall mount up like the lifting up of smoke [*when destruction comes it will come rapidly like wildfire*].

19 Through the wrath of the Lord of Hosts is the land darkened [*bad conditions prevail*], and the [*wicked*] people shall be as the fuel of the fire; no man shall spare his brother [*when people turn so wicked, they are no longer loyal, even to family members*].

20 And he shall snatch on the right hand and be hungry; and he shall eat on the left hand and they shall not be satisfied; they shall eat every man the flesh of his own arm [*the wicked will turn on each other*]—

21 Manasseh, Ephraim; and Ephraim, Manasseh; they together shall be against Judah. For all this

his anger is not turned away, **but his hand is stretched out still** [*you can still repent; please do!*].

2 NEPHI 20

Background
In the heading to chapter 20 in your Book of Mormon, you will find the phrase, *"Destruction of Assyria is a type of destruction of wicked at the Second Coming."* The word "type" means something that is symbolic of something else. For example, both Joseph who was sold into Egypt and Isaac were "types" of Christ, that is to say, many of the things that happened to them were symbolic of the Savior. The following charts show some of the ways in which these great prophets were types of Christ.

Joseph in Egypt	Christ
Was sold for the price of a common slave	Was sold for the price of a common slave
Was thirty years old when he began his mission as prime minister to save his people	Was thirty years old when He began His formal mission to save His people
Gathered food for seven years to save his people	Used seven "days" to create the earth in which to offer salvation to us
Forgave his persecutors	Forgave His persecutors

Isaac	Christ
Was the only begotten of Abraham and Sarah	Is the Only Begotten of the Father
Was to be sacrificed by his father	Was allowed to be sacrificed by His Father
Carried the wood for his sacrifice	Carried the cross for His sacrifice
Volunteered to give his life (Abraham was too old to restrain him.)	Gave His life voluntarily

Even in Leviticus 14, the priest is a "type" of Christ as he presents the privilege of being cleansed to the leper (who is a "type" of all sinners—that is to say, the leper can be symbolic of the need we all have to be cleansed from sin) We will include Leviticus 14:1–9 here as a brief lesson on the power of understanding the use of "types" in the scriptures.

Leviticus 14:1–9

1 And the LORD spake unto Moses, saying,

2 This shall be the law of the leper [*a "type" for all sinners; symbolic of serious sin and great need for help and cleansing*] in the day of his cleansing: He shall be brought unto the priest [*authorized servant of God; bishop, stake president, etc.; can also be a "type" of Christ—symbolic of Christ*]:

3 And the priest shall go forth out of the camp [*the person with leprosy did not have fellowship with the Lord's people and was required to live outside the main camp of the Children of Israel; the bishop, symbolically, goes out of the way to help sinners who want to repent*]; and the priest shall look, and, behold, if the plague of leprosy be healed in the leper [*the bishop serves as a judge to see if the repentant sinner is ready to return to full membership privileges*];

4 Then shall the priest command to take for him that is to be cleansed [*the person who has repented*] two

birds [*one represents the Savior, the other represents the person who has repented*] alive and clean, and cedar wood [*symbolic of the cross*], and scarlet [*associated with mocking Christ before his crucifixion, Mark 15:17*], and hyssop [*associated with Christ on the cross, John 19:29*]:

5 And the priest shall command that one of the birds [*a "type" for the Savior; symbolic of the Savior*] be killed in an earthen vessel [*Christ was sent to earth to die for us*] over running water [*Christ offers "living water," John 7:37–38, which cleanses us*]:

6 As for the living bird [*a "type," representing the person who has repented*], he [*the priest; symbolic of the bishop, stake president*] shall take it [*the living bird*], and the cedar wood, and the scarlet, and the hyssop [*all associated with the Atonement*], and shall dip them and the living bird in the blood of the bird that was killed over the running water [*representing the Savior's blood which was shed for us*]:

7 And he shall sprinkle upon him that is to be cleansed from the leprosy [*cleansed from sin, symbolically*] seven times [*seven is the number which, in numeric symbolism, represents perfection*], and shall pronounce him clean, and shall let the living bird [*the person who has repented*] loose into the open field [*representing the wide open opportunities again available in the kingdom of God for the

person who truly repents].

8 And he that is to be cleansed shall wash his clothes, and shave off all his hair [*symbolic of becoming like a newborn baby; fresh start*], and wash himself in water [*symbolic of baptism*], that he may be clean: and after that he shall come into the camp [*rejoin the Lord's people*], and shall tarry abroad out of his tent seven days.

9 But it shall be on the seventh day, that he shall shave all his hair off his head and his beard and his eyebrows, even all his hair he shall shave off [*symbolic of being "born again"*]: and he shall wash his clothes, also he shall wash his flesh in water [*symbolic of baptism*], and he shall be clean [*a simple fact, namely that we can truly be cleansed and healed by the Savior's Atonement*].

Having considered the use of "types" [*sometimes called "types and shadows"*] in the scriptures, we will now continue with Isaiah's teachings and watch as Assyria is used as a "type" of the destruction of the wicked at the Second Coming.

1 Wo unto them [*political leaders; kings*] that decree unrighteous decrees [*unrighteous laws*], and that write grievousness [*laws designed to oppress their people*] which they have prescribed;

2 To turn away the needy from judgment [*designed to keep the needy from fair treatment*], and to take away the right from the poor of my people, that widows may be their prey [*victims*], and that they may rob the fatherless [*they are greedy and brutal*]!

3 And what will ye [*the wicked*] do in the day of visitation [*punishment*], and in the desolation which shall come from far [*from Assyria; in other words, what will you wicked, greedy leaders do when the Assyrians attack you*]? to whom will ye flee for help? and where will ye leave your glory [*wealth, etc.*]?

4 Without me [*the Lord; without the help of the Lord*] they shall bow down under the prisoners [*huddle among the prisoners*], and they shall fall under the slain [*be killed*]. For all this his anger is not turned away, **but his hand is stretched out still** [*you can still repent*].

Now Isaiah gives a message from the Lord to the Assyrian king, Sargon. Sargon thinks that he is terrific in and of himself. He isn't.

5 O Assyrian, the rod [*tool of destruction used by the Lord to punish Israel*] of mine anger, and the staff in their hand is their indignation.

6 I will send him [*Assyria*] against a hypocritical nation [*Israel*], and against the people of my wrath [*Israel*] will I give him [*Assyria*] a charge [*an assignment*] to take the

spoil [*Israel's wealth*], and to take the prey [*Israel*], and to tread them [*Israel*] down like the mire [*mud*] of the streets [*see 2 Nephi 8:23*].

7 Howbeit he meaneth not so [*doesn't think so*], neither doth his heart think so [*the king of Assyria doesn't realize he is a tool in God's hand, thinks he doing it on his own*]; but in his heart it is to destroy and cut off nations not a few [*he is a wicked man, takes pleasure in destroying others*].

8 For he [*the Assyrian king*] saith [*boasts*]: Are not my princes [*military commanders*] altogether kings [*just like kings in other countries*]?

Isaiah portrays the Assyrian king, who is a "type" of Satan, naming off the cities he has easily conquered en route toward Jerusalem.

9 Is not Calno as Carchemish? Is not Hamath as Arpad? Is not Samaria as Damascus [*cities conquered by Assyria; see Map 10 in LDS Bible, first editions; see also 2 Kings 19:8–13 for Sennacherib's boastful letter to Hezekiah, King of Judah*]?

10 As my hand [*Assyria's*] hath founded [*Hebrew: acquired*] the kingdoms of the idols, and whose graven images did excel them of Jerusalem and of Samaria [*I've taken many cities whose idols are more powerful than those of Jerusalem and Samaria*];

11 Shall I not, as I have done unto Samaria and her idols, so do to Jerusalem and to her idols [*Assyria's king boasts that other nations' idols, gods, did not stop him and neither will Jerusalem's*]?

12 Wherefore it shall come to pass that when the Lord hath performed his whole work upon Mount Zion and upon Jerusalem [*when the Lord is through using Assyria to punish Israel*], I [*the Lord*] will punish the fruit of the stout heart of the king of Assyria, and the glory [*German Bible: pompousness*] of his high looks [*when I'm through using Assyria against Israel, then proud, haughty Assyria will get its deserved punishment*].

13 For he [*the Assyrian king*] saith: By the strength of my hand and by my wisdom I have done these things; for I am prudent; and I have moved the borders of the people, and have robbed their treasures, and I have put down the inhabitants like a valiant [*mighty*] man [*bragging*];

14 And my hand hath found as a nest the riches of the people; and as one gathereth eggs that are left have I gathered all the earth [*I'm mighty powerful!*]; and there was none that moved the wing, or opened the mouth, or peeped [*everybody is afraid of me!*].

Isaiah next uses some very fascinating imagery in describing the absurdity of the king of Assyria's taking credit to himself for his "amazing" accomplishments. There is an important message in this for all of us who might at times take or accept credit for accomplishments in the work of the Lord.

As you read verse 15, you might even find it a bit humorous.

15 Shall the ax [*king of Assyria*] boast itself against him [*the Lord*] that heweth [*chops*] therewith [*shall the ax brag that it is doing all the work by itself*]? Shall the saw magnify itself against [*German Bible: defy*] him that shaketh it [*uses it*]? As if the rod [*wooden club*] should shake itself against them that lift it up [*as if a wooden club should suddenly turn to the man who is swinging it and say, "Let go of me. I can do it myself!"*], or as if the staff should lift up itself as if it were no wood [*as if the staff were not simply a piece of wood*]!

16 Therefore [*because of the King of Assyria's wicked deeds and cocky attitude*] shall the Lord, the Lord of Hosts, send among his fat [*powerful*] ones, leanness [*Hebrew: disease, or trouble is coming to Assyria*]; and under his [*Assyria's*] glory he shall kindle a burning like the burning of a fire [*the Lord will trim Assyria down to size*].

17 And the light of Israel [*Christ*] shall be for a fire, and his [*Israel's*] Holy One [*Christ*] for a flame, and shall burn and shall devour his [*Assyria's*] thorns and his briers **in one day;**

The prophecy of destruction upon Assyria, given in verse 17, above, happened suddenly. 185,000 Assyrians died of devastating sickness in one night as they prepared to attack Jerusalem; see 2 Kings 19:35–37. The prophecy is continued with additional repetition in verses 18 and 19. We will use **bold** to point these out.

18 And **shall consume** the glory of **his forest** [*Assyria's armies*], and of **his fruitful field** [*his very productive military*], both **soul and body**; and they shall be **as when a standard-bearer fainteth** [*as when the last flag bearer falls, and the flag with him; your armies will be destroyed*].

19 And the **rest of the trees of his forest** [*the remnants of Assyria's army*] **shall be few**, that a child may write them [*so few Assyrians will remain that a small child could count them with his limited counting ability*].

20 And it shall come to pass in that day [*the last days*], that the remnant of Israel, and such as are escaped [*survive*] of the house of Jacob [*Israel*], shall no more again stay [*be dependent*] upon him [*Israel's enemies*] that smote them [*Israel*], but shall stay [*depend*] upon the Lord, the Holy One of Israel, in truth. [*In other words, the day will come in which Israel will become a righteous people who depend on and trust in the Lord.*]

Next, Isaiah again emphasizes

the future return of Israel to their God.

21 The remnant shall return, yea, even the remnant of Jacob, unto the mighty God [*Dual: 1. A remnant remains in the land after Assyrian destruction. 2. In the future, a righteous remnant of Israel will be gathered in; see 2 Nephi 21:11–12*].

22 For though [*although*] thy people Israel be as the sand of the sea, yet a remnant of them shall return [*German Bible: only a remnant will be converted; gathering*]; the consumption decreed [*destruction at the end of the world*] shall overflow [*will overcome the wicked*] with righteousness [*because of God's power or under God's direction; see the following verse*].

23 For the Lord God of Hosts shall make a consumption, even determined [*the decreed or prophesied destruction; see Isa. 10, footnote 23a*] in all the land.

Next, Isaiah emphasizes and repeats again the prophecy that the Lord will stop the Assyrians in their tracks. He adds that they will be stopped at the very last moment, just as they position themselves to enter Jerusalem.

24 Therefore, thus saith the Lord God of Hosts: O my people that dwellest in Zion, be not afraid of the Assyrian; he [*the Assyrian armies*] shall smite thee with a rod, and shall lift up his staff against thee, after the manner of Egypt

[*like Egypt did in earlier times*].

25 For yet a very little while, and the indignation [*the anger of the Lord against Israel*] shall cease, and mine anger in their destruction [*my anger will be directed toward the destruction of the Assyrians*].

26 And the Lord of Hosts shall stir up a scourge for him [*the Assyrians*] according to [*like*] the slaughter of Midian at the rock of Oreb [*Judges 7:23–25 where Gideon and his 300 miraculously defeated the overwhelming armies of the Midianites*]; and as his rod was upon the sea [*His power came upon the Red Sea to drown the Egyptian armies*] so shall he lift it up after the manner of Egypt [*God will stop Assyria like he did the Egyptians when they pursued the Children of Israel*].

27 And it shall come to pass in that day that his [*Israel's enemies, such as Assyria and others*] burden shall be taken away from off thy [*Israel's*] shoulder, and his yoke [*bondage*] from off thy neck, and the yoke shall be destroyed because of the anointing [*because of Christ, the "Anointed One"*].

As previously stated, Isaiah is a master of drama. Next, he will create a high degree of tension as he prophesies the advance of the Assyrian armies upon Jerusalem. It will look like Assyria will not be stopped; Assyrians will easily take several cities leading right up to the outskirts of

Jerusalem and it will look like Jerusalem is doomed despite Isaiah's prophecies to the contrary in verse 26. We will bold the names of the cities that the Assyrian king conquers as he heads toward Jerusalem.

28 He [*the Assyrian king with his powerful armies*] is come to **Aiath**, he is passed to **Migron**; at **Michmash** he hath laid up his carriages [*horses and carriages are symbolic of military might*].

29 They [*Assyria*] are gone over the passage [*they have come over the pass*]; they have taken up their lodging at **Geba**; **Ramath** is afraid; **Gibeah** of Saul is fled.

30 Lift up the voice [*weep!*], O daughter of **Gallim**; cause it to be heard unto **Laish**, O poor **Anathoth**.

31 **Madmenah** is removed; the inhabitants of **Gebim** gather themselves to flee.

32 As yet shall he [*Assyria*] remain at **Nob** [*just outside of Jerusalem*] that day; he shall shake his hand against the mount of the daughter of Zion [*Jerusalem*], the hill of Jeru-salem.

33 Behold, the Lord, the Lord of Hosts shall lop the bough with terror [*when Assyrian armies get right to Jerusalem, the Lord will "trim them down to size," "clip their wings," stop them in their tracks*]; and the high ones [*leaders of Assyrian armies*] of stature shall be hewn down; and the haughty shall be humbled.

34 And he shall cut down the thickets of the forests [*the Assyrian armies*] with iron [*an axe*], and Lebanon shall fall by a mighty one [*the Lord did stop Assyria by sending a sudden plague which killed 185,000 of them in one night as they camped outside Jerusalem; see 2 Kings 19:32–35*].

The Assyrian armies came up to Jerusalem, as prophesied, and were stopped suddenly by the Lord, as promised. This was one fulfillment of this prophecy.

However, this may be a dual prophecy, that is, one with more than one fulfillment. It also could refer to the attacks on Jerusalem and Israel in the last days, as powerful nations gather together to attempt to destroy them. In this case also, the Jews and Jerusalem will be spared also because of the Savior. He will appear on the Mount of Olives, which will split in two. The Jews will flee into the valley caused by the split and will see their Savior there. They will ask questions and He will answer. We will use prophecies recorded in Zechariah to review these future events and will use **bold** for teaching purposes.

Zechariah 12:8–9

8 In that day shall the LORD defend the inhabitants of Jeru-

salem; and he that is feeble among them at that day *shall be* as David; and the house of David shall be as God, as the angel of the LORD before them.

9 And it shall come to pass **in that day**, *that* **I will seek to destroy all the nations that come against Jerusalem**.

Zechariah 14:4–5

4 **And his** [*Christ's*] **feet shall stand in that day upon the mount of Olives**, which is before [*across the valley from*] Jerusalem on the east, **and the mount of Olives shall cleave** in the midst thereof **toward the east and toward the west**, *and there shall be* **a very great valley**; and half of the mountain shall remove toward the north, and half of it toward the south.

5 And **ye** [*the Jews*] **shall flee** *to* **the valley** of the mountains; for the valley of the mountains shall reach unto Azal: yea, ye shall flee, like as ye fled from before the earthquake in the days of Uzziah king of Judah: and the LORD my God shall come, *and* all the saints with thee.

Zechariah 13:6

6 And *one* **shall say unto him, What** *are* **these wounds in thine hands?** Then he shall answer, *Those* **with which I was wounded** *in* **the house of my friends**.

2 NEPHI 21

Background

This chapter compares to Isaiah 11 in the Bible. Joseph Smith said that Moroni quoted this chapter and said that it was about to be fulfilled. We find this statement in Joseph Smith—History, in the Pearl of Great Price, as follows (bold added for emphasis):

Joseph Smith—History 1:40

40 In addition to these, **he quoted the eleventh chapter of Isaiah, saying that it was about to be fulfilled.** He quoted also the third chapter of Acts, twenty-second and twenty-third verses, precisely as they stand in our New Testament. He said that that prophet was Christ; but the day had not yet come when "they who would not hear his voice should be cut off from among the people," but soon would come [*Joseph Smith—History 1:40*].

In this chapter, we are taught that powerful leaders will come forth in the last days to lead the gathering of Israel. We are instructed in Christlike qualities of leadership. We will be shown the peace that will abound during the Millennium and Isaiah will also teach about the last days gathering of Israel.

1 And there shall come forth a rod [*Hebrew: "twig"; D&C 113:3–4 defines this "rod" as "a servant in the hands of Christ, who is partly a descendant of Jesse as well as of*

Ephraim . . . on whom there is laid much power."] out of the stem of Jesse [*Christ; see D&C 113:1–2*], and a branch shall grow out of his roots.

Perhaps, the imagery here in verse one grows out of the last two verses of chapter 20, where the wicked leaders end up as "stumps" and have been destroyed. In the last days, new, righteous, powerful leaders will be brought forth to replace the "stumps" of the past and will have their origins from the "roots" of Christ. "Roots" can symbolically represent being solid and firmly rooted in God.

2 [*Christlike qualities of leadership described next.*] And the Spirit of the Lord shall rest upon him, the spirit of wisdom and understanding, the spirit of counsel and might, the spirit of knowledge and of the fear of the Lord;

3 And shall make him of quick understanding in the fear of the Lord; and he shall not judge after the sight of his eyes, neither reprove after the hearing of his ears.

4 But with righteousness shall he judge the poor, and reprove with equity for the meek of the earth; and he shall smite the earth with the rod of his mouth, and with the breath of his lips shall he slay the wicked.

5 And righteousness shall be the girdle of his loins, and faithfulness the girdle of his reins [*desires, thoughts*].

Isaiah now makes the transition directly into the Millennium.

6 The wolf also shall dwell with the lamb, and the leopard shall lie down with the kid [*young goat*], and the calf and the young lion and fatling together; and a little child shall lead [*herd*] them [*Millennial conditions*].

7 And the cow and the bear shall feed [*graze*]; their young ones shall lie down together; and the lion shall eat straw like the ox.

8 And the suckling child [*nursing child*] shall play on the hole of the asp [*viper*], and the weaned child [*toddler*] shall put his hand on the cockatrice's [*venomous serpent's*] den.

9 They shall not hurt nor destroy in all my holy mountain, for the earth shall be full of the knowledge [*Hebrew: devotion*] of the Lord, as the waters cover the sea. [*There will be great and wonderful peace on earth during the Millennium.*]

10 And in that day there shall be a root of Jesse [*probably Joseph Smith, but we don't know for sure*], which shall stand for an ensign of the people [*will signal that the gathering of Israel in the last days is about to begin*]; to it [*the "ensign" or flag signaling the beginning of an event*] shall the Gentiles seek; and his rest shall be glorious.

11 And it shall come to pass in that day that the Lord shall set his hand again the second time [*dual: a remnant returned after the Babylonian captivity / last days gathering of Israel*] to recover the remnant of his people which shall be left, from Assyria, and from Egypt, and from Pathros, and from Cush, and from Elam, and from Shinar, and from Hamath, and from the islands of the sea. [*In other words, in the last days, Israel will be gathered from every nation in the world.*]

12 And he shall set up an ensign [*the Church in the last days*] for the nations, and shall assemble the outcasts of Israel, and gather together the dispersed of Judah [*the Jews*] from the four corners of the earth.

As you will recall from your study of Isaiah so far, and from the history of the Holy Land, the twelve tribes split into two nations in a bitter dispute over high taxes, etc. after the death of Solomon. Over the years, Ephraim (the ten tribes whose nation was in the northern portion of the Holy Land) and Judah (the southern kingdom with Jerusalem as their capital city) became bitter enemies. Therefore, the prophecy that follows is marvelous! It is a prophecy that the day will come when the Jews and the descendants of Ephraim will get along well. We are seeing this today (**bold** added for emphasis).

13 The envy of Ephraim also shall depart, and the adversaries of Judah shall be cut off; **Ephraim shall not envy Judah, and Judah shall not vex Ephraim** [*the United States and others will be on good terms with the Jews*].

Next, Isaiah addresses conditions in the Middle East in the last days before the Second Coming of the Savior.

14 But they [*the Jews, with Ephraim's help*] shall fly upon the shoulders of the Philistines towards the west [*attack the western slopes that were once Philistine territory*]; they shall spoil them of the east together; they shall lay their hand upon Edom and Moab; and the children of Ammon shall obey them [*the Jews will be powerful against the enemy nations which surround them in the last days rather than being easy prey for their enemies as they have been throughout history*].

15 And the Lord shall utterly destroy the tongue of the Egyptian sea [*productivity of Nile River ruined?—see Isaiah 19:5–10*]; and with his mighty wind he shall shake his hand over the river, and shall smite it in the seven streams, and make men go over dry shod.

16 And there shall be a highway for the remnant of his people which shall be left, from Assyria, like as it was to Israel in the day that he came up out of the land of Egypt [*the Lord will establish His gospel which will serve as a "highway" for Israel to return to Him*].

2 NEPHI 22

Background

This chapter compares to Isaiah, chapter 12. It is a short but beautiful chapter referring to the Millennium. It describes the faithful who survive the destruction at the Second Coming of Christ as praising the Lord and rejoicing at the salvation that has come to them.

1 And in that day [*the Millennium*] thou [*Israel*] shalt say: O Lord, I will praise thee; though thou wast angry with me thine anger is turned away, and thou comfortedst me.

2 Behold, God is my salvation; I will trust, and not be afraid; for the Lord JEHOVAH [*Jesus*] is my strength and my song; he also has become my salvation.

3 Therefore, with joy shall ye draw water [*"living water", John 4:10; 7:38–39*] out of the wells of salvation.

4 And in that day shall ye say: Praise the Lord, call upon his name, declare his doings among the people, make mention that his name is exalted.

5 Sing unto the Lord; for he hath done excellent things; this is known in all the earth [*knowledge of the Lord will cover the earth*].

6 Cry out and shout, thou inhabitant of Zion; for great is the Holy One of Israel [*Christ*] in the midst of thee.

2 NEPHI 23

Background

In chapter 20, the destruction of Assyria was a "type" of [or symbolic of] the destruction of the wicked at the Second Coming of Christ. We discussed the definition of "type" in the notes at the beginning of that chapter. In this chapter, the destruction of Babylon is likewise a "type" of the destruction of Satan's kingdom at the time of the Second Coming.

It will be helpful to understand that the ancient city of Babylon was a huge city full of wickedness. Over time, Babylon has come to symbolize the wickedness of the world. A brief description of Babylon is given in your Bible Dictionary under "Babylon" as follows:

Babylon. The capital of Babylonia. According to Gen. 10:8–10 it was founded by Nimrod and was one of the oldest cities of the land of Shinar; in 11:1–9 we have the record of the Tower of Babel and the "Confusion of Tongues" [see Ether 1:3–5, 34–35]. During the Assyrian supremacy [see *Assyria*] it became part of that empire, and was destroyed by Sennacherib. After the downfall of Assyria, Babylon became Nebuchadnezzar's capital. He built an enormous city of which the ruins still remain. The city was square, and the Euphrates ran through the middle of it. According to Herodotus the walls were 56 miles in circumference, 335 ft. high, and 85 ft. wide. A large part of the city consisted of beautiful parks and gardens. The chief building was the famous temple of Bel. Inscriptions that have been recently deciphered show Babylonian accounts of the Creation and the Deluge in many ways similar to those given in Genesis. Other inscriptions recount events referred to in the Bible histories of the kingdoms of Israel and Judaea, and also give valuable information as to the chronology of these periods.

A sketch of the history of the Babylonian empire will be found under *Assyria*.

1 The burden of [*message of doom to*] Babylon, which Isaiah the son of Amoz did see.

Verses 2–5, next, describe how the Lord will gather his righteous forces together.

2 Lift ye up a banner upon the high mountain, exalt [*raise*] the voice unto them [*the righteous*], shake the hand [*wave the hand, signal*], that they may go into the gates of the nobles [*gather with the righteous*].

3 I have commanded my sanctified ones [*my saints*], I have also called my mighty ones, for mine anger is not upon them that rejoice in my highness.

4 The noise of the multitude in the mountains like as of a great people

[*the gathering*], a tumultuous noise of the kingdoms of nations gathered together, the Lord of Hosts mustereth the hosts of the battle.

5 They come from a far country, from the end of heaven, yea, the Lord, and the weapons of his indignation, to destroy the whole land [*the wicked*].

Next, Isaiah switches topics from the gathering of the righteous to fight together against wickedness to a strong warning to the wicked who will soon be facing the consequences of their evil ways.

6 Howl ye [*the wicked*], for the day of the Lord [*Second Coming*] is at hand; it shall come as a destruction from the Almighty.

7 Therefore shall all hands be faint [*hang limp*], every man's [*wicked men*] heart [*courage*] shall melt;

8 And they shall be afraid; pangs and sorrows shall take hold of them; they shall be amazed [*will look in fear*] one at another; their faces shall be as flames [*burn with shame*].

9 Behold, the day of the Lord [*Second Coming*] cometh, cruel [*it will appear cruel to the wicked*] both with wrath and fierce anger, to lay the land desolate; and he [*the Lord*] shall destroy the sinners thereof out of it [*a purpose of the Second Coming*].

10 For the stars of heaven and the

constellations thereof shall not give their light; the sun shall be darkened in his going forth, and the moon shall not cause her light to shine [*signs of the times preceding the Second Coming of Christ*].

11 And I will punish the world for evil, and the wicked for their iniquity; I will cause the arrogancy of the proud to cease, and will lay down the haughtiness [*pride*] of the terrible [*tyrants; typical Isaiah repetition to drive home a point*].

12 I will make a man more precious [*scarce*] than fine gold; even a man than the golden wedge of Ophir [*a land rich in gold, possibly in southern Arabia; there will be relatively few survivors of the Second Coming*].

13 Therefore [*because of the wickedness on earth prior to the Second Coming*], I will shake the heavens, and the earth shall remove out of her place, in the wrath of the Lord of Hosts, and in the day of his fierce anger.

14 And it [*dual: Babylon literally as a city; also the wicked in general*] shall be as the chased roe [*hunted deer*], and as a sheep that no man taketh up [*no shepherd, no one to defend it*]; and they shall every man turn to his own people, and flee every one into his own land [*foreigners who have had safety in Babylon, because of Babylon's great power, will return to their homelands because Babylon is no longer powerful and safe*].

15 Every one that is proud shall be thrust through [*stabbed*]; yea, and every one that is joined to the wicked shall fall by the sword.

16 Their children, also shall be dashed to pieces before their eyes; their houses shall be spoiled and their wives ravished [*fate of Babylon; innocent people suffer because of the wicked*].

Next, Isaiah gives a very specific prophecy regarding how the ancient city of Babylon was to be conquered.

17 Behold, I will stir up the Medes against them [*the Medes, from Persia, conquered Babylon easily in 538 B.C.*], which shall not regard silver and gold, nor shall they delight in it [*you Babylonians will not be able to bribe the Medes not to destroy you*].

18 Their bows shall also dash the young men to pieces, and they shall have no pity on the fruit of the womb [*babies*]; their eyes shall not spare children.

19 And Babylon, the glory of kingdoms, the beauty of the Chaldees' excellency, shall be as when God overthrew Sodom and Gomorrah.

Isaiah prophesied that Babylon would be completely destroyed and never inhabited again. And that is exactly what happened. It remains in ruins even today. The symbolism is clear. Satan's kingdom will be destroyed by the Savior at the time of His Second

Coming, and again after the "little season" at the end of the Millennium, never again to be rebuilt. (See D&C 88:111–14.)

20 It shall never be inhabited, neither shall it be dwelt in from generation to generation: neither shall the Arabian pitch tent there; neither shall the shepherds make their fold there.

21 But wild beasts of the desert shall lie there; and their houses [*the ruins*] shall be full of doleful creatures [*such as owls*]; and owls shall dwell there, and satyrs [*male goats*] shall dance there.

22 And the wild beasts of the islands shall cry in their desolate houses, and dragons [*hyenas, wild dogs, jackals*] in their pleasant palaces; and her time is near to come, and her day shall not be prolonged [*Babylon's time is up, her days are almost over*]. For I will destroy her speedily; yea, for I will be merciful unto my people [*the righteous*], but the wicked shall perish.

2 NEPHI 24

Background
Isaiah uses very colorful style and imagery as he now prophesies concerning the future downfall of the King of Babylon and, symbolically, the downfall of Satan's kingdom. Compare with Isaiah 14 in the Bible.

1 For the Lord will have mercy on Jacob [Israel], and will yet choose

Israel, and set them in their own land [*One historical fulfillment of this was when Cyrus the Great of Persia allowed Jewish captives in Babylon to return, 538 B.C.; another group returned in 520 B.C. This is also being fulfilled in our day.*]; and the strangers shall be joined with them [*foreigners will live with them*], and they shall cleave to the house of Jacob.

2 And the people [*many nations who will help Israel return*] shall take them [*Israel*] and bring them to their place; yea, from far unto the ends of the earth; and they [*Israel*] shall return to their lands of promise. And the house of Israel shall possess them and the land of the Lord shall be for servants and handmaids; and they [*Israel*] shall take them [*nations who used to dominate Israel*] captives unto whom they [*Israel*] were captives; and they [*Israel*] shall rule over their oppressors [*the tables will be turned in the last days*].

Notice that "lands" in verse 2, above, is plural. Among other things, this reminds us that in the last days there are to be several gathering places for Israel. In our day, members are being "gathered" into stakes of Zion throughout the world.

3 And it shall come to pass in that day [*Millennium*] that the Lord shall give thee [*Israel; the Lord's covenant people; the members of the Church*] rest, from thy sorrow, and from thy fear, and from the

hard bondage wherein thou wast made to serve [*Israel will finally be free from subjection by foreigners*].

Next, Isaiah paints a future scene with words in which he depicts two things, namely, the literal fall of Babylon and her wicked king, and also, symbolically, the future fall of Satan and his wicked kingdom. Such prophecies of Isaiah are known as "dual meaning" prophecies.

As he sets things up for his students, Isaiah creates interest and intrigue by telling them that downtrodden Israel will someday come to the point when they will see the king of Babylon (symbolic of wicked earthly leaders) as well as Satan himself trimmed down to size, with no more power to afflict and distress them. Isaiah then creates fascinating imagery to drive home his point that the faithful righteous will eventually triumph over all evil by staying close to God.

4 And it shall come to pass in that day, that thou [*Israel*] shalt take up this proverb [*taunting saying*] against the king of Babylon [*dual: literally King of Babylon. Refers also to Satan plus any wicked leader*], and say: How hath the oppressor ceased [*what happened to you!*], the golden city ceased [*your unconquerable city, kingdom, is gone*]!

In verse 5, below, Isaiah confirms

that it is the power of the Lord that will ultimately break the power of the wicked to afflict the righteous.

5 The Lord hath broken the staff of the wicked, the scepters [*power*] of the [*wicked*] rulers.

6 He [*dual: King of Babylon; Satan*] who smote the people in wrath with a continual stroke [*never ceasing*], he that ruled the nations in anger, is persecuted [*is now being punished*], and none hindereth [*nobody can stop it*].

7 The whole earth is at rest, and is quiet [*Millennium*]; they break forth into singing [*during the Millennium*].

8 Yea, the fir-trees [*people*] rejoice at thee [*at what has happened to Satan*], and also the cedars [*people*] of Lebanon, saying: Since thou art laid down [*since you got chopped down*] no feller [*tree cutter, lumberjack*] is come up against us.

9 Hell [*spirit prison*] from beneath is moved for thee [*is getting ready to receive you*] to meet thee at thy coming; it stirreth up the dead for thee, even all the chief ones [*dead wicked leaders*] of the earth; it hath raised up from their thrones all the [*wicked*] kings of the nations.

10 All they shall speak and say unto thee [*dual: Satan; King of Babylon*]: Art thou also become weak as we [*what happened to your power*]? Art thou become like unto us [*did you get your power taken away too, like us*]?

11 Thy pomp is brought down to the grave [*was destroyed with you*]; the noise of thy viols [*royal harp music*] is not heard; the worm is spread under thee, and the worms cover thee. [*Maggots are destroying your dead body just like they destroyed ours. You're no better off here in hell than we are, so hah, hah, hah! Refers to the King of Babylon since Satan has no mortal body.*]

Next comes one of the most famous quotes from Isaiah regarding Lucifer. It deals with his fall from heaven, after his rebellion in the premortal life.

12 How art thou fallen from heaven [*What happened to you?*], O Lucifer, son of the morning! Art thou cut down to the ground, which did weaken the nations [*you used to destroy nations; now your power is destroyed*]!

13 For thou hast said in thine heart [*these were your motives*]: I will ascend into heaven, I will exalt my throne above the stars of God [*I will be the highest*]; I will sit also upon the mount of the congregation, in the sides of the north [*mythical mountain in the north where gods assemble*];

14 I will ascend above the heights of the clouds; I will be like the Most High [*Moses 4:1 indicates he wanted to be the Most High!*].

15 Yet thou [*Lucifer*] shalt be brought down to hell, to the sides of the pit [*to the lowest part of the world of the dead, outer darkness*].

16 They [*the residents of hell*] that see thee [*Lucifer; King of Babylon*] shall narrowly look upon thee [*scorn you, mock you*], and shall consider [*look at*] thee, and shall say: Is this the man that made the earth to tremble, that did shake kingdoms?

17 And made the world as a wilderness, and destroyed the cities thereof, and opened not the house of his prisoners [*refused to free his prisoners*]?

18 All the kings of the nations, yea, all of them, lie in glory, every one of them in his own house [*all other kings have magnificent tombs*].

19 But thou [*dual: King of Babylon literally; Satan figuratively because he doesn't even have a physical body*] art cast out of thy grave like an abominable branch [*pruned off and thus worthless*], and the remnant of those that are slain [*you are just like any other dead wicked person*], thrust through with a sword, that go down to the stones of the pit [*to the very bottom*]; as a carcass trodden under feet.

20 Thou [*King of Babylon; Satan*] shalt not be joined with them in burial, because thou hast destroyed thy land and slain thy people; the seed of evil-doers shall never be renowned [*none of your evil family will survive, King of Babylon*].

21 Prepare slaughter for his [*King

of Babylon] children for the iniquities of their fathers, that they do not rise, nor possess the land, nor fill the face of the world with cities [none of your children will rule the earth like you have].

Next, Isaiah reiterates that it is ultimately the Lord who will stop Lucifer and all powerful wicked leaders and rulers. Note how thoroughly Isaiah defines the destruction. We will use **bold** to point it out.

22 For I will rise up against them [the Lord will stop Lucifer; King of Babylon], saith the Lord of Hosts, and **cut off** from Babylon the **name**, and **remnant**, and **son**, and **nephew** [I will destroy Babylon completely], saith the Lord.

One of Isaiah's favorite methods of driving home the point that a wicked kingdom will be destroyed completely is to picture it desolate, deserted—where only birds and animals live, avoiding humans. We see this technique in the next verse.

23 I will also make it [Babylon] a possession for the bittern [owls], and pools of water; and I will sweep it with the besom [broom] of destruction [a "clean sweep"], saith the Lord of Hosts.

Isaiah has finished with Babylon, and starts a new topic now, namely, the fate of Assyria.

24 The Lord of Hosts hath sworn [covenanted], saying: Surely as I

have thought [planned], so shall it come to pass [here is something else I will do]; and as I have purposed [planned], so shall it stand [it will happen]—

25 That I will bring the Assyrian in my land [Judah], and upon my mountains [the mountains of Judah] tread him [Assyria] under foot; then shall his yoke [Assyrian bondage] depart from off them [my people], and his burden depart from off their shoulders [dual: the Assyrian downfall in Judah, 701 B.C.; also, the forces of the wicked will be destroyed at the Second Coming and again at the end of the earth].

26 This is the purpose [the plan] that is purposed upon the whole earth; and this is the hand [the power of the Lord] that is stretched out upon all nations [the eventual fate of all wicked].

27 For the Lord of Hosts hath purposed [planned], and who shall disannul [prevent it]? And his [the Lord's] hand is stretched out, and who shall turn it back [who can stop the Lord]?

Isaiah has finished with the Assyrians and now switches to the Philistines.

28 In the year that king Ahaz died [about 720 B.C.] was this burden [message of doom to the Philistines].

29 Rejoice not [don't get all happy and start celebrating] thou, whole

Palestina [*Philistia*], because the rod [power] of him [*Shalmaneser, King of Assyria from 727–22 B.C.*] that smote thee is broken; for out of the serpent's root [*"snakes lay eggs,"or, from the same source, Assyria*] shall come forth a cockatrice [*one "snake" is dead—Shalmaneser—and a worse one will yet come—Sennacherib, King of Assyria, 705–687 B.C. The Philistines rejoiced when Sargon, King of Assyria from 722–705 B.C. took over at Shalmaneser's death. Sargon was not as hard on them as his predecessor was.*], and his fruit [*his son, Senacherib*] shall be a fiery flying serpent.

30 And the first-born of the poor shall feed, and the needy shall lie down in safety [*if you Philistines will join with the Lord, repent etc., you too can enjoy peace and safety, otherwise . . .*]; and I will kill thy [*Philistines*] root with famine, and he shall slay thy remnant [*you will be utterly destroyed*].

31 Howl, O gate; cry, O city; thou, whole Palestina [*Philistia*], art dissolved [*reduced to nothing*]; for there shall come from the north a smoke [*cloud of dust made by an approaching enemy army*], and none shall be alone in his appointed times [*the enemy army will have no cowards in it*].

32 What shall then answer the messengers of the nations [*what will one say when people ask "What happened to the Philistines?"*]? [*Answer:*] That the Lord hath founded Zion, and the poor of his people shall trust in it [*that the Lord is the one who caused the destruction of the wicked and established Zion*].

2 NEPHI 27

Background

This chapter compares with Isaiah 29 in the Bible. It was given by Isaiah about 700 B.C., near the end of his ministry. It deals with the last days, including the restoration of the gospel through the Prophet Joseph Smith including many specific details about the coming forth of the Book of Mormon. It is one of those chapters of scripture that bear extra strong witness of the truth of prophecies given by the Lord's prophets.

Isaiah begins by prophesying about the out-of-control wickedness that will prevail among all peoples upon the earth in the last days. Bold is used for teaching purposes.

1 But, behold, in the last days, or in the days of the Gentiles [*when the times of the Gentiles are being fulfilled; see Luke 21:24*]—yea, behold all the nations of the Gentiles and also the Jews, both those who shall come upon this land [*the land of the Book of Mormon*] and those who shall be upon other lands, yea, even upon all the lands of the earth, behold, they will be drunken [*out of control*] with iniquity and all manner of abominations—[*they will be hooked on*]

wickedness; wickedness will be very widespread]

2 And when that day shall come they shall be visited of the Lord of Hosts, with thunder and with earthquake, and with a great noise, and with storm, and with tempest, and with the flame of devouring fire [*the burning at the Second Coming; see D&C 5:19*].

Next, Isaiah prophesies that once the gospel is restored in the last days, none will be successful in stopping its progress.

3 And all the nations that fight against Zion [*the Lord's work and his people*], and that distress her, shall be as a dream of a night vision [*will be gone suddenly*]; yea, it shall be unto them [*wicked nations*], even as unto a hungry man which dreameth, and behold he eateth [*in his dream*] but he awaketh and his soul is empty [*he is still hungry*]; or like unto a thirsty man which dreameth, and behold he drinketh but he awaketh and behold he is faint [*still hungry and thirsty*], and his soul hath appetite; yea, even so shall the multitude of all the nations be that fight against Mount Zion [*the Lord's work; they, the wicked, will never be satisfied and will ultimately come up empty. Persecutors of the saints never feel satisfied, can't seem to leave them alone*].

4 For behold, all ye that doeth iniquity, stay yourselves and wonder [*stop and think*], for ye shall cry out, and cry; yea, ye shall be drunken [*out of control*] but not with wine, ye shall stagger but not with strong drink [*you will stagger about in wickedness because you reject the prophets; see verse 5*].

5 For behold, the Lord hath poured out upon you the spirit of deep sleep [*has had to withdraw His spirit; spiritual darkness; compare with Alma 12:11*]. For behold, **ye have closed your eyes**, and **ye have rejected the prophets**; and your rulers [*righteous leaders*], and the seers [*prophets*] hath he [*the Lord*] covered [*taken away*] because of your iniquity.

Next begins an incredibly detailed prophecy of the coming forth of the Book of Mormon.

6 And it shall come to pass [*in the last days; see verse 1*] that the Lord God shall bring forth unto you the words of a book [*the Book of Mormon*], and they shall be the words of them which have slumbered [*people who have already passed away such as Nephi, Mormon, and Moroni*].

7 And behold the book shall be sealed [*referring to the sealed portion of the plates; see verses 10, 21; also Ether 5:1*]; and in the book shall be a revelation from God, from the beginning of the world to the ending thereof.

8 Wherefore, because of the things which are sealed up, **the things which are sealed** [*the sealed*

portion of the plates] **shall not be delivered** [*translated*] **in the day of the wickedness and abominations of the people**. Wherefore, the book [*sealed portion*] shall be kept from them.

The fact that the sealed portion of the plates will not be translated and given to the people while "wickedness and abominations" exist makes us wonder if it might not be until the Millennium before we get the rest of the Book of Mormon.

9 But the book [*the gold plates*] shall be delivered unto a man [*Joseph Smith*], and he shall deliver [*translate*] the words of the book, which are the words of those who have slumbered in the dust [*Book of Mormon prophets*], and he [*Joseph Smith*] shall deliver these words unto another [*refers prophetically to the incident in which Martin Harris gave a copy of characters taken from the plates to Professor Charles Anthon; see JS–H 1:63–65*];

10 But the words which are sealed [*sealed portion of the plates*] he shall not deliver [*translate*], neither shall he deliver the book. For the book shall be sealed by the power of God, and the revelation which was sealed [*the sealed portion*] shall be kept in the book [*kept with the plates*] until the own due time of the Lord [*until the Lord says it is time to translate it; see verse 22*], that they [*the contents of the sealed portion*] may come forth; for behold, they reveal all things

from the foundation of the world unto the end thereof.

People often wonder what is in the sealed portion of the Book of Mormon plates. Verse 10, above, at least gives us a hint, namely, that they contain "all things from the foundation of the world unto the end thereof." What a treasure that will be!

11 And the day cometh that the words of the book which were sealed [*the sealed portion, see verses 8 and 10*] shall be read upon the house tops [*shall be made available to everyone*]; and they shall be read by the power of Christ; and all things [*compare with D&C 101:32–34*] shall be revealed unto the children of men which ever have been among the children of men, and which ever will be even unto the end of the earth.

Having spoken some about the sealed portion of the plates that Joseph Smith received from Hill Cumorah, next, Isaiah gives specific details about the coming forth of the Book of Mormon as we have it. He will begin by telling about the Three Witnesses to the Book of Mormon.

12 Wherefore, at that day when the book [gold plates] shall be delivered [*by Angel Moroni*] unto the man [*Joseph Smith*] of whom I have spoken, the book shall be hid from the eyes of the world [*no one will be allowed to see the gold plates*], that the eyes of none shall behold it save

[*except*] it be that three witnesses [*Oliver Cowdery, David Whitmer and Martin Harris; see D&C 17, heading and verse 1*] shall behold it, by the power of God, besides him [*Joseph Smith*] to whom the book shall be delivered; **and they shall testify to the truth of the book and the things therein.**

We will take a moment here and read the testimony of these three witnesses. Note how they adhered carefully to the guidelines given in Isaiah's prophecy, above. In fact, the Lord gave additional instructions to Martin Harris, Oliver Cowdery, and David Whitmer as to what they should say in their testimony, as follows (bold added):

D&C 17:3–6

3 And after that you have obtained faith, and have seen them with your eyes, **you shall testify of them, by the power of God**;

4 And this you shall do that my servant Joseph Smith, Jun., may not be destroyed, that I may bring about my righteous purposes unto the children of men in this work.

5 And **ye shall testify that you have seen them**, even as my servant Joseph Smith, Jun., has seen them; for it is by my power that he has seen them, and it is because he had faith.

6 **And he has translated the book**, even that part which I have commanded him, **and** as your Lord and your God liveth **it is true.**

Now, let us read the Testimony of Three Witnesses (bold used for emphasis):

THE TESTIMONY OF THREE WITNESSES

BE IT KNOWN unto all nations, kindreds, tongues, and people, unto whom this work shall come: That **we**, through the grace of God the Father, and our Lord Jesus Christ, **have seen the plates** which contain this record, which is a record of the people of Nephi, and also of the Lamanites, their brethren, and also of the people of Jared, who came from the tower of which hath been spoken. And **we** also **know** that they have been **translated by the gift and power of God**, for his voice hath declared it unto us; wherefore **we know of a surety that the work is true**. And we also testify that we have seen the engravings which are upon the plates; and **they have been shown unto us by the power of God**, and not of man. And we declare with words of soberness, that an angel of God came down from heaven, and he brought and laid before our eyes, that **we beheld and saw the plates, and the engravings thereon; and we know that it is by the grace of God the Father, and our Lord Jesus Christ, that we beheld and bear record that these things are true.**

And it is marvelous in our eyes. Nevertheless, the voice of the Lord commanded us that we should bear record of it; wherefore, to be obedient unto the commandments of God, **we bear testimony of these things**. And we know that if we are faithful in Christ, we shall rid our garments of the blood of all men, and be found spotless before the judgment–seat of Christ, and shall dwell with him eternally in the heavens. And the honor be to the Father, and to the Son, and to the Holy Ghost, which is one God. Amen.

OLIVER COWDERY
DAVID WHITMER
MARTIN HARRIS

13 And there is **none other which shall view it** [*the gold plates*], **save it be a few** [*the Eight Witnesses; see their witness at the beginning of your Book of Mormon*] **according to the will of God**, to bear testimony of his word unto the children of men; for the Lord God hath said that the words of the faithful [*Book of Mormon prophets*] should speak as if it were from the dead.

There is one other recorded witness of the gold plates who was not called upon to bear witness to the world, as directed in verse 13, but who, nevertheless, saw the gold plates. Her name was Mary Whitmer. She is the mother of David Whitmer. Her husband, Peter Whitmer, Senior, invited Joseph Smith and Oliver Cowdery to come to the family farm in Fayette, New York, and continue the work of translating the gold plates there, after persecution became too dangerous for them to remain in Harmony, Pennsylvania.

David Whitmer came with his horse and buggy to Harmony and transported Joseph and Oliver to Fayette. Emma Smith stayed behind to finish some details and soon joined Joseph at the Whitmer home in Fayette. Having extra people to feed and take care of was an extra burden for Mother Whitmer, which overwhelmed her at times, but she never complained. One evening, as she went to the barn to milk the cows, Moroni appeared to her and expressed appreciation for her kindness in hosting the Prophet and Oliver and offered to show her the plates so she would know for sure that she was helping with the work of the Lord. He did so. Mary Whitmer's son, David, reported this incident as follows:

> She was met out near the yard by the same old man [*the Angel Moroni seen earlier by David, judging by her description of him*] who said to her: "You have been very faithful and diligent in your labors, but you are tired because of the increase of your toil; it is proper therefore that you should receive a witness that

your faith may be strengthened." Thereupon he showed her the plates. [*Report of Elders Orson Pratt and Joseph F. Smith, pp. 772–73; spelling standardized.*] This quote is used in the Institute of Religion student manual for Church History, *Church History in the Fulness of Times,* Religion 341–43, published in 2000, chapter 5.

14 Wherefore, the Lord God will proceed to bring forth the words of the book; and in the mouth of as many witnesses [*missionaries, you, me*] as seemeth him good will he establish his word; and wo be unto him that rejecteth the word of God!

15 But behold, it shall come to pass that the Lord God shall say unto him [*Joseph Smith*] to whom he shall deliver the book: Take these words which are not sealed and deliver them to another [*Martin Harris*], that he may show them unto the learned [*Professor Charles Anthon and Dr. Mitchell; see JS–History 1:64–65*], saying: Read this, I pray thee. And the learned [*Charles Anthon*] shall say: Bring hither the book, and I will read them.

Isaiah even gives details as to the motives of Mitchell and Anthon.

16 And now, **because of the glory of the world and to get gain** will they [*Anthon and Mitchell*] say this, and not for the glory of God.

17 And the man [*Martin Harris*] shall say: I cannot bring the book, for it is sealed.

18 Then shall the learned say: I cannot read it.

19 Wherefore it shall come to pass, that the Lord God will deliver again the book and the words thereof to him [*Joseph Smith*] that is not learned; and the man that is not learned shall say: I am not learned.

20 Then shall the Lord God say unto him [*Joseph Smith*]: The learned shall not read [*translate*] them, for they have rejected them, and I am able to do mine own work; wherefore thou shalt read [*translate*] the words which I shall give unto thee [*with the help of the Urim and Thummim*].

21 Touch not the things which are sealed [*don't even peek at the sealed portion*], for I will bring them forth in mine own due time; for I will show unto the children of men that I am able to do mine own work.

22 Wherefore, when thou [*Joseph Smith*] hast read the words which I have commanded thee, [*finished the translation of the Book of Mormon plates*], and obtained the witnesses which I have promised unto thee, then shalt thou seal up the book again, and **hide it up unto me**, that I may preserve the words which thou hast not read [*the sealed portion*], until I shall see fit

in mine own wisdom to reveal all things unto the children of men.

With respect to the instruction to "hide it up unto me" in verse 22, above, it is interesting to note that as Joseph Smith finished the translation of the plates, he and Oliver Cowdery did just that. Brigham Young relates that they took the plates back to the Hill Cumorah where the hill opened up for them and they entered a large room filled with other plates and records. This incident is related by Brigham Young in the Journal of Discourses, Volume 19, page 38 as follows.

I will take the liberty to tell you of another circumstance that will be as marvelous as anything can be. This is an incident in the life of Oliver Cowdery, but he did not take the liberty of telling such things in meeting as I take. I tell these things to you, and I have a motive for doing so. I want to carry them to the ears of my brethren and sisters, and to the children also, that they may grow to an understanding of some things that seem to be entirely hidden from the human family. Oliver Cowdery went with the Prophet Joseph when he deposited these plates. Joseph did not translate all of the plates; there was a portion of them sealed, which you can learn from the Book of Doctrine and Covenants. When Joseph got the plates, the angel instructed him to carry them back to the hill Cumorah, which he did. Oliver says that when Joseph and Oliver went there, the hill opened, and they walked into a cave, in which there was a large and spacious room. He says he did not think, at the time, whether they had the light of the sun or artificial light; but that it was just as light as day.

They laid the plates on a table; it was a large table that stood in the room. Under this table there was a pile of plates as much as two feet high, and there were altogether in this room more plates than probably many wagon loads; they were piled up in the corners and along the walls. The first time they went there the sword of Laban hung upon the wall; but when they went again it had been taken down and laid upon the table across the gold plates; it was unsheathed, and on it was written these words: 'This sword will never be sheathed again until the kingdoms of this world become the kingdom of our God and his Christ.' I tell you this as coming not only from Oliver Cowdery, but others who were familiar with it, and who understood it just as well as we understand coming to this meeting, enjoying the day, and by and by we separate and go away, forgetting most of what is said, but remembering some things. So is it with other circumstances in life. I relate this to you, and I want you to understand it. I take this liberty of referring to those things so that they will not be forgotten and lost. (*Journal of Discourses*, 26 vols. [London: Latter-day Saints' Book Depot, 1854–86], 19: 38–39)

23 For behold, I am God; and I am a God of miracles; and I will show unto the world that I am the same yesterday, today, and forever [*I use the same gospel to save people; I am totally reliable, dependable*]; and **I work not among the children of men save it be according to their faith.**

Isaiah teaches an important lesson to us at the end of verse 23, above. It is basically that we determine how much the Lord is involved in our lives by our agency as we exercise faith in Him or as we chose not to exercise faith in Him.

24 And again it shall come to pass that the Lord shall say unto him [*Joseph Smith; see JS–H. 1:19*] that shall read [*translate*] the words that shall be delivered him:

Jesus quoted Isaiah, next, as He answered Joseph Smith's question as to which church to join, during the first vision.

25 Forasmuch as this people draw near unto me with their mouth, and with their lips do honor me, but have removed their hearts far from me, and their fear towards me [*their concept of God*] is taught by the precepts of men—

26 Therefore, I will proceed to do a marvelous [*Hebrew: "astonishing"*] work among this people, yea, a marvelous work and a wonder [*the Restoration of the gospel through Joseph Smith*], for the wisdom [*the false wisdom*] of their wise and learned shall perish, and the understanding of their prudent shall be hid [*pushed aside by revealed truth*].

27 And wo unto them [*the wicked*] that seek deep to hide their counsel [*evil plots*] from the Lord! And their works are in the dark; and they say: Who seeth us, and who knoweth us? And they also say: Surely, your turning of things upside down [*perversion of truth*] shall be esteemed as the potter's clay [*claiming they can get along without God, like the situation described in Isaiah 45:9 where the potter's clay tries to tell the potter what to do*]. But behold, I will show unto them [*the wicked*], saith the Lord of Hosts, that I know all their works. For shall the work [*the pot*] say of him [*the potter*] that made it, he made me not? Or shall the thing framed [*the building or whatever*] say of him [*the carpenter, craftsman*] that framed it [*built it*], he had no understanding [*he doesn't know me, or "God doesn't know us. We can be wicked and successfully hide from God." Or, "You wicked are just as foolish as potter's clay that claims it*

made itself into a pot and has no accountability to its maker."]?

Next, Isaiah will prophesy that Israel will blossom with literal forests and with truth, spiritual growth etc. after the Restoration. This is being very dramatically fulfilled, literally, today, as millions upon millions of trees are being planted in the southern portions of the Holy Land. It appears that significant spiritual growth is yet future.

28 But behold, saith the Lord of Hosts: I will show unto the children of men [*all people*] that it is yet a very little while [*after the Book of Mormon comes forth*] and Lebanon [*the Holy Land*] shall be turned into a fruitful field; and the fruitful field shall be esteemed as a forest.

Next, we are shown what the results of the coming forth of the Book of Mormon and the restoration of the true Church will be. (**Bold** added for emphasis.)

29 And in that day shall **the deaf hear** the words of the book, and the eyes of **the blind shall see** out of obscurity and out of darkness [*the spiritually deaf and blind will be healed as a result of the restoration, Book of Mormon*].

30 And **the meek also shall increase** [*shall gain strength and power with God*], and **their joy shall be in the Lord**, and **the poor among men shall rejoice in the**

Holy One of Israel [*the righteous will know the Savior again*].

31 For assuredly as the Lord liveth they shall see that the terrible one [*tyrant*] is brought to naught [*is reduced to nothing*], and the scorner [*one who ridicules the work of the Lord*] is consumed, and all that watch for iniquity [*in Church leaders and members; see D&C 45:50*] are cut off;

32 And they that make a man an offender for a word [*via corrupt lawyers and corrupt judicial system*], and lay a snare for him that reproveth in the gate [*Try to destroy the honest person who attempts to straighten out corrupt governments, etc. The "gate" was an alcove in Jerusalem's wall where officials and citizens met to discuss matters.*], and turn aside the just for a thing of naught [*destroy good people for unimportant matters*].

In a fascinating and ingenious way, Isaiah next portrays Jacob, the father of the twelve tribes of Israel, as having been embarrassed over the centuries to admit that the Israelites are related to him. However, in the last days, when Israelites [including us] are strong, faithful saints, Jacob is no longer embarrassed to claim us as his posterity. Rather, he is proud to be our ancestor.

33 Therefore, thus saith the Lord, who redeemed Abraham, concerning the house of Jacob [*Israel*]: **Jacob shall not now be ashamed,**

neither shall his face now wax pale. [*Father Jacob will no longer have to be embarrassed about the behavior of his posterity.*]

34 But **when he seeth his children** [*his posterity being faithful to God in the last days*], **the work of my** [*the Lord's*] **hands** [*now righteous*], in the midst of him, **they** [*righteous Israel*] **shall sanctify my** [*God's*] **name**, and sanctify the Holy One of Jacob, and **shall fear** [*respect*] **the God of Israel** [*Christ*].

Isaiah now summarizes the results of the restoration and the coming forth of the Book of Mormon in one final sentence.

35 They also that erred in spirit shall come to understanding, and they that murmured shall learn doctrine [*via truths of the restoration*].

MOSIAH 14

Background

Mosiah 14 compares to Isaiah, chapter 53, and is a wonderful chapter, showing that teaching and prophesying about Christ was a dominant part of the work of Old Testament prophets. Abinadi, in effect, brings Isaiah in as a "second witness" to what he has been teaching the priests of Noah.

1 Yea, even doth not Isaiah say: Who hath believed our report [*"Who listens to us prophets, anyway?"*], and to whom is the arm of the Lord revealed [*"Who sees God's hand in things"*]?

2 For he [*Jesus*] shall grow up before him [*the Father*] as a tender plant [*a new plant, a restoration of truth*], and as a root out of dry ground [*apostate Judaism*]; he hath no form nor comeliness [*German Bible: He has no special appearance or beauty*]; and when we shall see him there is no beauty that we should desire him [*normal people couldn't tell he was the Son of God just by looking at him*].

3 He is despised and rejected of men; a man of sorrows [*sensitive to peoples' troubles*], and acquainted with grief; and we hid as it were our faces from him [*wouldn't even look at him*]; he was despised, and we [*people in Judea*] esteemed him not [*even his own siblings rejected him at first; John 7, heading and verse 5*].

4 Surely he has borne our griefs, and carried our sorrows; yet we did esteem him stricken, smitten of God, and afflicted [*we didn't recognize him as the Great Atoner, rather thought he was being appropriately punished by God*].

5 But he was wounded for our transgressions, he was bruised for our iniquities; the chastisement of our peace was upon him [*he was punished so that we could have peace*]; and with his stripes

[*punishments*] we are healed [*the Atonement and its effects*].

6 All we, like sheep, have gone astray; we have turned every one to his own way [*every one of us has sinned; we all need the Atonement*]; and the Lord hath laid on him the iniquities of us all [*He took our sins upon himself*].

7 He was oppressed, and he was afflicted, yet he opened not his mouth; he is brought as a lamb to the slaughter, and as a sheep before her shearers is dumb [*can't speak*] so he opened not his mouth.

8 He was taken from prison and from judgment [*fair treatment*]; and who shall declare his generation [*who even cared about what happened to him*]? For he was cut off [*killed*] out of the land of the living; for the transgressions of my people was he stricken.

9 And he made his grave with the wicked [*died with convicted criminals*], and with the rich in his death [*a rich man donated his tomb, John 19:38–42*]; because he had done no evil, neither was any deceit in his mouth [*Christ was perfect*].

10 Yet it pleased the Lord [*it was the Father's will*] to bruise him [*to allow the Atonement*]; he hath put him to grief; when thou shalt make his soul an offering for sin he shall see his seed [*his loyal followers, success; Mosiah 15:10–12*],

he shall prolong his days, and the pleasure of the Lord shall prosper in his hand.

11 He shall see the travail [*labor to bring forth the Atonement*] of his soul, and shall be satisfied [*He will look upon the Atonement with satisfaction*]; by his knowledge shall my righteous servant justify [*save*] many; for he shall bear their iniquities.

12 Therefore will I divide him a portion with the great, and he shall divide the spoil [*Jesus will receive his reward*] with the strong [*the righteous*]; because he hath poured out his soul unto death [*because He gave His life*]; and he was numbered with the transgressors; and he bore the sins of many, and made intercession for the transgressors.

3 NEPHI 22

Background

In Third Nephi, chapters 20–21, the Savior quoted much from Old Testament prophets, especially Isaiah, concerning the promised gathering of Israel in the last days. He will now quote what we know as Isaiah, chapter 54. After doing so, He will command the people of Nephi to study Isaiah (3 Nephi 23:1–2). The imagery in verse 1, next, is that of a woman (Israel) who has not been able to bear children. The message is that Israel did not bear children who remained righteous, but in the last days, she will have righteous, faithful saints, who will make and keep covenants with the Lord. You are part of the fulfillment of this prophecy of Isaiah.

1 And then [*in the last days*] shall that which is written [*the prophecies concerning the gathering of Israel*] come to pass: Sing, O barren [*Israel, who has not produced*], thou that didst not bear [*righteous children*]; break forth into singing [*rejoice*], and cry aloud, thou that didst not travail [*go into labor*] with child [*in former days, you did not succeed in bringing forth that which you were supposed to, namely righteous people loyal to Christ*]; for more are the children of the desolate [*converts from scattered Israel*] than the children of the married wife [*perhaps meaning converts from Israelites who remained in the Holy Land*], saith the Lord [*now, in the last days, you've got more righteous Israelites than you ever thought possible*].

One of the characteristics of Isaiah's prophesying is that he repeats the main point of the prophecy, and then repeats again, and again. We see this next.

2 Enlarge the place of thy tent [*make the tent bigger; make more room for righteous Israel in the last days!*], and let them stretch forth the curtains of thy habitations [*make more room*]; spare not [*spare no effort in making more room*],

lengthen thy cords and strengthen thy stakes [*the Church will greatly expand in the last days as righteous Israel is gathered*];

3 For thou [*righteous Israel*] shalt break forth on the right hand and on the left [*righteous Israel will be popping up everywhere!*], and thy seed [*the descendants of Israel*] shall inherit the Gentiles [*will spread throughout the world in the last days*] and make the desolate cities [*cities without the gospel*] to be inhabited [*with righteous members of the Church*].

4 Fear not, for thou shalt not be ashamed [*you won't fail*]; neither be thou confounded [*stopped; confused*], for thou shalt not be put to shame [*you won't fail again*]; for thou shalt forget the shame of thy youth [*forget past failures—a major message of the Atonement*], and shalt not remember the reproach [*embarrassing times*] of thy youth, and shalt not remember the reproach of thy widowhood [*when you broke your covenants with the Lord and were thus left alone*] any more [*you can forget the failures of the past when Israel was apostate; the once "barren" Church is going to bear much fruit in the last days*].

5 For thy maker, thy husband, the Lord of Hosts [*the true God*] is his name [*you will return to your Creator, the Lord in the last days*]; and thy Redeemer, the Holy One of

Israel—the God of the whole earth shall he be called [*reference to the Millennium*].

6 For the Lord hath called thee as a woman forsaken and grieved in spirit [*Israel has been through some very rough, discouraging times*], and a wife of youth, when thou wast refused [*you didn't bear righteous children when you were young*], saith thy God.

7 For a small moment [*in the Lord's time*] have I forsaken thee [*because you apostatized*], but with great mercies will I gather thee [*the Atonement in action*].

8 In a little wrath I hid my face from thee for a moment [*when you rejected me*], but with everlasting kindness will I have mercy on thee, saith the Lord thy Redeemer.

9 For this, the waters of Noah unto me [*your situation is similar to the days of Noah and the Flood*], for as I have sworn [*promised, covenanted*] that the waters of Noah should no more go over the earth, so have I sworn that I would not be wroth with thee [*just as I (the Lord) promised not to flood the earth again, so have I promised to accept you back as you return to me in the last days*].

10 For the mountains shall depart and the hills be removed [*other things may change, over time*], but my kindness shall not depart from thee, neither shall the covenant of

my peace [*which brings lasting peace*] be removed, saith the Lord that hath mercy on thee.

God keeps promises; Isaiah is reminding us of the true nature of God, a very kind and merciful God indeed!

Isaiah continues to repeat the main message, which the Savior has emphasized in the past two chapters to the survivors of the destruction in America, namely, that God is merciful and that Israel can indeed be gathered because of the Atonement of Christ. This applies to us all.

11 O thou [*Israel*] afflicted, tossed with tempest, and not comforted [*you've had a rough past*]! Behold, I will lay thy stones with fair colors, and lay thy foundations with sapphires [*I will make your eternal homes with me in heaven very beautiful; compare with the description of the celestial kingdom in Revelation 21:18-21*].

12 And I will make thy windows of agates [*gem stones*], and thy gates of carbuncles [*a bright red precious stone in Isaiah's day*], and all thy borders of pleasant stones

[*the righteous will have it very good*].

13 And all thy children [*Israel*] shall be taught of the Lord; and great shall be the peace of thy children [*likely referring mainly to the Millennium*].

14 In righteousness [*through Christ*] shalt thou [*Israel*] be established [*gathered into the fold in the last days*]; thou shalt be far from oppression for thou shalt not fear, and from terror for it shall not come near thee [*Millennial conditions*].

15 Behold, they [*enemies of righteousness*] shall surely gather together against thee, not by me [*not brought by the Lord, as in times past when Israel was wicked; example: 2 Nephi 20:5–6*]; whosoever shall gather together against thee shall fall for thy sake [*I will protect you; you will finally have peace*].

Next, the Lord, through Isaiah, explains why He has power to bless and protect Israel, if they repent and return to Him. The explanation is simple. He is the Creator!

16 Behold, **I have created the smith** [*the blacksmith*] that bloweth the coals in the fire, and that bringeth forth an instrument [*who creates tools, weapons, etc.*] for his work; and I have created the waster to destroy [*I have power over those who choose to destroy, in other words, over the wicked; you will be safe with me*].

In verse 17, next, Isaiah repeats and summarizes the main message in the previous verses.

17 **No weapon that is formed against thee shall prosper**; and every tongue that shall revile against thee in judgment thou shalt condemn [*your righteous actions will bear witness against*]. This is the heritage of the servants of the Lord, and their righteousness is of me [*comes because of My Atonement and gospel and power to save*], saith the Lord [*in other words, there is safety for the righteous with Me*].

About the Author

David J. Ridges taught for the Church Educational System for thirty-five years and has taught for several years at BYU Campus Education Week. He taught adult religion classes and Know Your Religion classes for BYU Continuing Education for many years. He has also served as a curriculum writer for Sunday School, seminary, and institute of religion manuals.

He has served in many callings in the Church, including Gospel Doctrine teacher, bishop, stake president, and patriarch. He and Sister Ridges served a full-time eighteen-month mission, training senior CES missionaries and helping coordinate their assignments throughout the world.

Brother Ridges and his wife, Janette, are the parents of six children and make their home in Springville, Utah.